Selected Laws of Papua New Guinea

Selected Laws of Papua New Guinea Volume 3

Selected Laws of Papua New Guinea: Volume 3

Originally Published in Sydney by Thomson Legal & Regulatory Group Asia Pacific Limited as 1 volume.

This reprint has been published in 3 volumes:

Volume 1: ISBN-10 9980-939-47-8, ISBN-13: 978-9980-939-47-0
Volume 2: ISBN-10 9980-939-48-6, ISBN-13: 978-9980-939-48-7
Volume 3: ISBN-10 9980-939-49-4, ISBN-13: 978-9980-939-49-4

Copies are available from:

UPNG Press and Bookshop
Box 413
University Post Office
Papua New Guinea

Table of Contents

Volume 3

CHAPTER No 243

Motor Traffic Act

PART I – PRELIMINARY

PART II – ADMINISTRATION

PART III – REGISTRATION OF VEHICLES AND LICENSING OF DRIVERS, ETC

PART IV – METERED PARKING

PART IVA – CERTAIN FEES TO BE PAID TO PROVINCIAL GOVERNMENT BODIES, ETC

PART V – OFFENCES

Division 1 – Offences Generally

INDEPENDENT STATE OF PAPUA NEW GUINEA

CHAPTER No 243

[700]Motor Traffic Act

(Consolidated to No 51 of 1995)

Being an Act relating to motor traffic, and for other purposes.

PART I – PRELIMINARY

1 Interpretation

(1) In this Act, unless the contrary intention appears –

"driver" means, subject to Subsection (2), a person driving a motor vehicle;

"drug" means a dangerous drug within the meaning of the *Dangerous Drugs Act*;

"Inspector of Motor Traffic" means an Inspector of Motor Traffic appointed by or under Section 5;

[701]"learners's permit" means a permit granted under Section 3 of the *Motor Traffic Regulation*;

"licence" means a licence under the regulations;

"metered zone" means a public street or a part of a public street declared under Section 12(a) to be a metered zone;

"motor vehicle" means a motor car, motor carriage, motor cycle, motor truck, motor omnibus, motor tractor or other vehicle powered wholly or partly by –

(a) a volatile spirit; or

(b) steam, gas, oil or electricity; or

(c) any means other than human or animal power, and includes a trailer, but does not include a vehicle used on a railway or tramway;

---

[700]See, also, Land Transport Board Act.

[701]Definition "learners's permit" in Section 1(1) inserted by *Motor Traffic (Amendment) Act* 1987 (No. 16 of 1987), s1(a).

[702]"motor vehicle owned by the State" means a motor vehicle bearing number plates as provided by Section 19A(1)(e) of the *Motor Traffic Regulation*;

"Motor Vehicles Registry" means –

(a) a police station where an Inspector of Police is stationed; or

(b) a place appointed under Section 7 to be a Motor Vehicles Registry;

"owner", in relation to a motor vehicle that is the subject of a hire-purchase agreement, means the person in possession of the vehicle under the agreement;

"pedestrian" includes a person running, walking, sitting, standing or otherwise being on a road;

"public motor vehicle" means a motor vehicle used for carrying passengers for hire or reward;

"public motor vehicle licence" means a public motor vehicle licence under the regulations;

"public street" means a street, road, lane, thoroughfare, footpath, bridge or place –

(a) that is open to or used by the public; or

(b) to which the public have or are permitted to have access,

whether on payment of a fee or otherwise;

"registered" means registered under the regulations;

"the Superintendent" means the Superintendent of Motor Traffic appointed by Section 4;

"this Act" includes the regulations;

"trailer" means subject to Subsection (3) –

(a) a vehicle without motive power; or

(b) a machine that is mounted on wheels,

that is constructed or adapted for being drawn by a motor vehicle;

"vehicle" means any description of vehicle on wheels other than a vehicle used on a railway or tramway.

(2) For the purposes of this Act, the person driving a motor vehicle to which a trailer is attached shall be deemed to be driving the trailer.

(3) For the purposes of this Act, a vehicle without motive power

---

[702]Definition "motor vehicle owned by the State" in Section 1(1) inserted by *Motor Traffic (Amendment) Act* 1987 (No. 16 of 1987), s1(b).

constructed or adapted for being drawn by a motor vehicle shall not be deemed to be a trailer, but shall be deemed to be part of the motor vehicle by which it is drawn, if –

(a) it is constructed or adapted for attachment to a motor vehicle by means of a turntable or kingpin; and

(b) a substantial part of its weight and of the weight of its load rests on the motor vehicle.

2 Act to bind the State

This Act binds the State.

3 Saving of liability under other laws

This Act does not affect any liability of a person by virtue of any other law.

PART II – ADMINISTRATION

4 Superintendent of Motor Traffic

The Departmental Head of the Department responsible for the administration of all legislation pertaining to land transport matters –

(a) is the Superintendent of Motor Traffic; and

(b) under the Minister, is charged with the administration of this Act.

5 Inspectors of Motor Traffic

(1) Every commissioned officer of the Police Force is an Inspector of Motor Traffic.

[703](2) The Minister may, by notice in the National Gazette, appoint an officer of the Public Service to be an Inspector of Motor Traffic in any place.

6 Traffic Districts

Each province is a Traffic District for the purposes of this Act.

7 Motor Vehicles Registries

The Minister may, by notice in the National Gazette, appoint places to be Motor Vehicles Registries for the purposes of this Act.

8 Delegation

(1) The Superintendent may, by instrument under his hand, delegate to an Inspector of Motor Traffic all or any of his powers and functions under this Act (except this power of delegation).

[704](2) The Superintendent may, by instrument under his hand, delegate to a provincial government body or Area Authority his powers and functions in relation to the –

(a) application for; or

(b) grant or renewal of; or

(c) cancellation or suspension of,

a public motor vehicle licence.

---

[703]Amended by No. 9 of 1978, s1.

[704]Added by No. 9 of 1978, s2.

9 Australian Government vehicles

Notwithstanding this Act, if the Superintendent is satisfied that –

(a) a motor vehicle is the property of the Government of Australia; and

(b) the number-plates bearing the registration number of the vehicle were issued by the Department of Administrative Services of Australia,

it is not necessary for the vehicle to carry any number-plate in addition to those so issued.

PART III – REGISTRATION OF VEHICLES AND LICENSING OF DRIVERS, ETC

10 Registration, licensing, etc

The regulations shall make provision, in accordance with Section 47, for and in respect of –

(a) the registration of motor vehicles; and

(b) the licensing of drivers.

[705]11 Permits to drive unregistered vehicles

(1) Notwithstanding Section 22, the Superintendent may, in his discretion –

(a) on payment of the prescribed fee; and

(b) on production of third party insurance cover,

grant to a primary producer or motor vehicle dealer who owns an unregistered motor vehicle a permit in the prescribed form to drive the vehicle along a route or routes specified in the permit, for such purposes and during such period as the Superintendent thinks proper.

(2) A permit granted under Subsection (1) is subject to such conditions as the Superintendent thinks proper.

(3) A permit shall not be granted under Subsection (1) for a tractor unless the tractor –

(a) is equipped with pneumatic tyres; or

(b) in the opinion of the Superintendent, will not cause undue damage to roads.

(4) If a motor vehicle for which a permit under Subsection (1) is in force is driven on a road otherwise than in accordance with the terms and conditions of the permit, the person driving the vehicle is guilty of an offence.

Penalty: A fine not exceeding K500.00.

[705]Amended by No. 4 of 1981, s4.

PART IV – METERED PARKING

12 Metered zones

The Superintendent may –

(a) declare a public street or a portion of a public street to be a metered zone; and

(b) cause a traffic sign –

(i) indicating where metered parking is authorized; or

(ii) defining a metered space in a metered zone; or

(iii) indicating the maximum period during which a motor vehicle may be parked in a metered zone; or

(iv) indicating the hours in which or the days on which metered parking only is permitted in a metered zone; or

(v) defining a loading zone; or

(vi) defining a vehicle stand; or

(vii) necessary or desirable for the safe and effective regulation of traffic,

to be constructed, marked, placed, erected or affixed in or near a public road or part of a public road that is in a metered zone or that is a metered zone; and

(c) alter or remove a traffic sign constructed, marked, placed, erected or affixed under Paragraph (b).

13 Council parking meters

(1) A Local Government Council may install in a metered zone, and maintain, parking meters in accordance with this Part.

(2) A Local Government Council that has installed a parking meter in the area administered by the Council shall –

(a) collect the money inserted in the meter; and

(b) pay the amounts collected into the general revenue of the Council.

14 Government parking meters

(1) In an area where there is no Local Government Council, or no Local Government Council prepared to install and maintain parking meters in accordance with this Part, parking meters may be installed and maintained in a metered zone by the State.

(2) The amounts collected from the parking meters installed and maintained under Subsection (1) shall be paid into the Consolidated Revenue Fund.

15 Installation of parking meters

A parking meter installed under Section 13 or 14 shall be placed in a metered space defined under Section 12(b)(ii) in a position approved by the Superintendent.

16 Liability in respect of parking offences in metered zones

(1) Subject to Subsection (4), where an offence is committed in relation to the parking of a motor vehicle in a metered zone the person who at the time of the commission of the offence was the owner of the vehicle –

(a) shall be deemed to have committed the offence; and

(b) may be proceeded against for the commission of the offence.

(2) For the purposes of Subsection (1), the person in whose name the motor vehicle is registered shall be deemed to be the owner of the vehicle.

(3) The court hearing a complaint of an offence in relation to the parking of a motor vehicle in a metered zone shall, unless the contrary is proved, presume that the parking meter in respect of which the complaint has arisen was at all times and in all respects in good and correct working order and condition.

(4) Notwithstanding Subsection (1), the owner of a motor vehicle shall not, by virtue of that subsection, be deemed to be guilty of an offence not actually committed by him if he proves, to the satisfaction of the court –

(a) that the vehicle was sold before the date on which the offence was committed; or

(b) that, at the time of the offence, the vehicle was stolen or being unlawfully used without his consent.

[706]PART IVA – CERTAIN FEES TO BE PAID TO PROVINCIAL GOVERNMENT BODIES, ETC

16A Certain fees to be paid to provincial government bodies, etc

(1) Where the Superintendent has delegated to a provincial government body or an Area Authority his powers and functions under Section 8(2), the power, authority, function, duty or responsibility to collect fees in respect of –

(a) an application for a public motor vehicle licence; and

(b) a public motor vehicle licence; and

(c) a certificate of registration as a public hire car or a private hire car; and

(d) a temporary licence; and

(e) a certificate of registration as a motor omnibus,

under the *Motor Traffic Regulation*, is vested in the provincial government body or the Area Authority.

(2) Where any fees are collected under this section by a provincial government body or an Area Authority, the amounts so collected –

(a) shall be deemed not to be public moneys of the State, but shall be revenue of the provincial government body or Area Authority, as the case may be; and

(b) shall be paid into the general revenue of that provincial government body or Area Authority.

[706]Added by No. 9 of 1978 s4.

PART V – OFFENCES

Division 1 – Offences Generally

17 Dangerous driving and negligent driving

[707](1) A person who drives a motor vehicle on a public street negligently, furiously or recklessly, or at a speed or in a manner that is dangerous to the public, is guilty of an offence.

Penalty: A fine of not less than K15.00 and not exceeding K200.00 or imprisonment for a term not exceeding six months, or both.

[708](2) A person who drives a motor vehicle on a public street without due care and attention, or without reasonable consideration for other road users, is guilty of an offence.

Penalty: A fine not exceeding K500.00.

(3) In considering whether an offence has been committed against this section, the court shall have regard to all the circumstances of the case, including –

(a) the nature, condition and use of the street on which the offence is alleged to have been committed; and

(b) the amount of traffic that was or might reasonably have been expected to have been on the street at the time.

[709]18 Driving under the influence

A person who, while he is under the influence of intoxicating liquor or a drug –

(a) drives a motor vehicle on a public street; or

(b) occupies the driving seat of a motor vehicle on a public street and attempts to put the motor vehicle in motion,

is guilty of an offence.

Penalty: For a first offence – a fine not less than K50.00 and not exceeding K300.00 or imprisonment for a term not less than three months and not exceeding 12 months, or both a fine and imprisonment. For a second or subsequent offence – a fine not less than

[707]Amended by No. 111 of 1973, s3.
[708]Amended by No. 4 of 1981, s4.
[709]Amended by No. 111 of 1973, s5.

K400.00 and not exceeding K300.00 or imprisonment for a term not less than six months and not exceeding 12 months, or both a fine and imprisonment.

19 Prevention of driving under the influence, etc

(1) Subject to Subsection (2), where a member of the Police Force is of opinion on reasonable grounds that a person who is driving, or appears to him to be about to drive, a motor vehicle is by reason of his physical or mental condition incapable of having proper control of the vehicle, he may do all or any of the following things: –

(a) forbid the person to drive the vehicle while he is so incapable; or

(b) require him to deliver up immediately all ignition or other keys of the vehicle in his actual possession; or

(c) take such other steps as are in his opinion necessary to make the vehicle immobile or to remove it to a place of safety.

(2) Subsection (1) does not authorize –

(a) the detention of keys; or

(b) the immobilization or detention of a motor vehicle,

for any longer period than is necessary in all the circumstances of the case in the interests of the person or of any other person, or of the public.

(3) Subject to Subsection (4), a person who –

(a) contravenes or fails to comply with a prohibition or requirement made by a member of the Police Force under this section; or

(b) attempts to obstruct a member of the Police Force in the exercise of any power conferred on him by this section,

is guilty of an offence.

Penalty: For a first offence – a fine not exceeding Kl00.00.

For a second or subsequent offence – a fine not exceeding K200.00 or imprisonment for a term not exceeding six months.

(4) A person shall not be found guilty of an offence against this section unless the court is satisfied that the member of the Police Force concerned had reasonable grounds for believing that in all the circumstances of the case the action taken by him under Subsection (1) was necessary in the interests of the person or of any other person, or of the public.

20 Medical examination of arrested persons

A person who is arrested for an offence against Section 18 or 19 is entitled, on request made by him or on his behalf, to be examined by a medical practitioner, and where any such request is made the member of the Police Force making the arrest shall afford all reasonable facilities for the holding of the examination.

[710]21 Unlicensed drivers

(1) Subject to this Act, a person who drives a motor vehicle on a public street without being licensed for the purpose is guilty of an offence.

Penalty: A fine of not less than K10.00 and not exceeding K500.00.

(2) Subject to this Act, a person who employs or permits an unlicensed person to drive a motor vehicle on a public street is guilty of an offence.

Penalty: A fine not exceeding K500.00.

[711]22 Unregistered vehicles, etc

(1) Subject to this Act and in particular to Section 11, a person who drives, or causes or permits to be driven, on a public street, an unregistered motor vehicle is guilty of an offence.

Penalty: A fine of not less than K20.00 and not exceeding K500.00.

(2) Subject to this Act and in particular to Section 11, a person who drives, or causes or permits to be driven, on a public street a motor vehicle that –

(a) does not have the prescribed number-plate properly affixed to it; or

(b) has its number-plate obscured so that the numbers on the plate are not clearly visible; or

(c) has the original numbers on its number-plate obliterated by paint or any other material; or

(d) has its number-plate so damaged that the original numbers are not complete and distinctly visible,

is guilty of an offence.

Penalty: A fine not exceeding K500.00.

---

[710]Amended by No. 111 of 1973, s6 and No. 4 of 1981, s2 and s4.
[711]Amended by No. 111 of 1973, s6, No. 4 of 1981, s4.

(3) A person is not liable to a penalty for an offence against Subsection (1) and (2) if he proves to the satisfaction of the court that –

(a) the breach was the result of an accident; or

(b) the vehicle concerned –

(i) was being driven to the nearest Motor Vehicles Registry for the purpose of being registered; and

(ii) otherwise complied with the prescribed conditions.

[712]23 Vehicles carrying passengers

A person who causes or permits a motor vehicle (other than a vehicle in respect of which the prescribed public motor vehicle licence is in force) to be used for carrying passengers for hire or reward is guilty of an offence.

Penalty: A fine not exceeding K500.00.

[713]24 Stopping in case of accidents

Where injury or damage is caused to a person or to an animal or vehicle in the charge of a person because of an accident in which a motor vehicle is concerned, if the driver of the motor vehicle –

(a) fails to stop his vehicle; or

(b) fails, when required –

(i) by the person who is injured or whose animal or vehicle is injured or damaged; or

(ii) by a member of the Police Force,

to give –

(iii) his name and address; and

(iv) the name and address of the owner of the motor vehicle; and

(v) the registration number of the motor vehicle; or

(c) fails to report the accident to the officer-in-charge of the police station nearest the scene of the accident as soon as practicable, and in any case within 24 hours,

he is guilty of an offence.

Penalty: A fine not exceeding K500.00.

---

[712]Amended by No. 4 of 1981, s4.

[713]Amended by No. 4 of 1981, s4.

25 Unauthorized use of vehicles

(1) Subject to Subsection (2), a person who drives or uses a motor vehicle without first obtaining the consent of the owner is guilty of an offence.

Penalty: A fine not exceeding K2,000.00 or imprisonment for a term not exceeding five years, or both.

(2) Notwithstanding anything in this Act, Subsection (1) does not apply to a member of the Police Force in the execution of his duty.

[714]26 Unauthorized interference with vehicles

A person who interferes with or tampers with a motor vehicle or any part of a motor vehicle without the consent of the owner of the vehicle is guilty of an offence.

Penalty: A fine not exceeding K2,000.00 or imprisonment for a term not exceeding five years, or both.

27 Failure to pay fare

A person who, in respect of a journey in a public motor vehicle, refuses or fails, without reasonable excuse (proof of which is on him), to pay the regular charge or fare payable by him when demanded from him by the owner or the driver of the vehicle, or by an employee of the owner, is guilty of an offence.

Penalty: A fine not exceeding Kl0.00.

[715]28 Hiring of vehicle by fraud

A person who procures the use or hire of a motor vehicle by fraud or misrepresentation is guilty of an offence.

Penalty: A fine not exceeding K500.00.

[716]29 Limitation of speed

(1) The Minister may, by notice in the National Gazette, limit the speed at which a motor vehicle may travel –

(a) on a public street; or

(b) on any part of a public street; or

(c) in an area,

specified in the notice.

---

[714]Amended by No. 4 of 1981, s4.
[715]Amended by No. 4 of 1981, s4.
[716]Amended by No. 4 of 1981, s4.

(2) A person who drives a motor vehicle on a public street or a part of a public street, or in an area, specified in a notice under Subsection (1) at a speed greater than the speed permitted by the notice is guilty of an offence.

Penalty: A fine not exceeding K500.00.

[717]30 Production of licence, etc, on demand

(1) A driver of a motor vehicle who fails to produce his licence when required to do so by a member of the Police Force, or an Inspector of Motor Traffic in the execution of his duty under this Act is guilty of an offence.

Penalty: A fine of not less than K1.00 and not exceeding K500.00.

(2) A driver of a motor vehicle who, when required by a member of the Police Force, or an Inspector of Motor Traffic in the execution of his duty under this Act to state his name and place of abode –

(a) refuses to do so; or

(b) states a false name or place of abode,

is guilty of an offence.

Penalty: A fine not exceeding K500.00.

[718]31 Failure to assist in identification of offending driver

The owner of, or a passenger in, a motor vehicle who, when required by a member of the Police Force, or an Inspector of Motor Traffic to give any information that –

(a) it is in his power to give; and

(b) may lead to the identification of the person who was driving the vehicle when an offence against this Act is alleged to have been committed,

refuses or fails to give the information is guilty of an offence.

Penalty: A fine not exceeding K500.00.

[717]Section 30 amended by:

- No 111 of 1973 s4; and
- No 9 of 1978, s3; and
- No 4 of 1981, s1 and s4.

[718]Amended by No. 9 of 1978, s3 and No. 4 of 1981, s4.

[719]32 Miscellaneous offences relating to licences, registration, etc

A person who –

(a) by a false statement or misrepresentation obtains or attempts to obtain a licence, certificate of registration or permit under Section 11; or

(b) wilfully furnishes false or misleading information with regard to particulars required by this Act to be furnished in relation to a licence, certificate of registration or permit under Section 11; or

(c) without lawful excuse, has in his possession –

(i) a licence, certificate of registration, permit under Section 11, registration label or number-plate issued under this Act; or

(ii) an article –

(A) resembling a licence, certificate of registration, permit under Section 11, registration label or number-plate issued under this Act; and

(B) calculated to deceive; or

(d) forges, fraudulently alters or uses or fraudulently lends to, or allows to be used by, any other person a licence, permit under Section 11, number-plate or mark for identifying a motor vehicle under this Act; or

(e) owns or drives on a public street an unregistered motor vehicle having on it any numbers or number-plate –

(i) of a description prescribed to be affixed to motor vehicles; and

(ii) calculated to deceive; or

(f) except as authorized by this Act, transfers, or causes or permits to be transferred, a number-plate issued under this Act in respect of a motor vehicle to any other motor vehicle, or causes or permits such a number-plate to be on any other motor vehicle; or

(g) affixes to, or causes or permits to be affixed to, or to be on, an unregistered motor vehicle –

(i) a number-plate, or an article on which there is a number, resembling, but not being, a prescribed number-plate; or

[719]Amended by No. 4 of 1981, s4.

(ii) a prescribed number-plate that has been altered in contravention of this Act; or

(h) sells, disposes of or buys, or attempts to sell, dispose of or buy, a number-plate or certificate of registration, otherwise than as part of the sale, disposal or purchase of the vehicle in respect of which the number-plate or certificate of registration was issued; or

(i) sells, disposes of or buys, or attempts to sell, dispose of or buy, a permit under Section 11,

is guilty of an offence.

Penalty: A fine not exceeding K500.00.

[720]33 Production of licence to court

A licensed driver charged with an offence against this Act who fails, without reasonable excuse, to produce his licence to the court at the time of hearing is guilty of an offence.

Penalty: A fine not exceeding K500.00.

Division 2 – Summary Provision in Certain Cases

[721]34 On-the-spot fines

(1) Where it appears to a member of the Police Force or a prescribed officer that a person has committed a prescribed offence against this Act, the member of the Police Force or prescribed officer may serve on the person a notice in the prescribed form to the effect that if he does not desire to have the matter determined by a court he may pay to an officer specified in the notice, within the time specified in the notice, the amount of the penalty prescribed for the offence if dealt with under this section.

(2) A notice under Subsection (1) may be served –

(a) personally or by post; or

(b) by leaving it on or in, or attaching it to, the vehicle.

(3) A person alleged to have committed an offence to which Subsection (1) applies has the right to decline to be dealt with under this section.

(4) For the purposes of Subsection (3), a person who fails to pay, within the time specified in the notice or such further time as is allowed in any particular case, the penalty to which a notice under Subsection (1)

[720]Amended by No. 4 of 1981, s4.
[721]Amended by No. 4 of 1981, s4.

relates shall be deemed to have declined to be dealt with under this section.

(5) Where the amount of the prescribed penalty for an alleged offence is paid in accordance with this section, no person is liable to any further proceedings for the offence.

(6) Payment, in accordance with this section, of a penalty in respect of an alleged offence –

(a) shall not be regarded as an admission of liability for the purposes of; and

(b) does not affect or prejudice,

any criminal proceedings other than proceedings for the alleged offence or any civil claim, action or proceeding arising out of the same occurrence.

(7) The regulations may –

(a) prescribe the offences that are prescribed offences for the purposes of this section by –

(i) setting out the offences; or

(ii) referring to the provisions creating the offences; and

(b) prescribe the amount of, and the method of payment of, the penalty payable under this section for a prescribed offence.

(8) A penalty prescribed for the purposes of this section for a prescribed offence shall not exceed –

(a) the maximum amount of penalty that could be imposed for the offence by a court; or

(b) a fine of K500.00,

whichever is the less.

(9) Subject to Subsections (5) and (6), this section is supplementary to, and not in derogation of, any other provision of this Act or any other law in relation to proceedings that may be taken in respect of prescribed offences.

[722]*Division 3 – Traffic Infringement Summons*

34A Traffic Infringement Summons

(1) Where it appears to a member of the Police Force or a prescribed officer that a person has committed a prescribed offence against this Act, that member of the Police Force or prescribed officer may serve on the a person a Traffic Infringement Summons.

[722]Added by No. 4 of 1981, s3.

(2) A Traffic Infringement Summons shall be in the prescribed form and shall –

(a) be directed against the person named in the summons as the person alleged to have committed the prescribed offence; and

(b) specify the alleged offence; and

(c) specify the penalty prescribed for that offence; and

(d) specify the court to the Clerk of which the penalty may be paid within a period of 14 days commencing on the day following the day on which the Summons is served; and

(e) state that in the event of –

(i) payment of the penalty at the court and within the period specified, the case will not be called in court; and

(ii) non-payment of the fine at the court within the specified period, the case will be called on the first day on which the court sits following the expiry of the specified period; and

(iii) . . . [Omitted]

(iv) the person named in the Summons wishing to plead not guilty or otherwise wishing to be heard by the court, he should appear or be represented in the court on the first day on which the court sits following the expiry of the specified period.

(3) A person who serves a Traffic Infringement Summons shall immediately after service –

(a) make an affidavit, endorsed on the original Summons, stating the day and place of service; and

(b) transmit the original Summons to the Clerk of the Court specified in the Summons for subsequent production at the court if required in accordance with the provisions of this Act in the event of non-payment of the sum specified within the time specified.

(4) A Traffic Infringement Summons containing an affidavit purporting to be an affidavit of service is prima facie evidence of the service of the summons.

34B Procedure on Traffic Infringement Summons

(1) For the purpose of this section –

"defendant" means a person on whom a Traffic Infringement Summons has been served;

"specified" means specified in the Traffic Infringement Summons.

(2) Following the service of a Traffic Infringement Summons –

(a) where the defendant pays the specified penalty to the Clerk of the specified court within the specified period, the matter proceeds no further; or

(b) where payment is not made under Paragraph (a) – the case is called in the specified court on the first day on which the court sits following the expiry of the specified period; or

(c) where the case is called under Paragraph (b) and –

(i) the defendant is not present or represented, a plea of guilty shall be recorded and the matter dealt with in accordance with the procedure of the court; or

(ii) the defendant is present or represented, the matter shall be dealt with in accordance with the procedure of the court.

PART VI – EFFECT OF CONVICTION

[723]35 Automatic disqualification, etc

Where a person is convicted of an offence against Section 17(1) or 18, the court that convicts him shall disqualify him from holding and obtaining a licence for such period as it thinks proper, not being less than –

(a) in the case of a first offence –

(i) against Section 17(1) – three months; and

(ii) against Section 18 – six months; and

(b) in the case of a second or subsequent offence against either of those sections – 12 months.

36 Discretionary suspension, disqualification, etc

(1) Subject to Section 35, the court that convicts a person of an offence against this Act may, in addition to any other punishment to which the person is liable under this Act in respect of the offence –

(a) if he holds a licence or a permit under Section 11 –

(i) suspend the licence or permit for such time as the court thinks proper and, if the court thinks fit, also direct that no licence and no such permit be granted to him during such further time after the expiration of the licence or permit as the court thinks proper; or

(ii) cancel the licence or permit and, if the court thinks fit, declare him to be disqualified from obtaining a licence or such a permit for such time as the court thinks proper; and

(b) if he does not hold a licence or a permit under Section 11 – direct that no licence or permit be granted to him during such time as the court thinks proper.

(2) A person whose licence or permit under Section 11 is suspended is, during the period of suspension, disqualified from obtaining a licence or permit.

[724]36A Driving while disqualified

A person who drives a motor vehicle on a public street –

---

[723]Amended by No. 111 of 1973, s5.

[724]Section 36A inserted by *Motor Traffic (Amendment) Act* 1987 (No. 16 of 1987), s5.

(a) while disqualified by a court from holding or obtaining a –

(i) driving licence; or

(ii) learner's permit; or

(iii) permit under Section 11; or

(b) while his –

(i) driving licence; or

(ii) learner's permit; or

(iii) permit under Section 11,

has been suspended by order of a court,

is guilty of an offence.

Penalty: A term of imprisonment not less than three months.

[725]37 Endorsement of licence or permit

(1) Where the holder of a licence or of a permit under Section 11 is convicted of an offence against this Act, the court that convicts him shall cause particulars of the conviction to be endorsed on the licence or permit.

(2) Where the holder of a licence or of a permit under Section 11 is convicted of an offence against this Act, he must produce his licence or permit within a reasonable time for the purpose of endorsement.

Penalty: A fine not exceeding K500.00.

[726]38 Wrongfully obtaining, etc., licence, etc

If –

(a) a person who is disqualified under this Act from obtaining a licence or a permit under Section 11 applies for or obtains a licence or such a permit, or a renewal of a licence or of such a permit, while he is so disqualified; or

(b) a person whose licence or permit under Section 11 has been endorsed in accordance with Section 37 applies for or obtains a licence or such a permit, or a renewal of a licence or of such a permit, without giving particulars of the endorsement,

the licence or permit is of no effect and he is guilty of an offence.

Penalty: A fine not exceeding K500.00.

---

[725]Amended by No. 4 of 1981, s4.

[726]Amended by No. 4 of 1981, s4.

39 Particulars of convictions, etc

The court that makes a conviction or order under this Act shall cause particulars of the conviction or order to be forwarded to the prescribed officer.

PART VII – MISCELLANEOUS

40 Arrest without warrant

A member of the Police Force may, without warrant, arrest –

(a) a person in the act of committing, or immediately after having committed, an offence against Section 18, 19, 25, 26, 30(2) or 31; or

(b) a person whom he believes on reasonable grounds to have committed any such offence.

41 Offences due to accident

A person is not liable to be convicted of an offence against this Act if he proves to the satisfaction of the court hearing the case that the offence could not have been avoided by reasonable efforts on his part.

42 Records of registrations, licences, etc

(1) Particulars of the registration of motor vehicles and of the issue of certificates, permits under Section 11 and licences shall be recorded at the prescribed office or offices.

(2) An extract from or copy of any entry contained in a record kept in accordance with Subsection (1), certified by a prescribed officer, shall, in all courts and on all occasions, be –

(a) received as evidence; and

(b) deemed to be sufficient proof of all particulars contained in the entry,

without requiring the production of the books, permit, licence, requisition, notice or other document on which the entry was founded.

43 Evidence of registration and ownership

In any proceedings under this Act –

(a) proof that a motor vehicle has not on it the prescribed distinguishing number is prima facie evidence that the vehicle is not registered; and

(b) proof that a person registered a motor vehicle is prima facie evidence that he is the owner of the vehicle.

44 Powers and duties of police

(1) Every member of the Police Force shall do all things in his power to ensure that this Act is duly observed.

(2) In all cases not expressly provided for, a member of the Police

Force in the execution of his duty under this Act may give such reasonable directions –

(a) to persons driving motor vehicles or driving or riding other vehicles or animals; or

(b) to pedestrians,

on a public street as are in his opinion necessary for the safe and efficient regulation of the traffic on the street.

[727]44A Powers of police in relation to certain vehicles owned by the State, etc

(1) Where a motor vehicle owned by the State is being driven on a public street –

(a) outside the prescribed hours; and

(b) without bearing the prescribed label authorizing its being driven outside the prescribed hours,

a member of the Police Force may do all or any of the following things –

(c) order the driver of the motor vehicle to stop;

(d) forbid the driver to drive the motor vehicle;

(e) require the driver to supply particulars of his name, occupation and address;

(f) require the driver to deliver up immediately all ignition keys and other keys of the motor vehicle in his actual possession;

(g) take such other steps as are in the opinion of the member of the Police Force necessary to make the motor vehicle immobile or to remove it to a place of safety.

(2) Where a member of the Police Force has taken action under Subsection (1), he shall, as soon as is practicable, notify in the prescribed manner the Departmental Head of the Department of Personnel Management or a person authorized by the Departmental Head of the Department of Personnel Management for the purpose, of the action taken.

(3) A motor vehicle detained under Subsection (1) shall not be released except to a person authorized in writing by the Departmental Head of the Department of Personnel Management as a person authorized to collect motor vehicles so detained.

---

[727]Section 44A inserted by *Motor Traffic (Amendment) Act* 1987 (No. 16 of 1987), s6.

45 Service of notices

A notice under this Act shall be deemed to be duly served on an owner or driver of a motor vehicle if it is –

(a) served personally; or

(b) left at the last address specified in or endorsed on the licence of the owner or driver.

46 Speed-measuring and time-measuring devices

Where in any proceedings for an offence against Section 29 or any other law, the speed at which a motor vehicle travelled on the occasion of the alleged offence is relevant, evidence of the speed of the vehicle, as indicated or determined on that occasion by means of a prescribed speed-measuring or time-measuring device, used in the prescribed manner and subject to the prescribed conditions, is, without prejudice to any other mode of proof, prima facie evidence of the speed of the vehicle on that occasion.

[728]47 Regulations

The Head of State, acting on advice, may make regulations, not inconsistent with this Act, prescribing all matters that by this Act are required or permitted to be prescribed, or that are necessary or convenient to be prescribed for carrying out or giving effect to this Act, and in particular for –

(a) the regulation of the owners and drivers of motor vehicles; and

(b) the regulation of the registration of motor vehicles, and the manner, duration, suspension, cancellation, transfer and renewal of registration; and

(c) the granting of permits under Section 11; and

(d) the licensing of drivers of motor vehicles; and

(e) the regulation of the grant of licences, and of the renewal, transfer, suspension, cancellation and return of licences; and

(f) the replacement of lost licences; and

(g) the licensing of public motor vehicles; and

(h) the regulation of the grant of public motor vehicle licences, and of the renewal, transfer, suspension, cancellation and return of such licences; and

(i) prescribing maximum charges or fares to be made or charged in relation to public motor vehicles; and

---

[728]Amended by No. 9 of 1978, s5.

(j) prescribing the form, construction and equipment of public motor vehicles; and

(k) providing that a public motor vehicle licence shall not be granted or renewed except in respect of a motor vehicle the owner of which is insured as prescribed against his liability for damages in respect of the vehicle in case of injury to persons; and

(l) prescribing the qualifications of drivers of motor vehicles, and the age or ages at which persons may drive motor vehicles; and

(m) prescribing places for –

  (i) the registration of, and for application for the grant of permits under Section 11 in relation to, motor vehicles; and

  (ii) the licensing of drivers; and

(n) regulating the use of motor vehicles on public streets, and the conditions under which they may be so used; and

(o) regulating, subject to Section 29, the speed at which motor vehicles may travel; and

(p) regulating –

  (i) the weights of the loads and the numbers of passengers that may be carried on different kinds of motor vehicles; and

  (ii) the carrying on motor vehicles of long, large, heavy or projecting articles; and

(q) prescribing and regulating the carrying of lights on motor vehicles; and

(r) prescribing and regulating the affixing and use of horns or other means of alarm; and

(s) prescribing and regulating the affixing of efficient brakes on motor vehicles; and

(t) preventing or minimizing –

  (i) the noise; and

  (ii) the issue of smoke or fumes,

  from the working of the machinery or engines of motor vehicles; and

(u) prohibiting the use of motor vehicles that, owing to their construction or other cause, are unsuitable for safe use; and

(v) prescribing the rules of the road to be observed by drivers of motor vehicles; and

(w) the regulation of motor traffic both generally and in respect of particular localities or public streets; and

(x) the prohibition or restriction of motor traffic –

(i) in particular localities or public streets; and

(ii) for a specified period or otherwise; and

(iii) in respect of a class or all classes of motor vehicles; and

(y) providing that motor vehicles shall have separate distinguishing numbers, and regulating –

(i) the form of the numbers; and

(ii) the manner of affixing them on vehicles; and

(iii) the issue and return of them; and

(z) the erection of uniform signs and notices for the guidance of motor drivers; and

(za) the temporary registration of motor vehicles owned by persons residing outside the country and temporarily in the country, and the drivers of such vehicles; and

(zb) the issue of special number-plates to manufacturers of, or dealers in, motor vehicles for use on motor vehicles in their possession, on trial before or after completion, and prescribing the conditions under which such plates may be used; and

(zc) regulating or prohibiting the manufacture, repair, cleansing or assembling of motor vehicles in public streets; and

(zd) subject to the *Inflammable* [729]*Liquid Act*, regulating or prohibiting the conveyance of inflammable liquid in or on motor vehicles used for the carriage of passengers for hire or reward; and

(ze) the seizure and custody of motor vehicles that –

(i) are dangers or unreasonable obstructions to traffic; or

(ii) have been abandoned in a public street,

and for –

(iii) the recovery of any expenses incurred in the seizure and custody of any such vehicle; and

(iv) its disposal or destruction if the owner fails to claim it or to pay any expenses referred to in Subparagraph (iii) within the prescribed time; and

---

[729]The Act has "Liquids".

(zf) requiring the carrying of efficient fire extinguishers on specified classes of motor vehicles used for the carriage of passengers for hire or reward; and

(zg) making provision for or with respect to the marking of tyres of motor vehicles by means of crayon, chalk or a similar substance by members of the Police Force, or an Inspector of Motor Traffic for any purpose connected with the enforcement of any of the provisions of this Act; and

(zh) prohibiting or restricting any person (other than the driver or other prescribed person) from –

(i) parking, minding, caring for or taking charge of a motor vehicle on a public street; or

(ii) offering his services for any such purpose; and

(zi) prohibiting or regulating the setting up and use of stalls, stands and vehicles for –

(i) the sale of goods; or

(ii) the pursuit of any business, calling or employment,

in a public street; and

(zj) prohibiting loitering and the obstruction of traffic in the carriageways of public streets; and

(zk) regulating the use of trailers; and

(zl) prescribing rules for the taking up and setting down of passengers; and

(zm) appointing officers of the Public Service and commissioned officers of the Police Force to administer this Act, and defining their powers and duties; and

(zn) prescribing the manner in which registers shall be kept; and

(zo) prescribing the forms of –

(i) certificates of registration; and

(ii) permits under Section 11; and

(iii) licences and other documents,

issued and used under or for the purposes of this Act; and

(zp) the regulation of the parking of motor vehicles in metered zones; and

(zq) the operation and treatment of parking meters; and

(zr) the method of payment into parking meters; and

(zs) the number and denomination of coins to be inserted in a parking meter in respect of a metered space per hour or part of an hour; and (zt) prescribing the matters in relation to which fees are payable and the fees to be paid; and

(zu) imposing taxation on motor vehicles; and

(zv) prescribing penalties of fines not exceeding K50.00 for offences against the regulations made for the purposes of Part IV., or for failures to comply with traffic signs constructed, marked, placed, erected or affixed under that Part; and

(zw) prescribing penalties of fines not exceeding K500.00 or imprisonment for a term not exceeding six months, or both, and default penalties of fines not exceeding K50.00 for offences against the regulations.

[730](zx) prescribing the hours during which a motor vehicle owned by the State may be driven and the label authorizing its being driven outside those hours and the manner of reporting action taken under Section 44A.

[731](zy) making provision for the compulsory fitting of seat belts to motor vehicles and for the compulsory wearing of such seat belts by drivers and passengers.

---

[730]Section 47(zx) added by *Motor Traffic (Amendment) Act* 1987 (No. 16 of 1987), s7.

[731]Section 47(zy) added by *Motor Traffic (Amendment No. 2) Act* 1989 (No. 12 of 1989).

CHAPTER No 296

Motor Vehicles (Third Party Insurance) (Basic Protection Compensation) Act

PART I – PRELIMINARY

PART II – INQUIRIES

PART III – COMPENSATION

PART IV – MISCELLANEOUS

INDEPENDENT STATE OF PAPUA NEW GUINEA

CHAPTER No 296

Motor Vehicles (Third Party Insurance) (Basic Protection Compensation) Act

(Consolidated to No 28 of 1997)

Being an Act to provide for the speedy payment of a limited amount of compensation to the dependants of persons whose deaths are directly or indirectly attributable to the use of motor vehicles, without regard to any concept of negligence, and for related purposes.

PART I – PRELIMINARY

1 Interpretation

In this Act, unless the contrary intention appears –

"assessment officer" means an assessment officer appointed under Section 5, and includes a Magistrate of a District Court and a coroner;

"assessor" means an assessor appointed under Section 7;

"award" means an award of compensation made under Section 19;

"compensation" means compensation payable under this Act;

"deceased person" means a deceased person to whom this Act applies;

"dependent child", in relation to a deceased person, means –

(a) a child (including an ex-nuptial child) of the deceased person; and

(b) a person to whom the deceased person stood *in loco parentis*;

"dependent wife", in relation to a deceased person, means a wife of the deceased person who was wholly or in part dependent, by custom or otherwise, on the deceased person at the date of his death;

"entitled person", in relation to a deceased person, means the person to whom compensation is payable under Section 17;

"Government motor vehicle" means a motor vehicle the property of the State;

"immediate customary kinship group", in relation to a deceased person, means –

(a) any wife or child of the deceased who was not wholly or in part dependent on the deceased person at the time of his death; and

(b) any member of the family, extended family, sub-clan or clan to which he was most closely affiliated during his lifetime, who is entitled to a beneficial share in the customary estate of the deceased;

"inquiry" means an inquiry conducted under this Act;

"insured motor vehicle" means a motor vehicle that, at the relevant time –

(a) is insured by the successor company under this Act; or

(b) is a Government motor vehicle;

"motor vehicle" means a motor car, motor carriage, motor cycle, motor truck, motor omnibus, motor tractor or other vehicle propelled wholly or partly by a volatile spirit or by steam, gas, oil or electricity, or by means other than human or animal power, and includes a trailer, but does not include a vehicle used on a railway or tramway;

"the regulations" means any regulations made under this Act;

[732]"successor company" means the successor company nominated under Section 65 of the *Motor Vehicles (Third Party Insurance) Act* (Chpater 295);

"the Trust" . . .

"this Act" includes the regulations;

"uninsured motor vehicle" means a motor vehicle that is not an insured motor vehicle.

2 Application to the State

This Act binds the State.

---

[732]The definition of "successor company" inserted by *Motor Vehicles (Third Party Insurance) (Amendment) Act* 1997 (No. 28 of 1997), s 3 and Schedule 2.

3 Exclusion of certain deaths

This Act does not apply to or in relation to the death of a person that is directly or indirectly attributable to personal injury suffered by him as a result of a motor vehicle accident where the death occurred more than 90 days after the accident.

4 Saving of Coroners Act

This Act does not affect the operation of the *Coroners Act*, and a coroner is not bound by any decision given by an assessment officer under this Act.

PART II – INQUIRIES

5 Assessment officers

(1) The Minister may, by notice in the National Gazette –

(a) appoint an officer to be an assessment officer for the purposes of this Act; and

(b) specify the area within which he has jurisdiction, power and authority.

(2) An assessment officer appointed under Subsection (1) may conduct an inquiry relating to the death of a person where he has reasonable cause to believe that the death of that person was directly or indirectly attributable to the use of a motor vehicle in the area within which he has jurisdiction.

6 Magistrates and coroners to be assessment officers

A Magistrate of a District Court and a coroner are, by virtue of their offices, assessment officers and have jurisdiction, power and authority throughout the country.

7 Appointment of assessors

(1) An assessment officer may, where he thinks it necessary or desirable to do so in relation to any inquiry conducted or to be conducted under this Act, appoint not more than three persons to assist him with the inquiry.

(2) An assessor appointed under Subsection (1) has and shall perform such functions and duties, other than the making of a determination under Part III., as are directed by the assessment officer.

8 Establishment of inquiry

(1) Where an assessment officer has reasonable cause to believe that the death of a person was directly or indirectly attributable to the use of a motor vehicle, he –

(a) may, of his own motion; and

(b) shall, as soon as practicable after receiving a request to do so from an entitled person, a member of the Police Force or the Minister,

conduct a full inquiry into the cause of the death.

(2) Where an assessment officer is unable to conclude an inquiry held under Subsection (1) within two weeks after the date on which he receives a request from an entitled person, a member of the Police Force

or the Minister, he shall forward a report to the Minister setting out the reasons for his being unable to do so.

9 Inquiry to be conducted without regard to legal formalities

An inquiry under this Act shall be conducted without regard to legal forms and solemnities, and the assessment officer conducting the inquiry is not bound to apply technical rules of evidence but shall admit and consider such relevant information as is available, including hearsay.

10 Power to summon witnesses

(1) An assessment officer may summon before him any person for the purpose of giving evidence or producing documents.

(2) A summons under Subsection (1) shall be served, and proof of service given, in such manner and subject to such conditions as the assessment officer determines.

(3) A summons under this section may be oral or written, and in the case of an oral summons may be served by being communicated to the person concerned by the assessment officer or by a person authorized by the assessment officer for the purpose.

11 Representation

An entitled person is entitled to be represented before an assessment officer by any person other than a lawyer.

12 Contempt of assessment officer

A person who –

- (a) when summoned under Section 10 to appear before an assessment officer refuses or fails, without reasonable excuse (proof of which is on him), to do so; or
- (b) wilfully interrupts, interferes with or disturbs any proceedings before an assessment officer; or
- (c) wilfully obstructs or attempts to obstruct an assessment officer acting under this Act; or
- (d) refuses or fails to give evidence or to answer a lawful question when lawfully required to do so by an assessment officer,

is guilty of an offence.

Penalty: A fine not exceeding K200.00.

13 Transfer of proceedings

Where an inquiry has been commenced by an assessment officer, he may at any time before decision, of his own motion or otherwise, for reasons that shall be recorded, make an order staying the inquiry and, on such terms as seem to him just, transferring the inquiry for hearing by some other assessment officer.

14 Effect of transfer

Where an inquiry is ordered to be transferred to or heard before another assessment officer under Section 13, the assessment officer who instituted the inquiry shall report the proceedings to the other assessment officer, and thereupon the last-mentioned assessment officer shall proceed with the inquiry as though a request under Section 8 had been made to him.

PART III – COMPENSATION

15 Determination of cause of death

An assessment officer shall, after he has completed an inquiry under this Act, determine whether the death of the person or persons the subject of the inquiry, or any of them, is directly or indirectly attributable to the use of a motor vehicle.

16 Determination as to entitled persons, etc

Where an assessment officer determines under Section 15 that the death of a person the subject of the inquiry was directly or indirectly attributable to the use of a motor vehicle, he shall at the same time determine –

(a) where the deceased was not an occupant of a motor vehicle and where it is possible to do so, the motor vehicle or motor vehicles that was or were most closely associated with the death; and

(b) where compensation is payable under Section 17(*b*), the person who is for the time being the head of the deceased person's immediate customary kinship group.

17 Entitlement to compensation

Compensation awarded under Section 19 is payable –

(a) where the deceased died leaving a dependent wife or dependent child – to the wife or child; and

(b) in any other case – to the head of the deceased person's immediate customary kinship group as agent for all members of that group.

18 Maximum amount of compensation payable

The total amount of compensation awarded under this Act by an assessment officer in respect of the death of any person shall not exceed –

(a) in the case of a person who died leaving a dependent wife or dependent child or both – K5,000.00; and

(b) in any other case – K2,500.00.

19 Award of Compensation

(1) Subject to Sections 17 and 18, an assessment officer may award compensation to the entitled person, or each of the entitled persons, in such amount as he fixes.

(2) An award of compensation under Subsection (1) is subject to such conditions as the assessment officer specifies in the award.

(3) In assessing –

(a) the amount of compensation payable to an entitled person or entitled persons; or

(b) the proportionate amount of compensation payable to each entitled person,

under Subsection (1), the assessment officer shall have regard to –

(c) customary disposition of property on death; and

(d) any economic loss suffered by any or all of the entitled persons; and

(e) any other factor that he thinks relevant.

20 Payment of compensation

(1) Compensation is payable under this Act –

(a) in the case of the death of –

(i) an occupant of a motor vehicle; or

(ii) a person, in relation to whose death the assessment officer has determined under Section 16(*a*) that the vehicle most closely associated with the death was a vehicle other than a Government motor vehicle,

by the successor company; and

(b) in the case of the death of –

(i) an occupant of a Government motor vehicle; or

(ii) a person, in relation to whose death the assessment officer has determined under Section 16(a) that the motor vehicle most closely associated with the death was a Government motor vehicle,

by the State; and

(c) in any other case, by the successor company and the State in such proportions as are determined by the Minister.

(2) The assessment officer shall, in any award made by him under Section 19, specify whether the successor company, the State or both is or are liable under Subsection (1) for payment of the compensation.

(3) Subsection (1) applies to the successor company and the State

whether the motor vehicle, at the time of the occurrence of the accident in respect of which compensation is payable, was being used on a public street or otherwise.

(4) Compensation under this Act is payable within the prescribed time and in the prescribed manner.

[733](5) Where compensation is not paid within the prescribed time the person liable to pay the compensation shall pay, in addition to any other penalty, interest on the amount of the compensation outstanding at the rate of 5% per annum from the date of the last day on which the compensation should have been paid until the date on which the compensation is paid.

21 Distribution of copies of award

Where an award is made under this Act relating to the payment of compensation, the assessment officer shall, as soon as practicable after the making of the award, give or forward a copy of the award certified under his hand to –

(a) the Minister for Justice; and

(b) the Minister; and

(c) the entitled person or entitled persons in whose favour the award was made, or the person or persons appointed by the entitled person or entitled persons to represent him or them; and

(d) the successor company.

22 Enforcement of awards

(1) An award operates as an order for the payment of a sum of money under the *District Courts Act* (Chapter 40).

(2) For the purposes of Subsection (1), an award may be entered in such manner as is prescribed in the records at the District Court exercising jurisdiction at the place where the award was made.

23 Recovery by successor company, etc, in certain cases

(1) Subject to Subsection (2), any amount paid by the successor company or the State under this Act in relation to an uninsured, unidentified or unknown motor vehicle may be recovered by the successor company or the State, as the case may be, as a debt from the person who –

---

[733]Section 20(5) added by Motor Vehicles (Third Party Insurance) (Basic Protection Compensation) (Amendment) Act 1991 (No. 20 of 1991), s2.

(a) at the time of the occurrence of the event out of which the award was made – was the owner of the motor vehicle; or

(b) where at the time of the event some other person was driving the vehicle – from the owner and the driver jointly or from either of them severally.

(2) It is a sufficient defence in any proceedings under this section –

(a) against the owner (whether severally or jointly with the driver) – if he establishes to the satisfaction of the court that, at the time of the occurrence, some other person was driving the motor vehicle without his authority; or

(b) against the driver of an uninsured motor vehicle (whether severally or jointly with the owner) – if he establishes to the satisfaction of the court that, at the time of the occurrence –

(i) he was driving the motor vehicle with the authority of the owner or had reasonable grounds for believing, and did in fact believe, that he had such authority; and

(ii) he had reasonable grounds for believing, and did in fact believe, that the motor vehicle was an insured motor vehicle.

(3) Any amount recovered by the successor company under this section in relation to a payment made by it in connexion with an unidentified or unknown motor vehicle shall be paid by the successor company, in proportions determined by the Minister, to the State and to itself.

(4) In making a determination under Subsection (3), the Minister shall have regard as far as practicable to the proportion of the amount provided by the State or the successor company, as the case may be.

24 Recovery by successor company where decision of assessment officer subsequently overruled

Where the successor company has paid moneys under an award and subsequently a court of competent jurisdiction determines that the death of the person in respect of whom the award was made was not directly or indirectly attributable to the use of a motor vehicle, the successor company may recover from the State the amount paid under the award as a debt.

25 Saving of other rights of action

(1) An award of compensation made in favour of any person under this Act does not affect the right of that person –

(a) to commence proceedings under any other law for the recovery of damages for the death of the person in respect of whom the award was made; and

(b) any damages awarded to a person as a result of those proceedings shall be reduced by the amount of compensation awarded to the person under this Act.

(2) Subject to Subsection (1), this Act does not affect the operation of –

(a) the *Motor Vehicles (Third Party Insurance) Act*; or

(b) the *Workers' Compensation Act*; or

(c) the *Wrongs (Miscellaneous Provisions) Act.*

PART IV – MISCELLANEOUS

26 Judicial notice

All courts, Judges and persons acting judicially shall take judicial notice of –

(a) the official signature of a person who holds or has held the office of assessment officer; and

(b) the fact that the person holds or has held that office,

if the signature purports to be attached or appended to a decision or other document issued by the assessment officer.

27 Acts done on Sundays

No act, matter or thing done or suffered by or under the authority of an assessment officer shall be deemed to have been invalidly or unlawfully done or suffered merely by reason of the fact that it was so done or suffered on a Sunday.

28 Indemnity

(1) An assessment officer is not liable to be sued for an act done or an award made by him in the exercise of jurisdiction conferred by this Act, or for an act done by him beyond the limits of that jurisdiction, if, at the time when he did the act or made the award, he believed in good faith that he had jurisdiction to do the act or make the award.

(2) In any proceedings referred to in Subsection (1), the burden of proof of lack of good faith is on the person asserting it.

29 Regulations

The Head of State, acting on advice, may make regulations, not inconsistent with this Act, prescribing all matters that by this Act are required or permitted to be prescribed, or that are necessary or convenient to be prescribed for carrying out or giving effect to this Act, and in particular for prescribing –

(a) the manner of recording a decision of an assessment officer; and

(b) the time within which compensation is payable; and

(c) the manner in which compensation is payable; and

(d) the imposition of penalties of fines not exceeding K500.00 or imprisonment for terms not exceeding six months, or both, for offences against the regulations.

CHAPTER No 295

Motor Vehicles (Third Party Insurance) Act

PART I – PRELIMINARY

PART II – MOTOR VEHICLES INSURANCE (PNG) TRUST

PART III – THE GENERAL MANAGER

PART IV – THE SERVICE OF THE TRUST

PART V – PREMIUM-FIXING ADVISORY COMMITTEE

PART IV – MISCELLANEOUS

PART VI – THE MOTOR VEHICLES INSURANCE FUND

PART VII – FINANCE, ETC

PART VIII – THIRD-PARTY INSURANCE COVER

PART IX – CLAIMS AND ACTIONS FOR DAMAGES

PART X – OFFENCES

PART XI – MISCELLANEOUS

PART XII – TRANSFER OF UNDERTAKING OF THE SUCCESSOR COMPANY, ETC

SCHEDULE

OATH AND AFFIRMATION OF OFFICE

INDEPENDENT STATE OF PAPUA NEW GUINEA

CHAPTER No 295

Motor Vehicles (Third Party Insurance) Act

(Consolidated to No 28 of 1997)

Being an Act –

(a) . . .

[Repealed]

(b) to establish a Premium-Fixing Advisory Committee; and

(c) to require that owners and drivers of motor vehicles be insured against liability in respect of the death of or bodily injury to persons caused by or arising out of the use of motor vehicles,

and for related purposes.

PART I – PRELIMINARY

1 Interpretation

In this Act, unless the contrary intention appears –

"accident insurance business" means the business of undertaking liability under policies of insurance in respect of the happening of personal accidents (whether fatal or not), disease or sickness, or of any class of personal accidents, disease or sickness;

"annual pool account" means an account established under Section 45;

"the Commissioner" means the Insurance Commissioner appointed under Section 5(1) of the *Insurance Act* 1995;

"the Committee" means the Premium-Fixing Advisory Committee established Section 26;

"driver" includes the rider of a motor cycle and a person for the time being in charge of a motor vehicle;

"fiscal year", in relation to the successor company and to the annual pool account, means a period of 12 months commencing on 1 January and ending on 31 December;

"the Fund" means the Motor Vehicles Insurance Fund established under Section 32;

"insurance business" means the business of undertaking liability by way of insurance, including liability to pay damages or compensation contingent on the happening of a specified event, and includes any business incidental to insurance business, but does not include –

(a) life insurance business; or

(b) accident insurance business undertaken solely in connexion with life insurance business; or

(c) pecuniary loss insurance business carried on solely in the course of carrying on banking business, and for the purposes of that business, by a bank within the meaning of the *Banks and Financial Institutions Act*;

"insured motor vehicle" means a motor vehicle in relation to which there is in existence at all material times a third-party insurance cover;

"motor vehicle" means a motor car, motor carriage, motor cycle, motor truck, motor omnibus, motor tractor or other vehicle propelled wholly or partly by a volatile spirit or by steam, gas, oil or electricity, or by means other than human or animal power, and includes a trailer, but does not include a vehicle used on a railway or tramway;

"owner", in relation to a motor vehicle means –

(a) where a trader's plate is placed on the vehicle under Part VI. of the *Motor Traffic Regulation* – the person, firm or company to whom or to which the plate was issued; and

(b) subject to Paragraph (c), where the vehicle is registered – the person registered as the owner of the vehicle; and

(c) where a vehicle referred to in Paragraph (b) is sold or otherwise disposed of by the person registered as the owner of the vehicle, and he has given notice in accordance with Section 23(2) of the *Motor Traffic Regulation* – the purchaser; and

(d) where the vehicle is not registered – the person who is entitled to the immediate possession of the vehicle, whether solely or jointly or in common with some other person;

"pecuniary loss insurance business" means the business of undertaking liability by way or insurance against –

(a) risks of loss to the persons insured arising from the insolvency of their debtors or from the failure (otherwise than through insolvency) of their debtors to pay their debts when due; or

(b) risks of loss to the persons insured arising from their having to perform contracts of guarantee; or

(c) risks of loss to the persons insured attributable to interruptions of the carrying on of business carried on by them; or

(d) risks of loss to the persons insured attributable to their incurring unforeseen expenses;

"premium" means the amount received by the successor company or an agent of the successor company as consideration for the undertaking of a liability in the nature of insurance business in the country, whether –

(a) the contract of insurance is entered into; or

(b) the certificate of insurance is issued; or

(c) the premium is paid or received,

in the country or elsewhere;

"public street" means a street, road, lane, thoroughfare, footpath, bridge or place that is open to the public, or to which the public has or is permitted to have access, whether on payment of a fee or otherwise;

"registered" means registered under the *Motor Traffic Act*;

"the regulations" means any regulations made under this Act;

[734]"successor company" means the successor company nominated under Section 65;

"the Superintendent" means the Superintendent of Motor Traffic appointed by the *Motor Traffic Act*;

"third-party insurance cover" means an insurance cover issued by the successor company or an agent of the successor company under this Act;

"the Trust" . . .

"this Act" includes the regulations;

---

[734]Definition "successor company" inserted by *Motor Vehicles (Third Party Insurance) (Amendment) Act* 1997 (No. 28 of 1997), s2.

"uninsured motor vehicle" means a motor vehicle (including a trailer) that is not an insured motor vehicle, but does not include a motor vehicle that is –

(a) the property of the State or of any authority of the Government; or

[735](b) . . .

(c) in respect of which persons are exempted by or under this Act from the provisions of Section 48.

2 Application

(1) For the purposes of this Act, a motor vehicle in relation to which a permit under Section 11 of the *Motor Traffic Act* has been granted and is in force shall be deemed to be registered under that Act, when it is driven or drawn in accordance with that section and the permit.

(2) This Act does not apply to or in relation to a vehicle referred to in Subsection (1) when it is driven or drawn otherwise than in accordance with Section 11 of the *Motor Traffic Act* or the permit granted under that section in relation to it.

[735]Repealed by No. 29 of 1978, s. 1.

[736]PART II – MOTOR VEHICLES INSURANCE (P.N.G.) TRUST

[Repealed]

[737]3 Establishment of the Trust

[Repealed]

[738]4 Constitution of the Trust

[Repealed]

[739]5 Alternate directors of the Trust.

[Repealed]

[740]6 Chairman of the Trust

[Repealed]

[741]7 Calling of meetings

[Repealed]

[742]8 Procedure at meetings

[Repealed]

---

[736]Part II repealed by Motor Vehicles (Third Party Insurance) (Amendment) Act 1997 (No. 27 of 1997), s2.

[737]Section 3 repealed by Motor Vehicles (Third Party Insurance) (Amendment) Act 1997 (No. 27 of 1997), s2.

[738]Section 4

- Amended by No. 29 of 1978, s. 2.
- Repealed and replaced by Motor Vehicles (Third Party Insurance) (Amendment) Act 1996 (No. 47 of 1996), s2.
- Repealed by Motor Vehicles (Third Party Insurance) (Amendment) Act 1997 (No. 27 of 1997), s2.

[739]Section 5 repealed by Motor Vehicles (Third Party Insurance) (Amendment) Act 1996 (No. 47 of 1996), s3.

[740]Section 6 repealed by Motor Vehicles (Third Party Insurance) (Amendment) Act 1997 (No. 27 of 1997), s2.

[741]Section 7 repealed by Motor Vehicles (Third Party Insurance) (Amendment) Act 1997 (No. 27 of 1997), s2.

[742]Section 8 repealed by Motor Vehicles (Third Party Insurance) (Amendment) Act 1997 (No. 27 of 1997), s2.

[743]9 Disclosure of interest

[Repealed]

[744]10 Vacation of office

[Repealed]

[745]11 Powers of the Trust to deal with property

[Repealed]

[746]12 Oath and affirmation of office

[Repealed]

[747]13 Functions of the Trust

[Repealed]

[748]14 Powers of the Trust

[Repealed]

[749]15 Delegation

[Repealed]

---

[743]Section 9 repealed by Motor Vehicles (Third Party Insurance) (Amendment) Act 1997 (No. 27 of 1997), s2.

[744]Section 10 repealed by Motor Vehicles (Third Party Insurance) (Amendment) Act 1997 (No. 27 of 1997), s2.

[745]Section 11 repealed by Motor Vehicles (Third Party Insurance) (Amendment) Act 1997 (No. 27 of 1997), s2.

[746]Section 12 repealed by Motor Vehicles (Third Party Insurance) (Amendment) Act 1997 (No. 27 of 1997), s2.

[747]Section 13 repealed by Motor Vehicles (Third Party Insurance) (Amendment) Act 1997 (No. 27 of 1997), s2.

[748]Section 14

- Replaced by No. 29 of 1978, s. 5.
- Section 14(1A) inserted by Motor Vehicles (Third Party Insurance) (Amendment) Act 1996 (No. 47 of 1996), s4.
- Section 14 repealed by Motor Vehicles (Third Party Insurance) (Amendment) Act 1997 (No. 27 of 1997), s2.

[749]Section 15 repealed by Motor Vehicles (Third Party Insurance) (Amendment) Act 1997 (No. 27 of 1997), s2.

[750]16 Provisions relating to secrecy

[Repealed]

[751]17 Annual report

[Repealed]

[752]18 Agents of the Trust

[Repealed]

[753]19 Terms and conditions of Directors, etc

[Repealed]

---

[750]Section 16 repealed by Motor Vehicles (Third Party Insurance) (Amendment) Act 1997 (No. 27 of 1997), s2.

[751]Section 17 repealed by Motor Vehicles (Third Party Insurance) (Amendment) Act 1997 (No. 27 of 1997), s2.

[752]Section 18 repealed by Motor Vehicles (Third Party Insurance) (Amendment) Act 1997 (No. 27 of 1997), s2.

[753]Section 19

- Repealed and replaced by Motor Vehicles (Third Party Insurance) (Amendment) Act 1996 (No. 47 of 1996), s5.
- Repealed by Motor Vehicles (Third Party Insurance) (Amendment) Act 1997 (No. 27 of 1997), s2.

[754]PART III – THE GENERAL MANAGER

[Repealed]

[755]20 Appointment, etc., of General Manager

[Repealed]

[756]21 Vacation of office of General Manager

[Repealed]

[757]22 Public Service rights of General Manager

[Repealed]

[758]23 Functions of General Manager

[Repealed]

---

[754]Part III repealed by Motor Vehicles (Third Party Insurance) (Amendment) Act 1997 (No. 27 of 1997), s2.

[755]Section 20 repealed by Motor Vehicles (Third Party Insurance) (Amendment) Act 1997 (No. 27 of 1997), s2.

[756]Section 21 repealed by Motor Vehicles (Third Party Insurance) (Amendment) Act 1997 (No. 27 of 1997), s2.

[757]Section 22 repealed by Motor Vehicles (Third Party Insurance) (Amendment) Act 1997 (No. 27 of 1997), s2.

[758]Section 23 repealed by Motor Vehicles (Third Party Insurance) (Amendment) Act 1997 (No. 27 of 1997), s2.

[759]PART IV – THE SERVICE OF THE TRUST

[Repealed]

[760]24 Appointment of officers

[Repealed]

[761]25 Temporary and casual employees

[Repealed]

[759]Part IV repealed by Motor Vehicles (Third Party Insurance) (Amendment) Act 1997 (No. 27 of 1997), s2.
[760]Section 24 repealed by Motor Vehicles (Third Party Insurance) (Amendment) Act 1997 (No. 27 of 1997), s2.
[761]Section 25 repealed by Motor Vehicles (Third Party Insurance) (Amendment) Act 1997 (No. 27 of 1997), s2.

PART V – PREMIUM-FIXING ADVISORY COMMITTEE

26 Appointment, etc, of Premium-Fixing Advisory Committee

(1) For the purposes of this Part, a body by the name of the "Premium-Fixing Advisory Committee" is established.

(2) The Committee shall consist of –

(a) the Commissioner; and

(b) a representative of the successor company appointed by the Minister, by notice in the National Gazette, on the nomination of the successor company; and

(c) two other persons appointed by the Minister, by notice in the National Gazette, of whom one shall be appointed on the nomination of the successor company.

(3) The Minister shall, by notice in the National Gazette, appoint one of the members of the Committee to be the Chairman of the Committee.

27 Meetings of Committee

(1) Meetings of the Committee shall be held annually and at such other times and places as are directed by the Minister.

(2) At a meeting of the Committee –

(a) two members are a quorum; and

(b) the Chairman, or in his absence a person elected by the members present from their own number, shall preside; and

(c) all questions shall be decided by a majority of votes of the members present and voting; and

(d) the person presiding has a deliberative and, in the event of an equality of votes on a matter, also a casting vote.

(3) The Committee shall cause minutes of its meetings to be kept.

(4) Subject to this Part, the procedures of the Committee are as determined by the Committee.

28 Powers of inspection

(1) For the purposes of the performance of its functions under this Part, the Committee or a person authorized by the Committee may –

(a) require any person to produce or make available to the Committee or authorized person any books, documents, records or information in the possession of or under the control of the person relating to third-party insurance; and

(b) take copies of or extracts from any such books, documents or records.

(2) A person who –

(a) when required to do so under Subsection (1), refuses or fails, without reasonable excuse (proof of which is on him), to produce or make available any books, documents, records or information; or

(b) hinders or obstructs the Committee or an authorized person in the exercise of its or his powers or the performance of its or his functions under this Act,

is guilty of an offence.

Penalty: A fine not exceeding K100.00.

Default penalty: A fine not exceeding K10.00.

29 Statistical and other returns

(1) The Committee may require a participating licensed insurer or the successor company to provide it with such statistics, statistical returns and other returns as, in the opinion of the Chairman of the Committee, are necessary for the purpose of the performance of its functions under this Part.

(2) A participating licensed insurer or the successor company, as the case may be, who, when required to do so under Subsection (1), refuses or fails, without reasonable excuse (proof of which is on him or it), to provide the statistics or returns is guilty of an offence.

Penalty: A fine not exceeding K200.00.

Default penalty: A fine not exceeding K20.00.

30 Report of Committee to Minister

The Committee shall, at least once in each year and at such other times as are directed by the Minister, report to the Minister –

(a) on the levels of premiums charged for third-party insurance; and

(b) on such other matters connected with third-party insurance as it thinks fit or as are directed by the Minister.

31 Level of premiums, etc

After receiving a report from the Committee, the minister may, by notice in the National Gazette, fix the level of premiums payable and the classification of vehicles in respect of the issue of third-party insurance cover, generally or in relation to a class or classes of motor vehicles.

PART VI – THE MOTOR VEHICLES INSURANCE FUND

32 Establishment of the Fund

(1) A Fund to be known as the "Motor Vehicles Insurance Fund" shall be established.

(2) There shall be paid into the Fund such moneys as are specified by this or any other Act

(3) The Fund shall be administered by the successor company.

(4) Whether or not he has paid any amount into the Fund, no person is entitled to any part of the Fund, and no person is entitled to receive any payment or benefit from the Fund except in accordance with this Part.

[762]33 Participation in the Fund

[Repealed]

34 Payments into the Fund

There shall be paid into the Fund –

(a) all moneys appropriated by Act for the purpose; and
(b) all moneys received as contributions or insurance premiums by the successor company; and
(c) any other moneys received by the successor company for the purposes of this Act.

35 Payments out of the Fund

There shall be paid out of the Fund –

(a) all moneys that the successor company is entitled or required to pay in payment or discharge of expenses, obligations and liabilities of the successor company arising under this Act; and
(b) all moneys required for the payment of remuneration or allowances payable to a director, the General Manager or an officer or employee of the successor company; and
(c) any other costs of administering the Fund.

---

[762]Section 33

- Added by No. 29 of 1978, s. 4.
- Repealed by Motor Vehicles Insurance (PNG) Trust (Administrative Arrangements) Act 1996, (No. 48 of 1996), s10.

[763](d) annual dividends to the State of an amount determined by the Board and paid annually.

36 Remission of amounts to the successor company

An agent of the successor company shall, on the last day of each month or at such other times as are agreed on between the successor company and the agent, remit to the successor company all amounts collected by it on behalf of the successor company.

37 Investment of money standing to the credit of the Fund

Money standing to the credit of the Fund may be invested –

(a) in any securities or class of securities approved by the Minister for the purpose; or

(b) on deposit with a licensed bank; or

[764](c) in any manner authorized by Section 57 of the *Public Finances (Management) Act* 1995.

[765]38 Distribution of excess and payment of deficiency

[Repealed]

[766]39 Winding-up of the Trust

[Repealed]

---

[763]Section 35(d) added by Motor Vehicles (Third Party Insurance) (Amendment) Act 1996 (No. 47 of 1996), s6.

[764]Section 37(c) added by Motor Vehicles (Third Party Insurance) (Amendment) Act 1996 (No. 47 of 1996), s7.

[765]Section 38 repealed by Motor Vehicles Insurance (PNG) Trust (Administrative Arrangements) Act 1996, (No. 48 of 1996), s11.

[766]Section 39 repealed by Motor Vehicles Insurance (PNG) Trust (Administrative Arrangements) Act 1996 (No. 48 of 1996), s12.

PART VII – FINANCE, ETC

[767]40 Percentage interest of licensed insurer in the Fund

[Repealed]

41 Bank accounts

(1) The successor company shall –

(a) open and maintain an account or accounts with a licensed bank; and

(b) maintain at all times at least one such account.

(2) The successor company shall pay all its money into an account referred to in Subsection (1).

42 Advances

(1) The successor company may accept an offer by the Departmental Head to advance such money as are from time to time lawfully available for the purposes of the successor company on such terms as are agreed on between the successor company and the Departmental Head.

(2) The successor company shall repay, in accordance with the terms on which an advance under Subsection (1) is made, such portion of the advance as is repayable.

43 Private treaty loans

(1) The successor company may, with the consent of the Minister, borrow, for the purposes of the successor company, money from a person on such terms as are agreed on between the successor company and that person.

(2) The successor company shall repay a loan made under Subsection (1) in accordance with the terms on which it is made.

44 Accounts and records

The successor company shall –

(a) cause to be kept proper accounts and records of its transactions and affairs to recognized international standards; and

(b) do all things necessary to ensure that –

[767]Section 40 repealed by Motor Vehicles Insurance (PNG) Trust (Administrative Arrangements) Act 1996 (No. 48 of 1996), s13.

(i) all payments out of its money are properly authorized and correctly made; and

(ii) adequate control is maintained over its assets and other assets in its custody, and over the incurring of liabilities by it.

[768]45 Annual pool accounts

[Repealed]

46 Audit

(1) The successor company shall arrange for an inspection and audit of the accounts and records of the successor company by a qualified company auditor at least once in each year.

(2) [769]Section 176 of the Companies Act, with the necessary modifications, applies to the successor company and the auditor of the successor company.

[770]47 Reports to participating licensed insurers

[Repealed]

---

[768]Section 45 repealed by Motor Vehicles (Third Party Insurance) (Amendment) Act 1996 (No. 47 of 1996), s9.

[769]Note that the corresponding provision in the *Companies Act* 1995 now applies.

[770]Section 47 repealed by Motor Vehicles Insurance (PNG) Trust (Administrative Arrangements) Act 1996, (No. 48 of 1996), s14.

PART VIII – THIRD-PARTY INSURANCE COVER

48 Insurance by owners of motor vehicles

(1) Subject to this Act, the owner of a motor vehicle must at all times during the registration and renewal of registration of the motor vehicle indemnify himself and keep himself indemnified with the successor company against the sums specified in Section 49(2)(a) for which he or his estate may become liable by way of damages for the death of or bodily injury to a person caused by, or arising out of the use of, the motor vehicle.

Penalty: A fine not exceeding K200.00.

(2) The third-party insurance cover shall not be revoked during the period of registration of the insured motor vehicle unless the registration or renewal of registration, as the case may be, is sooner cancelled or surrendered.

49 Manner of effecting third-party insurance

(1) In order to comply with the requirements of this Act, a third-party insurance cover shall –

(a) in the area of the Central Traffic Registry – be issued by the successor company to the owner of a motor vehicle on the owner lodging with the Superintendent –

(i) an application for registration or re-registration, as the case may be; and

(ii) the appropriate amount of insurance premium in respect of the motor vehicle; and

(b) in any other area – be issued by the successor company to the owner of a motor vehicle on the owner obtaining from an agent of the successor company a certificate in a form approved by the successor company stating that the appropriate amount of insurance premium in respect of the motor vehicle has been paid.

(2) A third-party insurance cover issued under Subsection (1) –

(a) where it is issued in relation to a particular motor vehicle, insures the owner of the motor vehicle and any other person who at any time drives the motor vehicle, whether with or without the authority of the owner, jointly and each of them severally against all liability incurred by the owner and the other person jointly or by either of them severally in respect of the death of or bodily injury to a person caused by, or arising out of the use of, the motor vehicle, to an amount not exceeding –

(i) K100,000.00 in respect of the death of or bodily injury to any one person in any one case; and

(ii) K500,000.00 in the case of any one accident or series of accidents arising out of the one event; and

(b) becomes effective on the date of registration or re-registration, as the case may be, of the motor vehicle in respect of which it is issued; and

(c) continues in force –

(i) where the registration is renewed within 15 days after the expiry of the preceding period of registration – until the date of renewal; and

(ii) in any other case – until 15 days after the date on which the registration expires.

50 Payment of third-party premiums

The Superintendent shall not register or re-register a motor vehicle unless –

(a) in the case of a motor vehicle situated in the area of the Central Traffic Registry – he has received the amount of third-party insurance premium payable in respect of the motor vehicle; and

(b) in any other case – he has received a certificate issued under Section 49(1)(b) in respect of the motor vehicle.

51 Exclusion of certain liabilities

A third-party insurance cover issued under this Act does not extend to insure the owner or driver of the motor vehicle against –

(a) a liability to pay compensation, under a law in relation to workers' compensation, to a worker employed by him; or

(b) a liability incurred by him under an agreement, unless the liability is one that would have arisen in the absence of the agreement.

52 Change of ownership

A third-party insurance cover enures in favour of the owner for the time being and the driver of the vehicle, notwithstanding any change in the ownership of the vehicle.

53 Duties of owner and driver

(1) Where the death of or bodily injury to a person is caused by, or arises out of the use of, a motor vehicle in respect of which a third-party insurance cover is in force –

(a) the owner must, as soon as practicable after the occurrence that resulted in the death or injury, or if he was not then driving the motor vehicle as soon as practicable after he became aware of the occurrence, give a written notification of the occurrence, with particulars as to the date, nature and circumstances, to the successor company; and

(b) if, at the time of the occurrence, the driver of the motor vehicle was not the owner of the motor vehicle, the driver must as soon as practicable give a written notification –

(i) to the owner of the motor vehicle; or

(ii) to the successor company,

of the occurrence, with particulars as to the date, nature and circumstances; and

(c) the owner and the driver, or either of them, must give such information, in addition to the information referred to in Paragraphs (a) and (b), and take such steps, as the successor company reasonably requires, whether or not a claim has been made in respect of the death or bodily injury; and

(d) the owner or the driver must not, without the written consent of the successor company, make an offer, promise, payment or settlement, or an admission of liability, in respect of the death or bodily injury; and

(e) the owner or the driver must immediately give to the successor company a written notification of every notice of intention to make a claim given to him, and of every claim made or action brought against him, in respect of the death or bodily injury; and

(f) where the owner becomes aware that notice of intention to make a claim has been given to, or a claim has been made or an action brought against, the driver in respect of the death or bodily injury, he must immediately give to the successor company a written notification of the notice or claim; and

(g) the owner or the driver must not, without the written consent of the successor company, enter on, or incur expense in relation to, litigation in respect of any liability against which he is insured under the third-party insurance cover.

Penalty: A fine not exceeding K100.00.

(2) It is a sufficient compliance with a requirement of Subsection (1) as to the giving of a notification by the owner or the driver if the notification is given by a person on his behalf.

(3) A notification given under this section is not subject to discovery and is not admissible in evidence in any proceedings (whether or not for an offence against this or any other Act) except proceedings for failure to comply with this section.

(4) This section does not apply where –

(a) the person suffering the death or bodily injury was the owner of the motor vehicle; and

(b) the motor vehicle was at the time of the occurrence being driven by the owner.

PART IX – CLAIMS AND ACTIONS FOR DAMAGES

54 Claims for damages

(1) Subject to Subsection (2), any claim for damages in respect of the death of or bodily injury to any person caused by, or arising out of the use of –

- (a) a motor vehicle insured under this Act; or
- (b) an uninsured motor vehicle in a public street; or
- (c) a motor vehicle on a public street where the identity of the motor vehicle cannot after due inquiry and search be established,

shall be made against the successor company and not against the owner or driver of the motor vehicle and, subject to Subsection (5), any proceedings to enforce any such claim for damages shall be taken against the successor company and not against the owner or driver of the motor vehicle.

(2) Subsection (1) does not apply to a claim for damages made under the *Motor Vehicles (Third Party Insurance) (Basis Protection Compensation) Act.*

(3) A claim under Subsection (1)(a) or (b) may be made, and any proceedings to enforce such a claim may be taken, notwithstanding that the owner or driver of the motor vehicle –

- (a) is dead; or
- (b) cannot be found; or
- (c) is the spouse of the person whose death, or to whom bodily injury, has been caused.

(4) The inquiry and search under Subsection (1)(c) for the purpose of establishing the identity of the motor vehicle may be proved orally or by the affidavit of the person who made the inquiry and search.

(5) Where an award of damages is made by a court in respect of a claim under Subsection (1) that exceeds the amount of liability of the successor company specified in Section 49(2)(a), the court shall, at the time when it makes the award, determine against whom (if anyone) the excess shall be awarded, and an award under this subsection operates as a judgement against that person for all purposes.

(6) No action to enforce any claim under this section lies against the successor company unless notice of intention to make a claim is given by the claimant to the successor company within a period of six months

after the occurrence out of which the claim arose, or within such further period as –

(a) the Commissioner; or

(b) the court before which the action is instituted,

on sufficient cause being shown, allows.

(7) For the purposes of this Act, if the owner of a motor vehicle or his estate becomes liable, by way of damages, in respect of a motor vehicle for the death of or bodily injury to a person who is a worker within the meaning of any law relating to workers compensation, compensation under that law in respect of which a person is entitled to be indemnified by the owner or his estate is damages.

55 Representation of owner and driver in action for compensation

Where a claim for damages under Section 54(1) is made against the successor company, a copy of the claim shall, where possible, be served on the owner, and where the owner is not the driver also on the driver, and the owner and driver may be represented on the hearing of the claim as though they were parties to the action.

56 Reimbursement of the successor company

Where in relation to a claim under Section 54(1)(c) the successor company properly pays any amount in satisfaction of the claim made or judgement recovered against it and the amount of any costs and expenses properly incurred by it in relation to the claim, the Departmental Head shall, out of money lawfully available for the purpose, pay to the successor company such proportion of the amount as the Minister fixes.

57 Recovery by the successor company in certain cases

(1) Subject to Subsection (2), the successor company may recover –

(a) any amount properly paid by the successor company in satisfaction of a claim under Section 54(1)(b) or (c) or, judgement recovered against it under such a claim; and

(b) the amount of any costs and expenses properly incurred by it in relation to any such claim or to the proceedings in which judgement was obtained,

as a debt from the person who, at the time of the occurrence out of which the claim arose or in respect of which the judgement was obtained, was the owner of the motor vehicle, or, where at the time of the occurrence some other person was driving the vehicle, from the owner and the driver jointly or from either of them severally.

(2) It is a sufficient defence in any proceedings under this section –

(a) against the owner (whether severally or jointly with the driver) – if he establishes to the satisfaction of the court before which the action is instituted that, at the time of the occurrence, some other person was driving the motor vehicle without his authority; or

(b) against the driver of an uninsured motor vehicle (whether severally or jointly with the owner) – if he establishes to the satisfaction of the court before which the action is instituted that, at the time of the occurrence –

(i) he was driving the motor vehicle with the authority of the owner or had reasonable grounds for believing, and did in fact believe, that he had such authority; and

(ii) he had reasonable grounds for believing, and did in fact believe, that the motor vehicle was an insured motor vehicle.

(3) Any amount properly paid by the successor company in satisfaction of a claim under Section 54(1)(a) or a judgement recovered against it under such a claim. and the amount of any costs and expenses properly incurred by it in relation to any such claim or to the proceedings in which judgement was obtained, may, where the driver of the vehicle in relation to which the claim was made or the judgement recovered has been convicted of an offence under Section 40 of the [771]*Motor Traffic Act* relating to the incident from which the claim arose, be recovered by the successor company as a debt from the driver of the vehicle.

(4) Any amount recovered by the successor company under [772]Section 54(1)(c) shall be paid by the successor company, in proportions determined by the Minister, to the State and the Fund.

(5) In making a determination under Subsection (4), the Minister shall have regard, as far as practicable, to the respective proportions of the amount provided by the State and the successor company.

(1) The successor company –

---

[771]The original provision referred to offences "under" Section 19 of the pre-Independence M*otor Traffic Act* 1960, which corresponded to Section 40 of the *Motor Traffic Act.* That section does not create offences, so possibly "referred to in" was intended instead of "under".

[772]*Sic.* No amounts are recoverable by the Trust under Section 54(1)(c), and possibly the intention was to refer to recoveries by the Trust (under Section 57(1)) of amounts paid by it under Section 54(1)(c).

(a) may undertake the settlement of a claim against it or any other person under this Act; and

(b) shall indemnify a person insured under this Act against all costs and expenses incidental to proceedings under this Act to the relevant amount specified in Section 49(2)(a).

(2) The person referred to in Subsection (1) shall sign all such warrants and authorities as the successor company requires for the purpose of enabling it to have the defence or conduct of any proceedings referred to in that subsection and, in default of his so doing, the court in which the proceedings are taken or had may order that they be signed by the successor company on his behalf.

(3) Nothing said or done by or on behalf of the successor company in connexion with the settlement of any such claim or the defence or conduct of any such proceedings shall be regarded as an admission of liability in respect of, or in any way prejudices, any other claim, action or proceedings arising out of the same occurrence.

PART X – OFFENCES

59 Use of uninsured vehicle

(1) Subject to this section, a person who uses, or causes or permits any other person to use, an uninsured motor vehicle is guilty of an offence.

Penalty: A fine not exceeding K500.00 or imprisonment for a term not exceeding 12 months, or both.

(2) It is a defence to a charge of an offence against Subsection (1) if the defendant proves to the satisfaction of the court hearing the case that at the time when the vehicle was used he had reasonable grounds for believing, and in fact believed, that the vehicle was insured under this Act.

60 Soliciting instructions, etc

(1) A person who, directly or indirectly, for personal gain –

(a) solicits instructions or authority to act on behalf of any other person in respect of the making or commencement of a claim or action for damages or compensation for the death of or bodily injury to a person caused by, or arising out of the use of, a motor vehicle, or in respect of negotiation, compromise or settlement of any such claim or action; or

(b) on behalf of any other person, makes or commences, or causes to be made or commenced, a claim or action for damages or compensation referred to in Paragraph (a), or negotiates, settles or compromises any such claim when made or commenced,

is guilty of an offence.

Penalty: A fine not exceeding K200.00.

(2) Subsection (1)(b) does not apply to a lawyer properly acting in the course of his profession.

(3) An agreement to pay to a person who contravenes Subsection (1) money for work done or services rendered in respect of a matter referred to in that subsection is void, and money so paid is recoverable by action brought in a court of competent jurisdiction by the person who paid it.

61 Saving of other remedies

No proceedings or conviction for an offence against, contravention of or neglect or failure to comply with this Act affects any remedy to which a person aggrieved or injured by the act or omission to which the proceedings or conviction relates is entitled against the successor company, or against the person who committed the act or was responsible for the omission.

62 Avoidance of certain contracts

(1) In this section, "public motor vehicle" means a public motor vehicle as defined in the *Motor Traffic Act*.

(2) A contract for the conveyance of a passenger in a public motor vehicle is void so far as it purports to negative or to restrict the liability of the successor company or a person in respect of claims that may be made against the successor company or the person in respect of the death of or bodily injury to the passenger while being carried in, entering or alighting from the vehicle, or purports to impose a condition with respect to the enforcement of any such liability.

63 Statement by owner as to insurance

(1) The owner of a motor vehicle in respect of which a claim is made in relation to a death or bodily injury arising out of or caused by the use of the motor vehicle shall, on demand by or on behalf of the person making the claim, state whether or not he is or was insured under this Act, or would have been so insured if the successor company had not avoided or cancelled the certificate.

(2) A person who, without reasonable excuse, fails to comply with Subsection (1), or wilfully makes a false statement in reply to a demand under that subsection, is guilty of an offence.

Penalty: A fine not exceeding K500.00.

PART XI – MISCELLANEOUS

64 Regulations

The Head of State, acting on advice, may make regulations, not inconsistent with this Act, prescribing all matters that by this Act are required or permitted to be prescribed, or that are necessary or convenient to be prescribed for carrying out or giving effect to this Act.

PART XII – TRANSFER OF UNDERTAKING OF THE SUCCESSOR COMPANY, ETC

[773]65 Minister may appoint transfer date and nominate company

The Minister may, by notice in the National Gazette –

(a) appoint a day (hereinafter referred to as "the transfer date"); and

(b) nominate a company or companies incorporated under the *Companies Act* (Chapter 146) (hereinafter referred to as "the successor company"), for the purposes of this Part.

[774]66 Shares in successor company on transfer date

(1) The successor company shall, on the transfer date, be wholly owned by the State.

(2) The shares in the successor company shall be held by the Minister on behalf of the State.

67 Transfer of assets, etc, of Trust to successor company on transfer date

(a) all assets held by, and all obligations and liabilities imposed on, the successor company are transferred to the successor company; and

(b) all contracts and agreements (including contracts of employment) entered into, made with or addressed to the successor company are, to the extent they were immediately before the transfer date binding on and enforceable against the successor company binding on and of full force and effect against or in favour of the successor company as if the successor company had been a party to them or bound by them or entitled to the benefit of them; and

(c) all licences held by the successor company are transferred to, and deemed to be held by, the successor company for the unexpired period of such licences; and

[773]Section 65 inserted by Motor Vehicles (Third Party Insurance) (Amendment) Act 1997 (No. 28 of 1997), s1.

[774]Section 66 inserted by Motor Vehicles (Third Party Insurance) (Amendment) Act 1997 (No. 28 of 1997), s1.

(d) any arbitration, action or proceeding pending or existing by, against or in favour of the successor company does not abate or discontinue, but may be prosecuted, continued or enforced by, against or in favour of the successor company.

[775]68 Formal transfer of land, etc, unnecessary

Where any asset falling to be transferred under Section 67(a) is land registered under the *Land Registration Act* (Chapter 191), the Registrar of Titles shall, without formal transfer and without fee, on application by the successor company, enter or register the successor company in the register kept under the Act and, on entry and registration, grant a certificate of title, lease or other instrument evidencing title to the land within that Act.

[776]69 Minister empowered to sell shares in successor company

The Minister is, on and in accordance with the terms of the direction of the National Executive Council, empowered to sell the shares of the successor company.

[777]70 Tax and duties

(1) For the purposes of the *Income Tax Act* 1959, the successor company shall be deemed to have acquired the assets, obligations and liabilities referred to in Section 67(a) at a value equal to their written down book value in the books of the successor company as at the transfer date.

(2) The successor company shall be entitled to tax depreciation and to any other applicable tax deduction in respect of assets, obligations and liabilities referred to in Section 67(a) as if the successor company had owned such assets, rights and liabilities since such assets, rights and liabilities were first acquired by the successor company.

(3) Shares issued to the Minister responsible for finance matters on behalf of the State shall be deemed to have been fully paid and issued for valuable consideration other than cash.

(4) The transfer to the successor company of the assets, rights and

---

[775]Section 68 inserted by Motor Vehicles (Third Party Insurance) (Amendment) Act 1997 (No. 28 of 1997), s1.
[776]Section 69 inserted by Motor Vehicles (Third Party Insurance) (Amendment) Act 1997 (No. 28 of 1997), s1.
[777]Section 70 inserted by Motor Vehicles (Third Party Insurance) (Amendment) Act 1997 (No. 28 of 1997), s1.

liabilities specified in the allocation statement shall be exempt from any stamp duty, fee, tax, charges or other duty payable under any Act, including without limitation, the *Land Registration Act* (Chapter 191).

(5) No registration fee shall be payable in respect of the authorized capital of the successor company, and no tax or duty shall be payable on the issue of shares, to the Minister responsible for finance matters on behalf of the State.

SCHEDULE

Act. Sec. 12

OATH AND AFFIRMATION OF OFFICE

Oath.

I, . . . , do swear that I will well and truly serve the Independent State of Papua New Guinea in the office of director of the Motor Vehicles Insurance (P.N.G.) Trust.

So help me God!

Affirmation.

I, . . . , do solemnly and sincerely promise and declare that I will well and truly serve the Independent State of Papua New Guinea in the office of director of the Motor Vehicles Insurance (P.N.G.) Trust

CHAPTER No 377

National Provident Fund Act

PART I – PRELIMINARY

PART II – NATIONAL PROVIDENT FUND BOARD

PART III – THE SERVICE OF THE BOARD

PART IV – NATIONAL PROVIDENT FUND

PART V – CONTRIBUTIONS

PART VI – PROTECTION OF CONTRIBUTIONS AND PAYMENTS

PART VII – EXEMPTIONS

PART VIII – TRANSFER OF ACCOUNTS

PART IX – WITHDRAWALS AND PAYMENTS FROM THE FUND

PART X – MISCELLANEOUS

THE INDEPENDENT STATE OF PAPUA NEW GUINEA

CHAPTER No 377

National Provident Fund Act

(Consolidated to No 27 of 1990)

Being an Act to provide for the institution and management of a National Provident Fund for employees in establishments and for related purposes.

PART I – PRELIMINARY

1 Compliance with Constitutional requirements

(1) This Act, to the extent that it regulates or restricts a right or freedom referred to in Subdivision III.3.C (*qualified rights*) of the *Constitution*, namely –

(a) the freedom from arbitrary search and entry conferred by Section 44 of the *Constitution*; and

(b) the freedom of assembly or association conferred by Section 47 of the *Constitution*; and

(c) the freedom of employment conferred by Section 48 of the *Constitution*; and

(d) the right to privacy conferred by Section 49 of the *Constitution*,

is a law that is made for that purpose.

(2) The purpose of this Act is a public purpose.

(3) For the purposes of Section 29 of the *Organic Law on Provincial Government*, it is declared that this law relates to a matter of national interest.

2 Interpretation

(1) In this Act, unless the contrary intention appears –

"affected establishment" means an establishment to which, –

(a) in terms of Section 3; or

(b) as a result of a decision under Section 4,

this Act applies;

"Board" means the National Provident Fund Board of Trustees established under Section 5;

"the commencement date" means –

(a) in relation to so much of the *National Provident Fund Act* as allowed the appointment of the National Provident Fund Board of Trustees and the making of Rules and administrative arrangements to facilitate the operation of the National Provident Fund – 25 September 1980; and

(b) in relation to the remainder of the Act – 26 March 1981;

"contribution" means a contribution payable in respect of a member under this Act;

[778]"court" means the District Court;

"Director" means the Managing Director of the National Provident Fund appointed under Section 15;

"employee" means any person who –

(a) is employed for wages in any kind of work, manual or otherwise, in or in connexion with the work of an establishment; and

(b) receives his wages directly or indirectly from the employer,

and includes any person employed by or through a contractor or agent in or in connexion with the work of the establishment;

"employer" means –

(a) in relation to an establishment which is a factory – the owner or occupier of the factory, including the agent of the owner or occupier, or the legal representative of a deceased owner or occupier; and

(b) in relation to any other establishment –

(i) the person who, or the authority which, has the ultimate control over the affairs of the establishment; and

[778]Definition "court" in Section 1 inserted by *National Provident Fund (Amendment) Act* 1990 (No. 27 of 1990), s1(a).

(ii) where the affairs are entrusted to a manager, managing director or managing agent – the manager, managing director or managing agent;

"establishment" means an organization which employs persons between whom and the establishment, the relationship of employer and employee exists;

"exempted employee" . . .

"exempted establishment" . . .

"Fund" means the National Provident Fund established under Section 25;

"Inspector" means a person appointed to be an Inspector under Section 22;

"member" means a member of the Fund;

"pay" means all emoluments which are –

(a) earned by an employee while on duty or on leave with pay in accordance with the terms of contract of employment; and

(b) paid or payable in cash to him; and

(c) gross wages, remuneration and commission,

but does not include overtime pay, allowances and bonuses and compensation receivable in relation to employment of service of an employee or any presents made by an employer;

[779]"Premiers' Council" means the Premiers' Council established by Section 82 of the *Organic Law on Provincial Government*;

[780]"Rules" means the rules made by the Board in accordance with Section 61;

"this Act" includes the Rules;

"Trustee" means a Trustee of the National Provident Fund Board of Trustees.

(2) Where an establishment consists of different departments or has branches, whether situated in the same place or in different places, all the departments and branches shall be treated as one establishment.

---

[779]This definition has become redundant following the repeal and replacement of the *Organic Law on Provincial Government* by the *Organic Law on Provincial Governments and Local-level Governments*. In fact there was/is no reference in any substantive provision to the "Premiers' Council".

[780]Definition "Rules" in Section 1 inserted by *National Provident Fund (Amendment) Act* 1990 (No. 27 of 1990), s1(d).

3 Application

(1) Subject to this section this Act applies to –

(a) every establishment in which 25 or more persons are employed except –

(i) an establishment which is covered under the Public Officers Superannuation Fund established under the *Public Officers Superannuation Act*; or

(ii) an establishment to which the *Defence Force Retirement Benefits Act* applies; or

(iii) . . .

(b) every employer in relation to an affected establishment; and

(c) every employee who –

(i) is a citizen; and

(ii) is, and has been for the prescribed period, an employee of an affected establishment; and

(iii) . . .

(d) every employee who –

(i) is a non-citizen; and

(ii) is, and has been for the prescribed period, an employee of an affected establishment; and

(iii) has opted in the prescribed manner to be a member of the Fund.

(2) The Minister may, after giving two months' notice in the National Gazette, apply this Act to all or any establishments employing such number of persons less than 25 as is specified in the notice.

(3) Where the employer and the majority of the employees of an establishment have –

(a) agreed that the provisions of this Act should apply to the establishment; and

(b) made application to the Minister accordingly,

the Minister may, by notice in the National Gazette, apply this Act to the establishment.

(4) An affected establishment shall continue to be subject to this Act notwithstanding that the number of persons employed in it at any time falls below 25 for any reason.

(5) Where immediately before this Act becomes applicable to an establishment, there is in existence a provident fund which is common to the employees of that establishment and the employees in any other

establishment, the Minister may, by notice in the National Gazette, apply this Act to the other establishment.

(6) . . .

4 Director to decide whether Act applies, etc

(1) The Director, or any officer authorized by him, shall investigate and decide any question as to –

(a) whether the Act applies in the case of an establishment where this is disputed; or

(b) the amount due by an employer under this Act where this is disputed,

and his decision is final.

(2) For the purposes of carrying out an investigation under Subsection (1), the Director, or any officer authorized by him, shall have the same powers as a court for obtaining evidence, enforcing the attendance of persons to give evidence and requiring the discovery and production of documents.

PART II – NATIONAL PROVIDENT FUND BOARD

5 National Provident Fund Board

(1) The National Provident Fund Board of Trustees is hereby established.

(2) The Board –

(a) is a corporation with perpetual succession; and

(b) shall have a seal; and

(c) may acquire, hold and dispose of property; and

(d) may sue and be sued in its corporate name.

(3) All courts, Judges and persons acting judicially shall take judicial notice of the seal of the Board affixed to a document and shall presume that it was duly affixed.

6 Constitution of the Board

(1) The Board shall consist of the following Trustees: –

(a) the Chairman, appointed by the National Executive Council, after consideration of recommendations by the Minister; and

(b) the Departmental Head of the Department responsible for finance and planning matters or his nominee; and

(c) the Departmental Head of the Department responsible for labour and employment matters or his nominee; and

(d) the Managing Director; and

(e) two persons (who are themselves employees) representing employees of affected establishments, appointed by the Minister from a list of names submitted to him from the employees in affected establishments as in the opinion of the Minister represent the employees; and

(f) two persons (who are themselves employers) representing employers of affected establishments, appointed by the Minister from a list of names submitted to him from employers in affected establishments as in the opinion of the Minister represent the employers.

(2) Appointments under Subsection (1)(a), (e) and (f) shall be notified in the National Gazette.

(3) Subject to this Act, the terms and conditions of the Trustees appointed under Subsection (1)(a), (e) and (f) are as determined by the Minister from time to time.

(4) The Trustees appointed under Subsection (1)(a), (e) and (f) shall be appointed for a period of three years and are eligible for re-appointment.

[781](5) The Trustees shall appoint a person other than a Trustee to be Secretary to the Board.

7 Acting Chairman

(1) Where the Chairman is absent (whether from the country or from a meeting) or is unable or is otherwise unavailable to act, the Board may elect from among their own number an Acting Chairman.

(2) The Acting Chairman has and may exercise all the powers and perform all or any of the functions of the Chairman and this Act applies accordingly.

8 Leave of absence of Trustees

The Chairman may grant leave of absence to a Trustee on such terms and conditions as he determines.

9 Declaration of Office

(1) Before entering on the duties of his office, a Trustee shall make the Declaration of Office provided by the *Constitution*.

(2) The Declaration of Office shall be made by a Trustee before the Minister or a person appointed by the Minister for the purpose.

10 Vacation of office of Trustee

(1) If a Trustee –

- (a) dies; or
- (b) becomes permanently incapable of performing his duties; or
- (c) resigns his office by writing under his hand addressed to the Minister; or
- (d) absents himself from three consecutive meetings of the Board without the written consent of the Chairman; or
- (e) becomes of unsound mind as that expression is used in the *Public Health Act*; or
- (f) is guilty of moral turpitude,
- [782](g) being a person appointed under Section 6(1)(e), ceases to be an employee; or

---

[781]Section 6(5) amended by *National Provident Fund (Amendment) Act* 1986 (No. 40 of 1986), s1(b).

[782]Section 10(1)(g) inserted by *National Provident Fund (Amendment) Act* 1990 (No. 27 of 1990), s5.

[783](h) being a person appointed under Section 6(1)(f), ceases to be an employer,

the Minister shall terminate his appointment.

(2) The Minister may, at any time, terminate the appointment of a Trustee for inability, inefficiency, incapacity or misbehaviour.

(3) Where the appointment of a Trustee is terminated under this section, the Minister shall, by notice in the National Gazette, declare his office vacant.

(4) Where an office is declared vacant under Subsection (3), the vacancy shall be filled in accordance with Section 6.

11 Vacancy not to affect powers or functions

The exercise or performance of a power or function of the Board is not invalidated by reason only of a vacancy in the membership of the Board.

12 Meetings of the Board

(1) Subject to Subsection (3), the Board shall meet as the Chairman determines, provided that the Board meets at least three times in each year.

(2) Subject to Subsection (3), the Secretary shall, if requested to do so by not less than one third of the Trustees, call a meeting of the Board as soon as practicable after receiving the request.

(3) The Secretary shall give to all Trustees at least 15 days' notice of a meeting of the Board.

(4) At a meeting of the Board –

(a) a quorum is the Chairman and at least four other Trustees of whom –

(i) one shall be from those appointed under Section 6(1)(e); and

(ii) one shall be from those appointed under Section 6(1)(f); and

(b) the Chairman or Deputy Chairman shall preside; and

(c) matters arising shall be decided by a majority of the votes of the Trustees present and voting; and

(d) the person presiding has a deliberative and, in the event of an equality of votes on a matter, also a casting vote,

[783]Section 10(1)(h) inserted by *National Provident Fund (Amendment) Act* 1990 (No. 27 of 1990), s5.

[784]provided that if all the Trustees agree in writing on each occasion this period of notice may be reduced or waived.

(5) The Board shall cause minutes of its meetings to be recorded and kept.

(6) Subject to this Act, the procedures of the Board are as determined by it.

13 Indemnity of Trustees

A Trustee is not personally liable for any act of the Board or of a Trustee acting as such, done in good faith.

14 Functions of the Board

The Board shall administer the Fund in such manner as is provided under this Act and shall perform such other functions as are required under this Act.

[785]14A Delegation by the Board

The Board may delegate to the Chairman, Managing Director or any other person or body, all or any of its functions or powers (except this power of delegation) under this Act.

[784]Section 12(4) end line inserted by *National Provident Fund (Amendment) Act* 1986 (No. 40 of 1986), s2.

[785]Section 14A inserted by *National Provident Fund (Amendment) Act* 1990 (No. 27 of 1990), s7.

PART III – THE SERVICE OF THE BOARD

15 Appointment, etc, of Managing Director of the National Provident Fund

(1) There shall be a Managing Director of the National Provident Fund who shall –

(a) be appointed by the Minister by notice in the National Gazette after prior consultation with the Board; and

(b) be appointed for such period as the Minister determines;

(c) be the Chief Executive of the Board; and

(d) be the head of the staff of the Board.

(2) The salary and other terms and conditions of employment of the Managing Director are as determined by the Minister from time to time, acting with the advice of the Board.

16 Vacation of office of Director, etc

(1) If the Director –

(a) becomes permanently incapable of performing his duties; or

(b) resigns his office by writing under his hand to the Board; or

(c) engages, without the consent of the Board, in any paid employment outside the duties of his office; or

(d) becomes bankrupt, applies to take the benefit of any law for the relief of bankrupt or insolvent debtors, compounds with his creditors for remuneration for their benefit; or

(e) is guilty of moral turpitude,

the Board shall terminate his appointment.

(2) The Board may, at any time, with the approval of the Minister, terminate the appointment of the Director for inability, inefficiency, incapacity or misbehaviour.

17 Public Service rights of Director to continue

Notwithstanding anything in the *Public Service Act*, where an officer or employee of the Public Service is appointed to be the Director, his service as Director shall be counted as service in the Public Service for the purpose of determining his rights (if any) in respect of –

(a) leave of absence on the ground of illness; and

(b) furlough or pay instead of furlough (including pay to dependents on the death of the officer).

18 Functions of the Director

(1) The Director shall manage the staff and administration of the Fund for the Board and shall act in accordance with the policy and directions of the Board.

(2) The Director shall advise the Board on any matter relating to the staff or administration referred to him by the Board.

(3) The Director has such other functions as the Board from time to time determines.

[786]18A Delegation by the Director

Except, where delegation by him is expressly prohibited –

(a) under law; or

(b) by the Board,

the Director may delegate to any person or body, any or all his powers and functions relating to finance and administration of the Fund (except this power of delegation), under this Act or the rules.

19 Appointment of officers

(1) The Board may, on the recommendation of the Director, appoint to be officers of the Board such persons as it thinks fit and necessary for the purposes of the administration of its functions.

(2) The Director and officers constitute the staff of the Board.

(3) Subject to this Part and to the Rules, officers hold office on such terms and conditions as the Board determines.

(4) Notwithstanding anything in the *Public Service Act*, where an officer appointed under this section was, immediately before his appointment an officer or employee of the Public Service, his service as an officer of the Board shall be counted as service in the Public Service for the purpose of determining his rights (if any) in respect of –

(a) leave of absence on the ground of illness; and

(b) furlough or pay instead of furlough (including pay to dependents on the death of the officer).

[786]Section 18A inserted by *National Provident Fund (Amendment) Act* 1990 (No. 27 of 1990), s9.

20 Rules for the staff of the Board

The Rules may make provision in relation to the staff of the Board and, in particular, may prescribe the terms and conditions of employment.

21 Other employees

(1) The Director may, with the approval of the Board, appoint such other employees as he thinks necessary for the purposes of this Act.

(2) Employees appointed under Subsection (1) shall be employed on such terms and conditions as the Board determines.

22 Inspectors

The Minister may, by notice in the National Gazette, appoint officers of the Board to be Inspectors for the purposes of this Act.

23 Powers of Inspector

For the purposes of –

(a) inquiring into the correctness of any information furnished in connexion with this Act; or

(b) ascertaining whether the provisions of this Act are being or have been complied with; or

(c) ascertaining whether the provisions of this Act are applicable to any person or establishment,

an Inspector may –

(d) require an employer to furnish such information as he considers necessary; and

(e) enter on the premises of an establishment for the purposes of examining any accounts, books, registers, records or other documents relating to the employment of persons or the payment of persons in the establishment; and

(f) examine, with respect to any matter relevant to the employment of persons and the payment of persons in the establishment, the employer, his agent or servant or any person found in charge of the establishment or the premises, or who the Inspector has reasonable cause to believe is or has been an employee in the establishment; and

(g) make copies of, or take extracts from, any accounts, books, registers, records or other documents that he may consider relevant.

24 Obstruction of Inspector

A person who –

(a) hinders or obstructs an Inspector in the execution of his duty under this Act; or

(b) fails to comply with a lawful requirement made by an Inspector under this Act; or

(c) refuses an Inspector entry to premises which the Inspector may, under this Act, lawfully enter; or

(d) impersonates an Inspector,

is guilty of an offence.

Penalty: A fine not exceeding K500.00.

PART IV – NATIONAL PROVIDENT FUND

25 National Provident Fund

(1) A fund to be called the National Provident Fund is hereby established.

(2) All contributions required to be made under this Act shall be paid into the Fund and all payments authorized to be made under this Act shall be met by the Fund.

(3) Income derived from the investment of the Fund is part of the Fund.

(4) The Fund is a provident fund for the purposes of Section 28 of the *Income Tax Act* 1959 (Adopted).

26 Board to be Trustee of Fund

(1) The Board shall be the Trustee of the Fund and all moneys belonging to the Fund shall be –

(a) deposited in a bank or banks as prescribed in accounts as prescribed; or

(b) invested by the Board in accordance with investment guidelines issued under Subsection (2).

(2) The Minister may from time to time issue guidelines as to the manner in which moneys held by the Board shall be invested.

[787]27 Expenses

All expenses incurred by the Board in connexion with the performance of its functions under this Act shall be met from the Fund.

28 Accounts and records to be kept

The Board shall –

(a) keep or cause to be kept proper accounts and records of its transactions and affairs; and

(b) do all things necessary to ensure that –

(i) all payments out of its moneys are properly made and properly authorized; and

(ii) adequate control is maintained over its assets or assets in its custody, and over the incurring of liabilities by

[787]Replaced by No. 27 of 1982, s1.

it.

[788]29 Audit

(1) For the purposes of this section, "subsidiary company", in relation to the Board, shall have the meaning given to a subsidiary company in relation to a public body under Section 1A of the *Public Bodies (Financial Administration) Act.*

(2) Subject to this section, the Auditor-General shall –

(a) inspect and audit the accounts and records of financial transactions of the Board and of any subsidiary company and records relating to its assets or assets in its custody; and

(b) promptly draw the attention of the Minister to any irregularity disclosed by the inspection and audit that is, in the opinion of the Auditor-General, of sufficient importance to justify his doing so.

(3) The Auditor-General may, in his discretion, dispense with the whole or any part of the detailed inspection and audit of any accounts referred to in Subsection (2).

(4) The Auditor-General shall, at least once in each year, report to the Minister the result of the inspection and audit of any accounts referred to in Subsection (2).

(5) The Auditor-General may, at his discretion, for the purpose of assisting him in an audit and inspection under Subsection (2), employ a registered company auditor who shall act under the direction of the Auditor-General and on the terms and conditions determined by the Auditor-General.

(6) The Auditor-General, or a person carrying out, or assisting in carrying out an inspection or audit under this section –

(a) is entitled at all reasonable times to full and free access to all accounts, records, documents and papers of the Board and of any subsidiary company relating directly or indirectly to the receipt or payment of moneys by it, or to the acquisition, receipt, custody or disposal of assets by it; and

(b) may make copies of, or take extracts from, any such accounts, records, documents or papers; and

---

[788]Replaced by No. 27 of 1982, s2, amended by No. 8 of 1983, s6.

(c) may require any person to furnish him with such information in his possession or to which he has access as the Auditor-General or the person carrying out or assisting in carrying out the inspection or audit, thinks necessary for the purposes of the functions of the Auditor-General under the *Constitution* and this Act.

(7) A person who contravenes Subsection (6)(c) is guilty of an offence.

Penalty: A fine not exceeding K200.00.

30 Reports and financial statements

(1) The Board shall, as soon as practicable after 31 December in each year prepare and furnish to the Minister a report of its operations during the year ended on that date, together with financial statements in respect of that year in such form as the Minister approves.

(2) Before furnishing financial statements to the Minister, the Board shall submit them to the auditor who shall report to the Minister –

(a) whether the statements are based on proper accounts and records; and

(b) whether the statements are in agreement with the accounts and records; and

(c) whether the receipt and expenditure and the investment of moneys, and the acquisition and disposal of assets, by the Board during the year are in accordance with this Act; and

(d) as to such other matters arising out of the statements as the auditor considers should be reported to the Minister.

(3) The Minister shall cause the report and financial statements, together with the report from the auditor, to be laid before the Parliament at its first meeting after their receipt by the Minister.

(4) When the report or financial statements of the Board are reproduced for publication or for other purposes, the report of the auditor shall be included in the reproduction.

(5) The first report and financial statements of the Board under this section shall be furnished as soon as practicable after 1 January following the commencement date.

PART V – CONTRIBUTIONS

31 Contributions by employer

Subject to Section 33, every employer to whom this Act applies shall pay to the Fund, in respect of each of his employees to whom this Act applies, a contribution at the rate of 7% of the pay actually drawn during the whole month, whether paid on a daily, weekly, fortnightly or monthly basis.

32 Contributions by employee

(1) Subject to Subsection (2) and to Section 33, every employee to whom this Act applies shall pay to the Fund a contribution at the rate of 5% of the pay actually drawn during the whole month, whether paid on a daily, weekly, fortnightly or monthly basis.

(2) An employee to whom this Act applies may, with the permission of the Director, pay to the Fund a further contribution in addition to that payable under Subsection (1) but the total contribution paid shall not be at a greater rate than 10% of the pay actually drawn during the whole month, whether paid on a daily, weekly, fortnightly or monthly basis.

33 Calculation of contributions

Each contribution payable under Sections 31 and 32 shall be calculated to the nearest toea, a half toea or more being counted at the next highest toea.

34 Payment of contributions

Every employer to whom this Act applies shall pay to the Board in the prescribed manner –

(a) the contributions payable by himself under Section 31; and

(b) on behalf of his employees – the contributions payable by his employees under Section 32.

35 Contributions to be paid into Fund

(1) All contributions paid under this Part shall be paid into the Fund in the prescribed manner.

(2) The Board shall cause to be credited to each member of the Fund the amount of every contribution paid on his behalf.

36 Employer not to reduce wages, etc

An employer shall not, by reason of his liability to pay contributions under this Part, reduce, directly or indirectly, the wages or salary or other benefits or emoluments to which an employee is entitled under his contract of employment or any other law.

37 Power to recover penal interest on default

(1) Where an employer defaults in making any payment due by him to the Fund, the Director may, by written notice, require the employer to give reasons why he should not make the payment due together with penal interest at the prescribed rate from the date on which payment was due until the date of payment.

(2) On receipt of a written notice under Subsection (1), an employer may make representations to the Director as to why penal interest should not be charged and, if the Director is satisfied that the reasons for late payment were unavoidable or acceptable, he may limit the rate of penal interest to an amount not less than the actual loss incurred by the Fund.

(3) Where an employer is aggrieved by a decision of the Director under Subsection (2) he may appeal in writing to the Chairman of the Board, whose decision is final.

PART VI – PROTECTION OF CONTRIBUTIONS AND PAYMENTS

38 Protection against attachment

The amount standing to the credit of any member in the Fund or of any exempted employee in a provident fund shall not –

(a) in any way be capable of being assigned or charged; and

(b) be liable to attachment under any decree or order of any court,

in respect of any debt or liability incurred by the member or the exempted employee.

39 No claim under Insolvency Act

The official trustee under the *Insolvency Act* shall not be entitled to any claim on the amount standing to the credit of any member in the Fund or of any exempted employee in a provident fund.

40 Amount to be paid from Fund on death of member to be free from debt, etc

Any amount standing to the credit of a member in the Fund or of an exempted employee in a provident fund at the time of his death and payable to his nominee under the terms of the provident fund or this Act, shall, subject to any deduction authorized by this Act, vest in the nominee free from debt or any other liability incurred by the deceased or the nominee before the death of the member or of the exempted employee.

41 Priority of payment of contributions over other debts

[789](1) Where an employer is adjudged insolvent, or being a company, is the subject of a winding-up order, the amount due –

(a) by an employer in relation to an affected establishment – by way of contributions, penal interest, accumulations or other charges under this Act; or

(b) by an employer in relation to an exempted establishment – by way of contributions to the provident fund of that exempted establishment or penal interest or other charges under this Act,

which has become due prior to the date of adjudication of insolvency or

[789]pngInLaw editorially inserted.

of the winding-up order, shall be deemed to be included among those debts which are to be paid in priority to other debts.

[790](2) For the purposes of Subsection (1), a certificate in writing under the hand of the chairman certifying that –

(a) the –

(i) person named in the certificate is, or was on a date specified in the certificate, an employer in relation to an affected establishment; and

(ii) sum specified in the certificate was, on a date specified in the certificate, due by that person by way of contributions, penal interest, accumulations or other charges under this Act; or

(b) the –

(i) person named in the certificate is, or was on a date specified in the certificate, an employer in relation to an exempted establishment; and

(ii) sum specified in the certificate was, on a date specified in the certificate, due by that person by way of penal interest or other charges under this Act,

is evidence of the matters stated in the certificate.

---

[790]Section 41(2) inserted by *National Provident Fund (Amendment) Act* 1986 (No. 40 of 1986), s4.

[791]PART VII – EXEMPTIONS

[Repealed No. 27 of 1990.]

[791]Part VII repealed by *National Provident Fund (Amendment) Act* 1990 (No. 27 of 1990), s10.

PART VIII – TRANSFER OF ACCOUNTS

47 Transfer from affected establishment to establishment to which Act does not apply

The amount of accumulations to the credit in the Fund of an employee in an affected establishment who leaves his employment and obtains re-employment in an establishment to which this Act does not apply shall –

(a) where the employee so desires; and

(b) where the rules of the provident fund of the establishment in which he is re-employed so permit,

be transferred in the prescribed time and manner to that provident fund.

48 Transfer from establishment to which Act does not apply to affected establishment

The amount of accumulations to the credit in a provident fund of an employee in an establishment to which this Act does not apply who leaves his employment and obtains re-employment in an affected establishment shall –

(a) where the employee so desires; and

(b) where the rules of the provident fund so permit,

be transferred to the credit of his account in the Fund.

PART IX – WITHDRAWALS AND PAYMENTS FROM THE FUND

49 Advance from the Fund for the purchase of a dwelling house, etc

(1) In this section –

"approved builder" means a builder approved by the Director;

"approved vendor" means a vendor approved by the Director;

(2) The Director may, on the application of a member, permit the payment to or on behalf of the member from the Fund of an amount not exceeding –

(a) 24 times the member's monthly pay; or

(b) the total amount of the contributions standing to the credit of the member's account,

whichever is the lesser amount, for the purpose of –

(c) purchasing from an approved vendor a dwelling – house or site for a dwelling house, either outright or on a deposit and instalment basis; or

(d) payment of the construction by an approved builder of a dwelling house, either outright or on a deposit and instalment basis; or

(e) payment of the cost of materials for use in the construction of a dwelling house, either outright or on a deposit and instalment basis; or

(f) any combination of the purposes referred to in Paragraphs (c), (d) and (e),

for the use of the member.

(3) A payment made under Subsection (2) is made subject to any conditions which the Director thinks fit and to the rules governing payments of this nature.

50 Recovery of payment

Where a payment has been made under Section 49 and the Director is satisfied that –

(a) the payment has been utilized for a purpose other than that for which it was made; or

(b) the conditions of the payment or the rules governing the payment have been contravened; or

(c) there is a reasonable apprehension that the conditions of the payment or the rules governing the payment will be contravened,

he may immediately take steps to recover the payment made, with interest at the rate of 2% above the rate of interest as determined from time to time by the Board, from the pay of the member in such instalments as the Director thinks fit.

51 Payment under Section 49 non-refundable

(1) Subject to Subsection (2), a payment made under Section 49 is not refundable.

(2) Where a member so desires, he may refund a payment made to him under Section 49 by such number of instalments not exceeding 36 as the Director fixes.

52 Circumstances in which accumulations in the Fund are payable to a member

(1) A member may withdraw the full amount standing to his credit in the Fund (or such other amount as is prescribed) –

(a) on retiring from his employment after attaining the age of 55 years; or

(b) on attaining the age of 55 years having previously retired from his employment; or

(c) on retirement on account of permanent and total incapacity for work due to bodily or mental infirmity duly certified as prescribed; or

(d) immediately before emigrating from Papua New Guinea for permanent settlement abroad; or

(e) not being a citizen, on his leaving Papua New Guinea for a period of at least two years; or

(f) on termination of employment in the case of retrenchment; or

(g) in such other circumstances as may be prescribed.

(2) The form of application for payment, the requirements for evidence in support of the application and the manner of payment shall be as prescribed.

53 Withdrawal by nominee

(1) The Board shall after the death of a member and on application by a person nominated under Section 54 pay to the applicant such part of the amount standing to the credit of the member as is stipulated in the nomination.

(2) An application under Subsection (1) shall be in the prescribed form and shall be accompanied by such evidence in support as is prescribed.

54 Nomination

(1) For the purposes of this section –

"children" includes adopted children where the Director is satisfied that the adoption is in accordance with the custom of the member;

"family" means –

(a) in the case of a man – his wife (except where, in accordance with any law or the custom of the community to which the spouses belong, the wife is no longer entitled to maintenance), his children (whether married or unmarried), his dependant parents and his deceased son's widow and children; and

(b) in the case of a woman – her husband and his dependant parents (except where the member by written notice to the Director excludes her husband from the family), her children (whether married or unmarried), her dependant parents and her deceased son's widow and children.

(2) Each member shall, in the prescribed manner, nominate a person or persons to receive in his or their own right such portions of the amount payable on the death of the member as are specified by the member.

(3) Where, at the time of making a nomination, a member has a family, the nomination shall be in favour of each member of the family equally, and a nomination in favour of any other person shall be null and void.

(4) Where, at the time of making a nomination, a member –

(a) has no family but subsequently acquires family; or

(b) has a family, but subsequently acquires further family,

his original nomination shall be deemed null and void and he shall immediately make a fresh nomination in favour of each member of his family equally.

(5) A nomination under this section in favour of a child who is a minor may appoint a person of full age in his family to be guardian.

(6) A nomination under this section may be amended at any time by a member after giving written notice in the prescribed form.

55 Procedure where no nominee

Where, at the time of the death of the member, no valid nomination has been made or no nominee is still alive, the amount standing to the credit of the member's account in the Fund shall be paid to persons determined by the Director in the manner determined by the Director.

[792]55A Other benefits

(1) The Board may authorize the payment to the members and their dependents of such other benefits as the Board determines in such manner as the Board determines.

(2) For the purposes of this section, the Board –

(a) may establish and maintain such fund or funds as it considers necessary for the purpose of this section; and

(b) shall pay into the fund or funds such amount, determined by the Board from the amounts received under Sections 31 and 32 determined by the Board; and

(c) shall pay out of the fund or funds, only for the purpose for which the fund or funds were established.

---

[792]Section 55A inserted by *National Provident Fund (Amendment) Act* 1990 (No. 27 of 1990), s14.

PART X – MISCELLANEOUS

56 Offences

A person who –

(a) for any purpose connected with this Act –

(i) knowingly makes a false statement; or

(ii) produces or furnishes or causes to be produced or furnished any document which he knows to be false in a material particular; or

(b) fails to pay to the Fund within such period as may be prescribed any amount which he is liable to pay under this Act in respect of or on behalf of any employee in any month; or

(c) obstructs any officer or servant of the Board in the discharge of his functions as such; or

(d) fails to comply with any rules made under this Act; or

(e) fails to transfer to the Fund any sum which he is required to transfer to it by virtue of Section 45 or 48 within such time as he is required by that section to transfer it; or

(f) fails to comply with any other requirements of this Act,

is guilty of an offence.

Penalty: For the first offence – a fine not exceeding K1,000.00 or imprisonment for a term exceeding one year.

For a second or subsequent offence – a fine not exceeding K2,000.00 or imprisonment for a term not exceeding two years.

Default penalty: A fine not exceeding K100.00.

57 Offence by corporation

Where a corporation does any act or makes any omission that is an offence under this Act, every person who at the time of the act or omission was a director or member of the governing body of the corporation or was concerned in the management of the corporation, and who authorized or knowingly permitted the act or omission, shall, for the purposes of this Act be deemed to have committed the offence.

58 Power of court to make orders

Where a person is convicted of an offence under Section 56(b) the court may, in addition to any sentence of fine or imprisonment, order him to pay to the Fund the amount in respect of the non-payment of which he was convicted.

59 Liability in case of transfer of establishment

Where an employer, in relation to an establishment, transfers that establishment, in whole or in part, by sale, gift, lease or in any other manner, the employer and the person to whom the establishment is transferred shall jointly and severally be liable to pay any contributions and other sums due from the employer under this Act in respect of the period up to the date of the transfer.

60 Protection for acts done in good faith

A suit or other legal proceedings shall not lie against an Inspector or other person in respect of anything which is, in good faith, done or intended to be done under this Act.

61 Rules

(1) The Board may make rules not inconsistent with this Act to provide for –

(a) all matters that are referred to in this Act as being prescribed; and

(b) all aspects of the administration of the Fund; and

(c) the employees or class of employees who shall join the Fund, and the conditions under which employees may be exempted from joining the Fund or from making any contribution; and

(d) the time and manner in which contributions shall be made to the Fund by an employer and by, or on behalf of, employees (whether employed by him directly or by or through a contractor), the contributions which an employee may, if he so desires, make under Section 32, and the manner in which such contributions may be recovered; and

(e) the constitution of any committee for assisting the Board; and

(f) the opening of offices of the Fund under the Board; and

(g) the manner in which accounts shall be kept, the investment of moneys belonging to the Fund in accordance with any directions issued or conditions specified by the National Government, the preparation of the budget, the audit of accounts and the submission of reports to the National Government or to any specified authority; and

(h) the conditions under which withdrawals from the Fund may be permitted and any deduction or forfeiture may be made and the maximum amount of such deduction or forfeiture; and

(i) the fixation by the Board of the rate of interest payable to members; and

(j) the form in which an employee shall furnish particulars about himself and his family whenever required; and

(k) the nomination of a person to receive the amount standing to the credit of a member after his death and the cancellation or variation of such nomination; and

(l) the registers and records to be maintained with respect to employees and the returns to be furnished by employers; and

(m) the form or design of any identity card, token or disc for the purpose of identifying any employee, and for its issue, custody and replacement; and

(n) the fees to be levied for any of the purposes specified in the rules; and

(o) the further powers (if any) which may be exercised by Inspectors; and

(p) the manner in which accumulations in any existing provident fund shall be transferred to the Fund under Part VIII, and the mode of valuation of any assets which may be transferred by the employers for that purpose.

(2) Rules made under Subsection (1) shall not have effect until they have been approved by the Head of State acting on advice, and notified in the National Gazette.

No 3 of 1997

Organic Law on National and Local-level Government Elections

PART I – PRELIMINARY

PART II – ADMINISTRATION

PART III – ELECTORATES

PART X – MISCELLANEOUS

PART IV – POLLING PLACES

PART V – ELECTORAL ROLLS

PART VI – QUALIFICATIONS AND DISQUALIFICATIONS FOR ENROLMENT AND FOR VOTING

PART VII – ENROLMENT

PART X – MISCELLANEOUS

PART VIII – OBJECTIONS

PART IX – APPEALS

PART X – WRITS FOR ELECTIONS

PART XI – THE NOMINATIONS

PART XII – VOTING BY POST

PART XIII – THE POLLING

Division 1 – Polling Schedule

Division 2 – General Provisions

Division 3 – Special Provisions in Certain Cases

Division 4 – Miscellaneous

PART XIV – THE SCRUTINY

Division 1 – Preliminary

Division 2 – Provisions relating to the Scrutiny of Ordinary Votes

Division 3 – Provisions Relating to the Scrutiny of Postal Votes

Division 4 – Provisions relating to the Scrutiny of Votes under Division 3 of Part XIII

Division 5 – Mode of Determining the Result of the Scrutiny

Division 6 – Re-count of Ballot-paper

PART XV – INTERPRETERS

PART XVI – THE RETURN OF THE WRITS

PART XVII – OFFENCES

PART XVIII – DISPUTED ELECTIONS, RETURNS, ETC

Division 1 – Disputed Elections and Returns

Division 2 – Qualifications and Vacancies

PART XIX – LOCAL-LEVEL GOVERNMENT ELECTIONS

Division 1 Preliminary

Division 2 – Administration

Division 3 – Electoral Rolls

Division 4 – Qualifications and Disqualifications for Enrolmentand for Voting

Division 5 – Enrolment

Division 6 – Objections

Division 7 – Appeals in relation to Enrolment

Division 8 – Writs for Elections

PART X – MISCELLANEOUS

SCHEDULE 1

INDEPENDENT STATE OF PAPUA NEW GUINEA

No 3 of 1997

Organic Law on National and Local-level Government Elections

Being an Organic Law to implement Section 125 (*electorates*) Section 126 (*elections*) and Section 187C (*Constitution, functions, etc., of Provincial Governments and Local-level Governments*) of the *Constitution* by providing for –

(a) a Boundaries Commission; and

(b) the defining of boundaries of National Electorates; and

(c) an Electoral Commission; and

(d) the holding of National Elections; and

(e) the holding of Local-level Government Elections,

and to repeal the *Organic Law on National Elections* and other laws and to make consequential amendments to the *Organic Law on Provincial Governments and Local-level Governments* and for related purposes,

MADE by the National Parliament.

PART I – PRELIMINARY

1 Compliance with Constitutional requirements

This Organic Law, to the extent that it regulates or restricts a right or freedom referred to in Subdivision III.3.C (*qualified rights*) of the *Constitution*, namely –

(a) the right to freedom from arbitrary search and entry conferred by Section 44 of the *Constitution*; and

(b) the right to freedom of conscience, thought and religion conferred by Section is of the *Constitution*; and

(c) the right to freedom of expression conferred by Section 46 of the *Constitution*; and

(d) the right to freedom of assembly and association conferred by Section 47 of the *Constitution*; and

(e) the right to privacy conferred by Section 49 of the *Constitution*; and

(f) the right to vote and stand for public office conferred by Section 50 of the *Constitution*; and

(g) the right to freedom of information conferred by Section 51 of the *Constitution*, is a law that is made for the purpose of giving effect to the public interest in public safety, public order and public welfare.

2 Application of this Law

Subject to Part XXII, Section 3 and Parts II to XVIII inclusive of this Law –

(a) apply to and in respect of elections to the National Parliament; and

(b) apply to and in respect of elections to Local-level Governments –

(i) only to the extent authorized by Part XIX; and

(ii) subject to such modification as is authorized by Part XIX.

3 Interpretation

(1) In this Law, unless the contrary intention appears –

"candidate", in Parts II and XVII, includes a person who, within three months before the first day of the polling period, announces himself as a candidate for election as a member of the Parliament;

"elector" means a person whose name appears on a Roll as an elector;

"electoral officer'' includes the Electoral Commissioner, a Returning Officer, presiding officer, substitute presiding officer, assistant presiding officer, poll clerk, interpreter and doorkeeper;

"electorate" includes –

(a) a provincial electorate; and

(b) an open electorate;

"electronic advice" means communication by any electronic means;

"member" means a member of the Parliament;

"officer" means an officer or employee of the National Public Service, a member of the Defence Force, a member of the Police Force, a member of the Correctional Service, an officer or employee of a Provincial Government or an officer or employee of a Local-level Government or an officer or employee of a governmental body;

"polling booth" means the polling place or part of the polling place determined by the presiding officer to be a polling booth under Section 118(2);

"polling period", in relation to an election, means the period for polling the first and last days of which are specified in the writ for that election and includes any extension of that period granted under Section 176;

"population" means –

(a) in the case where a National Census of Population has, in the opinion of the National Statistician, been completed and –

(i) from which in his opinion he is able to provide satisfactory estimates of population; and

(ii) in relation to which a redistribution has not previously been carried out,

the population as at the date of that National Census of Population as estimated by the National Statistician; and

(b) in any other case – the population as estimated by the National Statistician as at such date prior to the date of the redistribution as in the opinion of the National Statistician is the most recent date at which he can give a satisfactory estimate;

"Province" includes the National Capital District;

"Roll" means an Electoral Roll under this Law;

"the Boundaries Commission" means the Boundaries Commission established by Section 26;

"the Committee" means the Electoral Commission Appointments Committee established by Section 6;

"the Electoral Commission" means the Electoral Commission continued in establishment by Section 5;

"the Electoral Commissioner" means the Electoral Commissioner appointed under Section 5;

"the Parliament" means the National Parliament;

"the Returning Officer", in relation to an electorate, means the Returning Officer for that electorate;

"this Law" includes any regulations made under this Law.

(2) Notwithstanding any other law, where a time limit is imposed under this Law for the taking of an action, then unless the contrary intention appears, that time limit is mandatory.

(3) An opinion given by the National Statistician as to the population is non-justiciable.

4 Reference of certain questions to National Court

Any question as to whether a person has been validly elected as a member of the Parliament or whether the seat of a member has become vacant shall be determined by the National Court.

PART II – ADMINISTRATION

5 Electoral Commission

(1) The Electoral Commission established under the *Organic Law on National Elections* (repealed by this Law) continues in establishment.

(2) The Electoral Commission shall consist of the Electoral Commissioner.

(3) The Electoral Commissioner shall be appointed by the Head of State, acting with, and in accordance with, the advice of the Committee, by notice published in the National Gazette.

6 Electoral Commission Appointments Committee

There is hereby established an Electoral Commission Appointments Committee

consisting of –

(a) the Prime Minister or a Minister appointed by him, who shall be Chairman; and

(b) the Leader of the Opposition or in his absence the Deputy Leader of the Opposition; and

(c) the Chairman of the appropriate Permanent Parliamentary Committee; and

(d) the Chairman of the Public Services Commission.

7 Meetings of the Electoral Commission Appointments Committee

(1) The Committee shall meet at such times and places as, in the opinion of the Chairman, are necessary for the efficient conduct of its affairs.

(2) Questions arising at a meeting of the Committee shall be decided by a majority of the votes of the members.

(3) The Chairman has a deliberative vote and, in the event of an equality of votes on a question, also a casting vote.

(4) The procedures of the Committee are as determined by the Committee.

8 Casual vacancy, etc

(1) At any time when –

(a) the office of Electoral Commissioner is not filled on a permanent basis; or

(b) the Electoral Commissioner is away from the country or for any reason is not able to carry out his duties,

the Head of State, acting with, and in accordance with, the advice of the Committee, may appoint a person to act in the office of Electoral Commissioner for a period not exceeding six months.

(2) An acting Electoral Commissioner has and may exercise and perform all the powers, duties and functions of the Electoral Commissioner.

(3) This Law applies to an acting Electoral Commissioner in the same way as it applies to the Electoral Commissioner.

9 Term of office

The Electoral Commissioner shall be appointed for a term of six years and is eligible for re-appointment.

10 Declaration of office

Before entering upon the duties of his office, the Electoral Commissioner shall make the Declaration of Office before the Chief Justice or a Judge of the National Court appointed by the Chief Justice.

11 Disqualifications from office

A person is not qualified to be, or to remain, the Electoral Commissioner if he is –

(a) a member of the Parliament; or

(b) a member of a Provincial Assembly; or

(c) a member of a Local-level Government; or

(d) an office holder in a registered political party; or

(e) an undischarged bankrupt or insolvent; or

(f) of unsound mind within the meaning of any law relating to the protection of the person and property of persons of unsound mind; or

(g) under sentence of death or imprisonment.

12 Special conditions of employment

(1) The Electoral Commissioner shall not –

(a) actively engage in politics; or

(b) except on leave granted by the Head of State, or because of illness, absent himself from duty for more than 14 consecutive days or more than 28 days in any period of 12 months; or

(c) subject to Subsection (3), acquire by way of a gift or otherwise, or use or hold in any other manner, any interest in any property of Papua New Guinea or solicit, accept or receive any other benefit in addition to his terms and conditions of employment.

(2) Nothing in Subsection (1) prevents the Electoral Commissioner from holding office in a professional body in relation to which his qualifications are relevant.

(3) Subject to any Organic Law made for the purposes of Division III.2 (*leadership code*) of the *Constitution*, the Electoral Commissioner may purchase, lease or otherwise acquire land in the same manner and subject to the same conditions as any other citizen.

13 Resignation

(1) The Electoral Commissioner may resign by giving three months notice in writing of his intention to do so to the Head of State.

(2) The period of three months referred to in Subsection (1) shall be deemed to commence on the twenty-second day after the receipt of the notice by the Head of State except where the Head of State, acting with, and in accordance with, the advice of the Committee, by notice in writing to the Electoral Commissioner, fixes an earlier date for the commencement.

(3) The Electoral Commissioner may withdraw his resignation at any time before the period of three months referred to in Subsection (1) commences.

14 Retirement

(1) Subject to Subsection (2), a person who has attained the age of 55 years shall not be appointed or re-appointed as the Electoral Commissioner and a person shall not be appointed or re-appointed for a period that extends beyond the date on which he will attain the age of 55 years.

(2) The Head of State, acting with, and in accordance with, the advice of the Committee, may, for special reasons in a particular case, appoint or re-appoint a person who is over 55 years of age to be the Electoral Commissioner but in no case shall the Electoral Commissioner continue to act as the Electoral Commissioner after he has attained the age of 60 years.

15 Prime function of the Electoral Commission

It is the prime function of the Electoral Commission to organize and conduct all elections for the Parliament and the legislative arms of the Local-level Governments.

16 Department responsible for personnel matters to make staff available

The Department responsible for personnel matters shall, when so requested by the Electoral Commission make available to the Electoral Commission and to each Returning Officer such staff as may be necessary for the discharge of the functions conferred on the Electoral Commission.

17 Application of *Public Finances (Management) Act* 1995

Part VIII of the *Public Finances (Management) Act* 1995 applies to and in relation to the Electoral Commission.

18 Delegation

(1) The Electoral Commission may, by instrument in writing, delegate to an officer all or any of its powers and functions under this Law (except this power of delegation and any prescribed power and function), so that the delegated powers or functions may be had, exercised and performed by the delegate in relation to such electorate or electorates, or to such matters or class of matters, or to the whole of the country or such part of the country, as is specified in the instrument of delegation.

(2) Every delegation under Subsection (1) is revocable, in writing, at will.

(3) No delegation under this Section prevents the exercise or performance of a power or function by the Electoral Commission.

19 Returning Officers

The Electoral Commission shall, by notice in the National Gazette, appoint a Returning Officer for each electorate, who shall be charged with the duty of giving effect to this Law within or for his electorate, subject to any directions of the Electoral Commission.

20 Assistant Returning Officer

(1) Subject to this section, the Electoral Commission may, by notice published in the National Gazette, appoint a person to be an Assistant Returning Officer for a portion of an electorate.

(2) A person appointed to be an Assistant Returning Officer for a portion of an electorate may, subject to this Law and to the Regulations and to the control of the Returning Officer, perform the functions and exercise the powers of the returning Officer, in, or in relation to, that portion of the electorate.

(3) An Assistant Returning Officer shall not be appointed for a portion of an electorate for which less than 100 electors are enrolled.

(4) Where the services of an Assistant Returning Officer are required for the purposes of one election only, the appointment may be made by the Returning Officer by instrument in writing, and in that case the appointment terminates upon the completion of the election.

21 Appointment in cases of emergency

(1) Subject to Subsection (2), in the event of a vacancy occurring in an office of Returning Officer or Assistant Returning Officer, or in the absence from duty of any such officer, the Electoral Commission may, by notice in writing, appoint a person to perform the duties of the office during the period of the vacancy or absence.

(2) The Electoral Commission shall publish each notice under Subsection (1) in the National Gazette.

(3) In the event of a vacancy occurring in an office of Assistant Returning Officer appointed under Section 20(4), or in the absence from duty of any such officer, the Returning Officer may, by instrument in writing, appoint a person to perform the duties of the office during the period of the vacancy or absence.

(4) An appointment under Subsection (1) is temporary only, and does not confer on the appointee any right or claim to be permanently appointed to the position.

22 Date from which appointments are to take effect

A person appointed to be a Returning Officer or an Assistant Returning Officer under Section 21 shall be deemed to have been appointed as from the date specified in his appointment, or, if no such date is specified, as from the date of his appointment.

23 Candidates not to be Electoral Officers

No candidate shall be appointed an electoral officer, and if an electoral officer becomes a candidate he thereby vacates his office.

24 Keeping of Forms

All Returning Officers shall keep forms of claim for enrolment and transfer and such other forms as are prescribed, and shall without fee supply them to the public and assist the public in their proper use.

PART III – ELECTORATES

25 Election of Members to the Parliament

(1) Subject to this Law, for the purposes of elections to the Parliament there shall be such electorates in the country as are provided by this Law.

(2) One member shall be elected for each electorate by electors entitled to vote in respect of that electorate.

26 Boundaries Commission

For the purposes of a redistribution of Papua New Guinea into electorates, there is hereby established a Boundaries Commission consisting of –

(a) the Electoral Commissioner who shall be Chairman; and

(b) the Surveyor-General; and

(c) the National Statistician; and

(d) two persons, other than officers, appointed by the Head of State, acting with, and in accordance with, the advice of the Electoral Commission.

27 Term of office

A member of the Boundaries Commission referred to in Section 26(1)(d) shall be appointed for a term of six years.

28 Disqualifications from office

A person is not qualified to be, or to remain, a member of the Boundaries Commission if he is –

(a) a member of the Parliament; or

(b) a member of a Provincial Assembly; or

(c) a member of a Local-level Government; or

(d) an office-holder in a registered political party; or

(e) an undischarged bankrupt or insolvent; or

(f) of unsound mind within the meaning of any law relating to the protection of the person and property of persons of unsound mind; or

(g) under sentence of death or imprisonment.

29 Special conditions of employment

(1) A member of the Boundaries Commission shall not –

(a) actively engage in politics; or

(b) except on leave granted by the Head of State, or because of illness, absent himself from duty; or

(c) subject to Subsection (3), acquire by way of gift or otherwise, or use or hold in any other manner any interest in any property in Papua New Guinea or solicit, accept or receive any other benefit in addition to his terms and conditions of employment.

(2) Nothing in Subsection (1) prevents a member of the Boundaries Commission from holding office in a professional body in relation to which his qualifications are relevant.

(3) Subject to any Organic Law made for the purposes of Division III.2 (*leadership code*) of the *Constitution*, a member of the Boundaries Commission who is a citizen may purchase, lease or otherwise acquire land in the same manner and subject to the same conditions as any other citizen.

30 Resignation

(1) A member of the Boundaries Commission, other than a member referred to in Section 26(a), (b) or (c) may resign by giving three months' notice in writing of his intention to do so to the Head of State.

(2) The period of three months specified in Subsection (1) shall be deemed to commence on the twenty-second day after the receipt by the Head of State of the notice except where the Head of State. acting with, and in accordance with, the advice of the Committee, by notice in writing to the member. fixes an earlier date for the commencement.

(3) A member of the Boundaries Commission may withdraw his resignation at any time before the period of three months referred to in Subsection (1) commences.

31 Retirement

(1) Subject to Subsection (2), a person who has attained the age of 55 years shall not be appointed or re-appointed as a member of the Boundaries Commission and a person shall not be appointed or re-appointed for a period that exceeds beyond the date on which he will attain the age of 55 years.

(2) The Head of State, acting with, and in accordance with, the advice of the National Executive Council, may, for special reason in a particular case, appoint or re-appoint a person who is over 55 years of

age to be a member of the Boundaries Commission but in no case can any member of the Boundaries Commission continue to act as a member after he attained the age of 60 years.

32 Acting Appointments to the Commission

(1) At any time when a position of a member of the Boundaries Commission is not filled on a permanent basis, or when a permanent member of the Boundaries Commission is away from the country or for any reason is not able to carry out his duties, the Head of State, acting with, and in accordance with, the advice of the Electoral Commission may appoint a person to be an acting member of the Boundaries Commission.

(2) Subsection (1) does not apply to the position of a member of the Boundaries Commission who has been appointed in accordance with Section 26(1)(d).

(3) In a case referred to in Subsection (2) the Head of State, acting with, and in accordance with, the advice of the Electoral Commission may appoint a person to be an acting member of the Boundaries Commission.

(4) The appointment of an acting member of the Boundaries Commission continues until a permanent member is appointed or the permanent member returns to the country or becomes able again to carry out his duties, as the case may be.

(5) An acting member of the Boundaries Commission has and may exercise and perform all the powers, duties and functions of the position on the Boundaries Commission to which he was appointed.

(6) This Law applies to an acting member of the Boundaries Commission in the same way as it applies to a permanent member who held the position to which he was appointed.

33 Proceedings at meetings

(1) At a meeting of the Boundaries Commission, the Chairman shall preside if he is present.

(2) In the absence of the Chairman from a meeting of the Boundaries Commission, the members of the Commission present shall appoint one of their number to preside at the meeting.

(3) At a meeting of the Boundaries Commission, three members of the Commission form quorum.

(4) Questions arising before the Boundaries Commission shall be decided by a majority of votes of the members present and voting.

(5) The person presiding at a meeting of the Boundaries Commission has a deliberative vote, and, in the event of an equality of votes on a question, also a casting vote.

34 Provincial Electorates

(1) There shall be one provincial electorate for each Province.

(2) The boundaries of each provincial electorate are the boundaries of the Province for which it is the provincial electorate.

(3) A change in the boundaries of any Province shall, for the purposes of this Law, take effect only after the next following redistribution of electorates.

35 Open Electorates

(1) The number of open electorates shall be as determined by the Boundaries Commission but in no case shall the number of open electorates be less than 81 or more than 91.

(2) There shall be at least one open electorate in each Province.

36 Size of Open Electorates

(1) For the purposes of a proposed redistribution of the country into open electorates, the Boundaries Commission shall determine a population quota by the following formula: –

$$Q = \frac{P}{N}$$

where –

Q is the population quota for the electorate; and

P is the total population of the country; and

N is the provisional number of open electorates as determined by the Boundaries Commission within the limited specified in Section 35.

(2) Subject to Subsection (3), in drawing the boundaries of open electorates, the Boundaries Commission shall not draw them in such a way that –

(a) the population of any electorate is more than 20 per centum more than or less than 20 per centum less than the population quota prescribed by Subsection (1) except in circumstances which in the opinion of the Boundaries Commission would otherwise lead to an unreasonable result; or

(b) the boundaries of an open electorate cut across the boundary of a provincial electorate.

(3) Where the Boundaries Commission has –

(a) at a meeting determined the provisional number of electorates and proceeded to determine the population quota calculated for that number of electorates and proceeded to determine the population quota calculated for that number of electorates in accordance with Subsection (1); and

(b) a later meeting determines that there be more or less electorates than the provisional number determined at the earlier meeting,

the Boundaries Commission shall not redetermine the population quota.

(4) In determining the degree of variation of size between electorates (within the 20 per centum plus or minus allowable) the Boundaries Commission shall give due consideration to –

(a) density of population; and

(b) physical features and communications; and

(c) existing electoral boundaries; and

(d) Local-level Government and provincial and other administrative areas; and

(e) the community and diversity of interest, where it considers it relevant to do so.

37 Notice of proposed redistribution

Before baking its report, the Boundaries Commission shall cause a map with a description of the boundaries of the proposed electorates to be exhibited at such National, Provincial and Local-level Government offices as will give the people of the country a reasonable opportunity of seeing it and invite public attention to the map by advertisement in the National Gazette and by such other means as to it seems proper.

38 Objections and suggestions

Objections or suggestions in writing may be lodged with the Chairman of the Boundaries Commission not later than two months after the first advertisement in the National Gazette, and the Boundaries Commission shall consider all objections and suggestions so lodged before making its report.

39 Report of Boundaries Commission

(1) The Boundaries Commission shall, as soon as practicable after the expiration of the period of two months referred to in Section 38, forward to the Minister a report of its proposals for the re-distribution of the country into electorates, together with a map signed by not less than

three members of the Boundaries Commission showing the boundaries of each proposed electorate.

(2) The report shall state, as nearly as can be ascertained, the population in each proposed electorate.

40 Report to be laid before the Parliament

The report and map forwarded under Section 39 shall be presented by the Minister to the Parliament within seven sitting days after its receipt by him.

41 Determination of new Electorates

(1) A resolution of the Parliament accepting the recommendations of the Boundaries Commission for a proposed redistribution constitutes a determination of the number of open electorates and their boundaries, and those electorates until altered together with the provincial electorates, shall, subject to Subsection (3), be the electorates for the purposes of the election of members to the Parliament.

(2) The Minister shall cause the number of open electorates and their boundaries determined in accordance with Subsection (1) to be published in the National Gazette.

(3) Until the dissolution or expiration of the Parliament next following a determination under Subsection (1), the redistribution shall not affect the election of a new member to fill a vacancy happening in the Parliament, but for the purposes of any such election the electorates as previously existing, and the Rolls in respect of those electorates, shall continue to have full force and effect, notwithstanding that new Rolls for the new electorates may have been prepared.

(4) If the Parliament passes a resolution rejecting a proposed redistribution, or negatives a motion for the acceptance of a proposed redistribution, the Boundaries Commission shall within three months of the resolution rejecting or negativing an acceptance for a proposed redistribution make new recommendations for the redistribution of the country into electorates or confirm its previous recommendations and forward a copy of its new recommendations or its confirmation, as the case may be, to the Minister together with, in the case of any new recommendations, a map signed by not less than three members of the Commission showing the boundaries of each proposed electorate.

(5) Where the Boundaries Commission makes new recommendations under Subsection (4), it is not necessary for it to cause the action required by Section 37 to be taken.

(6) The new recommendations referred to in Subsection (4) shall state, as nearly as can be ascertained, the population in each proposed electorate.

(7) The new recommendations and map or the confirmation forwarded under Subsection (4) shall be presented to the Parliament by the Minister within seven sitting days after its receipt by him.

(8) If the Parliament passes a resolution rejecting the new or confirmed recommendations for a redistribution or negatives a motion for the acceptance of the new or confirmed recommendations, the matter lapses and the electorates for the purposes of the next succeeding general election shall be the electorates determined after the redistribution conducted immediately prior to that redistribution.

42 Change of Electors from one Roll to another

(1) When boundaries of an electorate are alerted, such changes as are thereby rendered necessary for the transfer of the names of the electors from one Roll to another shall be made by removing the names of those electors from the Roll from which they are changed, and by inserting the names so removed in the Roll to which they are changed.

(2) The transfer of names of electors from one Roll to another Roll under this Section shall be notified by the Electoral Commission in the National Gazette and in a newspaper circulating in the part of the country concerned.

(3) If the Electoral Commission considers that a notification in accordance with Subsection (2) is not effective as notice to a particular elector whose enrolment has been transferred, it may cause notice of the transfer to be sent by post or otherwise to the elector, or may take such other action as it considers desirable to ensure adequate publicity.

PART IV – POLLING PLACES

43 Polling places

(1) The Electoral Commission may, by notice published in the National Gazette or in a newspaper circulating in the electorate –

(a) appoint such number of polling places for each electorate as it thinks necessary and practicable; and

(b) abolish a polling place.

(2) No polling place shall be abolished after the issue of the writ and before the time appointed for its return.

PART V – ELECTORAL ROLLS

44 Rolls

There shall be a Roll for each electorate.

45 Form of Rolls

(1) A Roll shall be in such form as is determined by the Electoral Commission, and shall set out the name, address and occupation (or other prescribed particulars) and sex of each elector, and shall contain such further particulars as are prescribed or as the Electoral Commission directs.

(2) A direction under Subsection (1) may relate to the whole or a part of the country.

46 New Rolls

(1) All persons who are entitled to be enrolled on a Roll shall, subject to this Law, be so enrolled.

(2) New Rolls for any electorates shall be prepared whenever the Electoral Commission, by notice published in the National Gazette, directs.

(3) Subject to Subsection (4), a notice under Subsection (2) may specify the manner in which the Rolls shall be prepared, and may require any person, or member of a class of persons, entitled to enrolment on a new Roll and whose name does not appear on it to sign and send to the proper officer a form of claim for enrolment and otherwise to comply with the provisions of this Law relating to compulsory enrolment.

(4) Notwithstanding anything in Subsection (3), where an elector is enrolled in respect of an address in an electorate for which he is entitled to be enrolled, he shall not be required to sign and send in any further claim for enrolment in connection with the preparation of a new Roll under this section.

(5) The Electoral Commission shall, as soon as it is practicable to do so after the preparation of new Rolls, by notice published in the National Gazette, notify that the new Rolls have been prepared.

47 Additions, etc, to New Rolls

Upon the receipt by the Returning Officer of a new Roll for an electorate, the Returning Officer shall –

(a) make additions, alterations and corrections in it; and

(b) remove names from it,

in accordance with information received by him between the date of the notice directing the preparation of new Rolls and the date of the notification that the Rolls have been prepared, where the additions, alterations or corrections have not already been made in, or the removals have not been made from, the Roll.

48 Objections and notices to have effect in relation to New Rolls

Where objections have been lodged or notices of objection have been issued and action in respect of those objections or notices has not been completed before the notification of the preparation of new Rolls, the objections or notices have effect in relation to the new Rolls as if those Rolls had been in existence at the time of the lodging of the objections or the issuing of the notice.

49 Printing of Rolls

(1) Rolls shall be printed whenever the Electoral Commission so directs.

(2) Supplemental Rolls, setting out additions since the latest print of the Rolls, may, as necessary, be prepared and printed immediately after the issue of the writs for an election, and at such other times as the Electoral Commission directs.

50 Inspection

(1) Copies of the latest print of the electorate Roll and of all supplemental prints shall be open for public inspection at the office of the Returning Officer at all convenient times during his ordinary office hours without fee, and at such other places as the Returning Officer appoints for the purpose.

(2) Copies of the latest print of the electorate Roll and of all supplemental prints shall be obtainable at the office of the Returning Officer on payment of the prescribed fee.

51 Officers and others to furnish information

All officers and all occupiers of habitations and all persons who are, or appear to be, entitled to enrolment shall upon application furnish to the Electoral Commission or to a Returning Officer, or to an electoral officer acting under the directions of the Electoral Commission or the Returning Officer, all information that it or he requires in connection with the preparation, maintenance or revision of the Rolls.

PART VI – QUALIFICATIONS AND DISQUALIFICATIONS FOR ENROLMENT AND FOR VOTING

52 Persons entitled to enrolment

(1) All persons who have a right to vote under Section 50 (*right to vote and stand for public office*) of the *Constitution* who comply with the requirements of Part VII for enrolment for an electorate are entitled to enrolment.

(2) All persons whose names are on the Roll for an electorate shall, subject to this Law and to the provisions of any other law in force, vote at elections of a member for the electorate, but no person is entitled to vote more than once at an election, or at more than one election held at the same time.

(3) Subsection (2) does not prevent a person voting for a provincial electorate and an open electorate where the elections are being held at the same time.

PART VII – ENROLMENT

53 Officers

(1) The Electoral Commission may appoint persons to assist in the compilation and revision of the Rolls.

(2) A person appointed under Subsection (1) has such functions and duties as are prescribed or as the Electoral Commission directs.

54 Addition of names to Rolls

In addition to any other method provided for by law, names may be added to Rolls in accordance with claims for enrolment or transfer of enrolment.

55 Claims for enrolment

(1) Subject to this Section and to Section 52, a person who –

(a) has resided in the area of an electorate for a period of not less than six months immediately preceding the date of his claim for enrolment; or

(b) is nominated for an electorate for which he is not enrolled and was either born in the electorate or lived in the electorate for five years at any time, is entitled to have his name placed on the Roll for that electorate.

(2) Where the name of a person is placed on a Roll in accordance with Subsection (1)(a), he shall be enrolled in respect of the address of his last residence in the electorate.

(3) Where the name of a person is placed on a Roll in accordance with Subsection (1)(b), he shall be enrolled in respect of his last-known place of residence in the electorate.

(4) The Electoral Commission may, in relation to a person or class of persons, direct that a claim for enrolment be in the prescribed form and, if in the prescribed form, shall be signed by the claimant and attested by a prescribed person who shall sign his name as witness in his own handwriting.

56 Witness to application must satisfy himself of truth of statement

A person witnessing a claim for enrolment or transfer of enrolment shall, before he affixes his signature to it, satisfy himself, by inquiry from the claimant or otherwise, that the statements contained in the claim are true, unless he knows that the statements contained in the claim are true.

Penalty: A fine not exceeding K400.00.

57 Compulsory enrolment and transfer

(1) A person who is entitled to have his name placed on the Roll for an electorate, whether by way of enrolment or transfer of enrolment, and whose name is not on that Roll shall, at the first reasonably practicable opportunity, make a claim in the prescribed form to the Returning Officer for that electorate.

(2) A person who is entitled to have his name placed on the Roll for an electorate, whether by way of enrolment or transfer of enrolment, and whose name is not on that Roll on the expiration of 21 days from the date on which he became so entitled, is guilty of an offence unless he proves that his non-enrolment is not in consequence of his failure to comply with the provisions of Subsection (1).

(3) It is a defence to a charge of an offence against Subsection (2), if the defendant shows that he did not know, and had no reasonable opportunity of knowing, that his name was not on a Roll for which he was entitled to be enrolled.

(4) A person who is enrolled for the electorate in which he is residing and who changes his place of residence from one address in the electorate to another address in that electorate, and who has failed to notify, in the prescribed form, the new address to the Returning Officer for that electorate at the first reasonably practicable opportunity, is guilty of an offence.

(5) A person who is guilty of an offence against this Section is punishable, upon conviction –

- (a) in the case of a first offence – by a fine not exceeding K10.00; or
- (b) in any other case – by a fine not exceeding K25.00.

(6) A prosecution for an offence against this Section shall not be instituted without the consent of the Electoral Commission.

58 Registration of claim

(1) Upon receipt of a claim for enrolment or transfer of enrolment, notification of change of address within an electorate, or application for the alteration or correction of particulars of an existing enrolment, the Returning Officer shall note the date of its receipt by him, and if the claim, notification or application is in order and he is satisfied that the claimant is entitled to be enrolled or to have his name transferred or the particulars of his enrolment altered or corrected, as the case may be, the Returning Officer shall, subject to Section 60 –

(a) enter on the Roll kept by him the name of the claimant and the particulars relating to him; and
(b) notify the claimant in writing that he has been enrolled; and
(c) in the case of a transfer of enrolment, give notice of the transfer to the Returning Officer keeping the Roll from which the elector's name has been transferred.

(2) An interim acknowledgment of the receipt, after the issue of the writ for an election and before the close of the polling at the election, of a claim for enrolment or transfer of enrolment may be issued to the claimant by the Returning Officer in a form approved by the Electoral Commission.

(3) The Returning Officer keeping the Roll from which an elector's name has been transferred shall, upon receipt of notice of the transfer in the prescribed form, remove the elector's name from the Roll kept by him.

59 Notification of rejection of claim

The Returning Officer, on receipt of a claim, shall, subject to Section 60, after making such inquiry as he considers necessary if he is satisfied that the claimant is not entitled to enrolment or transfer of enrolment in accordance with the claim, notify the claimant as soon as practicable in the prescribed manner that his claim has been rejected, specifying the reason for the rejection, and advise the claimant that he is entitled, at any time within three months after the receipt of the notification, to appeal against the rejection in accordance with this Law.

60 Time for altering Rolls

Notwithstanding anything in this Law –
(a) claims for enrolment or transfer of enrolment which are received after 4 p.m. on the day of the issue of the writ for an election shall not be registered until after the end of the polling period for the election; and
(b) except by direction of the Returning Officer, no name shall be removed from a Roll under a notification of transfer of enrolment received after 4 p.m. on the day of the issue of the writ for an election and before the end of the polling period for the election.

61 Penalty on officer neglecting to enrol claimants

An officer who receives a claim for enrolment or transfer of enrolment and who, without just excuse, the burden of proof of which lies upon him, fails to do everything necessary on his part to be done to secure the enrolment of the claimant in pursuance of the claim is guilty of an offence.

Penalty: A fine not exceeding K1,000.00.

62 Alteration of Rolls

(1) In addition to other powers of alteration conferred by this Law, a Returning Officer may alter a Roll kept by him by –

(a) correcting a mistake or omission in the Roll; and

(b) correcting a mistake or omission in the particulars of the enrolment of an elector; and

(c) altering, on the application of an elector, the original name, address or occupation of the elector on the same Roll; and

(d) removing the name of a deceased elector; and

(e) striking out the superfluous entry where the name of the same elector appears more than once on the same Roll; and

(f) reinstating a name removed by mistake; and

(g) reinstating a name removed as the result of an objection where he is satisfied that the objection was based on a mistake as to fact and that the person objected to still retains and has continuously retained his right to the enrolment in respect of which the objection was made; and

(h) removing a name from the Roll where he is satisfied that the elector has ceased to be qualified for enrolment on the Roll and has secured enrolment on another Roll.

(2) Where the name of an elector has, in error, been incorrectly placed on the Roll for an electorate for which he is not entitled to be enrolled, and the elector is entitled to have his name placed on the Roll for another electorate, the Returning Officer for the electorate for which the elector is wrongly enrolled shall remove the name of the elector from that Roll and shall notify the Returning Officer for the electorate for which the elector is entitled to be enrolled accordingly, and that last-mentioned Returning Officer shall place the name of the elector on his Roll and shall notify the elector of the change of enrolment.

(3) No alteration under this Section shall, without the authority of the Returning Officer, be made at any time after 4 p.m. on the day of the issue of the writ for an election and before the end of the polling period for the election.

63 Special provisions for certain nominations

Notwithstanding anything in this Law, where a person who is entitled to do so has nominated for an electorate other than the electorate for which he is enrolled –

(a) the Returning Officer for the electorate for which he nominates shall place his name on the Roll for that electorate and notify the Returning Officer for the electorate for which he is enrolled who shall remove his name from the Roll for that electorate; and

(b) if the nomination is withdrawn, the Returning Officer for the electorate for which he was nominated shall remove his name from the Roll for that electorate and notify the Returning Officer for the other electorate who shall (unless he has in the meantime nominated for some other electorate) restore his name to the Roll for that other electorate; and

(c) if he fails to be elected, the Returning Officer for the electorate for which he was nominated shall remove his name from the Roll for that electorate and notify the Returning Officer for the other electorate who shall restore his name to the Roll for that other electorate; and

(d) if he is elected and later ceases to be the member for the electorate, the Returning Officer for the electorate for which he was the member shall remove his name from the Roll for that electorate and notify the Returning Officer for the other electorate who shall restore his name to the Roll for that other electorate unless he has ceased to be eligible for enrolment in that electorate and has been enrolled in another electorate.

64 Incorrect enrolment

Where a person whose name has been placed on the Roll for an electorate is not entitled to enrol for that electorate and that person secured enrolment under a claim in which he made a false statement, the Returning Officer may, at any time between the date of the issue of the writ for an election for that electorate and before the end of the polling period for that election, remove the name of that person from that Roll.

65 Alterations to be initialled

Every alteration of a Roll shall be made in such manner that the original entry shall not be obliterated, and the reason for each alteration and the date of the alteration shall be set against the alteration, together with the initials of the Returning Officer or of the person who makes the alteration on behalf of the Returning Officer.

PART VIII – OBJECTIONS

66 Names on Roll may be objected to

(1) A name on a Roll may be objected to by objection in writing lodged with or made by the Returning Officer.

(2) A sum of K4.00 shall be deposited in respect of each objection lodged by a person other than an electoral officer, to be forfeited to Papua New Guinea if the objection is held by the Returning Officer to be frivolous.

67 Objection

An objection under Section 66 shall be in the prescribed form, and shall be signed by an elector enrolled on the same Roll as the person objected to, or by the Returning Officer or a prescribed officer.

68 Duty to object

It is the duty of the Returning Officer and of any prescribed officer to lodge or make an objection in writing, setting out the grounds of the objection, in respect of any name which he has reason to believe ought not to be retained on the Roll.

69 Notice of objection

(1) When an objection is made by or lodged with a Returning Officer, the Returning Officer shall, subject to Subsection (3), give notice as soon as practicable of the objection to the person objected to.

(2) A notice under Subsection (1) may be in the prescribed form. and may be served by being posted or delivered to the last-known place of abode of the person objected to.

(3) Where the Returning Officer is satisfied that the ground of objection stated in an objection is not a good ground of objection or is frivolous, he may dismiss the objection, in which case no notice of the objection need be given to the person objected to.

(4) An objection on the ground that a person does not reside in the electorate for which he is enrolled shall be deemed not to be good unless it alleges that the person objected to has not resided in the electorate for the period necessary to qualify him for enrolment for that electorate.

70 Answer to objection

A person objected to under this Part may, orally or in writing in the prescribed manner, answer the objection.

71 Determination of objection

(1) Subject to Subsection (2), the Returning Officer shall determine an objection under this Part as soon as practicable after receipt by him of the answer of the person objected to, or, if no answer is received within a period of one month after the posting or delivery of the notice referred to in Section 69(1) and if it appears that the person objected to is not entitled to be enrolled on the Roll in respect of which the objection has been made, the Returning Officer shall –

(a) remove the name of the person from the Roll; and

(b) cause a copy of the notice of determination to be posted to or served on the objector and the person objected to.

(2) No name shall be removed from a Roll under this Section after 4 p.m. on the day of issue of the writ for an election and before the end of the polling period for the election.

PART IX – APPEALS

72 Appeal to District Court

(1) A person –

(a) who has made a claim for enrolment or transfer of enrolment in accordance with this Law, and has not been enrolled; or

(b) whose name has been removed from a Roll by the Returning Officer after an objection,

may at any time within two months after the receipt of notice of the rejection of the claim or of notice of the determination of the objection, as the case may be, make application in the prescribed manner to a District Court for an order directing that his name be enrolled or reinstated on the Roll, as the case requires.

(2) Where an objection has been determined by the Returning Officer adversely to the person objecting, that person may in the prescribed manner apply to a District Court for an order sustaining the objection.

(3) Where an application under this Section has reference to the decision of the Returning Officer upon an objection, the applicant shall, as prescribed, serve the objector or the person objected to, as the case requires, with notice of the application, and the person so served may appear, or may in writing authorize any person to appear on his behalf, to resist the application.

(4) The court may hear and determine an application under this section, and may make such order as it thinks fit as to the costs of the application.

(5) Costs ordered by the court to be paid may be recovered in the same manner as the costs of any other proceeding before the court.

(6) The Clerk of the Court shall send by post to the Returning Officer a certified copy of the order of the court, and the Returning Officer shall make such entries (if any) upon the Roll as are necessary to give effect to the order.

PART X – WRITS FOR ELECTIONS

73 Writs for General Elections

The Head of State, acting with, and in accordance with, the advice of the Electoral Commission, shall issue his writ for a general election of members in accordance with the provisions of Section 105 (*general elections*) of the *Constitution*.

74 Writs for vacancies

In the case of an election under Section 106 (*by-election*) of the *Constitution*, the Head of State, acting with, and in accordance with, the advice of the Electoral Commission, shall, as soon as practicable after the vacancy occurs, issue his writ for the election of a new member.

75 Form of Writs

(1) The writs for elections shall be in Form 1 or Form 2, as the case requires, in Schedule I, and shall fix the date for –

(a) nominations; and

(b) the first and last days of the period during which polling shall take place, which period shall not exceed 14 days; and

(c) the return of the writ.

(2) The Electoral Commission shall, as soon as practicable after the issue of a writ –

(a) advertize its issue and particulars in at least one newspaper circulated in the electorate to which the writ relates; and

(b) forward a copy to each Provincial Government and Local-level Government in the electorate; and

(c) take such further steps as it considers desirable to ensure adequate publicity.

76 Time of issue of Writs

For the purposes of this Law, a writ shall be deemed to have been issued at the hour of 4 p.m. on the day on which the writ was issued.

77 Address of Writs

(1) Writs for election of members shall be addressed to the respective Returning Officers for the electorates for which the elections are to be held, and may be issued through the Electoral Commission.

(2) The Electoral Commission may advise any Returning Officer by electronic advice of the issue of the writ for an election and the

particulars of the writ, and for the purposes of Section 82 the Returning Officer may act on the advice as if the writ had been received by him.

78 Date and Period of Nomination

Nomination of the candidates shall commence on the date of the writ, and the period of nomination shall not exceed seven days, including the date of the writ.

79 Date of Polling

The date fixed for the commencement of the polling period shall be a Saturday and shall be not less than eight weeks not more than 11 weeks after the date of the writ.

80 Date of Return of Writ

The date fixed for the return of the writ shall not be more than 21 days after the end of the polling period.

81 General Election to be held on same day

In the case of a general election, the same day shall be fixed for the commencement of the polling period in each electorate, and all writs shall be made returnable on the same day.

82 Duty of Returning Officer on receipt of Writ

On the receipt of a writ, the officer to whom it is directed shall endorse on it the date of its receipt.

PART XI – THE NOMINATIONS

83 Candidates must be nominated

No person is qualified to be elected as a member unless he has been duly nominated.

84 Qualifications for nomination

No person is qualified for nomination for an electorate while he is nominated for another electorate and that last-mentioned nomination has not been withdrawn.

85 Mode of nomination

A nomination shall be in the prescribed form and shall –

(a) name the candidate, his place of residence and occupation; and

(b) set out the qualifications by virtue of which he is qualified for nomination; and

(c) be witnessed by a person to whom the candidate is personally known.

86 To whom nomination made

(1) Nominations of members may be made to the Returning Officer for the electorate for which the election is to be held, to an Assistant Returning Officer for that electorate, or to a person "hereunto authorized by the Electoral Commission.

(2) Nominations may be made at any time after the issue of the writ and –

(a) in the case of a nomination made to the Returning Officer – before the hour of nomination; and

(b) in the case of a nomination made –

(i) to an Assistant Returning Officer or other person referred to in Subsection (1); or

(ii) in respect of a person who is not enrolled for the electorate,

before the commencement of the period of 48 hours immediately preceding the hour of nomination.

(3) Where a nomination is made to an Assistant Returning Officer or other person referred to in Subsection (1), he shall immediately notify the Returning Officer by electronic advice, in the prescribed form, of the

details of the nomination and deposit and forward the nomination to the Returning Officer.

87 Requisites for nomination

No nomination is valid unless –

(a) the person nominated consents to act if elected, and declares that he is qualified under the laws of Papua New Guinea to be elected as a member; and

(b) the nomination paper, or the electronic advice referred to in Section 86(3), as the case may be, is received by the Returning Officer after the issue of the writ and before the hour of nomination; and

(c) at the time of the delivery of the nomination paper the person nominated or some person on his behalf pays to the Returning Officer or other person to whom the nomination is made the nomination fee of K1,000.00 in money or in a banker's cheque.

88 Form of consent to act

The consent and the declaration of qualifications referred to in Section 87(a) shall be sufficient if the candidate signs the form of consent and declaration in the nomination paper, but the Returning Officer receiving the nomination, or the electronic advice of the nomination, as the case may be, may accept any other form of consent and declaration, whether accompanying the nomination paper or not, that he considers satisfactory, and that acceptance is final.

89 Formal defects

No nomination shall be rejected by reason of a formal defect or error if the Returning Officer receiving the nomination, or the electronic advice of it, as the case may be, is satisfied that the provisions of this Law have been substantially complied with.

90 Nomination fee non-refundable

Subject to Section 95, the nomination fee paid by or on behalf of a candidate at an election is non-refundable.

91 Place of nomination

The office of the Returning Officer for the electorate is the place of nomination in that electorate.

92 Hour of nomination

The hour of nomination is 4 p.m. on the day of nomination.

93 Declaration of nominations

The Returning Officer for the electorate for which an election is being held shall, at the hour of nomination, attend at the place of nomination for the electorate, and shall there publicly produce all nomination papers and electronic advices of nominations received by him, and declare the names, addresses and occupations of all candidates nominated.

94 Withdrawal of nomination

(1) A candidate may withdraw his nomination by lodging with the Returning Officer for the electorate, or with an Assistant Returning Officer for the electorate or a person authorized for that purpose by the Electoral Commission, a notice of withdrawal in the prescribed form, and thereupon the nomination shall be cancelled and the deposit lodged shall be returned.

(2) A withdrawal of nomination may be made –

(a) in the case of a notice of withdrawal lodged with the Returning Officer – at any time before the hour of nomination; or

(b) in the case of a notice of withdrawal lodged with an Assistant Returning Officer or other person referred to in Subsection (1) – more than 24 hours before the hour of nomination.

(3) Where a notice of withdrawal of nomination is lodged with an Assistant Returning Officer or other person referred to in Subsection (1), he shall immediately notify the Returning Officer by electronic advice, in the prescribed form, of the withdrawal and forward the notice to the Returning Officer.

95 Return of nomination fee in case of candidate's death

In the case of the death of a candidate before the end of the polling period, the nomination fee paid by him shall be returned to his legal personal representative.

96 Proceedings on nomination day

(1) If one candidate only is nominated for an electorate, the Returning Officer shall declare that candidate duly elected.

(2) If in an election more candidates than one are nominated, the proceedings shall, subject to the provisions of this Law relating to voting before the commencement of the polling period, stand adjourned to the commencement of the polling period.

97 Failure of Election

(1) Subject to this Law, whenever an election fails a new writ shall be issued for a supplementary election by the Head of State, acting with, and in accordance with, the advice of the Electoral Commission, as soon as practicable after the failure occurs.

(2) An election shall be deemed to have failed if no candidate is nominated or returned as elected.

PART XII – VOTING BY POST

98 Application by Electors for a Postal Vote Certificate and Postal Ballot-Paper

(1) An elector who –

(a) will not, throughout the polling period –

(i) be within the electorate for which he is enrolled; or

(ii) be within 16km by the nearest practicable route of a polling booth open in the electorate for which he is enrolled; or

(b) will be travelling or be away from his residence under conditions which will preclude him from voting at a polling booth open in the electorate for which he is enrolled; or

(c) is seriously ill or infirm, and by reason of that illness or infirmity will be precluded from attending at a polling booth to vote, or, in the case of a woman, will by reason of approaching maternity or of the necessity for caring for her infant be precluded from attending at a polling booth to vote; or

(d) is, by reason of his membership of a religious order or of his religious beliefs –

(i) precluded from attending at a polling booth; or

(ii) precluded from voting at a reasonably accessible polling place; or

(e) is a citizen residing abroad,

may make application for a postal vote certificate and postal ballot-paper.

(2) An application under this section, setting out the grounds upon which the elector claims to vote by post, may be made in writing, in person or by letter or electronic advice after the tenth day after the issue of the writ for the election to the Returning Officer for the electorate for which the applicant is enrolled.

(3) An application under this Section shall not be deemed to have been duly made if it reaches the officer to whom it is made after the commencement of the polling period for the election for which the applicant is enrolled.

(4) An elector shall not make, and a person shall not induce an elector to make. a false statement in an application for a postal vote certificate and postal ballot-paper.

Penalty: A fine not exceeding K1,000.00 or imprisonment for a term not exceeding six months, or both.

99 Penalty for improperly inducing elector to apply for postal vote

A person shall not improperly persuade or induce, or associate himself with a person in improperly persuading or inducing, an elector to make application for a postal vote certificate and postal ballot-paper.

Penalty: A fine not exceeding K1,000.00 or imprisonment for a term not exceeding one month.

100 Issue of certificate and ballot-papers

(1) Subject to Subsection (2), the Returning Officer who receives an application under this Part, if he is satisfied that it is properly made, shall deliver or post to the applicant a postal vote certificate printed on an envelope addressed to the Returning Officer for the electorate for which the applicant declares that he is enrolled, a postal ballot-paper and the prescribed directions to the elector and the authorized witness.

(2) Before delivering or posting a postal vote certificate and postal ballot-paper under Subsection (1), the Returning Officer shall insert in the certificate the name, address, occupation and sex of the elector and, if necessary, shall insert the name of the electorate and the names of the candidates and complete the instructions on the ballot-paper.

(3) Where an application under this Part is received after 4 p.m. on the day preceding the first day of the polling period in the electorate for which the elector is enrolled, a Returning Officer shall not post to the elector a postal vote certificate or postal ballot-paper.

(4) The postal vote certificate and postal ballot-paper shall be in the prescribed form.

101 Inspection of applications

(1) All applications for postal vote certificates and postal ballot-papers received by a Returning Officer shall be kept by him.

(2) All applications for postal vote certificates and postal ballot-papers shall be open to public inspection at all convenient times during office hours from and including the third day after the last day of the polling period until the election can no longer be questioned.

102 Numbering of applications and certificates

(1) The Returning Officer shall number all applications for postal vote certificates and postal ballot-papers received by him in consecutive

order, and shall number each postal vote certificate with a number corresponding with the number of the application.

(2) The Returning Officer shall initial the back of all postal ballot-papers issued, in such a position as to be easily seen when the ballot-paper is folded so as to conceal the vote.

103 Returning Officer to notify issue of postal vote certificate and postal ballot-paper

(1) The Returning Officer for an electorate in respect of which postal vote certificates and postal ballot-papers have been issued shall, if there is time conveniently to do so, note on the certified lists of votes the names of all electors to whom postal vote certificates and postal ballot-papers have been issued.

(2) If there is not time conveniently to note on a certified list of voters the issue of a postal vote certificate and postal ballot-paper, the Returning Officer shall, if practicable and reasonable, advise the presiding officer to whom the certified list of voters has been furnished of the issue of the postal vote certificate and postal ballot-paper.

(3) An elector to whom a postal vote certificate has been issued is not entitled to vote at a polling booth unless he first delivers to the presiding officer for cancellation his postal vote certificate and postal ballot-paper.

104 Authorized witnesses

(1) Subject to Subsection (2), the following persons are authorized witnesses within the meaning of this Law: –

(a) an elector or person who is qualified to be an elector; and

(b) where the vote is recorded outside the country, a person to whom the elector is well known.

(2) A person who is a candidate at an election is not an authorized witness at that election or at any other election held at the same time.

105 Directions for postal voting

The following directions for regulating voting by means of postal ballot-papers shall be substantially observed: –

(a) the elector shall exhibit his postal ballot-paper (unmarked) and his postal vote certificate to an authorized witness; and

(b) the elector shall indicate the grounds on which he wishes to vote by post by striking out those grounds in the postal vote certificate which do not apply to his particular case; and

(c) the form of declaration printed on the envelope bearing the postal vote certificate shall, after being filled in, be signed by the elector in the space provided for the signature of the voter in the presence of the authorized witness; and

(d) the authorized witness shall then and there sign his name in his own handwriting in the declaration printed on the envelope bearing the postal vote certificate in the place provided for the signature of the authorized witness, and shall add the title under which he acts as an authorized witness and the date; and

(e) the elector shall then and there, in the presence of the authorized witness but so that the authorized witness cannot see the vote, mark his vote on the ballot-paper in the prescribed manner, fold the ballot-paper, place it in the envelope addressed to the Returning Officer for the electorate in which he is entitled to vote; and

(f) the elector shall promptly post or deliver the envelope or cause it to be posted or delivered, to the Returning Officer for the electorate in which he is entitled to vote; and

(g) in the case of an elector suffering from a disability referred to in Section 140 the authorized witness shall mark the elector's vote on the ballot-paper and shall than and there fold the ballot-paper so that the vote cannot be seen, place it in the envelope addressed to the Returning Officer, fasten the envelope, and hand it to the voter, who shall post or deliver it, or cause it to be posted or delivered, to the Returning Officer for the electorate in which he is entitled to vote; and

(h) the authorized witness shall not suffer or permit any person (other than the elector) to see or become acquainted with the elector's vote, or to assist the elector to vote, or to interfere in any way with the elector in relation to his vote.

106 Duty of authorized witness

(1) An authorized witness shall –

(a) comply with the provisions of Section 105 insofar as they are to be complied with on his part; and

(b) see that the directions in that Section are complied with by every elector voting by post before him, and by every person present when the elector votes; and

(c) refrain from disclosing any knowledge of the vote of an elector voting by post before him.

Penalty: A fine not exceeding K1,000.00 or imprisonment for a term not exceeding six months

(2) An authorized witness shall not influence, or attempt to influence, in any way the vote of an elector voting by post before him.

Penalty: A fine not exceeding K1,000.00 or imprisonment for a term not exceeding one year.

107 Penalty for unlawfully marking postal ballot-paper

No person other than –

(a) the elector to whom the postal ballot-paper has been issued; or

(b) an authorized witness, acting under Section 105, assisting an elector in accordance with that section,

shall mark a vote upon a postal ballot-paper.

Penalty: A fine not exceeding K1,000.00 or imprisonment for a term not exceeding one year.

108 Unlawfully opening postal ballot-paper

No person other than the Returning Officer for the electorate in respect of which a postal ballot-paper has been issued, or an officer acting under his directions, shall open the envelope in which a postal ballot-paper has been placed under Section 105 and which has been fastened by the elector or by an authorized witness in accordance with the provisions of that section.

Penalty: A fine not exceeding K500.00.

109 Penalty for failure to post or deliver postal ballot-paper

A person to whom an application for a postal vote certificate and postal ballot-paper, or an envelope containing or purporting to contain a postal ballot-paper, is entrusted by a voter for the purpose of posting or delivering to a Returning Officer or Assistant Returning Officer, or delivery to a presiding officer, and who fails as soon as practicable to post or deliver the application or envelope, is guilty of an offence.

Penalty: A fine not exceeding K500.00 or imprisonment for a term not exceeding three months.

110 Penalty for inducing elector to hand over postal ballot-paper

A person shall not persuade or induce an elector to hand over to him a postal ballot-paper upon which a vote has been recorded.

111 Duty of persons present when an elector votes by post

A person present when an elector is before an authorized witness for the purpose of voting by post shall –

(a) obey all directions of the authorized witness; and

(b) refrain from making any communication whatever to the elector in relation to his vote; and

(c) refrain from assisting the elector or in any manner interfering with him in relation to his vote; and

(d) refrain from looking at the elector's vote or from doing anything whereby he may become acquainted with the elector's vote.

Penalty: A fine not exceeding K1,000.00 or imprisonment for a term not exceeding six months.

112 Ballot-box for postal votes

The Returning Officer shall keep a locked ballot-box on which the words "Postal Ballot Box" are conspicuously marked, and shall place and deep in that ballot-box, until the preliminary scrutiny under Section 155, all envelopes containing or bearing a postal vote certificate and purporting to contain a postal ballot-paper issued in respect of his electorate which –

(a) are delivered to him before the end of the polling period; or

(b) are received by him through the post up to the end of the polling period.

PART XIII – THE POLLING

Division 1 – Polling Schedule

113 Polling Schedule

(1) Subject to any directions given by the Electoral Commission, the Returning Officer shall, as soon as practicable after the close of nominations, prepare a polling Schedule showing the anticipated dates and times, within the polling period for the electorate, during which the polling booths will open at the polling places in the electorate, in such manner as he considers will give all electors in the electorate a reasonable and sufficient opportunity to vote at the election.

(2) Nothing in Subsection (1) or in this Law shall be construed to mean that polling shall be conducted on each day throughout the polling period or on any particular day in the polling period.

114 Publication of Polling Schedule

(1) The polling Schedule shall be published in the National Gazette and in a newspaper circulating in the electorate, and the Returning Officer shall take such other action as he considers necessary or desirable, or as is directed by the Electoral Commission, to ensure adequate publicity for the polling schedule.

(2) A copy of the polling Schedule shall be forwarded to each Provincial Government and Local-level Government in the electorate and shall be exhibited at such other places in the electorate as the Returning Officer appoints.

(3) A copy of the polling Schedule for an electorate shall be forwarded to each candidate in the electorate.

115 Adherence to Polling Schedule

(1) As far as possible, polling booths shall be open in accordance with the polling schedule, and the Returning Officer and presiding officers shall take all such action as is necessary or desirable for that purpose, whether expressly authorized by this Law or not.

(2) Subject to any directions given by the Electoral Commission, the Returning Officer may, where it becomes impracticable to adhere to a polling schedule, vary the schedule, in which case the provisions of Section 114 shall, as far as practicable, be observed in relation to the variation.

(3) Subject to any directions given by the Returning Officer, a presiding officer may where in his opinion it is necessary or desirable in order to meet an [793]unforeseen contingency of emergency and it is impracticable for the Returning Officer to vary the polling Schedule under Subsection (2), depart from the polling Schedule in relation to a polling place, and shall advise the Returning Officer of the departure and of the reasons for it as soon as practicable.

(4) Where the presiding officer departs from the polling Schedule in relation to a polling place, he shall take such action as is practicable to ensure adequate publicity for that departure at that polling place and amongst the electors likely to vote at it.

116 Appeal

(1) An elector may, not less than 14 days before the commencement of the polling period for an electorate, appeal to the Electoral Commission for an order varying a polling Schedule on the ground that it does not give to all electors in the electorate or in a part of the electorate a reasonable opportunity for voting in the election.

(2) Notwithstanding an appeal under Subsection (1), but subject to Section 115, a polling Schedule remains valid and in force until varied by order of the Electoral Commission under Subsection (1).

(3) In making an order under Subsection (1) the Electoral Commission shall give such directions as it considers desirable and practicable to ensure adequate publicity for the order.

117 Election not open to challenge

An election shall not be challenged on the ground of failure to observe a polling Schedule or to comply with the provisions of Section 114, or of a variation or a departure from a polling schedule.

Division 2 – General Provisions

118 Returning Officer to make arrangements

(1) If, on the day of nomination, the proceedings stand adjourned to the commencement of the polling, the Returning Officer shall immediately make all necessary arrangements for taking the poll, and in particular shall –

(a) appoint a presiding officer to preside at each polling place and all necessary assistant presiding officers, poll clerks, and door-keepers; and

---

[793]The Law has "unforseen".

(b) provide and furnish proper polling booths and ballot-boxes; and

(c) provide ballot-papers and all necessary certified lists of voters.

(2) The presiding officer shall, on or before the day of polling, determine the whole or the part of the polling place that shall be the polling booth in relation to that polling place.

(3) In an emergency during the polling due to the absence of an assistant presiding officer, poll clerk or door-keeper, or to [794]unforeseen and continued pressure at the polling which cannot be met by the duly appointed electoral officers, the presiding officer may appoint a person to act as assistant presiding officer, poll clerk or door-keeper, and the person so appointed or acting shall be deemed to have duly been appointed if the Returning Officer afterwards ratifies the appointment.

(4) No person under the age of 18 years shall be appointed to be or to act as a presiding officer or assistant presiding officer.

(5) An assistant presiding officer may, subject to any directions of the presiding officer, exercise all or any of the powers of the presiding officer, and shall, in respect of the exercise of those powers, be deemed to be the presiding officer.

119 Substitute

A presiding officer may appoint a person not under the age of 18 years to be his substitute to perform his duties during his temporary absence, and the substitute may, while so acting, exercise all the powers of the presiding officer and shall, in the exercise of those powers, be deemed to be the presiding officer.

120 No licensed premises to be used

No part of any premises licensed, or the subject of a permit, under –

(a) the *Liquor (Licensing) Act* (Chapter 312); or

(b) a Provincial law relating to liquor licensing,

shall be used for the purpose of a polling booth.

121 Separate voting compartments

Polling booths shall have one or more separate voting compartments, constructed so as to screen the voters from observation while they are marking their ballot-papers, and each voting compartment shall be furnished with a pen for the use of voters.

---

[794]The Law has "unforseen".

122 Ballot-boxes

(1) Each polling booth shall be provided with the necessary ballot-box or ballot-boxes.

(2) A ballot-box shall have a cleft in the cover through which the ballot-papers may be deposited in the box, and shall be provided with means for securely closing the cleft so that, when the cleft is so closed, no ballot-papers or other matters or things can be deposited or placed in the box or withdrawn from it.

(3) A ballot-box shall be capable of being securely fastened with a lock.

123 Certified list of voters

The certified list of voters to be used by a presiding officer at a polling place shall be the list of the electors on the Roll enrolled for the electorate for which the polling place is prescribed certified by the Returning Officer, and shall before the hour of commencing the poll in the polling area be delivered to the presiding officer for his guidance during the polling.

124 Form of Ballot-papers

Ballot-papers to be used in an election shall be in the prescribed form.

125 Ballot-papers

In printing the ballot-papers to be used in an election –

(a) the names of all candidates duly nominated shall be printed in an order determined as follows –

(i) the Returning Officer shall, at the place of nomination, immediately after the close of nominations and before all persons present, make out in respect of each candidate a slip bearing the name of the candidate as shown on his nomination or the electronic advice on his nomination, enclose the respective slips in separate blank envelopes of exact similarity and deposit the several envelopes in a locked ballot-box; and

(ii) the Returning Officer shall then thoroughly shake and rotate the ballot-box and shall permit any other person, if he so desires, to do the same; and

(iii) the ballot-box shall then be opened and an officer shall take out and open the envelopes from the ballot-box one by one; and

(iv) the candidate whose name appears on the slip enclosed in the envelope first taken from the ballot-box shall be placed first on the ballot-papers, the candidate whose name appears on the slip enclosed in the envelope next taken from the ballot-box shall be placed next on the ballot-papers, and so on until the placing of all the candidates has been determined; and

(b) where similarity in the names of two or more candidates is likely to cause confusion, the names of those candidates may be set out with such description or addition as will distinguish them from one another; and

(c) except as otherwise prescribed, a square shall be printed opposite the name of each candidate.

126 Ballot-papers to be initialled

(1) No ballot-paper shall be delivered to a voter without being first initialled or affixed with an official mark as prescribed by the presiding officer, and an exact account shall be kept of all initialled ballot-papers.

(2) The initials of the presiding officer shall be placed on the back of the ballot-paper in such a position as to be easily seen when the ballot-paper is folded so as to conceal the names of the candidates.

127 Scrutineers at the Polling

(1) Scrutineers may be appointed by candidates to represent them at polling places during the polling, but so that not more than one scrutineer, other than relieving scrutineers, shall be allowed to each candidate at each polling booth or subdivision of a polling booth on any one day.

(2) Appointments of scrutineers shall be made by notice in writing or by electronic advice addressed to the Returning Officer or presiding officer, and the notice or electronic advice shall be signed by the candidate and shall give the name and address of the scrutineer.

128 Provisions relating to Scrutineer

(1) A scrutineer shall not –

(a) interfere with or attempt to influence an elector within the polling booth; or

(b) communicate with a person in the polling booth except so far as is necessary in the discharge of his functions; or

(c) enter a compartment of a polling booth whilst a voter is present in that compartment.

Penalty: A fine not exceeding K100.00.

(2) A scrutineer shall not be prevented from entering or leaving a polling booth during the polling, and during his absence, a relieving scrutineer may act in his place, but so that only one scrutineer for each candidate shall be present in the polling booth or a subdivision of the polling booth at any one time.

(3) A scrutineer who commits a breach of this section, or who misconducts himself or fails to obey the lawful directions of the presiding officer may be removed from the polling booth by a member of the Police Force or by a person authorized by the presiding officer to remove him.

(4) A scrutineer may not be used to assist any voter to vote under Section 140 or 143.

129 Persons present at polling

A candidate shall not in any way take part in the conduct of the polling, and no person, other than the presiding officer, assistant presiding officers, officers, poll clerks, interpreters, door-keepers and scrutineers, and the electors voting and about to vote, shall enter or remain or be permitted to enter or remain in the polling booth during the polling except by permission of, and on such conditions as are determined by, the presiding officer.

130 The Polling

(1) Subject to Subsections (2) and (3), the polling shall be conducted as follows: –

(a) before the first ballot-paper is placed in an empty ballot-box, the Returning Officer or, if he is not present, the presiding officer, shall exhibit the ballot-box empty, and shall then securely fasten its cover; and

(b) the poll shall open at each polling place at 8 a.m. on each day (other than a Sunday or a public holiday) during the period for taking the poll at that polling place, and shall not close until all electors present in the polling booth at 6 p.m. and desiring to vote, have voted; and

(c) the doors of the polling booth shall be closed at 6 p.m. and no person shall be admitted after that hour to the polling booth for the purpose of voting; and

(d) at the close of the polling on each day of the polling period at a polling place, the presiding officer shall, in the presence of the poll clerk and of any scrutineers who are in attendance, publicly close, fasten, lock and take charge of the ballot-box; and

(e) when a ballot-box is full or no longer required for the polling, or at the end of the polling period for all polling places for which he is the presiding officer, whichever first occurs, the presiding officer shall, with the least possible delay, forward the ballot-box for the purposes of scrutiny, and it shall on no account be opened except in accordance with this Law.

(2) Notwithstanding anything in Subsection (1), where –

(a) the Returning Officer or the presiding officer considers it necessary the polling may commence at any particular polling place at a time later than 8 a.m. and, except on the last day of the polling period for the electorate, may close at a time later than 6 p.m.; and

(b) the presiding officer considers that all electors entitled and likely to vote at any particular polling place have done so, or the Returning Officer so directs, the poll may close at that polling place at a time earlier than 6 p.m.

(3) Nothing in Subsection (2) shall be deemed to authorize the commencement of the scrutiny before the end of the polling period in every electorate.

131 Elections at which Electors are entitled to vote

(1) Subject to Division 3, an elector shall only be admitted to vote for the election of a member for the electorate for which he is enrolled.

(2) A person –

(a) whose name is on a Roll for an electorate; and

(b) who has, at some time after his name was entered on the Roll and before the issue of the writ for that electorate, qualified for enrolment in another electorate,

is not qualified to vote in the first-mentioned electorate.

(3) For the purposes of this section, the Rolls in force at the time of the election are, subject to Subsection (2), evidence of the right of each person so enrolled to vote at an election, unless he shows by his answer to a question prescribed by Section 134 that he is not entitled to vote.

132 Where Electors may vote

(1) An elector is entitled to vote at any prescribed polling place for the electorate for which he is enrolled while that polling place is open.

(2) Nothing in this Section authorizes an elector to vote more than once at an election.

133 Persons claiming to vote to give name and other particulars

A person claiming to vote at a polling booth shall –

(a) state his full name or names; and

(b) if so desired by the presiding officer for the purpose of identifying the name under which the vote is claimed, give any other particulars necessary to be stated in the Roll or to enable him to be identified in the Roll.

134 Questions to be put to Voter

(1) Subject to this Law, the presiding officer –

(a) may, and at the request of a scrutineer shall, put to a person claiming to vote the following questions: –

(i) "Have you already voted either here or elsewhere in this election (or these elections, as the case requires)?"; and

(ii) "Did you reside within this electorate for a period of more than six months before your claim for enrolment?"; and

(iii) "Are you at least 18 years of age?"; and

(iv) "Are you a citizen of Papua New Guinea?"; and

(v) "Are you qualified to vote?"; and

(b) may, and at the request of a scrutineer shall, also put to any person claiming to vote, whose name appears on the certified list of voters the following question: –

"Are you the person whose name appears as (here state name) on the certified list of voters for this electorate?".

(2) If a person claiming to vote to whom any of the questions specified in Subsection (1) are put –

(a) refuses to answer fully a question so put to him; and

(b) does not answer the question prescribed in Subsection (1)(a)(i) absolutely in the negative, if so put to him; or

(c) does not answer the question prescribed in Subsection (1)(a)(ii) absolutely in the affirmative when put to him; or

(d) does not answer a question specified in Subsection (1)(a)(iii), (iv), (v) or (b) absolutely in the affirmative when put to him,

his claim to vote shall be rejected unless he is a candidate for election for that electorate.

(3) The voter's answer to a question put to him by the presiding officer under this Section is conclusive, and the matter shall not, subject to this section, be further inquired into during the polling.

135 Certain errors not to forfeit vote

No error or omission in the Roll for an electorate of part of a name or entry of a wrong name, address or occupation and no mistake in the spelling of a name warrants the rejection of a claim to vote, and no person shall be disqualified from voting under the name appearing on the Roll because of a change of name.

136 Right of Elector to receive Ballot-paper

(1) The presiding officer or a poll clerk shall, at the polling, hand to each person claiming to vote a ballot-paper duly initialled or affixed with an official mark as prescribed by the presiding officer –

- (a) if the name under which he claims to vote is on the certified list of voters for the polling place and his right to vote is not challenged; or
- (b) if the name under which he claims to vote is on the certified list of voters for the polling place and his right to vote is challenged, and his answers to the prescribed questions show that he is entitled to vote; or
- (c) if he claims to vote under Division 3 and complies with the provisions of that Division.

(2) The presiding officer, at the request of a scrutineer, shall note any objection by the scrutineer to the right of a person to vote, and shall keep a record of that objection.

(3) If the presiding officer puts to a person all or any of the prescribed questions, his right to vote shall be deemed to have been challenged.

137 List of voters to be marked on issue of Ballot-paper

Immediately upon handling the ballot-paper to a person claiming to vote, the presiding officer or a poll clerk shall place a mark against the person's name on the certified list of voters.

138 Vote to be marked in private

Except as otherwise prescribed, a voter upon receipt of a ballot-paper shall without delay –

- (a) retire alone to some unoccupied compartment of the booth, and in there, in private, mark his vote on the ballot-paper in the prescribed manner; and

(b) fold the ballot-paper so as to conceal his vote and to show clearly the initials of the presiding officer or the affixed mark and exhibit it so folded to the presiding officer, and then openly, and without unfolding it, deposit it in the ballot-box; and

(c) quit the booth.

139 Method of marking Ballot-paper

Subject to this Law, an elector shall record his vote on his ballot-paper by placing an "X" in the square opposite the name of the candidate for whom he wishes to vote in such a way as to indicate clearly his preference for that candidate only.

140 Assistance to certain Voters

(1) If a voter satisfies the presiding officer that –

(a) his sight is impaired; or

(b) that he is so physically incapacitated that he is unable to vote without assistance; or

(c) that he is so illiterate that he is unable to vote without assistance,

the presiding officer shall permit such number of persons appointed by the voter to enter an unoccupied compartment of the booth with the voter, and mark, fold and deposit the voter's ballot-paper for him.

(2) A person appointed under Subsection (1) to assist a voter shall restrain from disclosing any knowledge of the vote of the voter.

Penalty: A fine not exceeding K400.00 or imprisonment for a term not exceeding three months.

Division 3 – Special Provisions in Certain Cases

141 Voter claiming to vote whose name on Roll has been marked

(1) Notwithstanding anything in this Law, where a voter, against whose name on the certified list of voters used at a polling place prescribed for the electorate for which he is enrolled a mark has been placed in accordance with Section 137, claims to vote in an election at that polling place he may, subject to Sections 52 and 134 and to the Regulations be permitted to vote.

(2) The ballot-paper of a voter voting under this Section shall be dealt with as prescribed.

142 Person claiming to vote whose name is noted as person to whom postal vote certificate, etc, issued

(1) Where a person whose name has been noted on the certified list of voters used at a polling place prescribed for the electorate for which he is enrolled as an elector to whom a postal vote certificate and postal ballot-paper have been issued, claims to vote in an election at that polling place and states, when requested to deliver to the presiding officer for cancellation his postal vote certificate and postal ballot-paper, that he has not received a postal vote certificate and postal ballot-paper, he may, subject to this Law, be permitted to vote, if he makes a declaration in the prescribed form before the presiding officer at the polling place.

(2) The ballot-paper of a voter voting under this Section shall be dealt with as prescribed, but no such ballot-paper shall be scrutinized unless the Returning Officer is satisfied that the voter is entitled to vote in the election, and that a postal vote certificate or postal ballot-paper has not been received by him.

143 Blind or physically incapacitated Voters

(1) If a voter who claims to vote under Section 141 or 142 satisfies the presiding officer that his sight is so impaired or that he is so physically incapacitated that he is unable to vote without assistance, the presiding officer shall –

(a) fill in the form of declaration with the required particulars relating to the enrolment of the voter as required by the voter; and

(b) read over to the voter the form of declaration; and

(c) require the voter to sign the form of declaration –

(i) in his own handwriting if he is able to do so; or

(ii) with his mark as his personal signature if he is unable to sign his name in his own handwriting; and

(d) cause the signature of the voter, if made by means of a mark, to be witnessed by a scrutineer present, or if no scrutineer be present, by the poll clerk; and

(e) complete and attest the declaration; and

(f) permit such number of persons appointed by the voter to enter an unoccupied compartment of the booth with the voter and to mark and fold the ballot-paper for the voter; and

(g) enclose the ballot-paper in the envelope bearing the declaration of the voter, securely fasten the envelope and deposit it in the ballot-box.

(2) If a voter to whom Subsection (1) applies fails to appoint a person under that subsection, the presiding officer shall take action in accordance with Subsection (1)(a) to (e) (inclusive) and shall, in the presence of a person appointed by the voter for the purpose if the voter so desires, or, in the absence of any such appointment, the poll clerk –

(a) mark and fold the ballot-paper for the voter; and

(b) enclose the ballot-paper in the envelope bearing the declaration of the voter, securely fasten the envelope and deposit it in the ballot-box.

144 Dealing with voters, etc, under this Division

(1) The presiding officer shall, upon receiving a ballot-paper from a person voting under this Division, in the presence of the voter and of such scrutineers as are present and without unfolding the ballot-paper, enclose it in an envelope bearing the declaration of the voter under Section 143, and addressed to the Returning Officer, and shall securely fasten the envelope and deposit it in the ballot-box.

(2) An Assistant Returning Officer who is authorized under this Law to open the ballot-box shall, without opening the envelope, transmit it to the Returning Officer.

(3) Where the claim of a person to vote under this Division is refused, the presiding officer shall make a note in writing of the fact of the claim and the reasons for the refusal, and the presiding officer and a poll clerk shall sign a note in the presence of such scrutineers as are present, who may also sign the note.

Division 4 – Miscellaneous

145 Spoilt Ballot-papers

If a voter, before depositing his ballot-paper in the ballot-box, satisfies the presiding officer that he has spoilt the ballot-paper by mistake or accident, he may, on giving it up, receive a new ballot-paper from the presiding officer, who shall there and then cancel the spoilt ballot-paper, write the word “Spoilt” across the face of it, place it in an endorsed envelope and forward it to the Returning Officer after the polling.

146 Adjournment of Polling on account of riot

(1) The presiding officer may adjourn the polling from day to day where the polling is interrupted or obstructed by riot or open violence.

(2) If from any cause a polling booth at a polling place is not open on any day during the period for taking the poll at that polling place, the presiding officer may adjourn the polling for a period not exceeding

seven days but in no event beyond the end of the polling period, and shall forthwith give public notice of the adjournment.

(3) Where for any reason the polling is adjourned at a polling place, those electors only –

(a) who are enrolled for the electorate for which the polling place is prescribed; or

(b) who are otherwise entitled to vote as electors for the electorate,

and have not already voted, are entitled to vote at the adjourned polling at that polling place.

(4) Nothing in this Section shall be deemed to affect the provisions of Division 1.

PART XIV – THE SCRUTINY

Division 1 – Preliminary

147 Scrutiny

The result of the polling shall be ascertained by scrutiny.

148 Counting Centres

The scrutiny shall be conducted at such places, to be known as "counting centres", as are appointed by the Returning Officer for the purpose.

149 Officers to conduct scrutiny

The scrutiny at a counting centre shall be conducted by the Returning Officer or, in the absence of the Returning Officer from that counting centre, by an Assistant Returning Officer.

150 Scrutineers at scrutiny

(1) A candidate may appoint one or more scrutineers to represent him at the scrutiny, but only one such scrutineer for each candidate may be present in the counting centre at any one time during the scrutiny.

(2) The appointment of a scrutineer under this Section to represent a candidate at a counting centre –

(a) shall be made by notice in writing signed by the candidate, or by electronic advice signed by the candidate before it is tendered for transmission, given or sent to the officer who is to conduct, or who is sent to the officer who is to conduct, or who is conducting, the scrutiny at the counting centre; and

(b) shall specify the name and address of the scrutineer.

151 Conduct of scrutiny

The scrutiny shall be conducted as follows: –

(a) it shall commence as soon as voting in the electorate is completed; and

(b) any scrutineers duly appointed under Section 150 and any persons approved by the officer conducting the scrutiny, may be present; and

(c) all the proceedings at the scrutiny shall be open to the inspection of the scrutineers; and

(d) the scrutiny may be adjourned from time to time as necessary until the counting of the votes is complete.

152 Action on objections to ballot-papers

(1) If a scrutineer objects to a ballot-paper as being informal, the officer conducting the scrutiny shall mark the ballot-paper "Admitted" or "Rejected", according to his decision to admit or reject the ballot-paper.

(2) Nothing in this Section prevents the officer conducting the scrutiny from rejecting a ballot-paper as being informal although it is not objected to.

153 Informal Ballot-papers

(1) Subject to this section, and to the provisions of Divisions 3 and 4 and the Regulations, a ballot-paper is informal if –

(a) it is not authenticated by the initials of the presiding officer or by an official mark as prescribed; or

(b) subject to Subsections (2), (3) and (4) it has no vote indicated on it, or it does not indicate the voter's intention; or

(c) it has on it any mark or writing (not authorized by this Law to be put on it) by which, in the opinion of the officer conducting the scrutiny, the voter can be identified.

(2) Subsection (1)(a) does not apply to a mark or writing placed on a ballot-paper by an officer, notwithstanding that the placing of the mark or writing on the ballot-paper is a contravention of this law.

(3) Subject to Divisions 3 and 4, a ballot-paper shall not be informal for any reason other than a reason specified in this section.

(4) Notwithstanding the provisions of this Section and of Section 128, where the Returning Officer is satisfied that any mark made on a ballot-paper clearly indicates the intention of the voter and the candidate for whom he has given his name, the Returning Officer shall not determine that the vote is informal merely because the mark is not an 'X'.

Division 2 – Provisions relating to the Scrutiny of Ordinary Votes

154 Scrutiny of ordinary votes in elections

(1) In an election the scrutiny shall, subject to the provisions of Divisions 3 and 4 be conducted in accordance with the succeeding provisions of this section.

(2) The electoral officer conducting the scrutiny shall, in the presence of a presiding officer, poll clerk or an officer and of such authorized scrutineers as choose to attend and any other person approved by the Returning Officer –

(a) open all ballot-boxes received from polling places within the electorate; and

(b) reject all informal ballot-papers, and arrange the unrejected ballot-papers under the names of the respective candidates by placing in a separate parcel all those on which a vote is indicated for the same candidate; and

(c) count the votes given for each candidate on all unrejected ballot-papers; and

(d) make out and sign a statement (which may be counter-signed by the presiding officer, poll clerk or officer present and, if they so desire, by such scrutineers as are present) setting out the number of votes given for each candidate, and the number of informal ballot-papers; and

(e) place in a separate parcel all the ballot-papers which have been rejected as informal; and

(f) where an Assistant Returning Officer conducts the scrutiny, transmit the following information, by electronic advice or in some other expeditious manner. to the Returning Officer: –

(i) the number of votes given for each candidate; and

(ii) the total number of ballot-papers rejected as informal; and

(g) seal up the parcels and endorse on each parcel a description of the contents of it, and permit any scrutineers present, if they so desire, to counter-sign the endorsement; and

(h) where an Assistant Returning Officer conducts the scrutiny, transmit the parcels to the Returning Officer with the least possible delay, together with the statement referred to in Paragraph (d).

Division 3 – Provisions Relating to the Scrutiny of Postal Votes

155 Scrutiny of Postal Votes

The scrutiny of postal votes shall be conducted by the Returning Officer with the assistance of an Assistant Returning Officer or an officer, in the presence of such authorized scrutineers as chosen to attend and any other persons approved by the Returning Officer.

156 Preliminary scrutiny of Postal Votes

(1) The Returning Officer conducting the scrutiny shall –

(a) subject to Subsection (2), as soon as practicable after the end of the polling period for an electorate, produce and open the postal voters' ballot-box in which the envelopes containing the voters' ballot-papers have been placed and produce unopened all envelopes containing postal votes received by him before the end of the polling period; and

(b) examine each certificate and, if satisfied that –

(i) the person making the vote is an elector enrolled for the electorate; and

(ii) the declaration purports to be witnessed by an authorized witness,

accept the ballot-paper for further scrutiny, and place a mark against the name of the elector on a certified copy of the Roll used by him for the purpose of the scrutiny, but, if not so satisfied, disallow the ballot-paper without opening the envelope in which it is contained; and

(c) place in one parcel the unopened envelopes bearing the duly signed and attested declarations of those persons whose ballot-papers have been accepted for further scrutiny; and

(d) place in another parcel the unopened envelopes bearing the declarations of those persons whose ballot-papers he has disallowed, fasten and seal the parcel, endorse on it the words "Postal voters' ballot-papers rejected at the preliminary scrutiny" and add the name of the electorate, his signature and the date; and

(e) place the envelopes containing the ballot-papers which he has decided to accept for further scrutiny before him on a table in such a manner that the address side of each envelope is visible; and

(f) number each envelope consecutively from one upwards in the top right-hand corner until all of the envelopes have been dealt with; and

(g) without further examining the certificate or declaration of any voter or permitting any other person to do so, withdraw from the envelope each ballot-paper contained in it, and, without inspecting or unfolding the ballot-paper or allowing any other person to do so, place on it a number corresponding with that placed on the envelope from which the ballot-paper has been withdrawn and deposit the folded ballot-paper in a locked ballot-box for further scrutiny; and

(h) place the envelopes in a parcel endorsed with the words "Envelopes bearing postal voters' declarations from which ballot-papers have been withdrawn for further scrutiny", fasten the parcel, and add the name of the electorate, his signature and the date.

(2) The Returning Officer shall, as far as practicable, keep in the Postal Voters' Ballot-box sufficient envelopes containing ballot-papers to ensure that all ballot-papers, when counted, shall be taken from a number sufficient to prevent the identity of voters from being disclosed.

157 Further scrutiny of Postal Votes

At the further scrutiny, the officer conducting the scrutiny shall, as soon as practicable after the preliminary scrutiny under Section 156 open the ballot-box referred to in Section 156(g), examine the postal voters' ballot-papers contained in the ballot-box, and take similar action to that set out in Section 154(2)(b), (c), (d), (e) and (g).

158 Mistakes

A postal vote shall not be rejected as informal merely because, in the case of a candidate, part only of his name has been written on it if there is no possibility of confusion with some other candidate, or by reason of a mistake in spelling or otherwise where there is no doubt as to the identity of the candidate and the elector's intention is clear.

Division 4 – Provisions relating to the Scrutiny of Votes under Division 3 of Part XIII

159 Conduct of scrutiny

The scrutiny of votes under Division XIII.3 shall be conducted by the Returning Officer and shall commence as soon as practicable after the end of the polling period for an electorate in the presence of an Assistant Returning Officer or an officer and such scrutineers as chosen to attend.

160 Action on receipt of Ballot-papers under Division XIII3

The Returning Officer shall produce unopened all envelopes containing ballot-papers used for voting under Division XIII.3 and shall, before opening an envelope or allowing any other person to do so, examine the declaration of the voter and, if it is in order and shall deal with the ballot-paper in accordance with this Division, and make such correction (if any) to the Roll as is necessary.

161 Preliminary scrutiny of votes cast under Division XIII3

(1) The Returning Officer shall, in relation to envelopes containing ballot-papers used for voting under Division XIII.3 –

(a) place in one parcel the envelopes bearing the declarations of persons who he is satisfied are entitled to vote in respect of the electorate, accept for further scrutiny the ballot-papers contained in the envelopes and in respect of envelopes under Sections 141 and 142, make a notation on a certified copy of the Roll used by him for the purposes of the scrutiny against the names of the persons voting that those persons have been permitted to vote under Section 141 or 142, as the case may be; and

(b) place in another parcel the envelopes bearing the declarations of persons who he is satisfied are not entitled to vote in respect of the electorate, or whose declarations are not signed and attested, fasten and seal the parcel, endorse thereon the words "Division 3 voters' ballot-papers rejected at the preliminary scrutiny", and add the name of the electorate, his signature and the date; and

(c) place the envelopes containing the ballot-papers accepted for further scrutiny before him on a table in such a manner that the face only of each envelope bearing the address of the Returning Officer is visible; and

(d) number each envelope consecutively from one upwards in the top right-hand corner until all of the envelopes have been dealt with; and

(e) without further examining the declaration of a voter, or permitting any other person to do so, withdraw from the envelope each ballot-paper contained in it, and, without inspecting or unfolding the ballot-paper or allowing any other person to do so, place on it a number corresponding with that placed on the envelope from which the ballot-paper has been withdrawn, and deposit the folded ballot-paper in a locked ballot-box for further scrutiny; and

(f) place the envelopes in a parcel, endorsed with the words "Envelopes bearing Division 3 voters declarations from which ballot-papers have been withdrawn for further scrutiny", fasten the parcel and add the name of the electorate, his signature and the date.

(2) A Division 3 voter's ballot-paper shall not be rejected at the preliminary scrutiny by reason only of the fact that the presiding officer has omitted to attest the declaration of the elector.

162 Further scrutiny

At the further scrutiny, the officer conducting the scrutiny shall, as soon as practicable after the preliminary scrutiny under Section 161, open the ballot-box referred to in Section 161(1)(e), examine the Division 3 voters' ballot-papers contained in the ballot-box, and take similar action to that set out in Section 154(2)(b) (c), (d), (e) and (g).

163 Informal Ballot-papers

In addition to the matters specified in Section 153, a Division 3 voter's ballot-paper is informal if it is not contained in an envelope bearing the declaration of the elector.

164 Parcelling of Ballot-papers

The officer conducting the scrutiny shall place in separate parcels –

(a) all Division 3 voters' ballot-papers allowed or admitted as formal; and

(b) all Division 3 voters' ballot-papers disallowed or rejected as informal, and shall fasten and seal each parcel, and endorse on it particulars of the contents of it and the name of the electorate, and add his signature and the date.

165 Opening of sealed parcels of Ballot-papers

The sealed parcels of Division 3 voters' ballot-papers may only be opened –

(a) for the purposes of an authorized re-count; or

(b) by direction of the National Court.

166 Opening of sealed parcels of Declarations

The sealed parcels of Division 3 voters' declarations may only be opened –

(a) by direction of the National Court; or

(b) as provided in the Regulations.

167 Preservation of Ballot-papers and Declarations

Subject to any action referred to in Section 165 or 166, the Returning Officer shall preserve the sealed parcels of –

(a) Division 3 voters' ballot-papers allowed or admitted to the scrutiny; and

(b) Division 3 voters' ballot-papers disallowed or rejected at the scrutiny; and

(c) envelopes bearing Division 3 voters' declarations from which ballot-papers have been withdrawn for further scrutiny; and

(d) envelopes bearing Division 3 voters' declarations and containing ballot-papers rejected at the preliminary scrutiny,

until their destruction has been authorized by the Electoral Commission.

Division 5 – Mode of Determining the Result of the Scrutiny

168 Scrutiny of votes in election

(1) The result of an election shall be determined by scrutiny in the following manner: –

(a) the Returning Officer shall ascertain the total number of votes given for each candidate;

(b) the candidate who has received the largest number of votes is elected;

(c) if two or more candidates have an equal number of votes, the Returning Officer shall decide, by drawing lots, who shall be elected.

(2) The procedure for drawing lots is as follows: –

(a) the Returning Officer shall immediately after the conclusion of the counting and before all persons present, make out in respect of each of the candidates having an equal number of votes a slip bearing the name of the candidate as shown on the ballot-paper, enclose the respective slips in separate blank envelopes of exact similarity and deposit the envelopes in a locked ballot-box; and

(b) the Returning Officer shall then thoroughly shake and rotate the ballot-box and shall permit any other person present, if he so desires, to do the same; and

(c) the ballot-box shall then be opened and an officer shall take out and open one of the envelopes; and

(d) the candidate whose name appears on the slip enclosed in the envelope taken from the ballot-box is elected.

169 Further provisions relating to scrutiny

The officer conducting the scrutiny shall, in respect of ballot-papers scrutinized by him –

(a) place in a separate parcel all the ballot-papers which have been rejected as informal; and

(b) place in a separate parcel the unrejected ballot-papers; and

(c) seal up the parcels and endorse on each parcel a description of its contents, and permit any scrutineers present, if they so desire to countersign the endorsement.

Division 6 – Re-count of Ballot-paper

170 Re-count

(1) Where on the final count, the margin of votes between the candidate who polled the highest number of votes and the candidate who polled the next highest number of votes does not exceed 0.25% of the number of votes polled by the candidate who polled the highest number of votes, the candidate who polled the next highest number of votes may, at any time before the declaration of the result of the election, request the Returning Officer to re-count the ballot-papers contained in a parcel.

(2) On receipt of a request under Subsection (1) the Returning Officer shall re-count the ballot papers contained in the parcel.

(3) The officer conducting a re-count has the same powers as if the re-count were the scrutiny, and may reverse any decision in relation to the scrutiny as to the allowance and admission or disallowance and rejection of any ballot-paper.

171 Reservation of disputed Ballot-papers

(1) The officer conducting a re-count may, and at the request of a scrutineer shall, reserve any ballot-paper for the decision of the Electoral Commission.

(2) The Electoral Commission shall decide whether a ballot-paper reserved for its decision under this Section is to be allowed and admitted or disallowed and rejected.

(3) In the event of the validity of the election being disputed, the National Court may consider any ballot-papers which were reserved for the decision of the Electoral Commission, but shall not order a further re-count of the whole or part of the ballot-papers in connection with the election unless it is satisfied that the re-count is justified.

172 Conduct of re-count

(1) Before proceeding to re-count any ballot-papers, the Returning Officer shall send to each candidate notice of the time and place of the re-count.

(2) The Returning Officer shall, at the time and place fixed for the re-count, in the presence of the scrutineer or scrutineers in attendance and of an officer, open every sealed parcel of ballot-papers to be re-counted and count the votes in it.

(3) Each parcel of ballot-papers to be re-counted shall be opened separately without destroying or rendering illegible any endorsement on the parcel, and every care shall be taken to prevent the ballot-papers in the parcel from being mixed with the ballot-papers in any other parcel.

(4) After a parcel has been opened and the votes in it counted, the Returning Officer shall replace the ballot-papers in their original cover, which he shall reseal, refasten and then place in a new cover which he shall also seal and fasten and endorse with the fact and date of the re-count, and the Returning Officer and such persons authorized to be present at the re-count as chosen to do so shall sign the endorsement.

(5) When any ballot-papers at a re-count are reserved for the decision of the Electoral Commission, the Returning Officer shall, in the presence of the scrutineer or scrutineers in attendance, place the ballot-papers in a properly fastened and sealed parcel bearing his signature and the signature or signatures of the scrutineer or scrutineers, together with an endorsement setting out the number of ballot-papers contained in the parcel, the name of the electorate and the date, and shall place the parcel in a fastened and sealed outer cover fully addressed to the Electoral Commission, and transport the parcel to it by hand or registered post.

(6) On receipt of the parcel, the Electoral Commission shall, in the presence of an officer and, if a candidate so desires, of a person appointed by the candidate, open the parcel and scrutinize the ballot-papers, and shall mark each ballot-paper "Admitted" or "Rejected", according to its decision to admit or reject the ballot-paper.

(7) When the Electoral Commission has given its decision on the ballot-papers reserved for its decision, it shall restore them to their original cover, refasten and reseal the cover and endorse on it –

(a) the number of ballot-papers contained in the cover; and

(b) a statement that the ballot-papers have been the subject of decision by it; and

(c) the signature of the Electoral Commissioner and the date,

and shall request the persons in whose presence it scrutinized the ballot-papers to add their signatures, and shall then place the parcel in a new cover, which it shall cause to be fastened, sealed and returned by hand or registered post to the Returning Officer.

(8) The Electoral Commission shall advise the Returning Officer, in writing, as to the number of ballot-papers admitted or rejected by it, and the decision of the Electoral Commission shall be accepted by the Returning Officer in completing his re-count of the ballot-papers.

(9) The receipt of every parcel of ballot-papers shall be acknowledged in writing by the Electoral Commission and the Returning Officer respectively.

PART XV – INTERPRETERS

173 Interpreters

(1) Notwithstanding the provisions of this Law, for the purposes of, and at any stage of, the proceedings at the polling or at the scrutiny, a person may, with the approval of the presiding officer or the officer conducting the scrutiny, as the case requires, make use of the services of a person as an interpreter.

(2) A candidate shall not be an interpreter, and a scrutineer shall not be an interpreter except for another scrutineer.

174 Duty of Interpreters

(1) An interpreter referred to in Section 173 shall –

(a) to the best of his ability, correctly interpret any matter which he is required to interpret; and

(b) comply with any directions given by the presiding officer of the officer conducting the scrutiny, as the case may be; and

(c) refrain from disclosing any knowledge of the vote of an elector for or to whom he interprets.

Penalty: A fine not exceeding K500.00 or imprisonment for a term not exceeding six months, or both.

(2) An interpreter shall not influence, or attempt to influence, in any way, the vote of an elector for or to whom he interprets.

Penalty: A fine not exceeding K1,000.00 or imprisonment for a term not exceeding six months, or both.

PART XVI – THE RETURN OF THE WRITS

175 Return of writs

(1) The Returning Officer shall, as soon as conveniently may be after the result of an election has been ascertained –

(a) at the place of nomination or any other place appointed by the Returning Officer, publicly declare the result of the election and the name of the candidate elected; and

(b) by endorsement under his hand certify on the writ the name of the candidate elected, and return the writ through the Electoral Commission to the Head of State who shall then forward all the writs to the Speaker of the Parliament.

(2) Where the Returning Officer cannot complete his inquiries into the facts set out in the declarations received by him under Section 141 or 142, without unduly delaying the declaration of the poll, and he is satisfied that the votes recorded on the ballot-papers could not possibly affect the result of the election, he may, subject to the concurrence of the Electoral Commission, declare the result of the election and return the writ without awaiting the receipt of the ballot-papers or the completion of inquiries, as the case may be.

176 Correction of errors

Any delay, error or omission in the printing, preparation, issue, transmission or return of any Roll, writ, ballot-paper or certified list of voters may be remedied, removed, rectified and supplied by the Electoral Commission by notice published in the National Gazette, specifying the matter dealt with and providing for the course to be followed, and that course shall be valid and sufficient.

177 Extension of time

(1) Subject to Subsections (2) and (3), within one month before or at any time during the polling period for an election, the Head of State, acting with, and in accordance with, the advice of the Electoral Commission may, where he is of the opinion that it is necessary to do so, provide for –

(a) extending the time –

(i) for holding the election; or

(ii) for returning the writ; or

(b) meeting any difficulty which might otherwise interfere with the due course or the election,

and provision so made shall be valid and sufficient.

(2) Where an extension of time granted under Subsection (1) does not apply to all electorates in which elections are being conducted at the same time –

(a) the last day of the polling period shall not be more than two weeks after the date originally fixed as the last day; and

(b) the date fixed for the return of the writ shall not be more than two weeks after the date originally fixed for its return.

(3) In the case of an extension of time under Subsection (1), public notice of the extension shall be immediately given in the electorate or the portion of the electorate for which the election is to be held.

PART XVII – OFFENCES

178 Illegal practices

(1) Subject to Subsection (2), the following are illegal practices at elections: –

(a) publishing an electoral advertisement, handbill or pamphlet or issuing an electoral notice (other than the announcement by advertisement in a newspaper of the holding of a meeting) without the name and address of the person authorizing the publication or issue being printed at the foot of it; and

(b) printing or publishing a printed electoral advertisement, handbill or pamphlet (other than an advertisement in a newspaper) without the name and place of business of the printer being printed at the foot of it; and

(c) printing, publishing or distributing an electoral advertisement, notice, handbill, pamphlet or card containing a representation of a ballot-paper or a representation apparently intended to represent a ballot-paper, and having on it any directions intended or likely to mislead or improperly interfere with an elector in or in relation to the casting of his vote; and

(d) printing, publishing or distributing an electoral advertisement, notice, handbill, pamphlet or card containing an untrue or incorrect statement intended or likely to mislead or improperly interfere with an elector in or in relation to the casting of his vote; and

(e) wilfully informing an elector during the polling period that he is not enrolled or entitled to be enrolled for a particular electorate, or is not entitled to vote, when as a fact he is enrolled or entitled to be enrolled, or is enrolled or entitled to be enrolled for that electorate, or is entitled to vote, as the case may be.

(2) Nothing in Subsection (1)(c) or (d) prevents the printing, publishing or distributing of a card not otherwise illegal, which contains instructions on how to vote for a particular candidate, so long as those instructions are not intended or likely to mislead an elector in or in relation to the casting of his vote.

(3) A person guilty of an illegal practice is liable to a penalty of a fine not exceeding K1,000.00 or imprisonment for a term not exceeding six months.

179 Heading to electoral advertisement

(1) The proprietor of a newspaper shall cause the work "advertisement" to be printed as a headline, in letters not smaller than 10 point or long primer, to each article or paragraph in his newspaper containing electoral matter, the insertion of which is or is to be paid for or for which a reward or compensation or promise of reward or compensation is or is to be made.

Penalty: A fine not exceeding K500.00.

(2) In Subsection (1), "electoral matter" includes all matter intended or calculated to affect the result of the election, and a report of the speech of a candidate if the report is or is to be paid for.

180 Articles to be signed

(1) On and after the date of issue and before the return of a writ for the election of a member, every article, report, letter or other matter commenting upon a candidate or political party, printed and published in a newspaper, circular, pamphlet or dodger shall be signed by the author, giving his true name and address at the end of the article report, letter or other matter, or where part only of the article, report, letter or matter appears in any issue of a newspaper, circular, pamphlet or dodger at the end of that part.

Penalty: A fine not exceeding K500.00.

(2) A newspaper editor or proprietor who permits, in a newspaper which he edits or owns, the publication of an unsigned article, report, letter or other matter commenting upon a candidate or political party, after the issue and before the return of any writ for the election of a member, is guilty of an offence.

Penalty: A fine not exceeding K500.00.

(3) This section does not apply to the publication in a newspaper of –

(a) a leading article; or

(b) an article which consists solely of a report of a meeting and does not contain any comment (other than comment made by a speaker at the meeting) upon a candidate or political party.

181 Matter broadcast

(1) On and after the date of issue and before the return of a writ for the election of a member, a person who broadcasts or permits to be broadcast, from a broadcasting station an announcement, statement or

other matter commenting upon a candidate or political party is, unless that announcement, statement or other matter includes the true name and address of the author of it, guilty of an offence.

Penalty: A fine not exceeding K500.00.

(2) Where an announcement, statement or other matter is broadcast in contravention of Subsection (1), the person who supplied the announcement, statement or other matter to the broadcasting station for broadcasting is, unless he proves that the true name and address of the author were included in the announcement, statement or other matter so supplied, guilty of an offence.

Penalty: A fine not exceeding K500.00.

(3) This section does not apply to the inclusion in a summary of news of a report of a meeting which contains no comment (other than comment made by a speaker at the meeting) upon a candidate or political party.

(4) For the purposes of this section, "broadcasting station" means a station broadcasting messages by means of wireless telegraphy.

182 Display of certain electoral posters prohibited

(1) Subject to this section, a person who writes, draws or depicts electoral matters directly on a roadway, footpath, building, vehicle, vessel, hoarding or place (whether it is or is not a public place or in a public place, and whether on land or water or in the air), is guilty of an offence.

Penalty: A fine not exceeding K500.00.

(2) The application of Subsection (1) extends in relation to an election although the writ for that election has not been issued.

(3) Nothing in this section prohibits –

(a) the posting up, exhibiting, writing, drawing or depicting of a sign or at the office or committee room of a candidate or political party indicating only that the office or room is the office or committee room of the candidate or party, and specifying the name of the candidate or the name of the party concerned; or

(b) the projection, by means of a cinematograph or other similar apparatus, of electoral matter on to a screen in a public theatre, hall or premises used for public entertainment.

(4) In this section –

"electoral matter" means any matter intended or calculated to affect the result of an election;

"electoral poster" means any material whatsoever on which electoral matter is written, drawn or depicted.

183 Removal of prohibited electoral posters

(1) A member of the Police Force may, and shall, if so directed by the Electoral Commission or by a Returning Officer –

(a) remove an electoral poster which appears to have been posted up or to be exhibited in contravention of Section 182; or

(b) obliterate electoral matter which appears to have been written, drawn or depicted in contravention of Section 182.

(2) A person shall not obstruct or hinder a member of the Police Force in the exercise or attempted exercise of any power or in the discharge or attempted discharge of any cut`, conferred or imposed upon him under this section.

Penalty: A fine not exceeding K500.00.

184 Loud-hailers, etc

(1) Subject to Subsection (2), a person, who uses a loud-hailer, megaphone or other similar device during the polling period, is guilty of an offence.

Penalty: A fine not exceeding K600.00.

(2) Subsection (1) does not apply to a police officer or electoral officer who uses a loud-hailer, megaphone or other similar device for the purposes of maintaining order or giving instructions.

185 Injunctions

For the purpose of ensuring compliance with Section 182, the National Court may, upon the application of an officer, grant an injunction –

(a) restraining an apprehended contravention of that section; or

(b) directing the removal of an electoral poster posted up or exhibited in contravention of that section, or the obliteration of electoral matter written, drawn or depicted in contravention of that section,

and may make an order incidental or supplementary to an order under this section, including an order as to costs.

186 Cards in polling booths

(1) A person who exhibits or leaves in a polling booth a card or paper having on it a direction or instruction as to how an elector should vote or as to the method of voting is guilty of an offence.

Penalty: A fine not exceeding K300.00.

(2) This section does not apply to official instructions exhibited by electoral officers at the direction of the Electoral Commission at a polling booth.

187 Untrue statement in electoral papers, etc

(1) A person who makes an untrue statement in an electoral paper, or in answer to a question under this Law or in information supplied to an officer for the purposes of the preparation, maintenance or revision of a Roll is guilty of an offence.

Penalty: A fine not exceeding K300.00.

(2) In Subsection (1), "electoral paper" includes a prescribed form.

188 Signature to electoral paper

(1) Every electoral paper which by this Law has to be signed by a person shall be signed by that person with his personal signature and in the case of the Electoral Commission by the personal signature of the Electoral Commissioner.

(2) Where a person who is unable to sign his name in writing makes his mark as his signature to an electoral paper, the mark shall be deemed to be his personal signature, if it is identifiable as such and is made in the presence of a witness who signs the electoral paper as a witness to the signature.

(3) A person who makes the signature of any other person on an electoral paper is guilty of an offence.

Penalty: A fine not exceeding K500.00.

(4) In this section, "electoral paper" includes a prescribed form.

189 Witnessing electoral papers

(1) A person who –

(a) signs his name as witness on a blank electoral paper; or

(b) signs his name as witness on an electoral paper which has been wholly or partly filled in unless it has been signed by the person intended to sign it; or

(c) signs his name as witness on an electoral paper unless he has seen the persons whose signature he purports to witness sign it; or

(d) writes on an electoral paper as his own name –

(i) the name of another person; or

(ii) any name not being his own name;

is guilty of an offence.

Penalty: A fine not exceeding K500.00.

(2) In Subsection (1), "electoral paper" includes a prescribed form.

190 Making marks on ballot-papers

Except where expressly authorized by or under this Law, a person, other than the elector to whom the ballot-paper has been lawfully issued, who makes a mark or writing on the ballot-paper of an elector is guilty of an offence.

Penalty: A fine not exceeding K500.00.

191 Electoral offences

The matters specified in Column 1 of the table in this section are electoral offences punishable in accordance with the provision in Column 2 of that table opposite the statement of the offence in Column 1.

TABLE OF ELECTORAL OFFENCES AND PUNISHMENTS

Nos.	Column 1Offences	Column 2 Punishments
1.	Voting more than once at the same election	K400.00 or imprisonment for three months.
2.	Wagering on the result of an election	K400.00.
3.	Wilfully defacing, mutilating, destroying or removing a notice, list or other document affixed by a Returning Officer or by his authority	K20.00.
4.	Knowingly making a false statement in a claim, application, return or declaration, or in answer to a question under this Law	Imprisonment for two years.
5.	Any contravention of this Law for which no other punishment is provided	K500.00.
6.	Falsely personating a person to secure a ballot-paper to which the personator is not entitled, or personating any other person for the purposes of voting	Imprisonment for two years.

7.	Fraudulently destroying or defacing a nomination paper or ballot-paper	Imprisonment for two years.
8.	Fraudulently putting a ballot-paper or other paper into a ballot-box	Imprisonment for six months.
9.	Fraudulently taking a ballot-paper out of a polling booth	Imprisonment for six months.
10.	Taking a ballot-paper out of a polling booth	K500.00.
11.	Forging, or uttering knowing it to be forged, a nomination paper or ballot-paper	Imprisonment for two years.
12.	In a polling booth during the polling, misconducting himself, or failing to obey the lawful directions of the presiding officer	K200.00 or imprisonment for one month.
13.	Supplying ballot-papers without authority	Imprisonment for six months.
14.	Unlawfully destroying, taking, opening, or otherwise interfering with ballot-boxes or ballot-papers	Imprisonment for six months.

192 Prohibition of canvassing near polling booth

(1) The following acts are, during the polling period and on all days to which the polling is adjourned, prohibited at an entrance of or within a polling booth, or within 7m of an entrance of a polling booth: –

(a) canvassing for votes; or

(b) soliciting the vote of an elector; or

(c) inducing an elector not to vote for a particular candidate; or

(d) inducing an elector not to vote at the election; or

(e) exhibiting a notice or sign (other than an official notice) relating to the election.

Penalty: A fine not exceeding K500.00.

(2) Where –

(a) a building used as a polling booth is situated in grounds within an enclosure; and

(b) the presiding officer at the polling booth causes to be displayed throughout the polling period at each entrance to those grounds a notice signed by him stating that those grounds are part of the polling booth,

those grounds shall, for the purposes of Subsection (1), be deemed to be part of a polling booth.

193 Badges or emblems in polling booths

An officer or scrutineer who wears or displays in a polling booth during the polling period a badge or emblem of a candidate or political party is guilty of an offence.

Penalty: A fine not exceeding K500.00.

194 Failure to transmit claims

A person who accepts a claim for enrolment or transfer of enrolment for transmission to a Returning Officer shall forthwith transmit the claim to the Returning Officer.

Penalty: A fine not exceeding K500.00.

195 Forging or uttering electoral papers

(1) A person who –

(a) forges an electoral paper; or

(b) utters a forged electoral paper, knowing it to be forged,

is guilty of an offence.

Penalty: Imprisonment for a term not exceeding two years.

(2) In Subsection (1), "electoral paper" includes a prescribed form.

196 Employers to allow employees leave of absence to vote

(1) If an employee who is an elector notifies his employer that he desires leave of absence to enable him to vote at an election, the employer shall, if the absence desired is necessary to enable the employee to vote at the election, allow him leave of absence without any penalty or disproportionate deduction of pay for such reasonable period as is necessary to enable the employee to vote at the election.

Penalty: A fine not exceeding K500.00.

(2) An employee who obtains leave of absence under this section under pretence that he intended to vote at the election but without the *bona fide* intention of doing so, is guilty of an offence.

Penalty: A fine not exceeding K500.00.

(3) This section does not apply to an elector whose absence may cause danger or substantial loss in respect of the employment in which he is engaged.

197 Protection of the official mark

(1) A person who, without lawful authority, the burden of proof of which lies upon him –

(a) makes an official mark on or in a paper; or

(b) has in his possession a paper bearing an official mark; or

(c) makes use of or has in his possession an instrument capable of making on or in a paper an official mark,

is guilty of an offence.

Penalty: A fine not exceeding K500.00.

(2) A person who, without lawful authority, the burden of proof of which lies upon him, makes on or in a ballot-paper, or on or in a paper purporting to be a ballot-paper, an official mark, shall be deemed to have forged a ballot-paper and is punishable accordingly.

(3) All paper bearing an official mark, and all instruments capable of making on or in paper an official mark, made or used by, or in the possession of, a person without lawful authority (the burden of proof of which authority lies upon him) is forfeited to Papua New Guinea, and may without warrant be seized by any member of the Police Force and destroyed or dealt with as prescribed.

(4) In this section, "official mark" means a prescribed mark to be placed or made on or in an electoral paper, and includes a mark so nearly resembling an official mark as to be likely to deceive.

198 Disorderly behaviour at meeting

(1) This section applies to any lawful public political meeting held in relation to an election between the date of the issue of the writ for the election and the date of the return of the writ.

(2) A person who, at a public meeting to which this section applies, acts in a disorderly manner for the purpose of preventing the transaction of the business for which the meeting is held is guilty of an offence.

Penalty: A fine not exceeding K500.00 or imprisonment for a term not exceeding two months.

(3) The Chairman of a public meeting to which this section applies may direct any member of the Police Force to remove from the room, building or place in which the meeting is being held a person who, in the opinion of the Chairman, is preventing the transaction of the business for which the meeting is held, and thereupon the member of the Police Force may take such steps as are necessary for the removal of the person from the room, building or place.

(4) A person –

(a) who has been removed from a room or building in accordance with a direction given under Subsection (3); or

(b) whose removal from a room, building or place has been directed under Subsection (3) and who has left that room, building or place,

and who, without the authority of the Chairman (proof of which authority lies upon that person) returns to that room or building while the meeting is in progress, is guilty of an offence.

Penalty: A fine not exceeding K500.00 or imprisonment for a term not exceeding two months.

(5) A member of the Police Force may arrest without warrant a person who commits an offence against Subsection (4).

199 Neglect to initial ballot-paper, etc

An officer who, contrary to his duty, fails to initial a ballot-paper or affix as official mark as prescribed, correctly to mark a certified list of voters, or properly to attest a declaration is guilty of an offence.

Penalty: A fine not exceeding K500.00.

200 Offender may be removed from polling booth

(1) A person who, in a polling booth during the polling, misconducts himself, or fails to obey the lawful direction of the presiding officer, may be removed from the polling booth by a member of the Police Force or by a person authorized by the presiding officer.

(2) A person who has been removed from a polling booth by direction of the presiding officer under Subsection (1) and who re-enters the polling booth without the permission of the presiding officer is guilty of a further electoral offence, punishable on conviction by twice the penalty prescribed by Section 191 for the original offence.

201 Defamation of candidate

(1) Subject to Subsection (2), a person shall not make or publish a false and defamatory statement in relation to the personal character or conduct of a candidate.

Penalty: A fine not exceeding K1,000.00 or imprisonment for a term not exceeding six months.

(2) It is a defence to a prosecution for an offence against Subsection (1), if the defendant proves that he has had reasonable ground for believing and did in fact believe the statement made or published by him to be true.

(3) A person who makes a false and defamatory statement in relation to the personal character or conduct of a candidate in contravention of this section may be restrained by injunction, at the suit of the candidate aggrieved. from repeating the statement or any similar false and defamatory statement.

202 Publication of matter regarding candidates

(1) Subject to this section, if, in any matter announced or published by a person, or caused by a person to be announced or published, on behalf of an association, league, organization or other body of persons, it is, without the authority of the candidate (the burden of proof of which authority lies upon that person) –

(a) claimed or suggested that a candidate in an election is associated with, or supports the policy or activities of, that association, league, organization or other body of persons; or

(b) expressly or impliedly advocated or suggested that candidate is the candidate for which a vote should be given,

that person is guilty of an offence.

Penalty: A fine not exceeding K500.00 or imprisonment for a term not exceeding three months.

(2) Where any matter, the announcement or publication of which by a person without the written authority of a candidate would be an offence against Subsection (1) on the part of that person, is announced or published by or on behalf of, or with the support of, an association, league, organization or other body of persons, every person who was an officer of that association, league, organization or body at the time of that announcement or publication shall be deemed to be guilty of an offence against that subsection.

(3) For the purposes of this section, where any matter purports expressly or impliedly to be announced or published by or on behalf of, or in the interests or with the support of, an association, league, organization or other body of persons the matter shall, in the absence of proof to the contrary, be deemed to be announced or published by or on behalf of, or with the support of, as the case may be, that association, league, organization or other body of persons.

(4) Nothing in the preceding provisions of this section applies to or in relation to an announcement or publication made or authorized by a *bona fide* political party or by a *bona fide* branch of a political party respecting a candidate who, by public announcement, has declared his candidature to be a candidature on behalf of or in the interests of that party.

203 Voting in an electorate when qualified to enrol in another electorate

A person who is enrolled in respect of an electorate and votes at an election in that electorate knowing that at some time after the date he was enrolled for that electorate and before the date of the issue of the writ for an election in that electorate he became qualified to enrol in, or to transfer his enrolment to, another electorate is guilty of an offence.

Penalty: A fine not exceeding K1,000.00 or imprisonment for a term not exceeding six months.

204 Liability for indirect acts

Every person is liable for an illegal practice or an offence against this Part committed directly or indirectly by himself, or by any other person on his behalf and with his knowledge or authority.

205 Application of Criminal Code

Nothing in this Law shall derogate or be deemed to derogate the provisions of the Criminal Code, but a person is not liable to be prosecuted or punished both under this Law and under the Criminal Code for the same offence.

PART XVIII – DISPUTED ELECTIONS, RETURNS, ETC

Division 1 – Disputed Elections and Returns

206 Method of disputing returns

The validity of an election or return may be disputed by petition addressed to the National Court and not otherwise.

207 Jurisdiction of National Court exercisable by single Judge

The jurisdiction of the National Court in relation to any matter under this Part may be exercise by a single Judge.

208 Requisites of petition

A petition shall –

(a) set out the facts relied on to invalidate the election or return; and

(b) specify the relief to which the petitioner claims to be entitled; and

(c) be signed by a candidate at the election in dispute or by a person who was qualified to vote at the election; and

(d) be attested by two witnesses whose occupations and addresses are stated; and

(e) be filed in the Registry of the National Court at Port Moresby or at the court house in any Provincial headquarters within 40 days after the declaration of the result of the election in accordance with Section 175(1)(a).

209 Deposit as security for costs

At the time of filing the petition the petitioner shall deposit with the Registrar of the National Court the sum of K2,500.00 as security for costs.

210 No proceedings unless requisites complied with

Proceedings shall not be heard on a petition unless the requirements of Sections 208 and 209 are complied with.

211 Right of returning officer to be represented

The Electoral Commission may, by leave of the National Court, enter an appearance in any proceedings in which the validity of an election or return is disputed, and be represented and heard in the proceedings, and in that case shall be deemed to be a party respondent to the petition.

212 Powers of court

(1) In relation to any matter under this part the National Court shall sit as an open court and may, amongst other things –

- (a) adjourn; and
- (b) compel the attendance of witnesses and the production of documents; and
- (c) grant to a party to a petition leave to inspect, in the presence of a prescribed officer, the Rolls and other documents (except ballot-papers) used at or in connection with an election and take, in the presence of the prescribed officer, extracts from those Rolls and documents; and
- (d) order a re-count of ballot-papers in an electorate; and
- (e) examine witnesses on oath; and
- (f) declare that a person who was returned as elected was not duly elected; and
- (g) declare a candidate duly elected who was not returned as elected; and
- (h) declare an election absolutely void; and
- (i) dismiss or uphold a petition in whole or in part; and
- (j) award costs; and
- (k) punish contempt of its authority by fine or imprisonment.

(2) The Judges of the National Court may make rules of court with respect of pre-trial conferences and procedures relating to procedures under this Part.

(3) The Court may exercise all or any of its powers under this section on such grounds as the Court in its discretion thinks just and sufficient.

(4) Without limiting the powers conferred by this section, the power of the Court to declare that a person who was returned as elected was not duly elected, or to declare an election absolutely void, may be exercised on the ground that illegal practices were committed in connection with the election.

213 Production of postal vote certificate, etc

(1) Without limiting the powers conferred by Section 212 –

(a) when it is proved that a ballot-paper issued under Section 100, 141, 142 or 143 has, in an election, been marked by a person who was not entitled to vote at the election, the Court may require the production of –

(i) the postal vote certificate delivered to or posted to that person; or

(ii) any other papers or documents relating to the ballot-papers issued under those sections,

as the case may be; and

(b) the Court may reject a ballot-paper.

(2) The production from proper custody of a ballot-paper purporting to have been used in an election and bearing an official number, and of a postal vote certificate or other papers or documents referred to in Subsection (1)(a)(ii) an official number corresponding to the official number on the ballot-paper, is *prima facie* evidence that the person who marked the ballot-paper was the person to whom the postal vote certificate was delivered or posted or who made the declaration, as the case may be.

(3) In Subsection (2), "official number" means a number purporting to have been placed on the ballot-paper or postal vote certificate, as the case may be, under this Law.

214 Inquiries by Court

The National Court shall inquire whether or not the petition is duly signed, and so far as Rolls and voting are concerned may inquire into the identity of persons and whether their votes were improperly admitted or rejected, assuming the Roll to be correct, but the Court shall not inquire into the correctness of a Roll.

215 Voiding election for illegal practices

(1) If the National Court finds that a candidate has committed or has attempted to commit bribery or undue influence, his election, if he is a successful candidate, shall be declared void.

(2) A finding by the National Court under Subsection (1) does not bar or prejudice a prosecution for an illegal practice.

(3) The National Court shall not declare that a person returned as elected was not duly elected. or declare an election void –

(a) on the ground of an illegal practice committed by a person other than the candidate and without the candidate's knowledge or authority; or

(b) on the ground of an illegal practice other than bribery or undue influence or attempted bribery or undue influence,

unless the Court is satisfied that the result of the election was likely to be affected, and that it is just that the candidate should be declared not to be duly elected or that the election should be declared void.

216 Court to report cases of illegal practice

Where the National Court finds that a person has committed an illegal practice, the Registrar of the Court shall promptly report the finding to the Speaker and to the Electoral Commission.

217 Real justice to be observed

The National Court shall be guided by the substantial merits and good conscience of each case without regard to legal forms or technicalities, or whether the evidence before it is in accordance with the law of evidence or not.

218 Immaterial errors not to vitiate election

(1) Subject to Subsection (2), an election shall not be avoided on account of a delay in the declaration of nominations, the polling, the declaration of the poll or the return of the writ, or on account of the absence or an error of, or an omission by, an officer which did not affect the result of the election.

(2) Where an elector was, on account of the absence or an error of, or an omission by, an officer, prevented from voting in an election, the National Court shall not for the purpose of determining whether the absence or error of, or the omission by, the officer did or did not affect the result of the election, admit evidence of the way in which the elector intended to vote in the election.

219 Evidence that person not permitted to vote

On the trial of a petition, the National Court shall not admit the evidence of a witness that he was not permitted to vote in an election during the hours of polling in the polling period unless the witness satisfied the Court –

(a) that he claimed to vote in the election, under that provision of this Law under which he was entitled or might be permitted to vote; and

(b) that he complied with the requirements of this Law relating to voting by electors in so far as he was permitted to do so.

220 Decision to be final

A decision of the National Court is final and conclusive and without appeal, and shall not be questioned in any way.

221 Copies of petition and order of court to be sent to the Parliament

The Registrar of the National Court shall promptly after the filing of a petition forward to the Clerk of the Parliament a copy of the petition, and after the trial of the petition shall promptly forward to the Clerk a copy of the order of the Court.

222 Counsel or solicitor

(1) A party to a petition shall not, except by consent of all parties or by leave of the National Court, be represented by counsel or solicitor.

(2) In no case shall more than one counsel appear on behalf of a party.

223 Costs

The National Court may award costs against an unsuccessful party to a petition.

224 Deposits applicable for costs

If costs are awarded to a party against the petitioner, the deposit lodged under Section 209 is applicable in payment of the sum ordered, but otherwise the deposit shall be paid to the petitioner.

225 Other costs

All other costs awarded by the National Court, including any balance above the deposit payable by the petitioner, are recoverable as if the order of the Court were a judgement of the National Court, and the order, certified by the Court, may be entered as a judgement of the National Court and enforced accordingly.

226 Effect of decision

Effect shall be given to a decision of the National Court as follows: –

- (a) if a person returned is declared not to have been duly elected, he shall cease to be a member; and
- (b) if a person not returned is declared to have been duly elected, he may take his seat accordingly; and
- (c) if an election is declared absolutely void a new election shall be held.

227 Definition of "petition"

In this Division, "petition" means a petition disputing an election or return.

Division 2 – Qualifications and Vacancies

228 Reference of question of qualification or vacancy

A question respecting the qualifications of a member or respecting a vacancy in the Parliament may be referred by resolution to the National Court by the Parliament and the Court shall thereupon have jurisdiction to hear and determine the question.

229 Speaker to state case

When a question is referred to the National Court under this Division, the Speaker shall transmit to the Court a statement of the question upon which the determination of the Court is desired, together with any proceedings, papers, reports or documents relating to the question in the possession of the Parliament.

230 Parties to the reference

The National Court may allow a person who, in the opinion of the Court, is interested in the determination of a question referred to it under this Division to be heard on the hearing of the reference, or may direct notice of the reference to be served on a person, and a person so allowed to be heard or so directed to be served shall be deemed to be a party to the reference.

231 Powers of courts

On the hearing of a reference under this Division, the National Court shall sit as an open court and has the powers conferred by Section 212 so far as they are applicable, and in addition has power –

(a) to declare that a person was not qualified to be a member; and

(b) to declare that a person was not capable of being chosen or of sitting as a member; and

(c) to declare that there is a vacancy in the Parliament.

232 Order to be sent to the Parliament

After the hearing and determination of a reference under this Division, the Registrar of the National Court shall promptly forward to the Clerk of the Parliament and the Electoral Commissioner a copy of the order or declaration of the National Court.

233 Application of certain sections

The provisions of Sections 217, 218, 219, 220, 221 and 222 apply so far as they are applicable, to proceedings on a reference to the National Court under this Division.

PART XIX – LOCAL-LEVEL GOVERNMENT ELECTIONS

Division 1 Preliminary

234 Application of this Part

(1) Subject to Part XXII, this Part applies to and in relation to elections of members of Local-level Governments.

(2) The Head of State, acting on advice, may determine that the heads of Local-level Governments be directly elected by electors, and where such a determination is made –

(a) the election of heads of Local-level Governments shall be in accordance with this Part subject to such modification as is prescribed or as is required in the circumstances; and

(b) where an election for a member of a Local-level Government and an election for the head of that Local-level Government are held simultaneously an elector may vote in respect of each election.

235 Interpretation

(1) In this Part, unless the contrary intention appears –

"approved form" means a form approved under [795]Section 240;

"Assistant Returning [796]Officer" means an officer provided under Section 237;

"ballot-box" means a box

(a) capable of being securely fastened with a lock; and

(b) having a cleft in the cover through which the ballot-papers may be deposited in the box and provided with means for securely closing the cleft so that, when the cleft is so closed, no ballot-papers or other matters or things can be deposited or placed in the box or withdrawn from it;

"ballot-paper" means a ballot-paper in accordance with this Law;

"candidate" means a candidate in an election;

"election petition" means a petition under Division 14.;

---

[795]The Law has "Secton".

[796]The Law has "Oficer".

"elector" means a person whose name appears on a roll and who is entitled to vote at the election in question;

"illegal practice" means an illegal practice specified in Division 13, and includes an offence under the *Criminal Code*;

"interpreter" means a person in respect of whom approval is given under Division 11.;

"Local-level Government" means a Local-level government established in accordance with Sections 26 and 27 of the *Organic Law on Provincial Governments and Local-level Governments*;

"official mark" means a mark authorized by the Returning Officer;

"polling booth" means a polling booth designated under Part IV.;

"Presiding Officer" means a Presiding Officer appointed under Section 238;

"the Returning Officer", in [797]relation to a Local-level Government, means the Returning Officer provided for that Local-level Government under Section 236;

"roll" means a roll of electors compiled under Division 3;

"writ" means a writ for an election issued under Section 271 and 272.

(2) Where under this Part, another Part of this Law is applied to and in relation to Local-level Government elections, words used in that other Part and defined in Subsection (1) shall have the meaning given to them in Subsection (1).

Division 2 – Administration

236 Returning officers

The Returning Officer, appointed under this Law for an open electorate, shall be the Returning Officer for Local-level Governments within that open electorate.

237 Assistant returning officers

(1) The Assistant Returning Officer appointed under this Law for an open electorate shall be the Assistant Returning Officer for Local-level Governments within that open electorate.

[797]The Law has "relationt".

(2) An Assistant Returning Officer may, subject to the control of the Returning Officer, exercise the powers and perform the duties of the Returning Officer.

238 Presiding officers, etc

(1) The Returning Officer may appoint one or more persons as Presiding Officers to assist, subject to the control of the Returning Officer, in the conduct of polling at an election.

(2) The Presiding officer may assist the Returning Officer in the scrutiny and counting of votes at the election.

(3) The Returning Officer may appoint one or more persons as Poll Clerks to assist, subject to the control of the Returning Officer, in the conduct of the polling.

239 General requirements

A person appointed under this Part shall –

(a) make such declarations as the Electoral Commissioner requires; and

(b) comply with any directions given by the Electoral Commissioner under his power of supervision under Section 19 of this Law.

240 Approved forms

The Electoral Commissioner may, by instrument, approve forms for the purposes of this Regulation.

241 Availability of forms

A Returning Officer shall –

(a) keep available copies of approved forms required by members of the public for the purposes of this Regulation; and

(b) without fee, supply them as required; and

(c) assist the public in their proper use.

Division 3 – Electoral Rolls

242 Rolls

The Roll in use for an open electorate for elections to the Parliament shall be used for elections to Local-level Governments within that open electorate.

243 Form of Rolls

(1) A Roll shall be in such form as is determined by the Electoral Commission, and shall set out the name, address and occupation (or other prescribed particulars) and sex of each elector, and shall contain such further particulars as are prescribed or as the Electoral Commission directs.

(2) A direction under Subsection (1) may relate to the whole or a part of the country.

244 New Rolls

(1) All persons who are entitled to be enrolled on a Roll shall, subject to this Law, be so enrolled.

(2) New Rolls for any wards shall be prepared whenever the Electoral [798]Commission, by notice published in the Local-level Government Gazette, directs.

(3) Subject to Subsection (4), a notice under Subsection (2) may specify the manner in which the Rolls shall be prepared, and may require any person, or member of a class of persons, entitled to enrolment on a new Roll and whose name does not appear on it to sign and send to the proper officer a form of claim for enrolment and otherwise to comply with the provisions of this Law relating to compulsory enrolment.

(4) Notwithstanding anything in Subsection (3), where an elector is enrolled in respect of an address in a ward for which he is entitled to be enrolled, he shall not be required to sign and send in any further claim for enrolment in connection with the preparation of a new Roll under this section.

(5) The Electoral Commission shall, as soon as it is practicable to do so after the preparation of new Rolls, by notice published in the Local-level Government Gazette, notify that the new Rolls have been prepared.

245 Additions, etc, to new Rolls

Upon the receipt by the Returning Officer of a new Roll for a ward, the Returning Officer shall –

(a) make additions, alterations and corrections in it; and

(b) remove names from it,

in accordance with information received by him between the date of the notice directing the preparation of new Rolls and the date of the notification that the Rolls have been prepared, where the additions,

---

[798]The Law has "Commisson".

alterations or corrections have not already been made in, or the removals have not been made from, the Roll.

246 Objections and notices to have effect in relation to new Rolls

Where objections have been lodged or notices of objection have been issued and action in respect of those objections or notices has not been completed before the notification of the preparation of new Rolls, the objections or notices have effect in relation to the new Rolls as if those Rolls had been in existence at the time of the lodging of the objections or the issuing of the notice.

247 Printing of Rolls

(1) Rolls shall be printed whenever the Electoral Commission so directs.

(2) Supplemental Rolls, setting out additions since the latest print of the Rolls, may, as necessary, be prepared and printed immediately after the issue of the writs for an election, and at such other times as the Electoral Commission directs.

248 Inspection

(1) Copies of the latest print of the electorate Roll and of all supplemental print; shall be open for public inspection at the office of the Returning Officer at all convenient times during his ordinary office hours without fee, and at such other places as the Returning Officer appoints for the purpose.

(2) Copies of the latest print of the electorate Roll and of all supplemental print; shall be obtainable at the office of the Returning Officer on payment of the prescribed fee.

249 Officers and others to furnish information

All officers and all occupiers of habitations and all persons who are, or appear to be, entitled to enrolment shall upon application furnish to the Electoral Commission or to a Returning Officer, or to an electoral officer acting under the directions of the Electoral Commission or the Returning Officer, all [799]information that it or he requires in connection with the preparation, maintenance or revision of the Rolls.

[799]The Law has "informaiton".

Division 4 – Qualifications and Disqualifications for Enrolment and for Voting

250 Persons entitled to enrolment

(1) All persons who have a right to vote under Section 50 (*right to vote and stand for public office*) of the *Constitution* who comply with the requirements of Division 5 for enrolment for a ward are entitled to enrolment.

(2) All persons whose names are on the Roll for a ward shall, subject to this Law and to the provisions of any other law in force, vote at elections of a member for the ward but no person is entitled to vote more than once at an election or at more than one election held at the same time.

Division 5 – Enrolment

251 Officers

(1) The Electoral commission may appoint persons to assist in the compilation and revision of the Rolls.

(2) A person appointed under Subsection (1) has such functions and duties as are prescribed or as the Electoral Commission directs.

252 Addition of names to Rolls

In addition to any other method provided for by law, names may be added to Rolls in accordance with claims for enrolment or transfer of enrolment.

253 Claims for enrolment

(1) Subject to this section and to Section 250, a person who –

(a) has resided in the area of a ward for a period of not less than six month immediately preceding the date of his claim for enrolment; or

(b) is nominated for a ward for which he is not enrolled and was either born the ward or lived in the ward for five years at any time,

is entitled to have his name placed on the Roll for that ward.

(2) Where the name of a person is placed on a Roll in accordance with Subsection (1)(a), he shall be enrolled in respect of the address of his last residence in the ward.

(3) Where the name of a person is placed on a Roll in accordance with Subsection (1)(b), he shall be enrolled in respect of his last-known place of residence in the ward.

(3) The Electoral Commission may, in relation to a person or class of persons, direct that a claim for enrolment be in the prescribed form and, if in the prescribed form, shall be signed by the claimant and attested by a prescribed person who shall sign his name as witness in his own handwriting.

254 Witness to application must satisfy himself of truth of statement

A person witnessing a claim for enrolment or transfer of enrolment shall, before he affixes his signature to it, satisfy himself, by inquiry from the claimant or otherwise, that the statements contained in the claim are true, unless he knows that the statements contained in the claim are true.

Penalty: A fine not exceeding K400.00.

255 Compulsory enrolment and transfer

(1) A person who is entitled to have his name placed on the Roll for a ward, whether by way of enrolment or transfer of enrolment, and whose name is not on that Roll shall, at the first reasonably practicable opportunity, make a claim in the prescribed form to the Returning Officer for that ward.

(2) A person who is entitled to have his name placed on the Roll for a ward, whether by way of enrolment or transfer of enrolment, and whose name is not on that Roll on the expiration of 21 days from the date on [800]which he became so entitled, is guilty of an offence unless he proves that his non-enrolment is not in consequence of his failure to comply with the provisions of Subsection (1).

(3) It is a defence to a charge of an offence against [801]Subsection (2) if the defendant shows that he did not know, and had no reasonable opportunity of knowing, that his name was not on a Roll for which he was entitled to be enrolled.

(4) A person who is enrolled for the ward in which he is residing and who changes his place of residence from one address in the ward to another address in that ward, and who has failed to notify, in the prescribed form, the new address to the Returning Officer for that electorate at the first reasonably practicable opportunity, is guilty of an offence.

---

[800]The Law has "wich".

[801]The Law has "Subsecton".

(5) A person who is guilty of an offence against this section is punishable, upon conviction –

(a) in the case of a first offence – by a fine not exceeding K10.00; or

(b) in any case – by a fine not exceeding K25.00.

(6) A prosecution for an offence against this section shall not be instituted without the consent of the Election Commission.

256 Registration of claim

(1) Upon receipt of a claim for enrolment or transfer of enrolment, notification of change of address within a ward, or application for the alteration or correction of particulars of an existing enrolment, the Returning Officer shall note the date of its receipt by him, and if the claim, notification or application is in order and he is satisfied that the claimant is entitled to be enrolled or to have his name transferred or the particulars of his enrolment altered or corrected, as the case may be, the Returning Officer shall, subject to Section 258 –

(a) enter on the Roll kept by him the name of the claimant and the particulars relating to him; and

(b) notify the claimant in writing that he has been enrolled; and

(c) in the case of a transfer of enrolment, give notice of the transfer to the Returning Officer keeping the Roll from which the elector's name has been transferred.

(2) An interim acknowledgement of the receipt, after the issue of the writ for an election and before the close of the polling at the election, of a claim for enrolment or transfer of enrolment may be issued to the claimant by the Retuning Officer in a form approved by the Electoral Commission.

(3) The Returning Officer keeping the Roll from which an elector's name has been transferred shall, upon receipt of notice of the transfer in the prescribed form, remove the elector's name from the Roll kept by him.

257 Notification of rejection of claim

The Returning Officer, on receipt of a claim, shall, subject to Section 258, after making such inquiry as he considers necessary if he is satisfied that the claimant is not entitled to enrolment or transfer of enrolment in accordance with the claim, notify the claimant as soon as practicable in the prescribed manner that his claim has been rejected, specifying the reason for the rejection, and advise the claimant that he is entitled, at any time within three month; after the receipt of the notification, to appeal against the rejection in accordance with the Law.

258 Time for altering Rolls

Notwithstanding anything in this Law –

(a) claims for enrolment or transfer of enrolment which are received after 3 p.m. on the day of the issue of the writ for an election shall not be registered until after the end of the polling period for the election; and

(b) except by direction of the Returning Officer, no name shall be removed from a Roll under a notification of transfer of enrolment received after 4 p.m. on the day of the issue of the writ for an election and before the end of the polling period for the election.

259 Penalty on officer neglecting to enrol claimants

An officer who receives a claim for enrolment or transfer of enrolment and who, without just excuse, the burden of proof of which lies upon him, fails to do everything necessary on his part to be done to secure the enrolment of the claimant in pursuance of the claim is guilty of an offence.

Penalty: A fine not exceeding K1,000.00.

260 Alteration of Rolls

(1) In addition to other powers of alteration conferred by this Law, a Returning Officer may alter a Roll kept by him by –

(a) correcting a mistake or omission in the Roll; and

(b) correcting a mistake or omission in the particulars of the enrolment of an elector; and

(c) altering, on the application of an elector, the original name, address or occupation of the elector on the same Roll; and

(d) removing the name of a decease elector; and

(e) striking out the superfluous entry where the name of the same elector appears more than once on the same Roll; and

(f) reinstating a name removed by mistake; and

(g) reinstating a name removed as the result of an objection where he is satisfied that the objection was based on a mistake as to fact and that the person objected to still retains and has continuously retained his right to the enrolment in respect of which the objection was made; and

(h) removing a name from the Roll where he is satisfied that the elector has ceased to be qualified for enrolment on the Roll and has secured enrolment on another roll.

(2) Where the name of an elector, has, in error, been incorrectly placed on the Roll for a ward for which he is not entitled to be enrolled,

and the elector is entitled to have his name placed on the Roll for another ward, the Returning Officer for the ward for which the elector is wrongly enrolled shall remove the name of the elector from that Roll and shall notify the Returning Officer for the ward for which the elector is entitled to be enrolled accordingly, and that last-mentioned Returning Officer shall place the name of the elector on his Roll and shall notify the elector of the change of enrolment.

(3) No alteration under this section shall, without the authority of the Returning Officer, be made at any time after 4 p.m. on the day of the issue of the writ for an election and before the end of the polling period for the election.

261 Special provisions for certain nominations

Notwithstanding anything in this Law, where a person who is entitled to do so has nominated for a ward other than the ward for which he is enrolled –

(a) the Returning Officer for the ward for which he nominates shall place his name on the Roll for that ward and notify the Returning Officer for the electorate for which he is enrolled who shall remove his name from the Roll for that ward; and

(b) if the nomination is withdrawn, the Returning Officer for the ward for which he was nominated shall remove his name from the Roll for that ward and notify the Returning Officer for the other ward who shall (unless he has in the meantime nominated for some other ward) restore his name to the Roll for that other ward; and

(c) if he fails to be elected, the Returning Officer for the ward for which h e was nominated shall remove his name from the Roll for that ward and notify the Returning Officer for the other ward who shall restore his name to the Roll for that other ward; and

(d) if he is elected and later ceases to be member for the ward, the Returning Officer for the ward for which he was the member shall remove his name from the Roll for that ward and notify the Returning Officer for the other ward who ;hall restore his name to the Roll for that other ward unless he has ceased to be eligible for enrolment in that ward and has been enrolled in another ward.

262 Incorrect enrolment

Where a person whose name has been placed on the Roll for a ward is not entitled to enrol for that ward and that person secured enrolment under a claim in which he made a false statement, the Returning Officer may, at any time between the date of the issue of the writ for an election for that ward and before the end of the polling period for that election, remove the name of that person from that Roll.

263 Alterations to be initialled

Every alteration of a Roll shall be [802]made in such [803]manner that the original entry shall not be obliterated, and the reason for each alteration and the date of the alteration shall be set against the alteration, together with the initials of the Returning Officer or of the person who makes the alteration on behalf of the Returning Officer.

Division 6 – Objections

264 Names on Roll may be objected to

(1) A name on a Roll may be objected to by objection in writing lodged with or made by the Returning Officer.

(2) A sum of K4.00 shall be deposited in respect of each objection lodged by a person other than an electoral officer, to be forfeited to Papua New Guinea if the objection is held by the Returning Officer to be frivolous.

265 Objection

An objection under Section 264 shall be in the prescribed form, and shall be signed by an elector enrolled on the same Roll as the person objected to, or by the Returning [804]Officer or a prescribed officer.

266 Duty to object

It is the duty of the Returning Officer and of any prescribed officer to lodge or make an objection in writing, setting out the grounds of the objection, in respect of any name which he has reason to believe ought not be retained on the Roll.

267 Notice of objection

(1) When an objection is made by or lodged with a Returning Officer, the Returning Officer shall, subject to Subsection (3), give notice as soon as practicable of the objection to the person objected to.

---

[802]The Law has "mde".
[803]The Law has "mannter".
[804]The Law has "Oficer".

(2) A notice under Subsection (1) may be in the prescribed form, and may be served by being posted or delivered to the last-known place of abode of the person objected to.

(3) Where the Returning Officer is satisfied that the ground of objection stated in an objection is not a good ground of objection or is frivolous, he may dismiss the objection, in which case no notice of the objection need be given to the person objected to.

(4) An objection on the ground that a person does not reside in the ward for which he is enrolled shall be deemed not to be good unless it alleges that the person objected to has not resided in the electorate for the period necessary to qualify him for enrolment for that electorate.

268 Answer to objection

A person objected to under this Part may, orally or in writing in the prescribed manner, answer the objection.

269 Determination of objection

(1) Subject to Subsection (2), the Returning Officer shall determine an objection under this Part as soon as practicable after receipt by him of the answer of the person objected to, or, if no answer is received within a period of one month after the posting or delivery of the notice referred to in Section 267(1) and if it appears that the person objected to is not entitled to be enrolled on the Roll in respect of which the objection has been made, the Returning [805]Officer shall –

(a) remove the name of the person from the roll; and

(b) cause a copy of the notice of determination to be posted to or served on the objector and the person objected to.

(2) No name shall be removed from a Roll under this action after 4 p.m. on the day of issue of the writ for an election and before the end of the polling period for the election.

Division 7 – Appeals in relation to Enrolment

270 Appeal to District Court

(1) A person –

(a) who has made a claim for enrolment or transfer of enrolment in accordance with this Law, and has not been enrolled; or

(b) whose name has been removed from a Roll by the Returning Officer after an objection,

[805]The Law has "Offier".

may at any time within two months after the receipt of notice of the rejection of the claim or of notice of the determination of the objection, as the case may be, make application in the prescribed manner to a District Court for an order directing that his name be enrolled or reinstated on the Roll, as the case requires.

(2) Where an objection has been determined by the Returning Officer adversely to the person objecting, that person may in the prescribed manner apply to a District Court for an order sustaining the objection.

(3) Where an application under this section has reference to the decision of the Returning Officer upon an objection, the applicant shall, as prescribed, served the objector or the person objected to, as the case requires, with notice of the application, and the person so served may appear, or may in writing authorize any person to appear on his behalf, to resist the application.

(4) The court may hear and determine an application under this section, and may make such order as it thinks fit as to the costs of the application.

(5) Costs ordered by the court to be paid may be recovered in the same manner as the costs of any other proceeding before the court.

(6) The Clerk of the Court shall send by post to the Returning Officer a certified copy of the order of the court, and the Returning Officer shall make such entries (if any) upon the Roll as necessary to give effect to the order.

Division 8 – Writs for Elections

271 Writs for general elections

The Minister responsible for Provincial and Local-level Government Affairs acting with, and in accordance with, the advice of the Electoral Commission, shall issue his writ for a general election so as to accord with the provisions of Section 34 of the *Organic Law on Provincial Governments and Local-level Governments*.

272 Writs for vacancies

In the case of the need for a by-election. acting with, and in accordance with, the advice of the Electoral Commission, shall, as soon as practicable after the vacancy occurs, issue his writ for the election of a new member.

273 Form of writs

(1) The writs for elections shall be in the prescribed form and shall fix the date for –

(a) nominations; and

(b) the first and last days of the period during which polling shall take place, which period shall not exceed 14 days; and

(c) the return of the writ.

(2) The Electoral Commission shall. as soon as practicable after the issue of a writ –

(a) advertise its issue and particulars in at least one newspaper circulated in the ward to which the writ relates; and

(b) forward a copy to the Provincial Government and Local-level Government in which the ward is [806]situated; and

(c) take such further steps as it considers desirable to ensure adequate publicity.

274 Time of issue of writs

For the purposes of this Law. a writ shall be deemed to have been issued at the hour of 4 p.m. on the day on which the writ was issued.

275 Address of writs

(1) Writs for election of members shall be addressed to the respective Returning Officers for the wards for which the elections are to be held, and may be issued through the Electoral Commission.

(2) The Electoral Commission may advise any Returning Officer by electronic advice of the issue of the writ for an election and the particulars of the writ, and for the purposes of Section 378 the Returning Officer may act on the advice as if the writ had been received by him.

276 Date and period of nomination

Nomination of the candidates shall commence on the date of the writ, and the period of nomination shall not exceed seven days, including the date of the writ.

277 Date of polling

The date fixed for the commencement of the polling period shall be a Saturday and shall be not less than eight weeks and not more than 11 weeks after the date of the writ.

---

[806]The Law has "situtated".

278 Date of return of writ

The date fixed for the return of the writ shall not be more than 21 days after the end of the polling period.

279 Duty of returning officer on receipt of writ

On the receipt of a writ, the officer to whom it is directed shall endorse, on it the date of its receipt.

280 General election to be held on same day

In the case of a general election, the same day shall be fixed for the commencement of the polling period in each electorate, and all writs shall be made returnable on the same day.

Division 9 – Nominations and Polling

281 Nominations

(1) Subject to Subsection (2), the provisions of Part XI of this Law (other than Sections 87(c), 90 and 95) shall apply as the provisions of this Law relating to Local-level Government elections.

(2) References in Part XI to an 'electorate' shall be read as references to 'a ward'.

(3) No nomination is valid unless at the time of delivery of the nomination the person nominated or some person on his behalf pays to the Returning Officer or other person to whom the nomination is made the sum prescribed by the Regulations in money or in a banker's cheque.

282 Polling

(1) Subject to Subsection (2), the provisions of Part XIII of this Law shall apply as the provisions of this Law relating to Local-level Government elections.

(2) References in Part XIII to an 'electorate' shall be read as references to a 'ward'.

Division 10 – Scrutiny

283 Scrutiny

(1) Subject to Subsection (2), the provisions of Part XIV of this Law shall apply as the provisions of this Law relating to Local-level Government elections.

(2) References in Part XIV to an 'electorate' shall be read as references to a 'ward'.

Division 11 – Interpreters

284 Interpreters

The provisions of Part XV of this Law shall apply as the provisions of this Law relating to Local-level Government elections.

Division 12 – Return of the Writs

285 Return of the writs

(1) Subject to Subsection (2), the provisions of Part XVI of this Law shall apply as the provisions of this Law to Local-level Government elections.

(2) References on Part XV to an 'electorate' shall be read as references to a 'ward'.

Division 13 – Offences

286 Illegal practices

(1) Subject to Subsection (2), the following are illegal practices: –

(a) publishing an electoral advertisement, handbill or pamphlet or issuing an electorate notice (other than the announcement by advertisement in a newspaper of the holding of a meeting) without the name and address of the person authorizing the publication or issue appearing at the end of it; and

(b) printing or publishing a printed electorate advertisement, handbill or pamphlet (other than an advertisement in a newspaper) without the name and place of business of the printer being printed at the foot of it; and

(c) printing, publishing or distributing a printed electoral advertisement, notice, handbill, pamphlet or card containing a representation of a ballot-paper, or a representation apparently intended to represent a ballot-paper, and having on it directions intended, or being likely, to mislead or improperly interfere with an elector in relation to the casting of his vote; and

(d) printing, publishing or distributing an electoral advertisement, notice, handbill, pamphlet or card containing an untrue or incorrect statement intended, or being likely, to mislead or improperly interfere with an elector in relation to the casting of his vote; and

(e) wilfully informing an elector during the election period that he is not –

(i) enrolled or entitled to be enrolled; or

(ii) enrolled or entitled to be enrolled for a particular ward; or

(iii) entitled to vote,

when, as a fact, he is enrolled or entitled to be enrolled, or is enrolled or entitled to be enrolled for the ward, or is entitled to vote, as the case may be; and

(f) before, [807]during or after an election, corruptly providing food, drink or lodging to or for a person on account of anything done, or to be done by an elector at an election; and

(g) being an elector, corruptly receiving food, drink or lodging on account of anything done at an election; and

(h) by force, threat, fraud, misrepresentation, undue influence or in any other manner inducing or attempting to induce another person to vote or fail to vote at an election, or to vote for a particular person at an election; and

(i) falsely personating a person to secure a ballot-paper to which the personator is not entitled, or personating any other person for the purpose of voting; and

(j) fraudulently destroying or defacing a nomination paper or ballot-paper; and

(k) fraudulently taking a ballot-paper out of a polling booth; and

(l) fraudulently putting a ballot-paper or other paper into a ballot-box; and

(m) taking a ballot-paper out of a polling booth; and

(n) forging, or uttering, knowing it to be forged, a nomination paper or ballot-paper; and

(o) in a polling booth during the polling, misconducting oneself, or failing to obey the lawful directions of the Returning Officer or the Presiding Officer; and

(p) supplying ballot-papers without authority; and

(q) unlawfully destroying, taking, opening or otherwise interfering with ballot-boxes or ballot-papers; and

---

[807]The Law has "duirng".

(r) voting more than once at the same election; and

(s) wagering on the result of an election; and

(t) wilfully defacing, mutilating, destroying or removing a notice, list or other document affixed by a Returning Officer or by his authority; and

(u) knowingly making a false statement in a claim, application, return or declaration, or in answer to a question under this Law; and

(v) distributing an advertisement, handbill or pamphlet published in contravention of Paragraph (a), (b), (c) or (d).

(2) Subsection (1)(c) or (d) does not prevent the printing, publishing or distributing of a card, not otherwise illegal, that contains instructions as to how to vote for a particular candidate, so long as the instructions are not intended, or likely, to mislead an elector in relation to the recording of his vote.

(3) A person who contravenes Subsection (1) is guilty of an offence.

Penalty: A fine not exceeding K500.00 or imprisonment for a term not exceeding one month or both.

Division 14 – Disputed Elections and Returns

287 Disputed elections and returns

(1) Subject to this section, the provisions of Part XVIII of this Law, other than Sections 208(e), 209, 210, 212(2), and 213, shall apply as the provisions of this law relating to disputed Local-level Government elections and returns.

(2) References in Part XVIII to –

(a) "Clerk of Parliament" shall be read as to "clerk of the Local-level Government"; and

(b) "electorate" shall be read as to a "ward"; and

(c) "member" shall be read as to "member of the Local-level Government"; and

(d) 'National Court" shall be read as to "District Court"; and

(e) "Registrar of National Court" shall be read as to "Clerk of the District Court"; and

(f) "Speaker" shall be read as to "head of the Local-level Government.

(3) A petition to dispute an election or return shall be filed at the District Court in the town in which are situated the headquarters of the

Provincial Government of the Province which includes the area of the Local-level Government in respect of which the election was held.

(4) At the time of filing the petition the petitioner shall deposit with the Clerk of the District Court the sum of K50.00 as security for costs.

(5) Proceedings shall not be heard on a petition unless the requirements of Subsections (3) and (4) and Section 208(a) to (d) inclusive are complied with.

PART XX – MISCELLANEOUS

288 Local government rules on advertising, etc

Any rule of a Local Level Government dealing with advertising, publishing of matter or any similar matter that: –

(a) discriminates or may discriminate against any candidate or class of candidates at an election; or

(b) gives preference or may give preference to be given to one candidate over another candidate in an election; or

(c) gives preference or may give preference to one registered political party over another registered political party; or

(d) allows a Local-level Government to do any of the matters specified in Paragraph (a), (b) or (c),

is to the extent that it discriminates, may discriminate, gives preference, may give preference, or allows a Local-level Government to discriminate or give preference void.

289 Institution of proceedings for defences

(1) The Electoral Commission shall, where the Public Prosecutor so advises, institute legal proceedings against a person committing an offence against this Law.

(2) Nothing in Subsection (1) affects the rights of any person to institute proceedings in respect of an offence against this Law.

290 Certificate evidence

On a prosecution under this Law, the certificate of the Electoral Commission or the Returning Officer that an election referred to in the certificate was duly held and that the person named in the certificate was a candidate at the election is evidence of the matters stated.

291 Electoral matter may be sent by electronic means

(1) In all cases where it is impracticable to communicate any electoral matter by post without occasioning undue delay, any electronic advice communicated in the ordinary course shall suffice for all the purposes of this Law as if the matter sent through electronic means had been communicated in the manner prescribed by this Law.

(2) Subject to Subsection (3), where, after the result of an election has been declared, the Returning Officer has certified by electronic means addressed to the Electoral Commission –

(a) that by reason of distance, or the infrequency of, or any interruption to, the postal services, the writ for the election, endorsed by the Returning Officer with the name of the candidate elected, cannot reach the Electoral Commission within 21 days; and

(b) the name of the candidate elected,

the Electoral Commission may endorse upon a copy of the writ a certified copy of the telegram received by it, and the copy so endorsed shall have the same force and effect as if it were the original writ duly endorsed by the Returning Office.

(3) If, upon the return of an original writ, any inconsistency is found to exist between the original writ and the copy of the writ endorsed under Subsection (2) as to the name of the candidate elected, the copy shall thereupon cease to have any force or effect, and action shall be taken in accordance with the endorsement on the original writ.

292 Averments deemed to be proved

In a prosecution in a court of summary jurisdiction in respect of a contravention of the provisions of this Law relating to compulsory enrolment, instituted by an officer or by a person acting under the direction of an officer, the averments of the prosecutor contained in the information or complaint shall be deemed to be proved in the absence of evidence to the contrary.

293 Defendant may be called upon to give evidence

Where a person has secured enrolment in pursuance of an electoral claim, or has made a claim for enrolment or transfer of enrolment, and proceedings arise in a court of competent jurisdiction in respect of the claim for enrolment or transfer of enrolment, the person may be called upon to give evidence upon oath to the court as to the truth of the statements contained in the claim for enrolment or transfer of enrolment.

294 Production of claims for enrolment, etc

(1) A person who is, or has been, an officer shall not, except for the purposes of this Law, be required –

(a) to produce in court, or give evidence of, a claim for enrolment or transfer of enrolment under this Law; or

(b) to divulge or communicate to a court any matter or thing in relation to a claim for enrolment or transfer of enrolment under this Law, being a matter or thing that has come to his notice in the performance of his duties or functions under this Law.

(2) In this section, "officer" includes any person performing duties, or exercising powers or functions, under or in relation to this Law.

295 Preservation of ballot-papers

(1) Subject to Subsection (2), all ballot-papers, certified lists of voters and declarations used at or in connexion with an election shall be preserved as prescribed until the election can no longer be questioned, when they shall be destroyed.

(2) Ballot-papers, certified lists of voters and declarations referred to in Subsection (1) shall be preserved for a period of 40 days after the date of the declaration of the poll.

296 Prescribed offences

For the purposes of Section 47(1)(b) (*right to vote and stand for public office*) of the *Constitution* the offences contained in the sections specified hereunder are prescribed offences: –

Sections 106, 107, 174(2), 178(1)(c), (d) and (e), 188(3), 191(1), (4), (7), (8), (9), (10), (12), (14) and (15), 195, 197(1) and 201.

297 Constitutional regulations

As authorized by Section 258 (*Constitutional Regulations*) of the *Constitution*, the Head of State, acting with, and in accordance with, the advice of the National Executive Council may make *Constitutional Regulations*, not inconsistent with this Law, prescribing all matters that by this Law are required or permitted to be prescribed, or that are necessary or convenient to be prescribed, for carrying out or giving effect to this Law, and in particular for prescribing –

(a) penalties not exceeding K200.00 for contraventions of the Regulations; and

(b) the procedure in relation to the imposition and recovery of penalties for offences against the compulsory enrolment provisions of this Law.

PART XXI – REPEAL AND CONSEQUENTIAL AMENDMENT

298 Repeal

The following laws are repealed: –

(a) *Organic Law on National Elections*;

(b) *Organic Law on National Elections (Amendment No. 1 Law)*;

(c) *Electoral Regulation* 1977;

(d) *Electoral (Marking of Votes) Regulation* 1982;

(e) *Electoral (Amendment) Regulation* 1987;

(f) Parts V.1 and 2 of the *Local Government Act* (Chapter 57);

(g) *Local Government (Electoral Provisions) Regulation* (Chapter 57);

(h) *Local Government (Urban Council Electoral Provisions) Regulation* (Chapter 57).

299 Consequential amendments to *Organic Law on Provincial Governments and Local-level Governments*

The *Organic Law on the Provincial* [808]*Governments and Local-level Governments* is amended –

(a) in Section 29(1) –

(i) in Paragraph (a) by inserting after the words "in accordance with" the following: –

"an Organic Law or"; and

(ii) in Paragraph (b), by inserting after the words "in accordance with" the following: –

"an Organic Law or"; and

(b) by repealing Section 34(1) and replacing it with the following: –

"(1) Wherever practicable, the term of a Local-level Government shall be the same as and run concurrently with the term of the Parliament, but in order to ensure the effective conduct of respective elections, this may be varied, provided that the date for the return of writs in a general election to Local-level Governments is

[808]The Law has "Governents".

fixed for a date not later than three months after the date fixed for the return of the writs of the general election to the Parliament."; and

(c) in Section 37, by inserting after the words "in accordance with" the following: –

"an Organic Law or".

PART XXII – SAVINGS AND TRANSITIONAL PROVISIONS

300 Interpretation

In this Part, "repealed laws" means the laws repealed by Section 298.

301 Electoral Commissioner

The Electoral Commissioner, appointed under the repealed laws and holding office immediately prior to the coming into operation of this Law, continues, after that coming into operation, to hold the office of Electoral Commissioner on the same terms and conditions for the remainder of the term for which he was appointed or until his appointment is earlier terminated according to law and the repealed laws do not operate so as to abolish the Office of Electoral Commissioner.

302 Returning Officers and Assistant Returning Officers

Returning Officers and Assistant Returning Officers appointed under the repealed laws and holding office as such immediately prior to the coming into operation of this law, continue, on that coming into operation, to hold the office for the remainder of the term for which they were appointed or where no term is specified until their appointment is revoked.

303 Staff

Staff made available under the repealed laws to the Electoral Commission by the Department responsible for personnel matters and serving as staff of the Electoral Commission immediately prior to the coming into operation of this law shall continue to serve as staff of the Electoral Commission.

304 Procedures relating to 1997 general election

All procedures of or pertaining to the general election to the Parliament and to the Local-level Government elections to be held during 1997 carried out under and in accordance with the repealed laws prior to the coming into operation of this law, are, on that coming into operation, deemed to have been [809]carried out under and in accordance with this Law, and in so far as such procedures have not been completed, shall be completed in accordance with the procedures of this Law.

---

[809]The Law has "caried".

305 Constitutional regulations pertaining to 1997 elections

In order to ensure compliance with –

(a) the Constitution, under which a general election to the Parliament falls to be held in 1997; and

(b) the *Organic Law on Provincial Governments and Local-level Governments*, under which the term of Local-level Governments shall be the same as and run concurrently with the term of the Parliament so that elections to Local-level Governments fall to be held in 1997,

the Head of State, acting on advice, may make Constitutional Regulations (as authorized by Section 258 (*Constitutional Regulations*) of the *Constitution*) –

(c) modifying this Law to such an extent; and

(d) making such incidental, consequential and supplementary amendments to this Law,

as may be necessary to enable the elections referred to in Paragraphs (a) and (b) to take place, and any such modifications and amendments have, in relation to those elections, full force and effect and on publication of the Constitutional Regulation shall apply in respect of those elections.

SCHEDULE 1

PAPUA NEW GUINEA

Organic Law on National and Local-level Government Elections

Sec. 73. Form 1

WRIT FOR A GENERAL ELECTION OF MEMBERS OF THE NATIONAL PARLIAMENT.

To: . . . , Returning Officer for . . . Electorate.

GREETING:

This is to command you to cause election to be made according to law of one Member of the National Parliament for the ... Electorate to serve in the Parliament, and I appoint the following dates for the purposes of the said election: –

1. For nomination 19...
2. For the first day of the polling period in the Electorate if the election is contested 19...
3. For the last day of the polling period in the Electorate if the election is contested 19...
4. For the return of the writ, on or before 19...

GIVEN under my hand at ... 19...

(*Head of State*).

PAPUA NEW GUINEA.

Organic Law on National and Local-level Government Elections

Sec. 74. Form 2.

WRIT FOR A ELECTION OF A MEMBER OF THE NATIONAL PARLIAMENT TO FILL A CASUAL VACANCY.

To: . . . , Returning Officer for . . . Electorate.

GREETING:

This is to command you to cause election to be made according to law of one Member of the National Parliament to fill the vacant office of Member for the . . . Electorate, and I appoint the following dates for the purposes of the said election: –

1. For nomination 19
2. For the first day of the polling period in the Electorate if the election is contested 19...
3. For the last day of the polling period in the Electorate if the election is contested 19...
3. For the return of the writ, on or before . . . 19...

GIVEN under my hand at . . . 19

(Head of State).

No 16 of 1992

Parole Act 1991

PART I – PRELIMINARY

PART II – PAROLE BOARD

PART III – PAROLE SERVICE

PART IV – PAROLE

PART V – MISCELLANEOUS

[810]INDEPENDENT STATE OF PAPUA NEW GUINEA

No 16 of 1992

Parole Act 1991

Being an Act to provide for a system of parole which will contribute to the maintenance of a just, peaceful and safe society by facilitating the reintegration of offenders into the community as law-abiding people; and for related purposes,

MADE by the National Parliament to come into operation in accordance with a notice published in the National Gazette by the Head of State, acting with, and in accordance with, the advice of the Minister.

PART I – PRELIMINARY

1 Compliance with constitutional requirements

This Act, to the extent that it regulates or restricts a right or freedom referred to in Subdivision III.3.C of the *Constitution*, namely –

(a) the right to freedom of assembly and association conferred by Section 47 of the *Constitution*; and

(b) the right to privacy conferred by Section 49 of the *Constitution*; and

(c) the right to freedom of information conferred by Section 51 of the *Constitution*; and

(d) the right to freedom of movement conferred by Section 52 of the *Constitution*,

is a law that is made for the purpose of giving effect to the public interest in –

(e) public safety; and

(f) public order; and

[810]Note that the *Corrective Institutions Act* (Chapter 63) has been repealed and replaced by the *Correctional Service Act* 1995 (No. 6 of 1995). No attempt has been made to cater for the implied amendments to this Act which were effected by the passing of the *Correctional Service Act* 1995.

(g) public welfare.

2 Interpretation

In this Act, unless the contrary intention appears –

"Board" means the Parole Board established under Section 3;

"Chairman" means the Chairman of the Board appointed under Section 3(2);

"Chief Parole Officer" means the Chief Parole Officer appointed under Section 11;

"Commissioner" means the Commissioner of Correctional Services;

"corrective institution" means premises declared under the *Corrective Institutions Act* (Chapter 63) to be a corrective institution;

"detainee" means a person who is, by reason of Section 20 of the *Corrective Institutions Act* (Chapter 63), deemed to be in the custody of the Commissioner;

"lawyer" means a person admitted to practice as a lawyer under the *Lawyers Act* 1986;

"Officer" means the Chief Parole Officer, a Parole Officer and a Voluntary Parole Officer;

"order" means an order for grant of parole made under Section 21 or varied under Section 25;

"Papua New Guinea Law Society" means the Papua New Guinea Law Society established under the *Lawyers Act* 1986;

"Parole Officer" means & Parole Officer appointed under Section 11;

"Parole Service" means the Parole Service established under Section 10;

"parolee" means a person in respect of whom an order for parole, which is still effective, has been granted;

"remission" means the remission of sentence of a detainee granted in accordance with the *Corrective Institutions Act* (Chapter 63);

"Voluntary Parole Officer" means a Voluntary Parole Officer appointed under Section 12.

PART II – PAROLE BOARD

3 Parole Board

(1) The Parole Board is hereby established.

(2) The Minister shall appoint as members of the Board the following three persons: –

(a) a lawyer, who shall be Chairman; and
(b) a person nominated by the Commissioner; and
(c) a person nominated by the Departmental Head.

(3) The lawyer referred to in Subsection (2)(a) shall be selected by the following process: –

(a) the President of the Papua New Guinea Law Society shall, following public advertisement –
   (i) select a panel of names from among applicants; and
   (ii) submit the panel to the Minister; and
(b) the Minister shall select the appointee from the panel of names.

(4) The persons referred to in Subsection (2)(b) and (c) shall have as many as possible of the following qualifications: –

(a) experience in social welfare matters;
(b) active involvement in community affairs;
(c) maturity and integrity;
(d) good standing in the community;
(e) appreciation and understanding of social issues and problems;
(f) interest or background in working with people in need of rehabilitation.

(5) The members of the Board shall –

(a) be appointed for a period not exceeding three years; and
(b) be eligible for reappointment.

(6) Subject to the *Salaries and Conditions Monitoring Committee Act* 1988, members of the Board are appointed on such terms and conditions as the Minister determines.

(7) Notwithstanding anything contained in the *Public Services (Management) Act* 1995, where an officer of the National Public Service is appointed to the Board, his service on the Board shall be counted as service in the National Public Service for the purpose of determining his rights (if any) in respect of –

(a) leave of absence on the ground of illness; and

(b) furlough or pay instead of furlough (including pay to dependents on the death of the officer).

(8) The provisions of the *Public Services (Management) Act* 1995 relating to leave to serve under another Act apply to the office of member of the Board.

(9) The Board shall have an official seal and all courts, Judges and persons acting judicially shall take judicial notice of the official seal of the Board affixed to a document and shall presume that it was duly affixed.

4 Leave of absence

(1) The Minister may grant leave of absence to a member of the Board on such terms and conditions as he determines.

(2) Where a member of the Board is on leave of absence or otherwise unable to act, the Minister may make a temporary appointment to the Board in accordance with Subsection (3) or (4) (as the case may be).

(3) Where the member referred to in Subsection (2) is the Chairman, the temporary appointee shall be a lawyer.

(4) Where the member referred to in Subsection (2) is not the Chairman, the temporary appointee shall have some or all of the qualifications referred to in Section 3(3).

5 Vacation of Office by Member of Board

(1) A member of the Board may resign his office by writing signed by him and delivered to the Minister.

(2) If a member of the Board –

(a) becomes permanently incapable of performing his duties; or

(b) resigns his office in accordance with Subsection (1) and the resignation is accepted by the Minister; or

(c) is absent from three consecutive meetings of the Board without the consent in writing of the Chairman, or, in the case of the Chairman, of the Minister; or

(d) is convicted of an offence and as a result of the conviction is sentenced to imprisonment or death,

the Minister shall terminate his appointment.

(3) The Minister may at any time, by written notice, advise a member of the Board that he intends to terminate his appointment on the grounds of inability, inefficiency, incapacity or misbehaviour.

(4) Within 14 days of the receipt of a notice under Subsection (3), the member may reply in writing to the Minister, who shall consider the reply and, where appropriate, terminate the appointment.

(5) Where the member does not reply in accordance with Subsection (4), his appointment is terminated.

6 Meetings of the Board

(1) The Board shall meet as often as required and at such times and places as it determines.

(2) The Chairman shall preside at all meetings of the Board.

(3) The quorum for a meeting of the Board is all the members.

(4) Subject to this Act, the procedures of the Board are as determined by the Board.

(5) Meetings of the Board shall not be open to the public.

7 Functions of the Board

(1) The functions of the Board are, in accordance with the provisions of this Act –

(a) to consider the cases of detainees who are eligible for parole in accordance with Section 17, and applications for parole under Section 22; and

(b) to grant orders for the release of detainees on parole where appropriate; and

(c) such other functions as are specified or required under this Act or any other law.

(2) In the performance of its functions, the Board shall apply the following criteria: –

(a) the protection of the public is the paramount consideration; and

(b) the detainee's release will cause no undue risk that he will reoffend before his sentence expires; and

(c) the detainee's release will contribute to the welfare and protection of the community by helping or furthering his reintegration into the community as a law-abiding person.

8 Powers of the Board

(1) The Board may do all things necessary or convenient to be done for, or in connection with, the performance of its functions.

(2) For the purpose of exercising the functions of the Board under this Act, the members of the Board have all the powers, authorities, protections and immunities conferred on a Commissioner under the *Commissions of Inquiry Act* (Chapter 31).

9 Chairman's report

As soon as possible after the close of each calendar year the Chairman shall, in respect of that year, submit to the Minister, for presentation to Parliament, a report in relation to –

(a) the number of detainees eligible for parole in accordance with Section 17; and

(b) the number of detainees eligible for parole who refused to be considered for parole in accordance with Section 19; and

(c) the number of detainees granted parole; and

(d) the number of detainees refused parole; and

(e) the number of detainees refused parole who have applied for the parole in accordance with Section 22; and

(f) the number of persons on parole; and

(g) the number of convictions for breach of parole; and

(h) the number of orders for grant of parole which were revoked; and

(i) the number of orders for parole discharged; and

(j) the operations generally of the Parole Board and of the system of parole; and

(k) the effect of the operation of this Act with respect to parole; and

(l) such other matters as he considers appropriate or as the Minister directs.

PART III – PAROLE SERVICE

10 Parole Service

A Parole Service is hereby established.

11 Officers of the Parole Service

(1) The Parole Service shall consist of –

(a) a Chief Parole Officer; and

(b) Parole Officers,

who will be officers of the National Public Service, and

(c) Voluntary Parole Officers.

12 Voluntary Parole Officers

(1) The Chief Parole Officer may, in writing, appoint a person to be a Voluntary Parole Officer.

(2) An appointment under Subsection (1) shall not be made where the person is the holder of an office or appointment that is inconsistent with the exercise of the powers, or the performance of the duties and functions, of an Officer of the Parole Service.

(3) The Chief Parole Officer may delegate his power of appointment under Subsection (1), including the power to revoke an appointment, to a Parole Officer.

(4) An appeal against a revocation of appointment by a delegate under Subsection (3) lies to the Chief Parole Officer who may confirm, vary or withdraw the revocation.

(5) A Voluntary Parole Officer is not entitled to a salary or other remuneration for services rendered by him under this Act, but may be reimbursed such expenses as are necessarily incurred by him in the proper performance of his duties and functions and at such rates as are determined by the Departmental Head.

(6) A Voluntary Parole Officer shall be deemed to be a worker employed by the State for the purposes of the *Workers Compensation Act* (Chapter 179).

13 Duties of the Chief Parole Officer

(1) The Chief Parole Officer shall be responsible for the efficient management of the Parole Service, and in particular shall –

(a) be responsible for the preparation of such reports of investigation and supervision as he considers necessary or as are required under this Act; and

(b) assign Officers to serve in such areas and for such cases as he determines; and

(c) direct and supervise the work of Officers and other employees assigned to him; and

(d) formulate and implement methods of investigation, supervision of. parolees, record keeping and reporting; and

(e) conduct training courses for Officers and other staff of the Parole Service; and

(f) develop policies and procedures for parole work; and

(g) prepare an annual report as required by Section 30; and

(h) have such other functions, powers, duties and responsibilities as are prescribed by or under this Act or any other law.

(2) The Chief Parole Officer has and may exercise any powers, or perform any duties or functions, of a Parole Officer.

14 Duties of Parole Officers

A Parole Officer shall –

(a) supervise all parolees placed under his supervision with a view to assisting their reintegration into the community as law-abiding people; and

(b) prepare for, and submit to, the Board reports in accordance with Section 19 to assist the Board in determining whether to grant, vary or revoke parole; and

(c) perform such other duties as are assigned to him under this Act or any other law; and

(d) perform such other duties as the Chief Parole Officer directs, including the making of investigations and reports as requested by the Board.

15 Duties of Voluntary Parole Officers

A Voluntary Parole Officer shall –

(a) as directed by a Parole Officer, supervise all parolees placed under his supervision with a view to assisting their reintegration into the community as law-abiding people; and

(b) aid and assist any Parole Officer as required; and

(c) prepare and submit to a Parole Officer such written reports and information with respect to any parolee as are required by a Parole Officer.

16 Extent of duties

(1) An Officer shall not, in the performance of his duties and functions under this Act or any other law, perform those duties and functions for a purpose other than the furtherance of the purposes for which the Parole Service is established.

(2) The Chief Parole Officer shall determine whether the performance of a duty or function in any general or particular circumstance is for the furtherance of the purposes referred to in Subsection (1).

PART IV – PAROLE

17 Eligibility for parole

(1) Subject to this Act, a detainee who –

(a) having been sentenced to a term of imprisonment of less than three years – has served not less than one year; or

(b) having been sentenced to a term of imprisonment of three years or more – has served not less than one third of the sentence; or

(c) having been sentenced to life imprisonment or detention during Her Majesty's pleasure – has served not less than ten years,

is eligible for parole.

(2) For the purposes of determining the length of a sentence under Subsection (1) –

(a) remission of sentence shall not be taken into account; and

(b) where a detainee has been sentenced to –

(i) two or more terms of imprisonment to be served concurrently – the longer or longest term (as the case may be) shall be considered; or

(ii) two or more terms to be served cumulatively – the total of these terms shall be considered.

18 Commissioner to provide particulars of detainees eligible for parole

At least six months before a detainee becomes eligible for parole in accordance with Section 17(1), the Commissioner shall provide the Board with the following particulars in the prescribed form: –

(a) the name of the detainee; and

(b) the date of his committal to the corrective institution; and

(c) particulars of the offence committed by him and of his conviction; and

(d) the length of the sentence imposed on him, and if more than one sentence has been imposed on him the lengths of the respective sentences and whether they were imposed to run concurrently or cumulatively; and

(e) particulars of any further sentences imposed on him since his committal to the corrective institution, including particulars of any sentences imposed on him for disciplinary offences while in detention; and

(f) the date on which he will become eligible for parole in accordance with Section 17,

and shall notify the detainee that this has been done.

19 Detainee may refuse to be considered for parole

(1) A detainee notified under Section 18 may refuse in writing to be considered for parole and the Commissioner shall advise the Board of the refusal.

(2) A detainee who has refused to be considered for parole under Subsection (1) may at any time withdraw his refusal in writing and the Commissioner shall advise the Board of the withdrawal.

(3) Where the Board has been notified of a refusal under Subsection (1), and unless it receives notice of a withdrawal under Subsection (2), it shall take no further action in the matter of parole of the detainee.

20 Reports on detainees eligible for parole

(1) Subject to Section 19(3), where the Board receives –

(a) information relating to a detainee in accordance with Section 18; or

(b) notice that a refusal has been withdrawn in accordance with Section 19(2); or

(c) an application for parole under Section 22,

the Board shall request –

(d) the Commissioner; or

(e) the Chief Parole Officer,

to provide it with reports on the detainee.

(2) The report of the Commissioner under Subsection (1) shall contain the following particulars in respect of the detainee: –

(a) an assessment of character and history during detention; and

(b) a report of a medical examination held within the previous three months; and

(c) a recent assessment by a psychiatrist or welfare officer; and

(d) where it is appropriate and available, a report of a resident or visiting chaplain; and

(e) details of any money, including wages, due to him; and

(f) an assessment of his attitude to the offence and to any victim of the offence; and

(g) a summary of progress while in detention, including a resume of achievements in academic and technical skills, and involvement in social, recreational and religious activities; and

(h) an assessment of relationships with other detainees and corrective institution staff; and

(i) an assessment of co-operation, behaviour and general attitude while in detention; and

(j) details of proposed plans, particularly in respect of education and training, employment, proposed housing, community and church involvement; and

(k) where the report is made in respect of an application for parole under Section 22, details of any apparent changes in behaviour and attitude since parole was refused.

(3) The report of the Chief Parole Officer under Subsection (1) shall contain the following particulars in respect of the detainee: –

(a) an assessment of character and history;

(b) previous convictions (if any);

(c) an assessment of his attitude to the offence;

(d) any matters of custom relevant to the offence committed;

(e) particulars of any disputes or disruptions within the community which have arisen as a result of the commission of the offence or which may be likely to arise if he is released on parole;

(f) the amount and nature of any compensation paid in relation to the offence;

(g) an assessment of the likelihood of his reoffending if he is placed on parole;

(h) an assessment of the probability of his successful reintegration into the community if he is released on parole;

(i) an assessment of his rehabilitation plans, particularly in respect of education and training, employment, proposed housing, community and church involvement, and the likelihood of future employment and education;

(j) an assessment of his financial situation, assets and property, family circumstances and marital status;

(k) any other particulars which the Chief Parole Officer thinks relevant in assisting the Board to decide whether to grant or refuse parole;

(l) where the report is made in respect of an application for parole under Section 22, details of any apparent changes in behaviour and attitude since parole was refused.

21 Orders granting parole, etc

(1) As soon as possible after receiving the reports under Section 20, the Board shall consider, in relation to the detainee reported on –

(a) those reports; and

(b) where available, the stated reasons and recommendations of the sentencing judge or magistrate; and

(c) other available information from the trial or sentencing; and

(d) any other available information which the Board considers relevant,

and shall decide whether to grant or refuse an order for parole, and, if an order is granted, what, if any, additional conditions are to be imposed in accordance with Section 24(2).

(2) An order granting parole takes effect from –

(a) such date as may be determined by the Board, not being a date before the date on which the detainee becomes eligible for parole; or

(b) where the Board makes no determination as to the date – from the date upon which the detainee becomes eligible for parole.

(3) Time spent on parole is deemed to be time served towards that part of the parolee's sentence that is remaining at the time of his release on parole.

(4) Notification of a decision under Subsection (1) shall be given to –

(a) the Commissioner; and

(b) the Chief Parole Officer; and

(c) the detainee.

22 Application after refusal of parole

(1) Subject to Subsection (2), a detainee who has been refused parole under Section 21 may apply in the prescribed form to the Board for parole.

(2) An application under Subsection (1) shall not be made within 12 months from the date of refusal to grant parole.

(3) Upon receipt of an application under Subsection (1), the Board shall request –

(a) the Commissioner; and

(b) the Chief Parole Officer,

to provide it with reports on the detainee in accordance with Section 20, and shall proceed to consider and decide whether to grant or refuse parole to the detainee in accordance with Section 21.

23 Release of parolee from detention

(1) Subject to Subsection (2), a parolee shall be released on parole upon the grant of parole in accordance with Section 21.

(2) Notwithstanding Subsection (1), a parolee shall not be released from detention –

(a) upon grant of parole under Section 21; or

(b) upon a decision in accordance with Section 27(5),

until he has been contacted by an Officer, who shall explain fully and in a language which the parolee understands the terms of his parole.

(3) Upon release from detention, a parolee shall report immediately to an office of the Parole Service nominated by a Parole Officer.

24 Conditions of parole

(1) An order for parole shall –

(a) specify the office to which the parolee is to report immediately upon release, in accordance with Section 23(2); and

(b) require the parolee to report to an Officer as and when he is required by the Officer to do so; and

(c) require the parolee to keep the peace and be of good behaviour; and

(d) require the parolee to follow any directions or instructions given to him by a Parole Officer; and

(e) require the parolee to inform a Parole Officer of his exact place of residence, which he shall not change unless –

(i) he has given to the Parole Officer reasonable notice of his intention to do so and the reasons for the proposed change; and

(ii) the Parole Officer has given him permission to change his residence; and

(iii) the parolee complies with any orders given to him by the Parole Officer in relation to his change of residence; and

(f) direct that the parolee shall give reasonable notice to a Parole Officer of his intention to change his employment and advise him of reasons for the change, and the nature and place of his proposed employment; and

(g) direct that the parolee shall give reasonable notice to a Parole Officer of any contracts, debts or financial undertakings which he proposes to incur or enter into, which might have a significant effect on his income or family situation; and

(h) require that the parolee shall, for the purposes of this Act, allow an Officer to enter his home during reasonable hours.

(2) In addition to the conditions set out in Subsection (1), the Board may impose such other conditions as are necessary in the circumstances of the case for ensuring compliance by the parolee with the conditions of the order and for his good conduct and welfare.

25 Variation of conditions

(1) The Board may –

(a) in its own discretion; or

(b) in considering a case of breach of parole under Section 27; or

(c) on the application of a parolee who has informed a Parole Officer of his intention to do so; or

(d) on the application of a Parole Officer,

suspend or vary any additional condition of parole under Section 24(2), or impose further conditions on the order for parole.

(2) Notification of any suspension, variation or addition of conditions under Subsection (1) shall be given to the Chief Parole Officer and to the parolee.

26 Breach of parole

(1) A parolee shall –

(a) comply with the requirement to report under Section 23(2); and

(b) comply with the conditions of his parole under Section 24, subject to any variation or addition under Section 25.

(2) A parolee who contravenes, or fails to comply with, a condition or requirement of his parole commits an offence.

(3) A member of the Police Force who, on reasonable grounds, believes that a parolee has committed a breach of, or has failed to comply with, his parole may, subject to the *Arrest Act* (Chapter 339) and the *Bail Act* (Chapter 340), arrest the parolee without a warrant.

(4) If, on information, it appears to a magistrate that a parolee has committed a breach of, or has failed to comply with, his parole, the magistrate may –

(a) issue a summons requiring the parolee to appear before a District Court; or

(b) where the information is on oath – issue a warrant for his arrest.

(5) An offence under Subsection (2) may be heard by a District Court, and where the parolee is convicted of the offence, the court shall –

(a) issue a certificate of conviction in the prescribed form; and

(b) remit the matter to the Board for consideration in accordance with Section 27; and

(c) subject to Subsection (6) – place the parolee in custody pending the decision of the Board.

(6) A parolee may not be held in custody under Subsection (5) for longer than the remainder of the term of imprisonment to which his parole order related.

27 Decision of Board in relation to breach

(1) Where a matter of breach of parole has been referred to it in accordance with Section 26, the Board shall –

(a) revoke the order; or

(b) not [811]revoke the order; or

(c) not revoke the order and vary, or impose additional conditions on, the order,

granting parole to the parolee.

(2) A decision under Subsection (1) shall be made as soon as is practicable after the arrest of a parolee under Section 26.

(3) Notification of a decision under Subsection (1) shall be given to –

(a) the Commissioner; and

(b) the Chief Parole Officer; and

(c) the parolee.

(4) Where the Board revokes an order for grant of parole under Subsection (1)(a), it shall remit the detainee to a corrective institution to serve the remainder of the term of imprisonment to which his parole order related.

(5) Where the Board does not revoke an order for grant of parole under Subsection (1)(b) or (c), it shall direct the Commissioner to release the parolee subject to the requirements of Section 23.

(6) Any time spent by a parolee in a corrective institution between

---

[811]The Act has "revole".

his arrest for breach of parole and the decision of the Board under Subsection (1) shall –

(a) where the order granting parole is revoked – be counted as part of the sentence served; or

(b) where the order granting parole is not revoked – be counted as part of the period of parole.

28 Discharge from parole

(1) Where a parolee's period of parole has expired, the Board shall discharge the order for parole.

(2) On the discharge of an order for parole under Subsection (1), the person to whom the order related is deemed to have served his sentence in full.

PART V – MISCELLANEOUS

29 Assistance to be given to officers

(1) Subject to any other law, a Parole Officer has a right to receive assistance and information from the State, a provincial government, an individual or other body for the proper performance of his duties and functions under this Act.

(2) A person who unlawfully –

(a) withholds information required by; or

(b) hinders or obstructs,

an Officer in the performance of his duties, is guilty of an offence.

Penalty: A fine not exceeding K200.00.

30 Report by Chief Parole Officer

As soon as is practicable after the close of each calendar year, the Chief Parole Officer shall submit to the Minister a report in respect of that year including –

(a) the number of persons on parole; and

(b) the number of parolees discharged from parole; and

(c) the number of reports made in respect of breaches of parole; and

(d) the effect of the operation of this Act with respect to parole; and

(e) particulars of the activities of the Parole Service.

31 Proceedings to be confidential

(1) Subject to Subsection (2), all evidence given to the Board relating to a detainee or parolee shall be and remain confidential.

(2) A copy of a written report by an Officer furnished to the Board may be made available to –

(a) any person or body who, in the opinion of the Chairman, has a legitimate professional interest in the information contained in the report; and

(b) the subject of the report and his lawyer; and

(c) the Departmental Head; and

(d) any person, as authorized by the Chief Parole Officer, for the purposes of research or study or for statistical reasons.

(3) A copy of a report made available –

(a) under Subsection (2)(b) – shall be made available before the meeting of the Parole Board at which it is to be considered and shall be returned to the Parole Board after that meeting; and

(b) under Subsection (2)(d) – shall be made available subject to such conditions as the Chief Parole Officer determines.

(4) A person who –

(a) publishes; or

(b) discloses; or

(c) makes available to any person,

any report or copy of any report or any part of it, except in accordance with this section, is guilty of an offence.

Penalty: A fine not exceeding K200.00 or imprisonment for a period not exceeding two months or both.

32 Indemnity

An Officer is not liable to any action, suit or other proceeding for any act or thing done or omitted by him to be done in good faith in the exercise of any power or the performance of any duty or function conferred or imposed upon him by or under this Act.

33 Regulations

The Head of State, acting on advice, may make regulations not inconsistent with this Act, prescribing all matters that by this Act are required or permitted to be prescribed for carrying out or giving effect to this Act, in particular for prescribing penalties of fines not exceeding K1,000.00 for offences against the regulations.

CHAPTER No 148

Partnership Act

PART I – PRELIMINARY

PART II – NATURE OF PARTNERSHIP

PART III – RELATIONS OF PARTNERS TO PERSONS DEALING WITH THEM

PART IV – RELATIONS OF PARTNERS TO ONE ANOTHER

PART V – MISCELLANEOUS

PART V – DISSOLUTION OF PARTNERSHIP AND ITS CONSEQUENCES

INDEPENDENT STATE OF PAPUA NEW GUINEA

CHAPTER No 148

Partnership Act

Being an Act to declare the law of partnership.

PART I – PRELIMINARY

1 Interpretation

(1) In this Act, unless the contrary intention appears –

"business" includes every trade, occupation or profession;

"court" means a court or Judge having jurisdiction in the case;

"partnership property" means, subject to Section 21, all property, and all rights and interests in property, originally brought into the partnership stock or acquired on account of the firm or for the purposes of, and in the course of, the partnership business.

(2) Persons who have entered into partnership with one another are, for the purposes of this Act, called collectively a firm, and the name under which their business is carried on is called the firm-name.

2 Saving of rules of the underlying law

The rules of the underlying law applicable to partnership continue in force except so far as they are inconsistent with the express provisions of this Act.

PART II – NATURE OF PARTNERSHIP

3 Definition of partnership

(1) Subject to Subsection (2), partnership is the relationship that subsists between persons carrying on a business in common with a view to profit.

(2) The relation between members of a company or association that is –

(a) registered as a company under any Act for the time being in force and relating to the registration of joint stock companies; or

(b) formed or incorporated by or under any other Act, letters patent or Royal Charter,

is not a partnership within the meaning of this Act.

4 Rules for determining existence of partnership

In determining whether a partnership exists, regard shall be had to the following rules: –

(a) joint tenancy, tenancy in common, joint property, common property or part-ownership does not of itself create a partnership as to anything held or owned jointly or in common, whether or not the tenants or owners share profits; and

(b) the sharing of gross returns does not of itself create a partnership, whether or not the persons sharing the returns have a joint or common right or interest in any property from which, or from the use of which, the returns are derived; and

(c) the receipt by a person of a share of the profits of a business is prima facie evidence only that he is a partner in the business, and the receipt of such a share, or of a payment contingent on or varying with the profits of a business, does not of itself make him a partner in the business, and in particular –

(i) the receipt by a person of a debt or other liquidated amount by instalments or otherwise out of the accruing profits of a business does not of itself make him a partner in the business or liable as such; or

(ii) a contract for the remuneration of a servant or agent of a person engaged in a business by a share of the profits of the business does not of itself make the servant or agent a partner in the business or liable as such; or

(iii) a person who is the widow or child of a deceased partner, and who receives by way of annuity a portion of the profits made in the business in which the deceased person was a partner, is not by reason only of the receipt a partner in the business or liable as such; or

(iv) the advance of money by way of loan to a person engaged or about to engage in any business on a written contract, signed by or on behalf of all the parties, that the lender will receive a rate of interest varying with the profits, or will receive a share of the profits arising from carrying on the business, does not of itself make the lender a partner with the person carrying on the business or liable as such; or

(v) a person receiving by way of annuity or otherwise a portion of the profits of a business in consideration of the sale by him of the goodwill of the business is not by reason only of the receipt a partner in the business or liable as such.

5 Postponement of rights of certain persons in case of insolvency

In the event of a person to whom money has been advanced in the circumstances referred to in Section 4(c)(iv), or a buyer of goodwill in consideration of a share of the profits of the business –

(a) being adjudicated insolvent; or

(b) entering into an arrangement to pay his creditors less than 100t in the kina; or

(c) dying in insolvent circumstances,

the lender is not entitled to recover anything in respect of his loan, and the seller of the goodwill is not entitled to recover anything in respect of the share of profits contracted for, until the claims of the other creditors of the borrower or buyer for valuable consideration in money or money's worth have been satisfied.

PART III – RELATIONS OF PARTNERS TO PERSONS DEALING WITH THEM

6 Power of partner to bind the firm

Each partner is an agent of the firm and of his other partners for the purpose of the business of the partnership, and the act of any partner who does any act for carrying on in the usual way business of the kind carried on by the firm of which he is a member binds the firm and his partners, unless –

(a) the partner so acting has in fact no authority to act for the firm in the particular matter; and

(b) the person with whom he is dealing knows that he has no authority or does not know, or does not believe, him to be a partner.

7 Partners bound by acts on behalf of firm

(1) An act or instrument relating to the business of a firm and done or executed in the firm-name, or in any other manner showing an intention to bind a firm, by any person authorized for the purpose, whether or not he is a partner, is binding on the firm and all the partners.

(2) Subsection (1) does not affect any general rule of law relating to the execution of deeds or negotiable instruments.

8 Partner using credit of firm for private purposes

Where a partner pledges the credit of the firm for a purpose apparently not connected with the firm's ordinary course of business, the firm is not bound unless he is in fact specially authorized by the other partners, but this section does not affect any personal liability incurred by a partner.

9 Notice of restriction on liability of firm

Where it is agreed between the partners that the power of any one or more of them to bind the firm is restricted, no act done in contravention of the agreement is binding on the firm with respect to persons having notice of the agreement.

10 Liability of partners

Each partner in a firm is liable jointly with the other partners for all debts and obligations of the firm incurred while he is a partner, and after his death his estate is, subject to the prior payment of his separate debts, liable in due course of administration for any of the debts and obligations that remain unsatisfied.

11 Liability of the firm for wrongs

Where, by any wrongful act of any partner acting in the ordinary course of the business of the firm, or with the authority of his co-partners, loss or injury is caused to a person who is not a partner in the firm, or a penalty is incurred, the firm is liable to the same extent as the partner.

12 Misapplication of property in custody of the firm

Where –

(a) a partner, acting within the scope of his apparent authority, receives money or property of another person and misapplies it; or

(b) a firm in the course of its business receives money or property of another person, and the money or property so received is misapplied by one or more of the partners while it is in the custody of the firm,

the firm is liable to make good the loss.

13 Liability under Sections 11 and 12

Each partner is liable jointly with his co-partners and also severally for everything for which the firm while he is a partner becomes liable under Section 11 or 12.

14 Improper employment of trust property for partnership purposes

(1) Subject to Subsections (2) and (3), if a partner who is a trustee improperly uses trust property in the business or on the account of the partnership, no other partner is liable for the property to the persons beneficially interested in it.

(2) This section does not affect any liability incurred by a partner by reason of his having notice of a breach of trust.

(3) This section does not prevent trust money from being followed and recovered from the firm if it is still in its possession or under its control.

15 Holding out

(1) Subject to Subsection (2), a person who, by word or conduct, represents himself, or who knowingly permits himself to be represented, as a partner in a firm, is liable as a partner to any one who has on the faith of any such representation given credit to the firm, whether or not the representation was made or communicated to the person giving credit by or with the knowledge of the apparent partner making the representation or permitting it to be made.

(2) Where after the death of a partner the partnership business is continued in the old firm-name, the continued use of the name, or of the deceased partner's name, as part of the firm-name does not of itself make his executor's or administrator's estate or effects liable for any partnership debts contracted after his death.

16 Admissions and representations of partners

An admission or representation made by a partner concerning the partnership affairs, and in the ordinary course of its business, is evidence against the firm.

17 Notice to partner

Notice of any matter relating to partnership affairs given to a partner who habitually acts in the partnership business operates as notice to the firm, except in the case of a fraud on the firm committed by or with the consent of that partner.

18 Liability of incoming and outgoing partners

(1) A person who is admitted as a partner into an existing firm does not become liable, by virtue of the admission, to the creditors of the firm for anything done before he became a partner.

(2) A partner who retires from a firm does not cease, by virtue of the retirement, to be liable for partnership debts or obligations incurred before his retirement.

(3) A retiring partner may be discharged from existing liabilities by agreement between himself and the members of the firm as newly constituted and the creditors, and such an agreement may be express or may be inferred as a fact from the course of dealing between the creditors and the firm as newly constituted.

19 Revocation of continuing guarantee, etc, by change in firm

A continuing guarantee or cautionary obligation given to a firm or to a third person in respect of the transactions of a firm is, in the absence of agreement to the contrary, revoked as to future transactions by any change in the constitution of the firm.

PART IV – RELATIONS OF PARTNERS TO ONE ANOTHER

20 Variations by consent of terms of partnership

The mutual rights and duties of partners, whether ascertained by agreement or defined by this Act, may be varied by the consent of all the partners, and such a consent may be express or may be inferred from a course of dealing.

21 Partnership property

(1) Partnership property shall be held and applied by the partners exclusively for the purposes of the partnership and in accordance with the partnership agreement.

(2) The legal estate or interest in any land that belongs to the partnership devolves according to its nature and tenure and the general rules of law applicable to such land, but in trust, so far as necessary, for the persons beneficially interested in the land under this section.

(3) Where co-owners of an estate or interest in any land that is not partnership property –

(a) are partners as to profits made by the use of the land; and

(b) purchase out of the profits other land to be used in like manner,

the land so purchased belongs to them, in the absence of agreement to the contrary, not as partners, but as co-owners for the same respective estates and interests as were held by them in the original land at the date of the purchase.

22 Property bought with partnership money

Unless the contrary intention appears, property bought with money belonging to the firm shall be deemed to have been bought on account of the firm.

23 Conversion into personal estate of land held as partnership property

Where land has become partnership property, it shall, unless the contrary intention appears, be treated –

(a) as between the partners (including the representatives of a deceased partner); and

(b) as between the representatives of a deceased partner,

as personal and not real estate.

24 Procedure against partnership property for a partner's separate judgement debt

(1) A writ of execution shall not issue against any partnership property except on a judgement against the firm.

(2) On the application of a judgement creditor of a partner, a court may –

(a) make an order charging the partner's interest in the partnership property and profits with payment of the amount of the judgement debt and interest; and

(b) by the same or a subsequent order appoint a receiver of his share of profits (whether already declared or accruing), and of any other money that may be coming to him in respect of the partnership; and

(c) direct all accounts and inquiries, and give all other orders and directions, that might have been directed or given if the charge had been made by the partner in favour of the judgement creditor, or that the circumstances of the case require.

(3) The other partner or partners may at any time redeem the interest charged, or if a sale is directed purchase the interest.

25 Rules as to interests and duties of partners

The interests of partners in the partnership property, and their rights and duties in relation to the partnership, shall be determined, subject to any express or implied agreement between the partners, by the following rules: –

(a) all the partners are entitled to share equally in the capital and profits of the business, and shall contribute equally towards the losses, whether of capital or otherwise, sustained by the firm; and

(b) the firm shall indemnify every partner in respect of payments made and personal liabilities incurred by him –

(i) in the ordinary and proper conduct of the business of the firm; or

(ii) in or about anything necessarily done for the preservation of the business or property of the firm; and

(c) a partner who makes, for the purpose of the partnership, any actual payment or advance beyond the amount of capital that he has agreed to subscribe is entitled to interest at the rate of 6% per annum from the date of the payment or advance; and

(d) a partner is not entitled, before the ascertainment of profits, to interest on the capital subscribed by him; and

(e) every partner may take part in the management of the partnership business; and

(f) no partner is entitled to remuneration for acting in the partnership business; and

(g) no person shall be introduced as a partner without the consent of all existing partners; and

(h) any difference arising as to ordinary matters connected with the partnership business may be decided by a majority of the partners, but no change may be made in the nature of the partnership business without the consent of all existing partners; and

(i) the partnership books shall be kept at the place of business of the partnership (or at the principal place of business, if there is more than one), and every partner may when he thinks fit, have access to, and may inspect and copy any of them.

26 Expulsion of partner

A majority of the partners have no power to expel a partner unless a power to do so has been conferred by express agreement between the partners.

27 Retirement from partnership at will

(1) Where no fixed term has been agreed on for the duration of the partnership, any partner may determine the partnership on giving notice of his intention to do so to all the other partners.

(2) Where the partnership was originally constituted by deed, a written notice signed by the partner giving it, is sufficient notice for the purposes of Subsection (1).

28 Presumption of continuance on old terms

(1) Where a partnership entered into for a fixed term is continued after the term has expired, without any express new agreement, the rights and duties of the partners remain the same as they were at the expiration of the term, so far as is consistent with the incidents of a partnership at will.

(2) A continuance of the business by the partners or such of them as habitually acted in it during the term, without any settlement or liquidation of the partnership affairs, shall be presumed to be a continuance of the partnership.

29 Duty of partners to render accounts, etc

Partners are bound to give true accounts and full information of all things affecting the partnership to any partner or the legal representatives of a partner.

30 Partners accountable for private profits

(1) Each partner shall account to the firm for any benefit derived by him, without the consent of the other partners, from any transaction concerning the partnership, or from any use by him of the partnership property, name or business connexion.

(2) Subsection (1) applies to transactions undertaken, by a surviving partner or by the representatives of the deceased partner, after a partnership has been dissolved by the death of a partner, and before the affairs of the partnership have been completely wound up.

31 Competition by partner with firm

If a partner, without the consent of the other partners, carries on any business of the same nature as and competing with that of the firm, he shall account for and pay over to the firm all profits made by him in that business.

32 Rights of assignee of share in partnership

(1) An assignment, whether absolute or by way of mortgage or redeemable charge, by any partner of his share in the partnership does not, as against the other partners, entitle the assignee, during the continuance of the partnership –

- (a) to interfere in the management or administration of the partnership business or affairs; or
- (b) to require any accounts of the partnership transactions; or
- (c) to inspect the partnership books,

but entitles the assignee only to receive the share of profits to which the assigning partner would otherwise be entitled, and the assignee must, except in case of fraud, accept the account of profits agreed to by the partners.

(2) In the case of a dissolution of the partnership, whether as respects all the partners or as respects the assigning partner, the assignee is entitled to receive –

(a) the share of the partnership assets to which the assigning partner is entitled as between himself and the other partners; and

(b) for the purpose of ascertaining that share, to an account as from the date of the dissolution.

PART V – DISSOLUTION OF PARTNERSHIP AND ITS CONSEQUENCES

33 Dissolution by expiration or notice

(1) Subject to any agreement between the partners, a partnership is dissolved –

(a) if entered into for a fixed term, by the expiration of the term; or

(b) if entered into for a single adventure or undertaking, by the termination of the adventure or undertaking; or

(c) if entered into for an undefined time, by any partner giving notice to the other of his intention to dissolve the partnership.

(2) In a case to which Subsection (1)(c) applies, the partnership is dissolved as from the date mentioned in the notice as the date of dissolution, or, if no date is mentioned, as from the date of the communication of the notice.

34 Dissolution by insolvency, death or charge

(1) Subject to any agreement between the partners, a partnership is dissolved as regards all the partners by the death or insolvency of a partner.

(2) A partnership may, at the option of the other partners, be dissolved if any partner permits his share of the partnership property to be charged under this Act for his separate debt.

35 Dissolution by illegality

A partnership is dissolved by the happening of any event that makes it unlawful for the business of the firm to be carried on, or for the members of the firm to carry it on in partnership.

36 Dissolution by the court

(1) On application in accordance with Subsection (2), a court may order a dissolution of a partnership where –

(a) a partner is shown to the satisfaction of the court to be of permanently unsound mind; or

(b) a partner, other than the partner applying for dissolution –

(i) becomes in any other way permanently incapable of

performing his part of the partnership contract; or

(ii) has been guilty of such conduct as, in the opinion of the court, regard being had to the nature of the business, is calculated to affect prejudicially the carrying on of the business; or

(iii) wilfully or persistently commits a breach of the partnership agreement, or otherwise so conducts himself in matters relating to the partnership business that it is not reasonably practicable for the other partner or partners to carry on the business in partnership with him; or

(c) the business of the partnership can only be carried on at a loss; or

(d) circumstances have arisen that, in the opinion of the court, make it just and equitable that the partnership be dissolved.

(2) Application for dissolution may be made –

(a) on the ground set out in Subsection (1)(a), by the committee or next friend, or a person having title to intervene, on behalf of the partner who is allegedly of unsound mind, or by any other partner; or

(b) on any other ground set out in Subsection (1), by any partner.

37 Rights of persons dealing with firm against apparent members of firm

(1) Where a person deals with a firm after a change in its constitution, he is entitled, until he has notice of the change, to treat all apparent members of the old firm as still being members of the firm.

(2) For the purposes of Subsection (1), an advertisement in the National Gazette is notice to persons who had dealings with the firm before the date of the dissolution or change so advertised.

(3) The estate of a partner who dies or who becomes insolvent, or of a partner who, not having been known to the person dealing with the firm to be a partner, retires from the firm, is not liable for partnership debts contracted after the date of the death, insolvency or retirement, as the case may be.

38 Rights of partners to notify dissolution

On the dissolution of a partnership or the retirement of a partner, any partner may publicly notify the fact, and may require the other partners to concur for that purpose in any necessary or proper act, that cannot be done without their concurrence.

39 Continuing authority of partners for purposes of winding-up

(1) Subject to Subsection (2), after the dissolution of a partnership the authority of each partner to bind the firm, and the other rights and obligations of the partners, continue, notwithstanding the dissolution, as far as is necessary to wind up the affairs of the partnership and to complete transactions begun but unfinished at the time of the dissolution.

(2) The firm is not bound by the acts of a partner who has become insolvent, but this subsection does not affect the liability of a person who has, after the insolvency, represented himself or knowingly suffered himself to be represented as a partner of the insolvent.

40 Rights of partners as to application of partnership property

(1) On the dissolution of a partnership, each partner is entitled, as against the other partners in the firm and all persons claiming through them in respect of their interests as partners –

(a) to have the property of the partnership applied in payment of the debts and liabilities of the firm; and

(b) to have the surplus assets after payment of those debts and liabilities applied in payment of what is due to the partners respectively after deducting what is due from them, as partners, to the firm.

(2) For the purposes of Subsection (1), a partner or his representative may, on the termination of the partnership, apply to the court to wind up the business and affairs of the firm.

41 Apportionment of premium where partnership prematurely dissolved

Where one partner has paid a premium to another on entering into a partnership for a fixed term, and the partnership is dissolved, otherwise than by the death of a partner, before the expiration of the term, the court may order the repayment of the premium, or of such part of the premium as, having regard to the terms of the partnership contract and to the length of time during which the partnership has continued, it thinks just, unless –

(a) the dissolution is, in the opinion of the court, wholly or chiefly due to the misconduct of the partner who paid the premium; or

(b) the partnership has been dissolved by an agreement containing no provision for a return of any part of the premium.

42 Rights on dissolution for fraud or misrepresentation

Where an agreement for a partnership is rescinded on the ground of the fraud or misrepresentation of one of the parties to it, the party entitled to rescind is, without prejudice to any other right, entitled –

(a) to a lien on, or a right of retention of, the surplus of the partnership assets, after satisfying the partnership liabilities, for any sum of money paid by him for the purchase of a share in the partnership and for any capital contributed by him; and

(b) to stand in the place of the creditors of the firm for any payments made by him in respect of the partnership liabilities; and

(c) to be indemnified by the person guilty of the fraud or making the misrepresentation against all the debts and liabilities of the firm.

43 Profits made after dissolution

(1) Subject to Subsection (2), where –

(a) a member of a firm dies or otherwise ceases to be a partner; and

(b) the surviving or continuing partners carry on the business of the firm with its capital or assets without any final settlement of accounts as between the firm and the outgoing partner or his estate,

in the absence of any agreement to the contrary the outgoing partner or his estate is entitled, at the option of himself or his representatives, to such share of the profits made after the dissolution as the court finds to be attributable to the use of his share of the partnership assets, or to interest at the rate of 5% per annum on the amount of his share of the partnership assets.

(2) Where by the agreement for partnership an option is given to the surviving or continuing partners to purchase the interest of a deceased or outgoing partner, and the option is duly exercised, the estate of the deceased partner, or the outgoing partner or his estate, as the case may be, is not entitled to any further or other share of profits.

(3) If a partner assuming to act in exercise of an option referred to in Subsection (2) does not in all material respects comply with the terms of the option, he is liable to account under Subsection (1).

44 Liability for retiring or deceased partner's share

Subject to any agreement between the partners, the amount due from surviving or continuing partners to an outgoing partner, or to the representatives of a deceased partner, in respect of the outgoing or deceased partner's share, is a debt accruing at the date of the dissolution or death.

45 Distribution of assets on final settlement of accounts

In settling accounts between the partners after a dissolution of partnership, the following rules shall, subject to any agreement, be observed: –

(a) losses, including losses and deficiencies of capital, shall be paid first out of profits, next out of capital, and lastly, if necessary, by the partners individually in the proportions in which they were entitled to share profits; and

(b) the assets of the firm, including the sums (if any) contributed by the partners to make up losses or deficiencies of capital, shall be applied in the following manner order: –

(i) in paying the debts and liabilities of the firm to persons who are not partners; and

(ii) in paying to each partner rateably what is due from the firm to him for advances as distinguished from capital; and

(iii) in paying to each partner rateably what is due from the firm to him in respect of capital,

and the ultimate residue (if any) shall be divided among the partners in the proportion in which profits are divisible.

CHAPTER No 381

Probation Act

PART I – PRELIMINARY

PART II – PROBATION SERVICE AND OFFICERS

PART III – PROBATION

PART IV – MISCELLANEOUS

INDEPENDENT STATE OF PAPUA NEW GUINEA

CHAPTER No 381

Probation Act

(Consolidated to No 19 of 1990)

Being an Act to establish a probation service, to provide for social rehabilitation of offenders and for related purposes.

PART I – PRELIMINARY

1 Compliance with Constitutional requirements

This Act, to the extent that it regulates or restricts a right or freedom referred to in Subdivision III.3.C (*qualified rights*) of the Constitution, namely –

(a) freedom of assembly and association conferred by Section 47 of the Constitution; and

(b) the right to privacy conferred by Section 49 of the Constitution; and

(c) the right to freedom of movement conferred by Section 52 of the Constitution,

is a law that is made for that purpose.

2 Interpretation

In this Act unless the contrary intention appears –

"Chief Probation Officer" means the Chief Probation Officer referred to in Section 5(1)(a);

"court" does not include a Village Court;

"declared area" means an area declared under Section 3;

"period of probation" means a period specified in a probation order in accordance with Section 16(2) and, includes, where the period has been extended under this Act, the extension;

"probationer" means a person in relation to whom a probation order is in force;

"probation officer" means a person referred to in Section 5(b);

"probation order" means an order made under Section 16(2);

"relevant court" in relation to an application, or other matter, connected with a probation order, means a court exercising the same jurisdiction as the court that made the order;

"Senior Probation Officer" means a person referred to in Section 5(b);

"Service" means the Probation Service established by this Act;

"this Act" includes the regulations;

"voluntary probation officer" means a person appointed under Section 6(1).

3 Application

(1) This Act applies to a declared area.

(2) The Minister, acting in accordance with the advice of the Departmental Head and the Chief Probation Officer, may, by notice in the National Gazette, declare an area of the country to be a declared area for the purposes of this Act.

PART II – PROBATION SERVICE AND OFFICERS

4 Establishment of Probation Service

The Probation Service is hereby established.

5 Appointment of officers

For the purposes of the Service, there shall be –

(a) a Chief Probation Officer; and

(b) such number of Senior Probation Officers and probation officers as are required,

who shall be officers or employees of the Public Service.

6 Appointment of voluntary probation officers

(1) Subject to Subsection (2), the Chief Probation Officer may, by writing, appoint a person to be a voluntary probation officer.

(2) An appointment under Subsection (1) shall not be made where the person is the holder of an office or appointment that is inconsistent with the exercise of the powers, or the performance of the duties and functions, of a probation officer.

(3) The Chief Probation Officer may delegate his power of appointment under Subsection (1), including the power to revoke an appointment, to a Senior Probation Officer and to a probation officer.

(4) An appeal against a revocation of appointment by a delegate under Subsection (3) lies to the Chief Probation Officer who may confirm, vary or rescind the revocation.

7 Terms and conditions of voluntary probation officers

(1) A voluntary probation officer shall be deemed to be a worker employed by the State for the purposes of the *Workers Compensation Act* (Chapter 179).

(2) A voluntary probation officer shall not be entitled to a salary or other remuneration for services rendered by him under this Act but may be reimbursed such expenses as are necessarily incurred by him in the proper performance of his duties and functions and at such rates as are determined by the Departmental Head in consultation with the Departmental Head of the Department of Personnel Management.

8 Duties of the Chief Probation Officer

The Chief Probation Officer shall be responsible for the efficient management of the Service and in particular shall –

(a) be responsible for preparation of such reports of investigation and supervision as are necessary; and

(b) assign probation officers to serve in such areas and for such cases as he determines; and

(c) direct and supervise the work of probation officers and other employees assigned to him; and

(d) formulate and implement methods of investigation, supervision of probationers, record keeping and reporting; and

(e) conduct training courses for staff of the Service; and

(f) develop policies and procedures for probation work.

9 Duties of Senior Probation Officer

It is the duty of a Senior Probation Officer –

(a) to supervise the work of probation officers as the Chief Probation Officer directs; and

(b) to perform such other duties as the Chief Probation Officer directs.

10 Duties of probation officer

It is the duty of a probation officer –

(a) to supervise, advise, assist and where possible to befriend, a probationer under him for the purposes of social rehabilitation of that probationer; and

(b) to perform such duties as are assigned to him under this Act or any other law; and

(c) to perform such other duties as the Chief Probation Officer directs.

11 Duties of voluntary probation officer

It is the duty of a voluntary probation officer –

(a) to advise, assist and where possible to befriend, a probationer as directed by a probation officer; and

(b) when required by a probation officer to do so – to prepare and submit written reports to that probation officer in respect of a probationer; and

(c) generally to assist a probation officer in the performance of his duties.

12 Extent of duties

(1) A probation officer shall not, in the performance of his duties and functions under this Act or under any other law, perform those duties and functions for a purpose other than for the furtherance of the principal purpose for which the Service is established, namely the social rehabilitation of offenders.

(2) Whether the performance of a duty or function in any general or particular circumstances is for the furtherance of the principal purpose referred to in Subsection (1) is as determined by the Chief Probation Officer.

13 Powers of probation officer

(1) In this section, "offence" does not include an offence for which a mandatory minimum sentence is provided for by any law.

(2) Where a court requests assistance in determining the most suitable method of dealing with a person convicted of an offence before it, the Chief Probation Officer may in his discretion –

(a) report, or order a probation officer to report, to that court on the personal history and character of the person; and

(b) advise, or order a probation officer to advise, the court –

(i) whether that person is likely to respond satisfactorily to probation; and

(ii) of any conditions that may be imposed on the release on probation of that person.

(3) A probation officer may commence, appear in or continue any proceedings in any court on behalf of any other probation officer.

14 Further powers, duties and functions

The Chief Probation Officer and Senior Probation Officer may exercise any powers, or perform any duties and functions, of a probation officer.

15 Reports to a person or body other than a court

The Chief Probation Officer may report to any person or body, not being a court, for the purposes of assisting that person or body review a sentence.

PART III – PROBATION

16 Probation order

(1) In this section, "offence" does not include an offence for which a mandatory minimum sentence is provided for by any law.

(2) Subject to Subsection (3), where a person, is convicted of an offence punishable by imprisonment or a fine or both imprisonment and a fine, the court convicting him may by probation order –

(a) impose a sentence but suspend committing him to imprisonment or a fine or both imprisonment and a fine; or

(b) defer sentencing him to imprisonment or a fine or both imprisonment and a fine,

and release him on probation for a period specified in the order, being a period of not less than six months and not more than five years.

(3) . . . [Repealed].

(4) Subsection (2) does not prevent the court –

(a) imposing and requiring the payment by the probationer of a fine authorized by law; or

(b) in accordance with any law – disqualifying the probationer from holding or obtaining a licence to drive a motor vehicle under the *Motor Traffic Act*.

(5) A probation order takes effect from such date as may be determined by the Court or, where the Court makes no determination as to the date, from the date of the making of the order.

(6) Subsection (2) shall not be construed as derogating from the powers of any court conferred by any other law to release a person on probation for such period and on such conditions as are specified in that law.

[812](7) Notwithstanding Subsection (6), where a law provides for –

(a) probation; or

(b) a person to be placed on probation,

this Act shall apply in the absence of any express provisions to the contrary in that law.

---

[812]Section 16(7) added by *Probate (Amendment) Act* 1990 (No. 19 of 1990), s3(e).

17 Conditions of probation

(1) A probation order shall –

(a) specify the address to which the probationer is to go and remain on release until he is contacted by a probation officer; and

(b) require the probationer to report to a probation officer as and when he is required by the probation officer to do so; and

(c) require the probationer to keep the peace and to be of good behaviour; and

(d) direct that –

(i) the probationer shall not change his address, other than the address referred to in Paragraph (a), unless he has given to a probation officer reasonable notice of his intention to do so and the reasons for the proposed change; and

(ii) where by virtue of the change of address, the probationer has moved to another declared area – he shall, within 48 hours of arrival, report to a probation officer in that area and advise that officer of the nature and place of his employment and of his new address in that area; and

(e) direct that the probationer shall give to a probation officer reasonable notice of his intention to change his employment and advise him of the nature and place of his proposed employment; and

(f) require that the probationer shall, for the purposes of this Act, allow a probation officer to enter his home during reasonable hours.

(2) In Subsection (1)(a), (b), (e) and (f), "probation office" includes a voluntary probation officer.

18 Additional conditions

(1) In addition to the conditions set out in Section 17(1), the court may impose all or any of the following conditions: –

(a) that a probationer shall not, except with the permission of a probation officer and in accordance with such directions as the probation officer may give, leave any specified area; and

(b) that a probationer shall pay, within such period and by such instalments as the court determines, damages for injury, or compensation for loss, suffered by any person by virtue of the offence for which the probationer is convicted or shall carry out work in restitution for such injury, compensation or loss; and

[813](c) that a probationer shall travel to and reside in a specific area; and

[814](d) that a probationer shall perform community work under the provisions of any law; and

[815](e) that a probationer shall pay, within such period and by such instalments as the court determines, compensation according to custom to any person or persons.

(2) Subsection (1) does not prevent the court imposing such other conditions as are necessary in the circumstances of the case for ensuring compliance by the probationer with the conditions of the order and for his good conduct and welfare.

[816](3) Where a probationer is performing community work or work by way of restitution, the probationer shall be deemed to be employed by the State for the purposes of the *Workers Compensation Act* (Chapter 179).

19 Variation and discharge of probation orders

(1) Subject to Subsection (6), a relevant court may, on application by a probationer, suspend or vary the conditions of the probation order which relates to that probationer.

(2) A probationer who has served not less than half the period of probation may, subject to Subsection (6), apply to a relevant court for the discharge of the probation order relating to him and the court may discharge the order.

(3) Subject to Subsection (6), a probation officer may, in relation to a probation order, apply to a relevant court for –

(a) suspension or variation of the conditions of the order; or

(b) imposition of additional conditions; or

---

[813]Section 18(1)(c) added by *Probation (Amendment) Act* 1990 (No. 19 of 1990), s4(a).

[814]Section 18(1)(d) added by *Probation (Amendment) Act* 1990 (No. 19 of 1990), s4(a).

[815]Section 18(1)(e) added by *Probation (Amendment) Act* 1990 (No. 19 of 1990), s4(a).

[816]Section 18(3) added by *Probation (Amendment) Act* 1990 (No. 19 of 1990), s4(d).

(c) extension of the period of probation where that period is less than five years; or

(d) the discharge of the order.

(4) On the hearing of an application under Subsection (3), the court, having regard to the information before it in relation to the probationer, may –

(a) do all, or any of the following things: –

(i) suspend or vary any conditions of the probation order; or

(ii) impose any additional conditions; or

(iii) subject to Subsection (5) – extend the period of probation; or

(b) discharge the order.

(5) A period of probation shall not be extended beyond the period of five years from the date when the probation order in which that period is specified first took effect.

(6) Except with the written consent of the Chief Probation Officer, an application under Subsection (1), (2) or (3) shall not be made to a court unless that court exercises jurisdiction in a declared area.

20 Breach of conditions of probation

(1) A probationer who contravenes, or fails to comply with, a condition of a probation order that relates to him commits an offence.

(2) An offence under Subsection (1) may be heard by a relevant court or a court exercising jurisdiction superior to the relevant court and the court may, on conviction of the probationer –

(a) extend the period of probation where that period is less than five years; or

(b) vary any condition of the probation order; or

(c) impose additional conditions; or

(d) where in accordance with Section 16(2)(a) sentence to imprisonment was suspended – commit the probationer to imprisonment for the whole or part of that sentence; or

(e) where in accordance with Section 16(2)(b) sentence was deferred – sentence the probationer to imprisonment for the offence for which he was originally convicted; or

[817](f) impose the penalty of a fine of not exceeding K200.00 or imprisonment for a term not exceeding four months.

[817]Section 20(2)(f) added by *Probate (Amendment) Act* 1990 (No. 19 of 1990), s5.

(3) Section 19(5) applies to an extension under Subsection (2)(a).

(4) Where the court has proceeded in accordance with Subsection (2)(d) or (e), the court shall discharge the probation order.

21 Arrest of probationers

(1) A member of the Police Force who, on reasonable grounds, believes that a probationer has committed a breach of a condition of a probation order relating to that probationer may, subject to the *Arrest Act* and the *Bail Act,* arrest him without a warrant.

(2) If, on information, it appears to a relevant court that a probationer has committed a breach of, or has failed to comply with, a condition of the probation order relating to him, the court may –

(a) issue a summons requiring the probationer to appear before it; or

(b) where the information is on oath – issue a warrant for his arrest.

22 Subsequent sentence

(1) Where a probationer is sentenced to imprisonment for a subsequent offence, other than an offence under Section 20, the period of probation shall continue to run while the probationer is under that imprisonment, and on release he shall serve the unexpired period of probation (if any).

(2) Subsection (1) does not prevent a court dealing with the probationer in accordance with Section 20 for an offence under that section.

PART IV – MISCELLANEOUS

23 Notice of proceedings relating to Probation Order

(1) In this section, "matter" does not include a bail application.

(2) Notice of an application under Section 19(3) shall be delivered to the probationer by the probation officer either before, or as soon as possible after, the application is lodged with the court.

(3) Immediately after an application under Section 19(1) or (2) is lodged with the court, a copy of that application shall be served by the court on the Chief Probation Officer and another copy on the probation officer under whose supervision the probationer has been placed.

(4) Where a probationer is brought before –

(a) a court in respect of an offence under Section 20; or

(b) a court (including a Village Court) in respect of any other offence,

the court before which he is brought shall, before the matter is determined, notify the Chief Probation Officer and the probation officer under whose supervision that probationer is, of the fact that the probationer has been brought before it in respect of the matter.

24 Distribution of order

A copy of a probation order or of an order discharging or varying a probation order shall, as the case requires, be given by the court making the order –

(a) to the probationer on the day on which it is made; and

(b) to the Chief Probation Officer and to the probation officer under whose supervision the probationer is to be or has been placed; and

[818](c) to the Chairman of the Village Court in the area in which the probationer resides.

25 Pre-sentence and other reports

(1) A report under Section 13 or any other report that a probation officer may make to a court in relation to a probationer is not a public record and shall be kept by the court receiving it as a separate record.

(2) A report referred to in Subsection (1) shall be available for inspection or use –

---

[818]Section 24(c) added by *Probate (Amendment) Act* 1990 (No. 19 of 1990), s6.

(a) by a court where the proceedings before it relate to the person the subject of the report; and
(b) by a person assisting the court in his professional capacity in relation to those proceedings; and
(c) by an official of a corrective institution acting in his official capacity in relation to those proceedings; and
(d) by the person the subject of the report or his legal representative – within the precincts of the court; and
(e) where applicable by the prosecution – within the precincts of the court; and
(f) by the Departmental Head or a person authorized by him in writing for that purpose; and
(g) by a probation officer in the course of his duties; and
(h) by a person authorized in writing by the Chief Probation Officer for the purposes of research, study or statistical data and on such conditions as the Chief Probation Officer specifies.

(3) A person who publishes or discloses the contents of, or makes available, a report to any person otherwise than in accordance with Subsection (2) is guilty of an offence.

Penalty: A fine not exceeding K200.00 or imprisonment for a term not exceeding two months.

26 Appeal by probationer

(1) A probationer may appeal or seek leave to appeal in respect of the offence for which he is convicted as if his release on probation were a sentence and where a fine has, in addition, been imposed, the fine shall for the purposes of the appeal or leave to appeal be deemed to form part of that sentence.

(2) While an appeal or application under Subsection (1) is pending, the probationer shall continue to serve his period of probation in accordance with the conditions of the probation order.

27 Discharge on expiry of period of probation

(1) A probation order is deemed to be discharged on the expiry of the period of probation and the person in relation to whom the order applies is discharged in respect of the offence for which he was originally convicted as if he had been sentenced in respect of that offence and had served the sentence.

(2) Notwithstanding Subsection (1), proceedings may be instituted against a person referred to in Subsection (1) –

(a) for any contravention of; or

(b) for failure to comply with,

a condition of a probation order under Section 20(1), within a period of six months after the expiration of the probation order in respect of a breach [819]occurring during the period of probation, and the court may on conviction impose any of the penalties under Section 20(2).

28 Assistance and information to be given to officers

(1) Subject to any other law, the Chief Probation Officer, a Senior Probation Officer and a probation officer has a right to receive assistance and information from the State, provincial government, an individual or other body, for the proper performance of his duties and functions under this Act.

(2) A person who unlawfully withholds information required by or hinders or obstructs a Chief Probation Officer, a Senior Probation Officer, a probation officer or a voluntary probation officer, in the performance of his duties, is guilty of an offence.

Penalty: A fine not exceeding K50.00.

29 Reports

As soon as possible after the close of each calendar year the Chief Probation Officer shall, in respect of that year, submit a report to the Minister in relation to –

(a) the number of persons released on probation; and
(b) the number of probation orders discharged; and
(c) the number of probationers convicted for breaches of probation orders including convictions for other offences committed by probationers; and
(d) the effect of the operation of this Act with respect to probation; and
(e) the particulars of the activities of the Service.

30 Immunity

The Chief Probation Officer, a Senior Probation Officer, a probation officer or a voluntary probation officer is not liable to any action, suit or other proceeding for any act or thing done or omitted to be done by him in good faith in the exercise of any power or the performance of any duty or function conferred or imposed on him by or under this Act.

[819]The Act has “occuring”.

31 Regulations

The Head of State, acting on advice, may make regulations not inconsistent with this Act prescribing all matters that by this Act are permitted or required to be prescribed or that are necessary or convenient to be prescribed for carrying out or giving effect to this Act.

No 19 of 1995

Public Services (Management) Act 1995

PART I – PRELIMINARY

PART II – THE PUBLIC SERVICES COMMISSION

PART III – REVIEW OF PERSONNEL MATTERS

PART IV – REVIEW OF ORGANIZATIONAL MATTERS

PART V – ORGANIZATION OF THE NATIONAL PUBLIC SERVICE

PART VA – CHIEF SECRETARY TO GOVERNMENT

PART VI – DEPARTMENTAL HEADS

Division 1 – General

Division 2 – Contracts of Employment

Division 3 – Acting Appointment of Departmental Heads

Division 4 – Reports

PART VII – CREATION OF OFFICES

PART VIII – QUALIFICATIONS

PART IX – RECRUITMENT

PART X – APPOINTMENTS AND PROMOTIONS

PART XI – CONTACT EMPLOYMENT

PART XII – TRAINING

PART XIII – SALARIES AND ALLOWANCES

PART XIV – DISCIPLINE

PART XV – RESIGNATION AND RETIREMENT

PART XVI – PROVINCIAL GOVERNMENT AND LOCAL-LEVEL GOVERNMENT ADMINISTRATION

PART XVII – GENERAL ORDERS

PART XVIII – MISCELLANEOUS

PART XIX – REPEAL

PART XX – TRANSITIONAL AND SAVING

SCHEDULE 1

OATH AND AFFIRMATION OF OFFICE OF OFFICERS

SCHEDULE 2

REPEALED ACTS

INDEPENDENT STATE OF PAPUA NEW GUINEA.

No 19 of 1995

Public Services (Management) Act 1995

(Consolidated to No 24 of 1998)

Being an Act –

(a) to make provision for the appointment, conditions of employment, constitution, powers, procedures and functions of the Public Services Commission in accordance with Section 190 (*Establishment of the Commission*) and 191 (*Functions of the Commission*) of the *Constitution*; and

(b) to implement Section 195 (*Organisation, etc., of the State Services*) of the *Constitution* in relation to the Public Service; and

(c) to implement the *Organic Law on Provincial Governments and Local-level Governments* insofar as an Act of the Parliament is required to make provision relating to the staffing of Provincial Governments and Local-level Governments; and

[820](d) to make provision for ensuring the implementation of decisions, directions and policies of the National Executive Council by the National Public Service and public bodies,

and for related purposes,

MADE by the National Parliament to come into operation –

(a) insofar as relating to Part XVI (and such other provisions as are directly relevant to the operation of Part XVI) – in accordance with the coming into operation of the *Organic Law on Provincial Governments and Local-level Governments*; and

[820]Paragraph (d) added by the *Public Services (Management) (Amendment) Act 1998* (No 24 of 1998), s2.

(b) insofar as relating to the remainder – in accordance with a notice in the National Gazette by the Head of State, acting with, and in connection with, the advice of the Minister.

PART I – PRELIMINARY

1 Compliance with constitutional requirements

(1) This Act, to the extent that it regulates or restricts a right or freedom referred to in Subsection III.3.C (*qualified rights*) of the *Constitution*, namely: –

(a) freedom of expression conferred by Section 46 of the *Constitution*; and

(b) freedom of assembly and association conferred by Section 47 of the *Constitution*; and

(c) the right to privacy conferred by Section 49 of the *Constitution*; and

(d) the right to vote and stand for public office conferred by Section 50 of the *Constitution*,

is a law that is mate for the purpose of giving effect to the public interest in public order and public welfare.

2 Interpretation

In this Act, unless the contrary intention appears –

"Chairman" means the Chairman of the Commission appointed under Section 5;

[821]"Chief Secretary to Government" means the Chief Secretary to Government under Section 21A;

"classification" means the arrangement of officers or offices in classes, and includes the allotment to officers or offices of salaries or limits of salary according to the value of the work;

"Commission" means the Public Services Commission;

"Departmental Head" means the Head of a Department of the Public Service and includes the persons referred to in Section 75 and any person deemed to be a Departmental Head under any other Act;

[821]The definition "Chief Secretary to Government" was added by the *Public Services (Management) (Amendment) Act* 1998 (No 24 of 1998), s3(a).

"District Administrator" means a District Administrator appointed under Section 73 of the *Organic Law on Provincial Governments and Local-level Governments*, and, in relation to a district, means the District Administrator for that district;

"employee" means a person employed to render temporary assistance in the Public Service, but does not include a person employed in an honorary capacity or a person remunerated by fees, allowances or commission only;

"family", in relation to an officer, means –

(a) a spouse of the officer; and

(b) children under the age of 16 years who are wholly dependent on and maintained by the officer; and

(c) relatives who are wholly dependent on and maintained by the officer in such circumstances that, in the opinion of the Departmental Head of the Department of Personnel Management, they should be regarded as forming part of the officer's family;

"General Orders" means the General Orders provided for by Section 70;

"office" means an office in the Public Service created under Section 22 or 33, or provided under Section 34;

"officer" means an officer in the Public Service, but does not include –

(a) an employee; and

(b) a person employed in an honorary capacity; or

(c) a person remunerated by fees, allowances or commission only;

"officer-in-charge" means an officer or employee who, by virtue of his office, is responsible for the supervision and general working of a branch or section of a Department, and includes an officer or employee who is responsible for the supervision of the work of other officers or employees not under the direct supervision of the officer in charge of the branch or section;

"pay" means salary, and in relation to any provision of this Act includes such allowances as are specified in the General Orders in relation to that provision;

"personnel matters" means decisions and other service matters concerning an individual whether in relation to his appointment, promotion, demotion, transfer, suspension, disciplining or cessation or termination of employment (except cessation or termination at the end of his normal period of employment as determined in accordance with law), or otherwise;

"Provincial Administrative Headquarters" means a Provincial Administrative Headquarters established by Section 72 of the *Organic Law on Provincial Governments and Local-level Governments* and, in relation to a province, means the Provincial Administrative Headquarters for that province;

"Provincial Administrator" means a Provincial Administrator appointed under Section 73(2) of the *Organic Law on Provincial Governments and Local-level Governments* and, in relation to a province, means the Provincial Administrator for that province;

"Provincial Governor" means the Provincial Governor of a province in accordance with the *Organic Law on Provincial Governments and Local-level Governments*, and, in relation to a province, means the Governor of that province;

[822]"public body" means any body, authority or instrumentality (corporate or unincorporate) established by or under an Act or Constitutional Law other than –

(a) a Constitutional Office-holder or the Office of a Constitutional Office-holder; or

(b) a body, authority or instrumentality incorporated or continued in existence under the *Companies Act* 1997;

"the repealed Acts" means the Acts specified in Schedule 2;

"seniority", in relation to an officer, means his seniority as determined in the prescribed manner;

"terms and conditions of service" means the obligations, entitlements and all benefits as specified in General Orders and Regulations;

"this Act" includes the Regulations and the General Orders;

"unattached officer" means an officer who is not occupying an office.

---

[822]The definition "public body" was added by the *Public Services (Management) (Amendment) Act* 1998 (No 24 of 1998), s3(b).

3 Application of this Act

This Act applies to and in relation to Officers, employees and all other persons otherwise employed or engaged under this Act, whether inside or outside Papua New Guinea.

4 Application of *Public Services Conciliation and Arbitration Act* (Chapter 69)

This Act does not affect the operation, in respect of officers and employees, of the *Public Services Conciliation and Arbitration Act* (Chapter 69) or any determination under it.

PART II – THE PUBLIC SERVICES COMMISSION

5 Appointment of Chairman

The Head of State, acting on advice, shall appoint one of the members of the Commission to be the Chairman of the Commission.

6 Conditions of employment

The salary and other conditions of employment of the Chairman and members of the Commission are as determined by the Salaries and Remuneration Commission.

7 Declaration of office

Before entering upon the duties of his office, a member of the Commission shall make the Declaration of Office before the Head of State or a person appointed by the Head of State.

8 Disqualification from office

A person is not qualified to be, or to remain, a member of the Commission if he is –

(a) a member of the Parliament; or
(b) a member of a Provincial Assembly; or
(c) a member of a Local-level Government; or
(d) an office holder in a registered political party; or
(e) an undischarged bankrupt or insolvent; or
(f) of unsound mind within the meaning of any law relating to the protection of the person and property of persons of unsound mind; or
(g) under sentence of death or imprisonment.

9 Special conditions of employment

(1) A member of the Commission shall not –

(a) actively engage in politics; or
(b) subject to Subsection (2), engage either directly or indirectly in the management or control of a corporation or other body of persons carrying on business for profit; or
(c) except on leave granted by the Head of State, or because of illness, absent himself from duty for more than 14 consecutive days or more than 28 days in any period of 12 months; or

(d) subject to Subsection (3), acquire by way of gift or otherwise, or use or hold in any other manner, any interest in any property in Papua New Guinea or solicit, accept or receive any other benefit in addition to his terms and conditions of employment.

(2) Nothing in Subsection (1)(b) or (d) prevents a member of the Commission from holding office –

(a) in a professional body in relation to which his qualifications are relevant; or

(b) as a nominee of Papua New Guinea in a corporation in which Papua New Guinea has a fiscal interest where –

(i) no direct or indirect financial benefit is received by the member as such a nominee; or

(ii) any direct or indirect financial benefit received by the member as such a nominee is paid by him to the Consolidated Revenue Fund.

(3) Subject to the *Organic Law on the Duties and Responsibilities of Leadership*, a member of the Commission may purchase, lease or otherwise acquire land in the same manner and subject to the same conditions as any other citizen.

10 Resignation

(1) A member of the Commission may resign by giving three months' notice in writing of his intention to do so to the Head of State.

(2) The period of three months referred to in Subsection (1) shall be deemed to commence on the twenty-second day after the receipt of the notice by the Head of State, except where the Head of State, acting on advice, given after receiving a report from the appropriate Permanent Parliamentary Committee, by notice in writing to the member, fixes an earlier date.

(3) A member of the Commission may withdraw his resignation at any time before the period of three months referred to in Subsection (1) commences.

11 Retirement

(1) Subject to Subsection (2), a person who has attained the age of 60 years shall not be appointed or re-appointed as the Chairman or a member of the Commission and a person shall not be appointed or re-appointed for a period that extends beyond the date on which he will attain the age of 60 years.

(2) The Head of State, acting on advice, given after consultation with any appropriate Permanent Parliamentary Committee, may, for special reasons in an appropriate case, appoint or re-appoint a person who is over 60 years of age to be the Chairman or a member of the Commission but in no case shall the Chairman or a member of the Commission continue to act as Chairman or a member of the Commission after he has attained the age of 65 years.

12 Acting Chairman and acting members of the Commission

(1) A member of the Commission may be appointed to be an acting Chairman of the Commission –

(a) to fill temporarily a vacancy; or

(b) in the case of the absence from duty for any reason of the Chairman.

(2) A person who is qualified under this Act for appointment may be appointed to be an acting member of the Commission –

(a) to fill temporarily a vacancy; or

(b) in the case of the absence from duty for any reason of a member of the Commission.

(3) Acting appointments under this section shall be made –

(a) in the case of an appointment made for a period of one month or less – by the Head of State, acting with, and in accordance with, the advice of the Minister; and

(b) in the case of an appointment for a period in excess of one month or an extension of an appointment – by the Head of State, acting on advice.

13 Powers of the Commission

(1) The Commission may at any time, for the purpose of performing its functions –

(a) enter premises occupied or used by –

(i) a Department of government; or

(ii) any State Service (other than the Defence Force); or

(iii) any Provincial Government; or

(iv) any other governmental service; and

(b) summons a person whose evidence appears to be material to the determining of any subject, inspection, inquiry, review or investigation being conducted by the Commission; and

(c) take evidence on oath or affirmation and for that purpose administer oaths and affirmations; and

(d) require any person to produce documents within his possession or subject to his control.

(2) A person shall not knowingly make any false or misleading statements in any evidence before the Commission.

Penalty: A fine not exceeding K200.00.

(3) Any officer who neglects or fails, without reasonable cause (the burden of proof of which lies upon him), to attend in obedience to a summons under Subsection (1), or to be sworn or answer questions or produce documents relevant to the subject of an inspection, inquiry or investigation when required to do so under that subsection, is guilty of an offence.

Penalty: A fine not exceeding K200.00.

(4) A person other than an officer who, after payment or tender of reasonable expenses, neglects or fails, without reasonable cause (the burden of proof of which lies upon him), to attend in obedience to a summons under Subsection (1) or to be sworn or answer questions or to produce a document relevant to the subject of an inspection, inquiry or investigation when required so to do under that subsection, is guilty of an offence.

Penalty: A fine not exceeding K200.00.

(5) Nothing in this section renders any person compellable to answer any question that might tend to incriminate him.

(6) In this section, "officer" means –

(a) an officer of the National Public Service; and
(b) a contract officer employed under the *Public Employment (Non-citizens) Act* (Chapter 342); and
(c) an officer of the Police Force; and
(d) an officer or employee of a provincial government; and
(e) an officer of any government service; and
(f) an employee of a service or force referred to in Paragraph (a), (c), (d) or (e); and
(g) an employee,

but does not include a member of the Defence Force.

14 Commission proceedings in camera

Where the Prime Minister certifies that the giving of any information or the answering of any question or the production of any documents or papers or things in public –

(a) may prejudice the security, defence or international relations of Papua New Guinea (including Papua New Guinea's relations with the Government or any other country or with any international organization) or the investigation or detection of offences; or

(b) may involve the disclosure of the proceedings, deliberations or decisions of the National Executive Council or of any Committee or that Council to matters of a secret or confidential nature and would be injurious to the public interest,

the Commission shall require the information or answer to be given, or as the case may be, the document, paper or thing to be produced in camera.

15 Procedures of the Commission

(1) The Commission shall meet at such times and places as are fixed by the Chairman.

(2) The Chairman shall preside at all meetings of the Commission if he is present.

(3) If the Chairman is not present at a meeting of the Commission, the member of the Commission most senior –

(a) in length of service as a Commissioner; or

(b) if all members present have equal length of service as Commissioner – in age,

shall preside at the meeting.

(4) The quorum at a meeting of the Commission is two.

(5) All matters before a meeting of the Commission shall be decided in accordance with the majority of votes of the members present and voting.

(6) In the event of an equality of votes on a matter, the member presiding has a casting, as well as a deliberative, vote.

(7) The Commission shall cause minutes or its meetings to be kept.

(8) Subject to this Act, the procedures of the Commission are as determined by the Commission.

16 Delegation by the Commission

(1) The Commission may, by instrument in writing under the hand of the Chairman, delegate to any person all or any of its powers and functions (other than this power of delegation or any prescribed power or function) so that the delegated powers and functions may be exercised and performed by the delegate in relation to the matter or class of matters specified in the instrument of delegation.

(2) Every delegation under Subsection (1) is revocable, in writing, at will, and no such delegation affects the exercise of a power or the performance of a function by the Commission.

17 Annual report by Commission

(1) The Commission shall, no later than 31 March in each year, give to the Head of State, for presentation to the National Parliament, a report on the work of the Commission and the National Public Service during the preceeding period of 12 months with such recommendations as to improvement as it thinks proper.

(2) Nothing in Subsection (1) prevents the Commission from making, on its own initiative, or at the request of the National Parliament or of the National Executive Council, other reports of the work of the Commission.

PART III – REVIEW OF PERSONNEL MATTERS

18 Review of personnel matters connected with the National Public Service

(1) The Commission shall review a personnel matter connected with the National Public Service either on its own initiative or following a complaint by an officer to the Commission where that officer has been affected by a decision in relation to that personnel matter.

(2) The Commission shall –

(a) complete the review of a personnel matter within 60 days of –

(i) the making of the complaint to the Commission under Subsection (1); or

(ii) where the Commission instigates the review, the instigation of the review; and

(b) shall consider whether the decision in relation to the personnel matter was an appropriate decision having regard to the nature of the decision and the views of the officer and of the Departmental Head; and

(c) recommend the confirmation, variation or revocation of the decision in relation to the personnel matter in writing to the Departmental Head and to the Departmental Head of the Department of Personnel Management.

(3) In carrying out a review of a personnel matter the Commission shall determine its own procedures but shall ensure that the views of the officer affected by the decision are put before it in relation to the personnel matter either in writing or orally.

PART IV – REVIEW OF ORGANIZATIONAL MATTERS

19 Review of organizational matters

(1) In the performance of its duty under Section 19(1)(b) (*Functions of the Commission*) of the *Constitution*, the Commission shall, before deciding whether advice should be given to the National Executive Council or other authority on a particular matter consider –

(a) the relative importance of that matter; and

(b) any advice, recommendations, opinions or views submitted by any governmental body.

(2) In formulating its advice the Commission shall have, as its [823]principal objective, the communication of the view of the individual members of the Commission as representatives of officers of long-standing and experience in the National Public Service.

[823]The Act has "principle".

PART V – ORGANIZATION OF THE NATIONAL PUBLIC SERVICE

20 Departments of the Public Service

(1) Subject to Subsection (2) there shall be –

(a) a Department of the Prime Minister and National Executive Council; and

(b) a Department of Personnel Management; and

(c) such other Departments as are established under Subsection (2).

(2) The Head of State, acting on advice, may, by notice in the National Gazette –

(a) establish a Department; or

(b) abolish a Department; or

(c) alter the name of a Department (including the Department of Personnel Management).

21 Functions of Departments

(1) Subject to Subsection (2), the functions of each Department, other than the Department of Personnel Management, are as determined by the Head of State, acting on advice, given after consideration of reports made to the National Executive Council by the Departmental Head of the Department of Personnel Management.

(2) Subject to Section 24(2), the functions of the Department of Personnel Management are as determined by the Head of State, acting on advice.

[824]PART VA – CHIEF SECRETARY TO GOVERNMENT

21A Chief Secretary to Government

(1) There is established within the National Public Service an office of Chief Secretary to Government.

(2) The Departmental Head of the Department of the Prime Minister and National Executive Council is the Chief Secretary to Government.

(3) The Chief Secretary to Government is the senior officer of the National Public Service.

21B Functions of Chief Secretary to Government

The functions of the Chief Secretary to Government are –

(a) to be the principal adviser to the Prime Minister and to the National Executive Council; and

(b) to co-ordinate policies and initiatives of the National Executive Council; and

(c) to ensure that decisions, directions and policies of the National Executive Council are implemented by the National Public Service and by public bodies; and

(d) to ensure that the National Public Service and public bodies perform effectively and are accountable to the National Executive Council and to the Parliament; and

(e) such other functions as are determined by the National Executive Council.

21C Powers of The Chief Secretary to Government

(1) The Chief Secretary to Government may at any time, for the purpose of the performance of his function under this Act or any other law –

(a) enter premises occupied or used by –

(i) a Department; or

(ii) a Provincial Government; or

(iii) a public body; and

[824]Part VA added by the *Public Services (Management) (Amendment) Act* 1998 (No 24 of 1998), s5.

(b) question a person who appears likely to have information relevant to the functions of the Chief Secretary to Government; and

(c) require any person to provide information relative to the functions of the Chief Secretary to Government; and

(d) require any person to produce documents within his possession or subject to his control where such documents are relevant to the functions of the Chief Secretary to Government; and

(e) issue directions relative to his functions to a Departmental Head and to the head of a public body.

(2) All Departmental Heads, heads of public bodies and officers of the National Public Service and of public bodies shall co-operate with the Chief Secretary to Government in the performance of his functions and the exercise of his powers under this Act.

21D Annual Report by Chief Secretary to Government

(1) The Chief Secretary to Government shall, no later than 31 March in each year, give to the Prime Minister, for presentation to the National Executive Council, a report in respect of implementation by the National Public Service and public bodies, during the year ending 31 December preceding, of Governmental policies and decisions.

(2) Nothing in Subsection (1) prevents the Chief Secretary to Government from making, on his own initiative or at the direction of the Prime Minister, other reports on the implementation, by the National Public Service and public bodies, of Governmental policies and decisions.

PART VI – DEPARTMENTAL HEADS

Division 1 – General

22 Departmental Heads

The Head of State, acting on advice, may, by notice in the National Gazette –

(a) create an office of Departmental Head; or

(b) abolish an office of Departmental Head; or

(c) alter the designation of an office of Departmental Head.

23 Delegation by Departmental Head

A Departmental Head (including the Departmental head of the Department of Personnel Management) may, in respect of an officer or employee or employees included in a class of officers or employees, by writing under his hand delegate to a person all or any of his powers and functions under this Act (except this power of delegation).

24 Responsibilities of Departmental Heads

(1) A Departmental Head –

(a) is responsible for the general working and efficient conduct of his Department; and

(b) shall report to the Departmental Head of the Department of Personnel Management whenever the necessity arises, any alterations that are, in his opinion –

(i) necessary or expedient for the more economical, efficient or convenient working of his Department or any branch of it; or

(ii) necessary in the salaries or allowances of any of the officers under his control; and

(c) shall bring to the attention of the Departmental Head of the Department of Personnel Management any matter, whether in relation to an officer or to the work of a branch or section of his Department, with which he thinks it desirable for the Departmental Head of the Department of Personnel Management to be acquainted; and

[825](ca) is responsible for ensuring that Governmental policies and decisions relative to his Department are implemented and for co-operating with, and complying with any directions issued by, the Chief Secretary to Government in this regard; and

(d) is otherwise responsible for such powers, functions and duties as may be delegated to him under this Act.

(2) The Departmental Head of the Department of Personnel Management –

(a) is responsible for –

(i) the proper administration of this Act; and

(ii) the application and interpretation of terms and conditions of employment in the National Public Service; and

(iii) the setting of terms and conditions of employment for the National Public Service and the setting and prescribing of conditions of service of the National Public Service; and

(iv) the conduct of industrial relations with public sector employee organizations; and

(v) the retrenchment of officers from the National Public Service; and

(vi) the formulating of General Orders under Section 70; and

(b) has such other functions and duties as are specified under Section 21(2) or otherwise in this Act; and

(c) is responsible for selection of –

(i) persons for appointment as officers; and

(ii) officers for appointment, promotion and transfer,

in accordance with the procedures specified in the General Orders.

(3) In the implementation of the functions specified in Subsection (2)(a)(iii), (iv) and (v), the Departmental Head of the Department of Personnel Management may consult with the Departmental Heads of the Departments of the Prime Minister and of the Department responsible for financial matters and of the Department responsible for planning matters.

---

[825]Section 24(1)(ca) added by the *Public Services (Management) (Amendment) Act* 1998 (No 24 of 1998), s6.

25 Filling of vacancies in certain offices of Departmental Head

Subject to Section 193 (*appointments to certain offices*) of the *Constitution*, a vacancy in an office or Departmental Head may be filled –

(a) by the promotion or transfer of an officer by the Head of State, acting on advice; or

(b) by an appointment in accordance with Section 27.

Division 2 – Contracts of Employment

26 Application

The Head of State, acting on advice, may, by notice in the National Gazette, specify the Departmental Heads to whom the provisions of this Division apply.

27 Appointments to offices of Departmental Head

(1) This section is subject to Section 193 (*appointments to certain offices*) of the *Constitution*.

(2) A Departmental Head shall be appointed by the Head of State, acting on advice, given after consultation with the Commission.

28 Contracts of employment

(1) A Departmental Head shall be employed under, and shall hold office in accordance with the terms and conditions of, a contract of employment with the State.

(2) A contract of employment under Subsection (1) shall be executed by the Head of State, acting on advice, on behalf of the State, and by the Departmental Head.

29 Employment under contract to constitute service

Employment under contract under this Division shall constitute service in the National Public Service for all purposes.

30 Cessation of employment in Public Service

A person who is appointed to be a Departmental Head and accordingly enters into a contract of employment under this Division, shall, on the termination of his employment in accordance with the contract of employment, cease to be an officer or employee of the Public Service.

Division 3 – Acting Appointment of Departmental Heads

31 Acting appointments of Departmental Heads

(1) Where a Departmental Head is absent from his office or unable to perform the duties of his office, or when there is a vacancy in an office of Departmental Head, the Head of State, acting on advice given after receiving a recommendation from the Minister, may appoint another officer to act in the place of the officer during his absence or inability, or may appoint an officer to fill the vacancy temporarily.

(2) A person appointed in an acting or temporary capacity under Subsection (1) shall not be employed in that capacity on a contract of employment under Section 28.

Division 4 – Reports

32 Reports

(1) Each Departmental Head shall –

(a) by 31 March in each year, prepare a report on the attainment of the planned objectives of his Department for the year ending 31 December preceding; and

(b) twice yearly, at such times as are specified in the General Orders, produce or cause to be produced an assessment of the ability and conduct of each officer in his Department; and

(c) produce or cause to be produced such further reports as may be required by

(i) the Departmental head of the Department of Personnel Management; or

(ii) the National Executive Council.

(2) Reports prepared under Subsection (1) shall be forwarded to the Departmental Head of the Department of Personnel Management.

(3) The reports prepared under Subsection (1)(a) shall be forwarded by the Departmental Head of the Department of Personnel Management to the Minister for presentation to the National Executive Council.

PART VII – CREATION OF OFFICES

33 Creation and abolition of offices

(1) This section does not apply to an office of Departmental Head.

(2) The Departmental Head of the Department of Personnel Management may, in relation to a Department –

(a) create an office and specify the qualifications for, and the duties of, the office; or

(b) abolish an office; or

(c) alter the designation of an office; or

(d) raise the classification of an office; or

(e) lower the classification of an office; or

(f) alter the qualifications for, or the duties of, an office; or

(g) transfer an office from one Department to another Department.

(3) Subject to Subsections (4) and (5), where a Department is re-organized, all offices in the Department are deemed to be vacant and shall be advertized in accordance with this Act.

(4) Where –

(a) a Department is re-organized; and

(b) the re-organization affects numbers of offices and/or designations of offices or of a class of offices,

the Departmental Head of the Department of Personnel Management may, by notice in the National Gazette, deem those offices or classes of offices not to be affected by the re-organization.

(5) Substantive occupants of offices or classes of offices the subject of a National Gazette notice under Subsection (4) shall retain their offices and such offices shall not be advertized.

34 Temporary offices

The Departmental Head of the Department of Personnel Management may, in his discretion –

(a) create or abolish an office and/or upgrade or downgrade the classification of an office; or

(b) appoint, transfer or redeploy a person from one office to another,

for the purpose of project implementation and other such purposes.

PART VIII – QUALIFICATIONS

35 Qualifications for admission to the Public Service

A person shall not be appointed under this Act as an officer unless –

(a) he provides evidence to the satisfaction of the Department of Personnel Management, of –

  (i) his health and physical fitness; and

  (ii) his possession of qualifications that will enable him to perform the duties of the office to which he is to be appointed; and

  (iii) his good character; and

(b) he makes and subscribes the oath or affirmation in Schedule 1.

PART IX – RECRUITMENT

36 Recruitment

(1) A Departmental Head may, by notice published in the National Gazette or elsewhere, invite persons to apply for appointment, promotion or transfer to a vacant office in the Department of which he is the Departmental Head.

(2) A Departmental Head shall specify in the notice –

(a) the office or class of offices in respect of which applications for appointment, promotion or transfer are invited; and

(b) the salaries, or limits of salaries, that will be applicable on appointment, promotion or transfer; and

(c) where applicable –

(i) the age limits for appointment; and

(ii) the qualifications required to be possessed for appointment, promotion or transfer and the period (if any) within which the qualifications or any of them must have been obtained; and

(iii) the date on which persons who obtain or have obtained the required qualifications during a period specified for the purposes of Subparagraph (ii) will cease to be qualified for appointment, promotion or transfer by virtue of those qualifications; and

(iv) that only males or only females will be appointed, promoted or transferred in particular proportions; and

(d) the manner of ascertaining the order in which offers of appointments, promotions or transfers will be made; and

(e) the date by which applications are required to be made; and

(f) such other matters (if any), not inconsistent with this Act, as the Departmental Head thinks desirable.

(3) Subject to Subsection (4), a Departmental Head shall not advertize and/or make an acting appointment against an office in his Department which has a substantive occupant.

(4) Where the substantive occupant of an office vacates the office for leave and/or study purposes, a Departmental Head may make an acting appointment to the office for the duration of the absence of the substantive occupant.

37 Temporary employment

(1) Where, in the opinion of the Departmental Head of the Department of Personnel Management, the business of a Department –

(a) warrants the engagement of temporary assistance to provide a particular skill or service to a Department; or

(b) has given rise to an unexpected workload which could not have been anticipated and is not expected to continue for more than six months,

the Departmental Head of the Department of Personnel Management may approve the employment of a person or persons to render temporary assistance to that Department.

(2) A person employed under Subsection (1) shall be employed on contract in a form specified in the General Orders.

(3) Notwithstanding the provisions of Subsection (1)(b), a person may be employed on contract under this section for a period in excess of six months where the Departmental Head of the Department of Personnel Management so authorizes.

(4) A National contract to which this section applies shall provide for a salary and for duty-related allowances, and discretionary allowance may be applied for by the National contract employee to the Departmental Head of the Department of Personnel Management and approved by that Departmental Head if he considers it warranted.

PART X – APPOINTMENTS AND PROMOTIONS

38 Effect of *Constitution*, Section 193

With regard to officers and offices to whom or to which Section 193 (*Appointment to Certain Offices*) of the *Constitution* applies, this Part shall be read subject to that section.

39 Acting appointments

Where an officer other than a Departmental Head is absent from his office or unable to perform the duties of his office for purposes specified in Section 36(4) or when there is a vacancy in an office other than an office of Departmental Head, the Departmental Head concerned may, if he thinks fit, appoint another officer to act in the place of the officer during his absence for inability, or may appoint an officer to fill the vacancy temporarily.

PART XI – CONTACT EMPLOYMENT

40 Designation of senior management offices

(1) The Minister may, pursuant to a directive of the National Executive Council, by notice in the National Gazette, designate an office, other than an office of Departmental Head created under Section 22, as a senior management office and the provisions of this Part shall apply to an office so designated.

(2) A notice under Subsection (1) shall specify, in relation to each senior management office, whether a person is to be appointed to that office by –

(a) the Head of State, acting on advice; or

(b) the Departmental Head of the Department of Personnel Management,

and an appointment shall be made in accordance with this Act.

(3) A person to be appointed to a senior management office shall –

(a) be an officer of the Public Service; or

(b) subject to Subsection (4), by virtue of his appointment, become an officer of the Public Service.

(4) A person referred to in Subsection (3)(b) shall only be appointed if he is eligible for appointment to the Public Service as otherwise required by this Act.

41 Contracts of employment

(1) An officer appointed to a senior management office shall be employed under, and shall hold office in accordance with, the terms and conditions of a contract of employment with the State, made subject to the *Salaries and Conditions Monitoring Committee Act* 1988.

(2) A contract of employment under Subsection (1) shall be executed on behalf of the State by –

(a) in respect of appointees under Section 40(2)(a) – the Head of State; and

(b) in respect of appointees under Section 40(2)(b) – the Departmental Head of the Department of Personnel Management,

and by the appointee.

(3) Notwithstanding the provisions of this Act relating to discipline of officers, a contract of employment under Subsection (1) shall make specific provision for discipline and an officer employed under a contract

of employment under Subsection (1) is exempted from the provisions of Part XIV.

(4) Notwithstanding the provisions of this Act relating to promotion and appointment, where –

(a) a contract of employment under Subsection (1) terminates or is terminated and is not subsequently renewed; and

(b) the appointee under that contract of employment is not re-appointed to another office under this Act,

his employment in the Public Service is terminated.

(5) The provisions of this Act shall apply to an officer employed on a contract of employment under this section only in so far as they are not inconsistent with the terms and conditions of the contract of employment.

42 Employment under contract to constitute service

Employment under contract under this Part shall constitute service in the Public Service for all purposes.

43 Administration of contracts

(1) The Departmental Head of the Department of Personnel Management shall, on behalf of the State, interpret any contract of employment made under this Part.

(2) An amendment to be made to a contract of employment under this Part –

(a) by reason of a directive of the National Executive Council; or

(b) to accord with General Orders; or

(c) for administrative purposes,

shall be authorized –

(d) in respect of contracts of employment to which Section 40(2)(a) refers – by the Minister; or

(e) in respect of contracts of employment to which Section 40(2)(b) refers – by the Departmental Head of the Department of Personnel Management.

PART XII – TRAINING

44 Training

(1) The Departmental Head of the Department of Personnel Management is responsible for initiating and co-ordinating manpower, career and training plans for the Public Service.

(2) A Departmental Head is responsible for –

(a) producing manpower, career and training plans for the Department of which he is Departmental Head; and

(b) submitting by 31 March of each year to the Departmental Head of the Department of Personnel Management plans produced under Paragraph (a).

(3) Any request for training, whether local or overseas, by or on behalf of an officer shall be consistent with the manpower, career and training plans of the Department of which he is an officer.

(4) An officer who is sent on study leave for promotion to a higher office shall, on successful completion of that study, be promoted to that higher office.

(5) An officer on a senior national contract who proceeds on study leave of more than three months shall forfeit all entitlements to the office for which he is contracted except –

(a) the substantive salary; and

(b) if he is not living in a State rent-free house, the housing allowance.

PART XIII – SALARIES AND ALLOWANCES

45 Salary classifications

(1) Offices shall be given such classifications as are fixed by the Departmental Head of the Department of Personnel Management.

(2) A classification under Subsection (1) may provide for a rate of annual salary or a scale of rates of annual salary.

(3) In fixing classifications under this section, the Departmental Head of the Department of Personnel Management shall comply with any general directions of the National Executive Council.

46 Allowances

Officers may be paid such allowances in such cases as are specified in the General Orders.

47 Deductions from officers' entitlements

Deductions may be made from the entitlement of officers and employees as specified in the General Orders, or as determined by the Minister, in relation to an officer or class of officer, or employee or class of employee for any service provided by the State or as a service to the officer or employee by the State.

48 Recovery of salary and allowances

(1) All amounts of salary and allowances payable to an officer may be recovered by the officer as a debt in any court of competent jurisdiction.

(2) The State nay, with the consent of an officer, effect deductions from the salary of an officer to recover debts due by the officer to the State.

49 Pay during suspension

Subject to Section 48, where an officer has been suspended in connection with a charge of an offence under this Act, he is entitled to receive his pay during the period of suspension, unless he absconds or the Departmental Head of the Department of Personnel Management, after receiving a report from the Departmental Head, orders otherwise.

PART XIV – DISCIPLINE

50 Disciplinary offences

An officer who –

(a) commits a breach of this Act; or

(b) except as authorized in the course of official duty, does or divulges, directly or indirectly, any confidential information concerning public business or any matters of which he has official knowledge; or

(c) except with the consent of the Head of State, acting on advice, or of an officer authorized for the purpose by the Head of State, acting on advice, publicly comments on administrative action or the administration of a Department; or

(d) wilfully disobeys or disregards a lawful order made or given by a person having authority to make or give it; or

(e) is negligent or careless in the discharge of his duties; or

(f) is inefficient or incompetent from causes within his own control; or

(g) uses intoxicating liquors or drugs to excess; or

(h) solicits or accepts a fee, reward, gratuity or gift in connection with the discharge of his official duties (other than his official remuneration); or

(i) is guilty of disgraceful or improper conduct in his official capacity or otherwise; or

(j) having taken an oath or made an affirmation in the form in Schedule 1, does or says anything in violation of it; or

(k) seeks the influence or interest of any person in order to gain promotion, transfer or other advantage; or

(l) supplies to another officer, for use for any purpose referred to in Paragraph (k), a certificate or testimonial relating to official capacity or the performance of official duties,

is guilty of a disciplinary offence and is liable to be dealt with and punished –

(m) in the case of a Departmental Head – under Part VI; and

(n) in the case of an officer other than a Departmental Head – under this Part.

51 Dealing with minor disciplinary offences

(1) If the Departmental Head, or an officer authorized by the Departmental Head to deal with minor offences, has reason to believe that an officer other than a Departmental Head has committed a disciplinary offence that, in his opinion, would properly be dealt with under this section, he may call on the officer for an explanation as to the alleged offence, and if, on consideration of the explanation, he is of the opinion that the offence has been committed, he may caution or reprimand the offending officer.

(2) A caution or reprimand by an officer other than the Departmental Head shall be immediately reported to the Departmental Head.

52 Dealing with serious disciplinary offences

(1) Where there is reason to believe that an officer other than a Departmental Head has committed a disciplinary offence other than an offence that may be dealt with under Section 51, the provisions of this section apply.

(2) The officer may –

(a) be charged by his Departmental Head or an officer authorized by the Departmental Head to lay charges under this Division; and

(b) if it is considered that the charge is of such a serious nature that the charged officer should not continue in the performance of his duty, be suspended by –

(i) his Departmental Head; or

(ii) in case of emergency – an officer authorized by the Departmental Head to lay charges under this Division.

(3) Suspension may be effected before, at the time of or after the laying of the charge, and may be removed at any time by the Departmental Head concerned pending determination of the charge, and where the charge has not been sustained shall be lifted immediately on a finding to that effect.

(4) On a charge being laid against an officer, he shall –

(a) promptly be given a copy of the charge; and

(b) be directed –

(i) to reply promptly in writing, stating whether he admits or denies the truth of the charge; and

(ii) to give any explanation that he desires to give in regard to it, and if a reply is not given by the officer within seven days after his receipt of the charge he may be deemed to have admitted the truth of the charge.

(5) If, after considering reports relating to the offence and charge, the reply and explanation (if any) of the officer charged and any further report that he thinks necessary, the Departmental Head concerned is of the opinion that the charge has been sustained, he may –

(a) fine the officer a sum not exceeding 20% of the officer's gross fortnightly pay; or

(b) reduce the officer's pay; or

(c) reduce the officer to an office having a lower classification, and to a salary within that classification; or

(d) in addition to or instead of imposing a punishment specified in Paragraph (a), (b) or (c), transfer the officer to some other office or locality; or

(e) dismiss the officer from the Public Service.

(6) The Departmental Head shall notify an officer of a punishment imposed or recommendation made by him under Subsection (5).

53 Officer charged with criminal offence

(1) Where an officer other than a Departmental Head is charged by Police with having committed a criminal offence he shall –

(a) where the criminal offence relates to the duties of his office – be suspended without pay by his Departmental Head; or

(b) where the offence does not relate to the duties of his office – be suspended on full pay by his Departmental Head.

(2) Where the officer is convicted of an offence which relates to the duties of his office by a court of competent jurisdiction, he shall be dismissed from the Public Service by the Departmental Head.

(3) Where the officer is convicted of an offence which does not relate to the duties of his office by a court of competent jurisdiction, he shall be dismissed by the Departmental Head, unless the Departmental Head otherwise determines.

54 Strikes

(1) An officer who aids, abets, forments or takes part in a strike that –

(a) interferes with or prevents; or

(b) is intended or calculated to interfere with or prevent,

the carrying on of any part of the public services or utilities of the country, or who attempts to do so, is deemed to have committed an illegal action against the peace and good order of the country.

(2) Any officer adjudged by the Departmental Head, after investigation and hearing, to be guilty of any action referred to in Subsection (1) may be summarily dismissed by the Departmental Head from the Public Service, without regard to the procedure prescribed in this Act for dealing with disciplinary offence.

PART XV – RESIGNATION AND RETIREMENT

55 Persons who have resigned from the Public Service to become candidates at elections

(1) An officer –

(a) who resigned or retired from the Public Service in order to become a candidate for election to –

(i) the National Parliament; or

(ii) a Provincial Assembly; and

(b) whose resignation or retiral was effected –

(i) in the case of a general election to be held at the expiry of the normal term specified for the Parliament or Provincial Assembly – at least six months before and not more than 12 months before the issue of writs for the election; or

(ii) in the case of a general election other than one referred to in Subparagraph (i) – within two weeks of the vote occasioning the election; or

(iii) in the case of a by-election – within two weeks or the event occasioning the by-election; and

(c) who was a candidate at the election; and

(d) who failed to be elected,

shall, upon application by him within two months after the declaration of the result of the election, and subject to the results of any medical examination under Subsection (3), be re-appointed to the Public Service in such office as the Departmental Head of the Department of Personnel Management directs.

(2) An officer –

(a) who resigned from the Public Service in order to become a candidate for election to –

(i) the National Parliament; or

(ii) a Provincial Assembly; and

(b) whose resignation or retiral was effected other than in accordance with Subsection (1)(b),

shall not be re-appointed to the Public Service.

(3) A person to be re-appointed under Subsection (1) may, at the discretion of the Departmental Head or the Department of Personnel

Management, be required to undergo medical examination.

(4) A person re-appointed under Subsection (1) shall be deemed to have continued in the Public Service as if he had not resigned or retired but had been on leave without pay during the period from the day on which his resignation became effective to and including the day immediately preceding the day on which he was re-appointed.

(5) The period referred to in Subsection (4) shall not be deemed to affect the continuity of the officer's service but, unless otherwise determined by the Departmental Head of the Department of Personnel Management, shall not, for any purpose, form part of any officer's service.

(6) The provisions of Part IX do not apply in respect of the re-appointment of a person under Subsection (1).

56 Age of retirement

(1) Subject to this section, an officer who has attained the age of 50 years is entitled to retire from the Public Service if he desires to do so, but such an officer may, subject to this Act, continue in the Public Service until he attains the age of 60 years.

(2) An officer who continues in the Public Service after he has attained the age at which he is entitled to retire –

(a) may be retired from the Service at any time before attaining the age of 60 years; and

(b) shall retire from the service on attaining the age of 60 years.

(3) A retirement under Subsection (2)(a) shall be affected by the Departmental Head of the Department of Personnel Management.

57 Retirement on account of infirmity or incapacity

(1) If a Departmental Head appears to the Head of State, acting on advice, after full investigation of the circumstances –

(a) to be, by reason of mental or bodily infirmity for any other reason, unfit to discharge or incapable of discharging the duties of his office efficiently; or

(b) to have ceased to have the qualifications specified for his office, or to be or to have become legally disqualified from carrying out those duties or legally incompetent to carry them out,

the Head of State, acting on advice given after receiving a report from the Departmental Head of the Department of Personnel Management, may retire the officer from the Public Service or transfer him to some other position of equal or lower status and pay.

(2) If an officer, other than a Departmental Head, appears to the Departmental Head, after full investigation of the circumstances –

(a) to be, by reason or mental [826]of bodily infirmity or for any other reason, unfit to discharge or incapable of discharging the duties of his office efficiently; or

(b) to have ceased to have the qualifications specified for his office, or to be or to have become legally disqualified from carrying out those duties or legally incompetent to carry them out,

the Departmental Head of the Department of Personnel Management after receiving a report from the Departmental Head, may retire the officer from the Public Service or transfer him to some other position of equal or lower status and pay.

(3) The retirement of an officer under this section shall not be deemed to be on account of mental or bodily infirmity unless it is so stated in the instrument affecting the retirement.

[826]The Act has "or".

PART XVI – PROVINCIAL GOVERNMENT AND LOCAL-LEVEL GOVERNMENT ADMINISTRATION

58 Provincial and Local-level Administrative organization

The Head of State, acting on advice, given after receiving a report from the Departmental Head of the Department of Personnel Management, may, by notice in the National Gazette –

(a) establish; or

(b) abolish; or

(c) alter the name of,

a provincial and local-level administrative organization in a province.

59 Functions of a Provincial and Local-level Administrative Organization

The functions of a provincial and local-level administrative organization in a province are –

(a) to effect the administration required by the *Organic Law on Provincial Governments and Local-level Governments*; and

(b) such other functions as are determined by the Head of State, acting on advice.

60 Appointment procedures in relation to Provincial Administrator

Where there is, or is likely to be, a vacancy in the office of Provincial Administrator in a province, the Departmental Head of the Department of Personnel Management shall submit to the Provincial Governor for the consideration of the Provincial Executive Council a list of persons suitable for appointment to the office.

61 Appointment procedures in relation to District Administrator

Where there is, or is likely to be, a vacancy in the office of a District Administrator, the Departmental Head of the Department of Personnel Management shall, in implementation of the consultation requirement in Section 73(3) of *the Organic Law on Provincial Governments and Local-level Governments* –

(a) give written notification of the vacancy or likely vacancy to the Departmental Head of the Department responsible for provincial and local-level government matters; and

(b) convene a selection hearing process as provided under General Orders in which process the relevant Provincial Administrator is to be involved; and

(c) thereafter notify the Departmental Head of the Department responsible for provincial and local-level government matters of the name of the officer (or names of the officers) recommended.

62 Terms and conditions of employment of Provincial Administrators and District Administrators

(1) A –

(a) Provincial Administrator; and

(b) District Administrator,

shall be –

(c) an officer of the Public Service; and

(d) subject to the *Salaries and Conditions Monitoring Committee Act* 1988, employed on terms and conditions determined by the Departmental Head of the Department of Personnel Management after consultation with the Provincial Governor of the province concerned.

(2) In any submission which he may make relative to the consultation under Subsection (1), the Provincial Governor shall give due consideration to –

(a) the equivalent job values in the National Public Service; and

(b) any special hardship conditions relating to his province.

63 Additional functions of Provincial Administrator

In addition to the functions specified in Section 74(1) of the *Organic Law on Provincial Governments and Local-level Governments*, the Provincial Administrator of a province –

(a) is the chief adviser to the Provincial Governor and to the Provincial Executive Council; and

(b) subject to relevant National laws is responsible to the Provincial Executive Council for strategic planning and financial and human resource management.

64 Additional functions of District Administrator

In addition to the functions specified in Section 74(2) of *the Organic Law on Provincial Governments and Local-level Governments*, a District Administrator –

(a) is the chief adviser to Local-level Governments in the district; and

(b) is responsible for planning at district level; and

(c) is responsible for the supervision of officers in the district.

65 Assignment of staff

(1) The Departmental Head of the Department of Personnel Management may [827]assign officer to a provincial and local-level administrative organization through procedures set out in this Act.

(2) An officer assigned under Subsection (1) is responsible to the Provincial Administrator.

66 Secondment of staff to and from other bodies

(1) Subject to Subsection (2), a Provincial Administrator may arrange for the secondment of –

(a) an officer from the provincial and local-level administrative organization to any other public or private body; or

(b) a person from any other public or private body to the provincial and local-level administrative organization,

for training or specialist service purposes.

(2) Before arranging a secondment under Subsection (1), a Provincial Administrator shall consult with –

(a) the Departmental Head of the Department of Personnel Management; and

(b) the Departmental Head of the Department responsible for provincial and local-level government matters.

67 Matters relating to Provincial Treasurers and other officers assigned to Provincial and District Treasuries

(1) A Provincial Treasurer shall be an officer of the Public Service.

(2) The recruitment, appointment, promotion, transfer, discipline and termination of the Provincial Treasurer and other officers of the Provincial and District Treasury are those applicable to officers under

---

[827]Sic.

this Act.

68 Provincial Government and Local-level Government Secretariats

(1) The Head of State, acting on advice, may, by notice in the National Gazette –

(a) establish; or
(b) abolish; or
(c) change the name of,

a Provincial Government and Local-level Government Secretariat for a province.

(2) The Head of State, acting on advice given after considering a recommendation from the Departmental Head of the Department of Personnel Management, may, by notice in the National Gazette –

(a) create; or
(b) abolish; or
(c) upgrade; or
(d) downgrade; or
(e) rename,

the Office of Head of a Provincial Government and Local-level Government Secretariat.

(3) Subject to Subsection (4), the Provincial Administrator may, after consultation with the Departmental Head of the Department of Personnel Management –

(a) create; or
(b) abolish; or
(c) upgrade; or
(d) downgrade; or
(e) alter the designation and/or classification of,

an office in the Provincial Government and Local-level Government Secretariat, other than the office of Head of the Secretariat.

(4) The size of the establishment for a Provincial Government and Local-level Government Secretariat shall not exceed –

(a) three offices to service the Provincial Executive Council; and
(b) four offices to service the Provincial Assembly; and
(c) six offices to service each Local-level Government.

(5) The Head of a Provincial Government and Local-level Government Secretariat is responsible to the Provincial Administrator for

the efficient performance of the functions of the Secretariat.

69 Appointments to offices in Provincial Governments and Local-level Governments Secretariats, etc

(1) The Provincial Administrator shall, on the recommendation of a Public Service Selection Committee constituted under this Act, appoint the Head of the Provincial Governments and Local-level Governments Secretariat.

(2) Procedures for selection, appointment, promotion, transfer, discipline and termination of staff of a Provincial Government and Local-level Government Secretariat are those applicable to officers of the Public Service and shall be administered by the Provincial Administrator.

(3) The Departmental Head of the Department of Personnel Management may assign officers to a Provincial Government and Local-level Government Secretariat for a specified period which may be extended.

(4) Staff seconded to a Provincial Government and Local-level Government Secretariat from a body other than the Public Service shall be seconded in accordance with provisions of that body relating to secondment.

PART XVII – GENERAL ORDERS

70 General Orders

(1) The Departmental Head of the Department of Personnel Management may give to officers directions (to be known as "General Orders"), not inconsistent with this Act, as to any matter prescribed by this Act to be so provided for or that is necessary or desirable for the efficient management and control of the Public Service.

(2) In formulating General Orders under Subsection (1), the Departmental Head of the Department of Personnel Management shall give effect to any relevant decisions on policy made by the National Executive Council.

PART XVIII – MISCELLANEOUS

71 Interpretation of Part XVIII

In this Part –

"designated position" means an office declared under Section 72 to be a designated position for the purposes of this Division;

"the Education Gazette" means the publication known as the Papua New Guinea Education Gazette published under the authority of the Departmental Head of the Department responsible for education matters;

"teacher" means a teacher within the meaning of the *Education Act* (Chapter 163).

72 Designated positions

The Departmental Head of the Department responsible for education matters may, by notice in the National Gazette, declare offices the occupants of which are required to be teachers, and teaching officers in the Department responsible for education matters for which teaching qualifications are desirable, to be designated positions for the purposes of this Division.

73 Appointment to designated positions

(1) Subject to the *Teaching Service Act* (Chapter 71) any member of the Teaching Service may be appointed to a designated position.

(2) An appointment referred to in Subsection (1) is not subject to probation.

(3) Subject to Subsection (2), Part IX applies to and in relation to an appointment in accordance with Subsection (1) as though it were a promotion.

(4) A member of the Teaching Service who is appointed to a designated position in accordance with this section is entitled, in place of any existing or accruing rights to which he was entitled in the Teaching Service immediately before the appointment, to such rights as are determined by the Departmental Head of the Department of Personnel Management and specified in his instrument of appointment.

(5) In Subsection (5), "existing or accruing rights" means rights or contingent rights in respect of –

(a) sick leave; and

(b) recreation leave; and

(c) furlough; and

(d) leave fares,

other than any such rights to the extent that he has already received benefits in respect of them in the Teaching Service.

(6) The service in the Teaching Service of a member of that Service who is appointed to a designated position in accordance with this section, and any previous service in the Public Service that was continuous with that service shall, for the purposes of this Act, be counted as service in the Public Service.

(7) This Act does not prevent a member of the Teaching Service who is appointed to a designated position in accordance with this section from being transferred or promoted to an office other than a designated position, but on promotion or transfer he shall be deemed, for all the purposes of this Act, to be an employee unless he was a transferred officer within the meaning of Section 125 of the *Teaching Service Act* (Chapter 71).

74 Eligibility for appointment to offices generally

(1) Notwithstanding this Act but subject to Subsection (2), a member [828]of the Teaching Service who ceased to be an officer by virtue of Section 126 of the Teaching Service Act (Chapter 71) is eligible to apply for promotion to any vacant office.

(2) For the purposes of this Part the pay, or scale of rates of pay, to which a member of the Teaching Service is entitled as such a member shall be taken into account as though it were the pay, or the scale of rates of pay, to which he is entitled in the Public Service.

75 Powers of Commissioner General of Internal Revenue and Auditor-General and Provincial Administrators

For the purposes of this Act –

(a) the Commissioner General of Internal Revenue; and

(b) the Auditor-General; and

(c) a Provincial Administrator; and

(d) such other officers or employees as are so specified by the Head of State, acting on advice,

shall, in relation to the officers and employees of, and offices in, the branches or sections of which they are respectively in charge, be deemed to be the Departmental Heads.

[828]The Act has "or".

76 Engagement in outside employment and acquisition of land

(1) Subject to this section, except with the permission of the Departmental Head of the Department of Personnel Management (which permission may be withdrawn at any time) an officer shall not –

(a) accept or continue to hold an office in or under the Government of another country or in or under any public or municipal corporation; or

(b) accept or continue to hold or discharge the duties of, or be employed in, a paid office in connection with any banking, insurance, agricultural, mining, mercantile or other commercial business, whether carried on by a corporation, a firm or an individual; or

(c) engage in or undertake any such business as principal or as agent; or

(d) engage or continue in the private practice of any profession, occupation or trade; or

(e) enter into any employment, whether remunerative or not, with any person, company or firm who or which is so engaged; or

(f) accept or engage in any remunerative employment other than in connection with the duties of his office or offices in the Public Service.

(2) Subject to the succeeding provisions of this section, Subsection (1) does not prevent an officer from becoming a member or shareholder only of an incorporated company or of a company or society or persons registered under a law of the country or elsewhere, but he shall not take any part in the conduct of the business of the company or society otherwise than by the exercise of his right to vote as a member or shareholder.

(3) The Departmental Head of the Department of Personnel Management may, by notice in the National Gazette, list companies and societies or persons which are authorized companies and societies for the purposes of this section.

(4) Except with the written consent of the Departmental Head of the Department of Personnel Management, an officer shall not personally or by his agent –

(a) hold shares in a company or society of persons operating in the country other than in a company or society authorized under Subsection (3); or

(b) acquire land in the country other than land on which a building is or is to be erected that is to be occupied by him as a resident or a dwelling-house for occasional use by him for purposes of health.

(5) For the purposes of Subsection (4), the wife of an officer shall be deemed to be the agent of her husband.

(6) Subsection (4) does not prevent an officer from acquiring land in accordance with custom.

(7) Notwithstanding this section, an officer may, with the approval of the Departmental Head of the Department of Personnel Management (which approval may at any time be withdrawn) act as a director of a co-operative company.

77 Air Insurance Cover

(1) Subject to Subsection (9), where an officer travels by air on official duty and suffers death or permanent and total incapacity arising as a result, the State is liable in accordance with this section.

(2) The amount of the liability of the State under this section is an amount, not being less than K4,000.00 nor more than K30,000.00 determined by the Head of State, acting on advice, on receipt of a report by a Committee of Inquiry appointed by the Minister.

(3) The amount of the liability of the State under Subsection (2) is reduced by any ticket insurance entitlement or by any payment in the nature of insurance due or received from the airline concerned, or by arrangement with it.

(4) In the case of the death of an officer, the State is not liable under this section where there are no dependants of the officer surviving him.

(5) In the case of the death of an officer leaving dependants, the amount payable under this section shall be apportioned between the dependants of the officer in such manner as is fixed by the Minister.

(6) Any amount that would otherwise be payable under this section shall be reduced by the amount of any damages received from the owner or operator of the aircraft involved.

(7) Where damages are received by the owner [829]or operator of the aircraft involved after payment has been made under this section, the amount by which the payment would otherwise have been reduced under this section may be recovered as a debt by the State from the person

[829]The Act has "of".

receiving the damages.

(8) Any payment made under this section is in addition to and not in substitution for or reduction of any liability of the State under the *Workers' Compensation Act* or otherwise.

(9) This section does not apply to an officer travelling in his own aircraft.

78 Regulations

The Head of State, acting on advice, may make regulations, not inconsistent with this Act, prescribing all matters that by this Act are required or permitted to be prescribed, or that are necessary or convenient to be prescribed for carrying out or giving effect to this Act, or for the more efficient control and management of the Public Service, and in particular for prescribing penalties.

PART XIX – REPEAL

79 Repeal

(1) Subject to Subsection (2), the Acts specified in Schedule 2 are repealed.

(2) The Acts repealed by Subsection (1) shall remain in operation after the coming into operation of this Act to the extent necessary to give effect to Sections 83, 84 and 85 of this Act.

PART XX – TRANSITIONAL AND SAVING

80 Transfer of Departments

The Departments established under the repealed Acts and in existence immediately before the coming into operation of this Act, shall, on that coming into operation, be deemed to be Departments established under Section 20.

81 Transfer of offices

All offices (including offices of Departmental Heads) established under the repealed Acts and in existence immediately before the coming into operation of this Act shall, on that coming into operation, be deemed to be offices created under this Act with –

(a) the same designation; and

(b) the same duties; and

(c) a requirement or the same qualifications; and

(d) the same classifications,

that they had, and in the same Departments as they were in, under the repealed Acts immediately before the coming into operation of this Act.

82 Transfer of officers

(1) A person who, immediately before the coming into operation of this Act, was a Departmental Head under the repealed Acts shall be deemed, on that coming into operation, to be a Departmental Head under this Act.

(2) An officer who, immediately before the coming into operation of this Act, was the substantive occupant of an office under the repealed Acts, shall be deemed, on that coming into operation, to have been appointed to the equivalent office under this Act.

(3) A person who, immediately before the coming into operation of this Act, was an unattached officer under any provision of the repealed Acts shall, on that coming into operation, be deemed to be an unattached officer under the equivalent provision of this Act.

(4) Where a person to whom Subsection (1), (2) or (3) applies was, immediately before the coming into operation of this Act, an officer on probation under the repealed Acts, he shall be deemed to be an officer on probation under this Act for the period of probation remaining unexpired immediately before that commencement.

(5) A person who, immediately before the coming into operation of this Act, was an employee under the repealed Acts shall, on that coming into operation, be deemed to be an employee under this Act.

(6) An officer or employee who was, immediately before the coming into operation of this Act, acting in an office by virtue of the provisions of the repealed Acts shall, on that commencement, continue so to act under this Act.

83 Disciplinary offences

(1) Where, prior to the coming into operation of this Act an officer has been charged with committing a disciplinary offence under the repealed Acts, and on that coming into operation the procedure set out for dealing with the disciplinary offence under the repealed Acts had not been completed, that disciplinary offence shall continue to be dealt with in accordance with the provisions of the repealed Acts.

(2) For the purposes of this Act, an offence against the repealed Acts committed prior to the coming into operation of this Act, but in respect of which no charge had been made at that coming into operation, shall be deemed to be a disciplinary offence under Section 50 of this Act.

84 Procedure in respect of appointments, etc

Where, procedure required in respect of an appointment, promotion or transfer commenced under the repealed Acts prior to the coming into operation of this Act has not been finalized at that coming into operation, the Departmental Head of the Department of Personnel Management may order –

(a) that the matter be finalized using the procedure under the repealed Acts; or

(b) that the matter be finalized under the procedure provided for in this Act and that so much of the procedure as was carried out under the repealed Acts be considered, in so far as appropriate, as procedure provided for under this Act; or

(c) that the procedure is so far as carried out under the repealed Acts be disregarded, and the matter proceed *ab initio* under the procedure provided for in this Act.

85 Acts, etc, done under repealed Acts

(1) All acts, matters and things done or suffered under or for the purposes of the repealed Acts or the Regulations or Determinations or General Orders made under the repealed Acts shall be deemed to have been done or suffered under the equivalent provisions of this Act or the Regulations or the General Orders.

(2) Without limiting the generality of Subsection (1), but subject to Section 83 and 84, that Subsection applies to any act, matter or thing relating to appointment, promotion, transfer or discipline.

86 Service

All periods that were counted as service of a person under the repealed Acts shall be counted as service for the equivalent purposes of this Act.

87 Provincial administration

Section 128 of the *Organic Law on Provincial Governments and Local-level Governments* in relation to administration shall apply for the purposes of this Act.

SCHEDULE 1

Sec. 35.

Oath and affirmation of office of officers

Oath

I, , do swear that I will well and truly serve the Independent State of Papua New Guinea as an officer of the National Public Service.

So help me God!

Affirmation

I, , do solemnly and sincerely promise and declare that I will well and truly serve the Independent State of Papua New Guinea as an officer of the National Public Service.

SCHEDULE 2

Repealed Acts

Sec. 7.

Public Services (Management) Act 1986.
Public Services (Management) (Amendment) Act 1987.
Public Services (Management) (Amendment) Act 1988.
Public *Services (Management) (Amendment) Act* 1993.

CHAPTER No 341

Search Act

PART I – PRELIMINARY

PART II – SEARCHES OF THE PERSON

PART III – SEARCHES OF PREMISES, AIRCRAFT, ETC

Division 1 – Searches without Warrant

Division 2 – Search Warrants

Division 3 – Powers in Aid of Manner of Search

Division 4 – Property Located During Search

PART IV – MISCELLANEOUS

INDEPENDENT STATE OF PAPUA NEW GUINEA

CHAPTER No 341

Search Act

Being an Act –

(a) to regulate or restrict certain rights or freedoms referred to in Subdivision III.3.C of the Constitution, namely –

(i) the freedom from arbitrary search and entry conferred by Section 44 of the Constitution; and

(ii) the right to privacy conferred by Section 49 of the Constitution,

so as to –

(iii) provide for searches of individuals, premises and property in certain cases; and

(iv) confer on persons making searches certain powers and duties; and

(b) to abolish certain rules of common law,

and for related purposes.

PART I – PRELIMINARY

1 Interpretation

(1) In this Act, unless the contrary intention appears –

"court" means any court, other than a Village Court, and includes a Judge or Magistrate of any court, other than a Village Court;

"craft" means –

(a) an aircraft or part of an aircraft; or

(b) a vessel or part of a vessel;

"information" includes a complaint for an offence;

"place of confinement" means a corrective institution, rural lock-up or police lock-up;

"policeman" means a member of the Police Force;

"vehicle" means any description of vehicle on wheels or runners;

"warrant" means a warrant issued under any law for the search of any place including premises, a vehicle, aircraft, vessel, luggage or freight.

(2) For the purposes of this Act, a person believes something on reasonable grounds if –

(a) he personally has that belief; and

(b) there are reasonable grounds for that belief.

[830]2 Application

(1) Subject to Subsection (2), this Act applies, [831]notwithstanding the provisions of any other law, to and in relation to any search whether by or under this Act or any other law.

(2) This Act does not apply to a search carried out under a warrant issued under the *National Intelligence Organization Act.*

[830]Section 2 replaced by No. 25 of 1984, s2.
[831]The Act has "notwithdtanding"".

PART II – SEARCHES OF THE PERSON

3 Circumstances where persons may be searched

(1) Where a policeman believes on reasonable grounds that a person has in his possession –

(a) anything that has been stolen or otherwise unlawfully obtained; or

(b) anything used or intended to be used in the commission of an indictable offence,

he may stop and search that person in accordance with Section 4 and, where applicable, exercise the power of seizure under Section 10(1).

(2) Subject to Section 4, where a policeman believes on reasonable grounds that it is necessary to do so, he may, at the time of arresting a person, search his person, the clothing he is wearing and any property under his immediate control –

(a) for the purpose of ascertaining whether he is concealing a firearm or other offensive weapon; or

(b) for the purpose of preventing the loss or destruction of evidence relating to the offence for which he was arrested, and, where applicable,

may exercise the power of seizure under Section 10(2).

(3) Where a person in lawful custody is to be detained in a place of confinement he may, immediately before he is so detained, be searched at that place of confinement by a policeman or a member of the Correctional Service, as the case requires in accordance with Section 4, who may, where applicable, exercise the power of seizure under Section 10(3).

(4) The owner of a craft or a person in command of a craft or a person authorized by either of them or a policeman may in accordance with Section 4, search a person intending to board the craft and, where applicable, may exercise the power of seizure under Section 10(3).

(5) Where a person in command of a craft suspects that a person on board the craft constitutes a danger to the safety of the craft he may, or persons authorized by him may, search that person in accordance with Section 4 and, where applicable, may exercise the power of seizure under Section 10(4).

4 Powers and duties relating to searches of persons

(1) Subject to this section, a person conducting a search of a person may touch the body and clothing of the person being searched.

(2) Searches of the person shall be conducted with due regard to decency.

(3) A person conducting a search of another person shall not use any greater force than is reasonable in the circumstances.

(4) Subject to Subsection (5), a search of a female shall only be carried out by or in the presence of an adult female.

(5) Where a policeman has reasonable grounds to believe that a female he has arrested is carrying a firearm or other offensive weapon he may, with due regard to decency, seize the weapon.

(6) Subsection (5) does not justify the use of greater force than is reasonable in the circumstances.

PART III – SEARCHES OF PREMISES, AIRCRAFT, ETC

Division 1 – Searches without Warrant

5 Circumstances where search may be made

(1) Where a policeman has reasonable grounds to believe that a vehicle or anything in a vehicle –

(a) has been stolen or otherwise unlawfully obtained; or

(b) has been used or is intended to be used in the commission of an indictable offence,

he may stop and search that vehicle and, where applicable, exercise the power of seizure under Section 10(1).

(2) Where a policeman believes on reasonable grounds that a person has in a vehicle that he is using at the time, a firearm or other offensive weapon, he may search the vehicle for the firearm or offensive weapon and, where applicable, exercise the power of seizure under Section 10(2).

(3) Where a policeman believes on reasonable grounds that it is necessary to do so, he may, at the time of arresting a person, search any vehicle the arrested person was using at the time of his arrest, for the purpose of preventing the loss or destruction of evidence relating to the offence for which he was arrested and, where applicable, may exercise the power of seizure under Section 10(2).

(4) Where the owner or the person in command of a craft or a policeman has reasonable grounds to suspect that a situation has arisen or is likely to arise involving the safety of the craft he may or persons authorized by him may search –

(a) the craft; and

(b) any luggage and freight on board or about to be placed on board the craft,

and, where applicable, may exercise the power of seizure under Section 10(4).

(5) Where a policeman is in immediate pursuit of a person whom he believes on reasonable grounds to have committed an indictable offence, he may, or persons authorized by him may, search any building or place in which he believes on reasonable grounds that the person being pursued –

(a) is concealed; or

(b) has, in the course of his pursuit, concealed or deposited anything.

Division 2 – Search Warrants

6 Issue of warrants

(1) If a court, other than a Local Court, is satisfied by information on oath that there are reasonable grounds for suspecting that there is in any building, craft, vehicle or place –

(a) any thing with respect to which any offence has been or is believed on reasonable grounds to have been committed; or

(b) any thing as to which there are reasonable grounds for believing it is likely to afford evidence of the commission of any such offence; or

(c) any thing as to which there are reasonable grounds for believing is intended to be used to commit any such offence,

it may issue a warrant to search that building, craft, vehicle or place.

(2) If a court other than a Local Court is satisfied by information on oath by a commissioned officer of the Police Force that there are reasonable grounds for suspecting that there is in any building or buildings in a village or in any part of a village or village garden any thing specified in Subsection (1)(a), (b) or (c), it may issue a warrant to search the building, buildings, village, part of the village or village garden.

(3) Where a warrant has been issued under Subsection (2) the person, policeman or policemen to whom the warrant is directed shall, where it is practicable to do so, before executing the warrant, endeavour to obtain the co-operation of those persons who, by custom, are regarded as the leaders of the village in respect of which the warrant has been issued.

(4) Subsection (1) or (2) does not justify the use of greater force than is reasonable in the circumstances.

7 Direction of warrant

A warrant may be directed to all or any of the following: –

(a) to a named person; or

(b) to the officer for the time being in charge of police in a particular province or place; or

(c) to all members of the Police Force.

8 Form of warrant

A warrant shall –

(a) describe the place to be searched; and

(b) state briefly the offence or matter of the information on which it is founded; and

(c) order the person to whom it is directed to search the place and seize any thing he may find in that place which relates –

(i) to the offence or the matter of the information on which the warrant is founded; or

(ii) to any other offence.

Division 3 – Powers in Aid of Manner of Search

9 Powers and duties relating to searches of premises, containers, etc

(1) A person conducting a search under Sections 5 and 6 in any place (other than in a baggage or freight container) and his assistants (if any) –

(a) have power –

(i) to enter and be in that place for the duration of the search and for that purpose to use such force as is reasonably necessary; and

(ii) to the least extent necessary with the least amount of damage – to interfere with the structure of the place for the purpose of search; and

(iii) to touch any article in that place; and

(iv) to stop and search any person found in that place in accordance with Section 4; and

(b) shall, within a reasonable period after the conclusion of the search, restore the place or cause the place to be restored as nearly as possible to the same state of cleanliness and neatness that existed immediately before the commencement of the search.

(2) A person conducting a search under Sections 5 and 6 in any baggage or freight container and his assistants (if any) –

(a) have power –

(i) to enter and be in the place where the baggage or freight container is situated and for that purpose to use such force as is reasonably necessary; and

(ii) to the least extent necessary and with the least amount of damage – to interfere with the structure of the container for the purpose of search; and

(iii) touch any article in the container; and

(b) shall, within a reasonable period after the conclusion of the search, restore the container and any article in the container as nearly as possible to the same state of cleanliness and neatness that existed immediately before the commencement of the search.

(3) Where a search of a container under Subsection (2) cannot otherwise be made, a person conducting a search referred to in that subsection and his assistants may destroy the container for the purpose of search.

(4) This section does not require the restoration of the structure of any place or container interfered with by virtue of the powers conferred by this section.

Division 4 – Property Located During Search

10 Certain property may be seized

(1) Where, during the course of a search that is authorized by this Act, a policeman finds any thing that he believes on reasonable grounds –

(a) has been stolen or otherwise unlawfully obtained; or

(b) has been used or is intended to be used in the commission of any indictable offence; or

(c) will provide evidence of an offence,

he may seize that thing.

(2) For the purposes of Sections 3(2), 5(2) and 5(3), where the person searching finds a firearm or offensive weapon he may seize it.

(3) For the purposes of Sections 3(3) and 3(4), where the person searching finds any thing which in his opinion may be dangerous or inexpedient to leave in the possession of the person searched he may seize that thing.

(4) For the purposes of Sections 3(5) and 5(4), where the person searching finds any thing that in his opinion –

(a) constitutes a danger or is capable of constituting a danger to the safety of the craft; or

(b) is capable of being used to threaten a person on the craft,

he may seize that thing.

11 Things seized may be handed to police, etc

(1) Where a person seizes any thing under this Act and in his opinion that thing may be evidence relating to an offence he may hand that thing to a policeman.

(2) Where the person in command of a craft is of the opinion that property seized under this Act, on board the craft during the journey may be evidence relating to an offence committed during that journey on the craft he may on behalf of the owner of the craft give possession of that property to the person he believes on reasonable grounds is a representative of the authority responsible for law enforcement in the country where the offence will be tried.

12 Police to maintain record of things seized, etc

Where any thing is seized by a policeman under this Act or is handed to a policeman, he shall enter in a permanent register of property –

(a) a full description of the thing including where appropriate, a note of any identification marks; and

(b) the time and date the thing was seized or received by him and in the case of things received by him the name and address of the person who handed the thing to him; and

(c) the place and the person from whom the thing was seized; and

(d) other details as are prescribed.

13 Possession of certain property

(1) Where any thing is seized under this Act by a policeman or is handed to policeman, the thing shall be deemed to be in the possession of the State.

(2) Where any thing is seized under Section 10(4) by a person, other than a policeman, the thing shall be deemed to be in the possession of the owner of the craft.

(3) Where any thing is seized under this Act, other than under Section 10(4), by a person other than a policeman –

(a) in the course of his employment – the thing shall be deemed to be in the possession of his employer; or

(b) in any other case – the thing shall be deemed to be in the possession of that person.

(4) Anything referred to in Subsection (1), (2) or (3) may be retained in possession in accordance with that subsection for the purpose of examination and investigation and in the event that a person is charged with an offence in relation to that thing or in relation to which that thing

is evidence the thing may, subject to any order to the contrary of a court, be retained in that possession until the charge and any subsequent proceedings on that charge have been determined.

14 Disposal of things seized under court order

(1) In this section –

"forgery equipment" means –

(a) any forged bank note, or any special paper, revenue paper, frame, mould, instrument, plate, wood, stone, material or other thing, of which the possession without lawful excuse is an offence; or

(b) any counterfeit coin, or any instrument, machine, tool, or other thing used or intended to be used for the purpose of coining, of which the possession with knowledge of its nature and without lawful excuse is an offence;

"seized property" means any thing, other than forgery equipment, that is seized by virtue of a power conferred by this Act.

(2) A court may order, on an application made to it by any person, that forgery equipment seized by virtue of a power conferred by this Act be forfeited, defaced or destroyed.

(3) Subject to Subsection (4), where any proceedings for an offence relating to seized property or in which seized property is used as evidence have been determined a court may order –

(a) that the seized property be delivered to the person appearing to the court to be entitled to it; or

(b) that the seized property be otherwise disposed of in such manner as the court thinks fit.

(4) Where a person is convicted on an offence relating to seized property and an order has been made under Subsection (3), the operation of that order is suspended until the determination of any appeal.

(5) On the hearing of any appeal the court may annul or vary an order made under Subsection (3).

15 Disposal of things seized in certain cases

(1) Where a policeman seizes any thing in a Corrective institution under Section 10(3) he may hand that thing to a correctional officer at the institution.

(2) Where a person seizes any thing on board a craft under Section 10(4), he may throw away, destroy or otherwise deal with that thing so that the craft and persons on board the craft are no longer endangered.

PART IV – MISCELLANEOUS

16 Powers of search conferred by other laws

The provisions of this Act that specify the circumstances in which a person may be searched are in addition to and not in derogation of a provision of any other Act or subordinate enactment that confers a power of search.

17 Civil remedy for wrongful exercise of powers conferred by this Act

(1) A person who –

(a) exercises a power to make a search in breach of this Act; or

(b) exercises a power conferred by this Act, other than a power of search, in breach of this Act; or

(c) performs a duty imposed by this Act in breach of this Act; or

(d) fails or refuses to perform a duty imposed by this Act,

may be liable in damages to the person aggrieved by that breach.

(2) An action under Subsection (1) may be brought –

(a) in the National Court; or

(b) in a District Court,

and in the case of a District Court the court has jurisdiction within the limits prescribed by Section 21 of the *District Courts Act*.

(3) In an action under Subsection (1) a court may award exemplary damages.

(4) The provisions of this section are in addition to and not in derogation of the provisions of the Constitution or any other law dealing with the enforcement of any constitutional right, power, duty, restriction or prohibition.

18 Certain acts deemed to be within course of employment

For the purposes of any civil proceeding, where the making of a search would otherwise be within the scope of a person's employment, the mere non-compliance by an employee with a provision of this Act does not, of itself, take any act of the employee, committed during the course of the search, outside the scope of his employment.

19 Abolition of certain common law powers and duties

(1) All powers at common law to issue search warrants are abolished.

(2) All duties and responsibilities imposed by the common law in relation to searches and search warrants are abolished.

20 Regulations

The Head of State, acting on advice, may make regulations not inconsistent with this Act, prescribing all matters that by this Act are required or permitted to be prescribed or that are necessary or convenient to be prescribed for carrying out or giving effect to this Act.

CHAPTER No 274

Sorcery Act

PREAMBLE

PART I – PRELIMINARY

PART II – PRINCIPLES, APPLICATION AND EFFECT OF ACT

PART III – OFFENCES, ETC, IN RELATION TO SORCERY

Division 1 – Offences

Division 2 – Forfeiture and Reparations

PART IV – DEFENCES ARISING OUT OF ACTS OF SORCERY

PART V – PROCEDURE, EVIDENCE, ETC

PART VI – MISCELLANEOUS

SCHEDULES

SCHEDULE 1

DEFINITION OF INNOCENT SORCERY

SCHEDULE 2

EVIDENCE, PROOF, ETC

INDEPENDENT STATE OF PAPUA NEW GUINEA

CHAPTER No 274

Sorcery Act

Being an Act to prevent and punish evil practices of sorcery and other similar evil practices, and for other purposes relating to such practices.

PREAMBLE

There is a widespread belief throughout the country that there is such a thing as sorcery [832]and that sorcerers have extraordinary powers that can be used sometimes for good purposes but more often for bad ones, and because of this belief many evil things can be done and many people are frightened or do things that otherwise they might not do.

Some kinds of sorcery are practised not for evil purposes but for innocent ones and it may not be necessary for the law to interfere with them, and so it is necessary for the law to distinguish between evil [833]sorcery and innocent sorcery.

There is no reason why a person who uses or pretends or tries to use sorcery to do, or to try to do, evil things should not be punished just as if sorcery and the powers of sorcerers were real, since it is just as evil to do or to try to do evil things by sorcery as it would be to do them, or to try to do them, in any other way.

Sometimes some people may act, or may believe that they are acting, under the influence of sorcery to such an extent that –

(a) their conduct may not be morally (and should not be legally) blameworthy; or

(b) actions that would ordinarily be regarded as customary offences may, in traditional social groups, be regarded as excusable or capable of being compensated for.

There is a danger that any law that deals fully with sorcery may encourage some evil-intentioned people to make baseless or merely spiteful or malicious accusations that their enemies are sorcerers solely to

[832]The Act has "ad".
[833]The Act has "srcery".

get them into trouble with other people, and this is a thing that the law should prevent.

PART I – PRELIMINARY

1 Interpretation

(1) In this Act, unless the contrary intention appears –

"act of sorcery" means any act (including a traditional ceremony or ritual) that is intended to bring, or that purports to be able or to be adapted to bring, powers of sorcery into action, or to make them possible or carry them into effect;

"forbidden sorcery" means sorcery other than innocent sorcery;

"harmful result" includes fear, intimidation or injury in mind, body or property;

"implement of sorcery" means any thing that –

(a) is designed or intended for use in acts of sorcery generally, or in a particular act or class of acts of sorcery; or

(b) has, by some ceremony, ritual or act (including an act of sorcery), been adapted for use in acts of sorcery generally, or in a particular act or class of acts of sorcery;

"innocent sorcery" means sorcery of a kind referred to in Schedule 1;

"social group" includes a family, an extended family, a lineage, a kinship group, a descent group and a local group or community;

"sorcerer" means a person who –

(a) claims to have powers of sorcery; or

(b) directly or indirectly pretends to have, holds himself out to have or professes to have, powers of sorcery;

"sorcery" includes (without limiting the generality of that expression) what is known, in various languages and parts of the country, as witchcraft, magic, enchantment, *puri puri*, *mura mura dikana*, *vada*, *mea mea*, *sanguma* or *malira*, whether or not connected with or related to the supernatural.

(2) A reference in this Act to custom shall be read as a reference to the relevant custom of the social group or groups concerned.

(3) A reference in this Act to proceedings brought by virtue of this Act shall be read as a reference to proceedings in which reliance is placed, for the purpose of bringing the proceedings, on any provision of

this Act, to the extent that the provision or its application is in question in the proceedings.

2 References to social groups

(1) A reference in this Act to a social group shall, in its application to any matter before a court under this Act, be read as a reference to the social group or groups that, in the opinion of the court, is or are of the most relevance.

(2) In this Act, a reference to a social group includes a reference to any settled community, or a part of that community, whether it is a traditional community or is composed of members of different traditional or other social groups.

(3) This Act does not prevent a person being regarded as a member of more than one social group or community.

PART II – PRINCIPLES, APPLICATION AND EFFECT OF ACT

3 Preamble as statement of objects and principles

Notwithstanding anything in any other law or rule of statutory construction, in the interpretation and application of this Act the provisions of the Preamble shall be taken fully into account in all cases, and each provision of this Act shall be read and construed as being intended to give effect to those provisions.

4 Innocent making of certain implements of sorcery

(1) Subsection (2) does not apply where –

(a) to the knowledge of the person relying on that subsection, the implement of sorcery concerned was made or adapted for use in a particular act of forbidden sorcery; or

(b) the implement of sorcery concerned was intended to be used in an act of forbidden sorcery.

(2) Notwithstanding this Act, the mere making of an implement of sorcery (including the adaptation of a thing so as to be an implement of sorcery) is not an act of sorcery, nor is a person who claims to have the power to make an implement of sorcery a sorcerer by virtue only of his claiming that power, if the implement is designed, intended or adapted for use both in acts of innocent sorcery and in acts of forbidden sorcery, depending on the use made of it in any given set of circumstances.

(3) The burden of proof that Subsection (2) applies in relation to an implement of sorcery is on the person relying on that subsection.

5 Existence and effectiveness of powers of sorcery

Even though this Act may speak as if powers of sorcery really exist (which is necessary if the law is to deal adequately with all the legal problems of sorcery and the traditional belief in the powers of sorcerers), nevertheless nothing in this Act recognizes the existence or effectiveness of powers of sorcery in any factual sense except only for the purpose of, and of proceedings under or by virtue of, this Act, or denies the existence or effectiveness of such powers.

PART III – OFFENCES, ETC, IN RELATION TO SORCERY

Division 1 – Offences

6 Sorcery generally

(1) This section does not apply in cases where the sorcery involved is innocent sorcery only.

(2) A person who, directly or indirectly, pretends to be, holds himself out to be, or professes to be a sorcerer is guilty of an offence.

(3) A person who influences or attempts to influence the acts of another person by the use or threatened use of the powers or services of a sorcerer as such is guilty of an offence.

Penalty: On conviction on indictment – imprisonment for a term not exceeding two years.

On summary conviction – imprisonment for a term not exceeding one year.

7 Criminal acts of sorcery

A person who –

(a) does any act of forbidden sorcery; or

(b) aids, abets, counsels or procures, or by act or omission is in any way knowingly concerned in or party to, the doing of any such act,

is guilty of an offence.

Penalty: On conviction on indictment – imprisonment for a term not exceeding five years.

On summary conviction – imprisonment for a term not exceeding one year.

8 Attempting to commit offence by means of sorcery

(1) If an act of sorcery is intended to produce or purports to produce any unlawful result, the person doing the act is guilty of an attempt to produce that result and is punishable accordingly.

(2) Notwithstanding anything in any other law, the fact that the unlawful result did in fact follow the act of sorcery does not prevent a

charge of an attempted offence being brought under Subsection (1), but nothing in this section affects the operation of Section 20.

9 Administering sorcerous substances, etc

(1) This section does not apply where the act of sorcery involved is an act of innocent sorcery only.

(2) A person who unlawfully administers to another person or to an animal –

(a) any substance that has been subjected to an act of sorcery; or

(b) any substance in the course of or in fulfilment of an act of sorcery,

is guilty of an offence.

Penalty: Imprisonment for a term not exceeding eight years.

10 False report of sorcery, etc

(1) This section does not apply in cases where the sorcery involved or allegedly involved is innocent sorcery only.

(2) The *Defamation Act* does not apply to or in relation to an offence against Subsection (3) or (4).

(3) A person who (except in the course of, or for the purpose of the institution of, legal proceedings or in any other case in which such an accusation or threat is privileged or excused by law) falsely accuses, to a third person, or threatens to accuse another person of –

(a) being or of having been a sorcerer; or

(b) performing or having performed an act of sorcery; or

(c) having been concerned in or a party to an act of sorcery,

is guilty of an offence.

(4) A person who spreads a false report that another person –

(a) is a sorcerer or performs or has performed an act of sorcery; or

(b) is or has been concerned in, or a party to, an act of sorcery,

is guilty of an offence.

Penalty: Imprisonment for a term not exceeding one year.

11 Possession of implement of forbidden sorcery

A person who, without lawful excuse (proof of which is on him), has in his possession an implement –

(a) made or adapted for use in a particular act of forbidden sorcery; or

(b) intended for use in an act of forbidden sorcery,

is guilty of an offence.

Penalty: Imprisonment for a term not exceeding one year.

Division 2 – Forfeiture and Reparations

12 Forfeiture of profits of sorcery

(1) Where a person –

(a) is convicted of an offence against this Act; or

(b) is convicted, by virtue of this Act, of an offence,

the court that convicts him may order any money or other thing that has been paid or given to him in consideration of the performance of an act of forbidden sorcery to be forfeited to the State and, subject to Section 14 –

(c) the money shall be paid into the Consolidated Revenue Fund; or

(d) the other thing may be dealt with in such manner as the Head of State, acting on advice, directs,

as the case may be.

(2) If the convicted person is no longer in possession of the money or thing, the amount of the money or the value of the thing, as assessed by the court, is a debt due to the State and the court may make an order for its payment.

13 Forfeiture of implement of sorcery

(1) Where a person –

(a) is convicted of an offence against this Act; or

(b) is convicted, by virtue of this Act, of an offence,

the court that convicts him may order any implement of sorcery owned by him or in his possession or under his control to be forfeited to the State.

(2) A court may at any time order any implement of sorcery that can be used in an act of forbidden sorcery to be forfeited to the State.

(3) An implement of sorcery forfeited to the State under this section shall be dealt with in such manner as the Head of State, acting on advice, directs.

14 Reparations

(1) Where a person is convicted of an offence involving an act of sorcery, the court that convicts him may order him to make such compensation as the court thinks proper to –

(a) any person at whom the act of sorcery was directed; or

(b) the social group to which any person at whom the sorcery was directed belongs or belonged at the time of the act.

(2) An order under Subsection (1) may be made at the time of conviction or sentence, or if the court thinks it proper to do so at a later date, and the court may in any event –

(a) admit further evidence, after conviction or sentence, in relation to the question of compensation; and

(b) adjourn the matter in order to enable the parties to reach agreement on the compensation to be made,

and may make such further or other order as it thinks proper.

(3) An order under this section may include an order that any money that has been or is liable to be forfeited to the State under Section 12(1), or any amount that is recovered or recoverable by the State under Section 12(2), be paid as part or all of the compensation.

PART IV – DEFENCES ARISING OUT OF ACTS OF SORCERY

15 Special defence in relation to charges of adultery

(1) In this section, "charge of adultery" means a charge of an offence against –

(a) Section 17 of the *Native Regulation (Papua)*; or

(b) Section 14 of the *Native Administration Regulation (T.N.G.)*,

or against any corresponding or analogous provision of any other law.

(2) It is a defence to a charge of adultery that an act of sorcery had been performed, without the consent (express or implied) of the accused person, of such a nature as to be generally believed, in the social groups of which the husband and the wife are respectively members, to have the effect –

(a) of inducing the accused person to have the sexual intercourse in question; and

(b) by custom, to excuse the act of intercourse in all the circumstances of the case.

(3) The burden of proof of a defence under Subsection (2) is on the accused person, and that burden need not be discharged beyond reasonable doubt.

(4) Subject to Subsection (5), the circumstances referred to in Subsection (2) include any circumstance (including any customary compensatory or conciliatory arrangement) that arose before the act of adultery, or that arose, or that the court dealing with the matter is satisfied will arise, after the act.

(5) The circumstances referred to in Subsection (2) do not include any act, matter or thing that –

(a) constitutes, or is an ingredient of, an offence committed by or on behalf of the accused person against any other law; or

(b) is repugnant to the general principles of humanity or is not in the public interest; or

(c) is, in the opinion of the court dealing with the matter, improper to be taken into account.

16 Sorcery as provocation

(1) An act of sorcery may amount to a wrongful act or insult within the meaning of Section 266 of the *Criminal Code*.

(2) It is immaterial that the act of sorcery –

(a) did not occur in the presence of the person allegedly provoked; or

(b) was directed at some person other than the person allegedly provoked.

(3) The likely effect of an act of sorcery relied on by virtue of this section shall be judged by reference, amongst other things, to the traditional beliefs of any social group of which the person provoked is a member.

(4) A defence provided by this section is in addition to and not in derogation of any defence that is –

(a) available by reason of any effect attributable, under any other law, to the act involved; or

(b) otherwise available to an accused person.

PART V – PROCEDURE, EVIDENCE, ETC

17 Evidentiary effect of possession of implement of sorcery

(1) For the purpose of any proceedings under or by virtue of this Act, evidence that a person has at any time owned or had in his possession or under his control, otherwise than in an official capacity or in a capacity not implying or suggesting the possession of powers of sorcery, an implement of sorcery is evidence that he has been at all relevant times a sorcerer.

(2) The burden of proof of a matter referred to in Subsection (1) is on the person alleging it.

(3) The provisions of Subsection (1) are in addition to and not in derogation of the other provisions of this Act.

18 Evidence, proof, etc

Schedule 2 applies to and in relation to proceedings brought under, or by virtue of this Act.

19 Saving of Customs Recognition Act

Except so far as this Act expressly provides to the contrary, this Act does not affect the operation of the [834]Customs Recognition Act.

---

[834]*See*, also, Constitution, Section Sch. 2.1.

PART VI – MISCELLANEOUS

20 Preservation of rights and liabilities under other laws, etc

Except where the contrary intention appears, nothing in this Act takes away from any person any defence, right or liability, whether civil or criminal –

(a) that is or has been available, acquired or incurred; or

(b) that will or may be available, acquired or incurred,

to or by him under any other law, but nothing in this section shall be deemed to show a contrary intention within the meaning of the *Interpretation Act* or to affect Section 16 of the Criminal Code, or any other similar law.

21 Regulations

The Head of State, acting on advice, may make regulations, not inconsistent with this Act, prescribing all matters that by this Act are required or permitted to be prescribed, or that are necessary or convenient to be prescribed for carrying out or giving effect to this Act.

SCHEDULES

SCHEDULE 1

Sec. 1(1).

DEFINITION OF INNOCENT SORCERY

Sch. 1.1. For the purposes of this Act, innocent sorcery is sorcery that –

(a) is protective or curative only, or is not intended to produce, and does not purport to be calculated or able or adapted to produce, any harmful or unlawful result, or to exert any harmful unlawful or undue influence on any person; and

(b) is generally regarded in the social groups of which –

(i) the accused person; and

(ii) the person at whom the act was directed; and

(iii) the person whose conduct was intended to be influenced,

are respectively members as being, by custom, legitimate or harmless and not offensive in all the circumstances of the case.

Sch. 1.2. Subject to Section Sch. 1.3. the circumstances referred to in Section Sch. 1.1. include any circumstance (including the courtship of an unmarried person by an unmarried person, betrothal, marriage, the fact that the act of sorcery was intended only to counteract or nullify the effect of a previous act of sorcery or any customary compensatory or conciliatory arrangement) that arose before the act of sorcery, or that arose, or that the court dealing with the matter is satisfied will arise, after the act.

Sch. 1.3. The circumstances referred to in Section Sch. 1.1. do not include –

(a) any act, matter or thing that constitutes, or is an ingredient of, an offence committed by or on behalf of the accused person against any other law; or

(b) any act, matter or thing that is repugnant to the general principles of humanity or is not in the public interest; or

(c) any other act, matter or thing that, in the opinion of the court dealing with the matter, is improper to be taken into account.

Sch. 1.4. For the purposes only of Section Sch. 1.3.(b) and (c), an act of sorcery shall not, simply as such, be deemed to be not in the public interest or improper to be taken into account.

Sch. 1.5. For the purpose of allowing any circumstance referred to in Section Sch. 1.1. to arise, if the court dealing with the matter considers it proper and in the interests of justice and the amicable settlement of social or personal disputes or differences to do so the court may by order adjourn the hearing of the matter for such period and on such terms and conditions (including the entering by any person into a recognizance for any purpose connected with the matter) as the court thinks proper.

SCHEDULE 2

Sec. 18.

EVIDENCE, PROOF, ETC

Sch. 2.1.(1) Evidence that –

(a) an act is, in the social group to which the doer of the act belongs, believed to be an act of sorcery; and

(b) a person believed that –

(i) the act was directed at him or at some other person; or

(ii) his conduct or the conduct of some other person was intended to be influenced by or as a result of the act,

is evidence that the act is an act of sorcery within the meaning of this Act and that the doer of the act knew it to be an act of sorcery.

(2) Where in a prosecution for an offence against this Act there is evidence of a general belief in the social group to which the doer of the act belongs that an act is an act of sorcery, the doer of the act shall, in the absence of evidence to the contrary, be presumed to have intended the act to be an act of sorcery.

Sch. 2.2. If in a prosecution for an offence against or in reliance on Section 8 the accused person is proved to have done an act of sorcery then –

(a) it is immaterial that the thing done was incapable of causing, or was not adapted to the fulfilment of, the result intended, if either –

(i) the accused person; or

(ii) the person at whom the act was directed; or

(iii) any person whose conduct was intended to be influenced,

believed that it was capable of producing the intended result or some similar result, and in the case of a person referred to in Subparagraph (ii) or (iii) the belief was known to the accused person; and

(b) until the contrary is proved, both the belief and the knowledge referred to in Paragraph (a) shall be presumed on the part of the accused person.

Sch. 2.3. (1) In considering for the purposes of this Act the question of the existence or effect of a traditional belief or of its being generally held in a social group, a court –

(a) is not bound to observe strict legal procedures or to apply technical rules of evidence; but

(b) shall –

(i) admit and consider such relevant information as is available (including hearsay and expressions of opinion); and

(ii) otherwise inform itself as it sees fit.

(2) For the purposes of deciding a question referred to in Subsection (1), a court –

(a) may refer to books, treatises, reports or other works of reference, or statements by Local Government Councils or committees of Local Government Councils, as to any custom (whether published or not), and may accept any matter or thing stated in them as evidence on the question; and

(b) may of its own motion call such evidence or require the opinions of such persons as it thinks fit,

but this section does not limit the discretion of the court in obtaining evidence or information for itself on the question.

Sch. 2.4. The burden of proof that an act of sorcery is an act of innocent sorcery is on the person alleging it.

CHAPTER No 202

Summary Ejectment Act

INDEPENDENT STATE OF PAPUA NEW GUINEA

CHAPTER No 202

Summary Ejectment Act

Being an Act to facilitate the recovery of possession of premises after determination of a tenancy, and for related purposes.

1 Interpretation

In this Act, unless the contrary intention appears –

"agent" means a person who is –

(a) usually employed by the lessor –

(i) in the letting of the premises; or

(ii) in the collection of the rents of the premises; or

(b) authorized by the lessor in writing to act –

(i) in the particular matter; or

(ii) as his attorney;

"lease" includes –

(a) a contract for the letting of land or premises, whether the contract is express or implied or is made orally, in writing or by deed; and

(b) a contract for the letting of land or premises, together with goods,

but does not include a lease –

(c) arising under an attornment clause in a mortgage; or

(d) in an agreement for the sale and purchase of land;

"lessor" and "lessee" means the parties to a lease or their respective successors in title, and include –

(a) a mesne lessor and a mesne lessee; and

(b) a sub-lessor and a sub-lessee; and

(c) in respect of premises that are subject to a mortgage, a mortgagee who enters or has entered into possession of the premises under the mortgage and a person who was the lessee of the premises immediately prior to the mortgagee entering into possession,

respectively, or their respective agents.

2 Application

This Act does not apply to customary land.

3 Proceedings for possession on determination of lease

(1) Where –

(a) the term or interest of a lessee of premises held by him has ended or has been duly determined; and

(b) the lessee, or (if the lessee does not actually occupy the premises or occupies only a part of the premises) a person by whom the whole or part of the premises is then actually occupied, neglects or refuses to quit and deliver up possession of the premises or of the part of the premises, as the case may be,

the lessor of the premises may make a complaint to a magistrate of a District Court against the person for the recovery of the premises, or of the part of the premises, and the magistrate may issue a summons in the prescribed form to that person.

(2) Where the person to whom the summons is directed under Subsection (1) –

(a) does not appear before a District Court at the time named in the summons; or

(b) appears and does not satisfy the Court that there is reasonable cause why he should not give possession of the premises or of the part of the premises of which he is then in possession,

and still neglects or refuses to deliver up possession of the premises or of the part of the premises of which he is then in possession, then on proof of the matter of the complaint the Court may order him to deliver up possession of the premises or of the part of the premises to the complainant, either immediately or on or before a day named in the order.

(3) Where an order made under Subsection (2) is not obeyed, a magistrate of a District Court may, at the request of the complainant, issue a warrant in the prescribed form directed to a member of the Police Force requiring him, within a period specified in the warrant, not being more than 30 clear days from the date of the warrant –

(a) to enter into the premises by force and with assistants if necessary; and

(b) to give possession of the premises or of the part of the premises to the complainant.

(4) In a complaint under this section against a lessee or occupier the complainant may add a claim not exceeding K500.00 for rent or mesne profits (or both) down to the day appointed for the hearing or to any preceding day named in the complaint, and any misdescription in the nature of the claim may be amended at the hearing.

(5) If the lessor does not appear at the time named in the summons, the Court shall dismiss the complaint.

4 Recovery of premises when rent in arrear

(1) Subject to this section, where the rent payable by a lessee holding premises by the week, month, or quarter, or a longer term not exceeding three years, is in arrear for –

(a) 10 days in the case of a weekly tenancy; or
(b) 21 days in the case of a monthly tenancy; or
(c) 30 days in the case of a quarterly tenancy; or
(d) 42 days in the case of a tenancy for a longer term,

the lessor may, without a formal demand or re-entry, make a complaint to a magistrate of a District Court who may issue a summons in the prescribed form directed to the lessee, and the service of the summons stands in place of a demand or re-entry.

(2) The power conferred on a lessor by Subsection (1) may be exercised only –

(a) if a right of re-entry for the non-payment of rent has not been expressly conferred on the lessor by agreement with the lessee, on the expiration of the relevant period referred to in Subsection (1)(a), (b), (c) or (d); or
(b) if a right of re-entry has been conferred on the lessor by agreement with the lessee –
   (i) on the accrual of the right of re-entry in accordance with the terms of the agreement; or
   (ii) at the expiration of the relevant period referred to in Paragraph (a),

whichever first occurs.

(3) Where there is a tenancy and no agreement as to its duration, the lessee shall, for the purposes of this section, be deemed to hold the premises by the month.

(4) If the lessee pays into a District Court all the rent in arrear and the costs at least five clear days before the day appointed for the hearing

of the complaint, the complaint shall be deemed to be withdrawn.

(5) If –

(a) the lessee does not make the payments specified in Subsection (4); and

(b) does not appear at the time named in the summons, or, if appearing, does not show reasonable cause why the premises should not be recovered,

the District Court may, on proof of the matter of the complaint, order the lessee to deliver up possession of the premises to the complainant, immediately or on or before a day named in the order.

(6) Where an order under Subsection (5) is not obeyed, a magistrate of a District Court may, at the request of the complainant issue a warrant in the prescribed form directed to a member of the Police Force requiring him, within a period specified in the warrant, not being more than 30 clear days from the date of the warrant –

(a) to enter by force and with assistants if necessary, into the premises; and

(b) to give possession of the premises to the complainant.

(7) From the time of the execution of the warrant issued under Subsection (6) –

(a) the complainant holds the premises discharged of the lease; and

(b) the lessee and all persons claiming by, through or under him are barred from all relief so long as the order under Subsection (5) is not reversed.

5 Recovery of possession by lessor

(1) Where –

(a) a lessee holding premises at a rent under a demise or agreement, written or oral, who is in arrear for two months, deserts the premises and leaves them uncultivated or unoccupied so that no sufficient distress can be had to countervail the arrears of rent; and

(b) no right or power of re-entry in case of the non-payment of rent is given or reserved by the demise or agreement, to the lessor,

a District Court may, at the request of the lessor, his lawyer or agent and on proof of the matters specified in Paragraphs (a) and (b), issue a warrant directed to a member of the Police Force requiring him –

(c) to enter and inspect the premises; and

(d) to affix or cause to be affixed on some conspicuous part of the premises a notice in writing specifying the day (not sooner than 14 days from the affixing of the notice) on which he will return to inspect the premises a second time.

(2) If the lessee or some person on his behalf pays the rent in a rear into the District Court that issued the warrant at least two clear days before the day specified in the notice affixed under Subsection (1)(d), the warrant shall be deemed to have been withdrawn.

(3) Where on the second inspection referred to in Subsection (1)(d) –

(a) the lessee or some person on his behalf does not appear and pay to the member of the Police Force the rent in arrear; or

(b) there is not a sufficient distress on the premises,

the District Court may issue a warrant directed to a member of the Police Force requiring him, on or before a day to be named in the warrant, to enter into the premises and put the lessor into possession of the premises.

(4) On the execution of a warrant under Subsection (3), the lease of the premises to the lessee as to any demise contained in the lease becomes void.

6 Recovery of premises held without right, etc

(1) Where a person without right, title or licence is in possession of premises, the owner may make a complaint to a magistrate of a District Court to recover possession of the premises, and the magistrate may issue a summons in the prescribed form to the person in illegal occupation.

(2) Where the person summoned under Subsection (1) –

(a) does not appear before the District Court at the time named in the summons; or

(b) appears and does not show reasonable cause why possession of the premises should not be given,

the Court may, on proof of the matter of the complaint, issue a warrant directed to a member of the Police Force requiring him, on or before a day specified in the warrant –

(c) to enter, by force and with assistants if necessary, into the premises; and

(d) to give possession of the premises to the complainant.

7 Notices between sub-lessor and sub-lessee

(1) A sub-lessor or sub-lessee –

(a) on whom a summons for the recovery of premises is served, or to whose knowledge it comes; or

(b) to whose knowledge the affixing of a notice under Section 5 comes,

shall, without delay, give notice of the summons or notice to his immediate sub-lessor or sub-lessee, as the case may be.

(2) If not already a party to any proceedings before the District Court, the sub-lessor or sub-lessee may, on receipt of notice specified in Subsection (1), apply to the Court to be added as a party to defend possession of the premises and the Court may allow him to be added.

(3) Where a summons is issued on the complaint of the lessor against a sub-lessor or sub-lessee, the District Court may, of its own motion and on reasonable notice being given to the sub-lessor or sub-lessee, as the case may be, add the sub-lessor or the sub-lessee as a party to defend possession of the premises.

(4) Where a sub-lessor or a sub-lessee has received notice under Subsection (1) or (3), the District Court may make an order for the recovery of possession against both the sub-lessor and the sub-lessee.

8 Warrant sufficient authority for entering premises

(1) A warrant under the hand of a magistrate of a District Court directed to a member of the Police Force and requiring him to give possession of premises authorizes him to enter, by force and with assistants if necessary, into the premises named in the warrant, and to give possession accordingly.

(2) An entry under a warrant shall not be made on a Sunday, Good Friday, Christmas Day or at any time other than between the hours of 9 a.m. and 4 p.m.

9 Procuring issue of warrant without right

Where, at the time of a granting of a warrant for the recovery of possession of any premises under this Act the person to whom it was granted had no lawful right to the possession of the premises, the obtaining of the warrant shall be deemed to be a trespass by him against the lessee or occupier of the premises only if–

(a) an entry is made by virtue of the warrant; or

(b) the complaint or request following which the warrant was issued was not bona fide.

10 Rights of outgoing tenant

This Act does not affect any right to which a person is entitled by law as outgoing lessee.

11 Stay of execution, etc, on giving security

(1) Where a lessee or occupier –

(a) against whom –

(i) an order is made under Section 3 or 4 to deliver up possession of premises; or

(ii) a warrant is issued under Section 5 or 6 for the recovery of possession of premises; and

(b) who offers at the time when the order is made or the warrant is issued to give security to defend an action of ejectment or other appropriate action, for recovery of possession of the premises in respect of which the order is made or the warrant is granted, brought against him in the National Court by or on behalf of the lessor by or for whom or on whose behalf the relevant complaint was made,

proceedings under the order or the execution of the warrant shall be suspended for three clear days.

(2) Where during the interval of three clear days referred to in Subsection (1) the lessee or occupier gives security by a joint and several bond of two sureties as prescribed in this section –

(a) proceedings shall not be taken under the order; or

(b) the warrant shall not be executed or put in force but is void.

(3) A bond entered into under Subsection (2) shall –

(a) be made to the lessor, and his heirs, executors and administrators; and

(b) be approved, and certified as being approved, by the District Court by which the complaint was heard, by a memorandum in writing on or annexed to the bond; and

(c) be in such sum as the Court, regard being had to –

(i) the value of the premises; and

(ii) the probable cost of the action; and

(iii) the probable length of time that must elapse before it can be determined,

thinks reasonable; and

(d) be conditioned to be void (in case the lessor, his heirs, executors or administrators succeed in the action) on payment of –

(i) all costs of suit awarded to or recovered by the lessor, or his heirs, executors or administrators in the action; and

(ii) all mesne profits of the premises accruing between the time when the order was made or the warrant was issued, as the case may be, and the time when the lessor, or his heirs, executors or administrators obtain possession of the premises by virtue of the action.

12 Relief to parties to bond

(1) On the application of a party bound by a bond specified in Section 11, or his heirs, executors or administrators, the National Court or a Judge may, in a summary way –

(a) give such relief to the person or persons making the application; or

(b) make such other order as it or he thinks just,

and a finding or order of the National Court or a Judge under this section operates as a defeasance of the bond.

(2) Where an unreasonable delay occurs in bringing or prosecuting the action of ejectment or other action for the recovery of the premises, the National Court or a Judge, on the application of a party bound by the bond, or his heirs, executors or administrators, may, in a summary way –

(a) order the bond to be cancelled and given up to the person or persons making the application; or

(b) make such other order as it or he thinks just.

(3) If the National Court or a Judge orders or directs the bond to be cancelled, the bond is void but without prejudice to any action or other remedy on it for a previous breach of the condition of defeasance of the bond.

(4) Where –

(a) the bond is forfeited; or

(b) on the hearing of the action in respect of which the bond was given the National Court or a Judge does not endorse on the record that the condition of the bond has been fulfilled,

the party to whom the bond has been made may make a complaint and recover on it.

(5) The District Court hearing a complaint under Subsection (4) may by order give such relief to the parties on the bond as appears to it just, and the order operates as a defeasance of the bond.

13 Protection of justices

An action or prosecution shall not be brought –

(a) against –

(i) a magistrate for issuing a warrant under this Act for the recovery of possession of any premises; or

(ii) a member of the Police Force for executing a warrant issued under this Act,

by reason only of the fact that the person on whose application the warrant was granted had no lawful right to the possession of the premises; or

(b) against a member of the Police Force by reason of an entry made by him under a warrant deemed to have been withdrawn under Section 4(2) if at the time he bona fide believed it to have been in force.

14 Effect of irregularity

(1) Where the person on whose application a warrant for the recovery of possession of premises was granted had, at the time of the granting of the warrant, a lawful right to the possession of the premises –

(a) he or his agent or any other person acting on his behalf; or

(b) a member of the Police Force bona fide executing or entering under the warrant,

shall not be deemed to be a trespasser by reason only of any irregularity or informality in the mode of proceeding for obtaining possession under this Act, but the party aggrieved is not debarred from –

(c) bringing an action in a court of competent jurisdiction for any special damage that he alleges he has sustained by reason of the irregularity or informality; and

(d) recovering full satisfaction for the special damage, with costs.

(2) If special damage is not proved, the defendant is entitled to a verdict, and, if damage is proved but is assessed by the court at a sum not exceeding K1.00, the complainant is not entitled to costs unless that court certifies that in its opinion full costs ought to be allowed.

15 Regulations

The Head of State, acting on advice, may make regulations, not inconsistent with this Act, prescribing all matters that by this Act are required or permitted to be prescribed, or that are necessary or convenient to be prescribed for carrying out or giving effect to this Act.

CHAPTER No 264

Summary Offences Act

PART I – PRELIMINARY

PART II – DRUNKENNESS

PART III – PROTECTION OF PERSONS

PART IV – PROTECTION OF THE NEIGHBOURHOOD

PART IX – OFFENCES RELATING TO CERTAIN TYPES OF VEHICLES

PART X – MISCELLANEOUS

INDEPENDENT STATE OF PAPUA NEW GUINEA

CHAPTER No 264

Summary Offences Act

Being an Act relating to summary offences.

PART I – PRELIMINARY

1 Interpretation

In this Act unless the contrary intention appears –

"boat" includes any ship, yacht, canoe, dinghy, raft, pontoon, and any water craft capable of carrying at least one occupant;

"brothel" means any premises used for the purposes of prostitution;

"court" means –

(a) a District Court; or

(b) a Local Court; or

(c) a Magistrate Grade III or IV; or

(d) a Magistrate Grade I or II;

"drunkenness" includes the state of a person who is so affected by alcoholic drink or drugs that his physical or mental faculties or his judgement are appreciably and materially impaired in the conduct of the ordinary affairs or acts of daily life;

"fight" means a fight in which two or more people are assaulting one another –

(a) in a manner that is likely to cause bodily injury to some other person; or

(b) so as to cause injury to the property of some other person;

"indictable offence" includes an indictable offence in relation to which a person may be dealt with summarily or a summary offence in relation to which a person may be dealt with on indictment.

"information" includes a complaint;

"offensive weapon" means –

(a) any article made or adapted for use for causing injury to the person; or

(b) any article intended by the individual having it with him for use for causing injury to the person;

[835](c) without prejudice to the general descriptions contained in Paragraphs (a) and (b) the following: –

(i) any imitation of a pistol, revolver, rifle, shotgun, machine gun or sub machine gun, unless such article is obviously a child's toy, of a type, class and description approved by the Registrar;

(ii) any article or device of a type or description commonly known as a knuckle duster or metal knuckles or any article or device made or adapted for use as such;

(iii) a sap glove or a studded glove;

(iv) a mace, knobkerry or similar device intended to be used as a blunt instrument, other than a ceremonial mace made or used solely as a symbol of authority on ceremonial occasions;

(v) any article or device in the form of a flail in which the striking part is armed with spikes or studded with any protruding matter, any whip or lash which is comprised wholly or partly of any form of metal, or any article commonly known as a cat of nine tails, whether or not it has nine leathers;

(vi) any article commonly known as kung fu sticks, otherwise known as Nunchiku or any similar article;

(vii) a pistol, capable of being concealed in the palm of the hand, but not including the standard 'pocket' or 'purse' pistol;

---

[835] Section (c) of the definition of "offensive weapon" was added by the Summary Offences (Amendment) Act 1986 (No. 36 of 1986), s2.

(viii) a firearm which substantially duplicates a walking stick, walking cane or umbrella;

(ix) a riding crop containing a knife or stiletto;

(x) a walking stick, walking cane or umbrella containing a knife, stiletto or sword;

(xi) a knife commonly known as a flick knife which has a blade which opens automatically on pressure of a button or similar release device;

(xii) a crossbow, other than an antique crossbow used for ornamental purposes;

(xiii) a cow prod, or similar device intended to cause an electrical shock upon the recipient;

(xiv) a sling shot or similar device such as the thing commonly known as a catapult;

"person" includes a member of the Police Force;

"premises" includes –

(a) any dwelling house, office, warehouse, store or shop; and

(b) any building or structure; and

(c) any factory, garage, workshop or hangar; and

(d) any pavilion, tent, or caravan; and

(e) any enclosed yard, garden or area; and

(f) any aircraft; and

(g) any vehicle; and

(h) any vessel,

and any part of such premises;

"public place" includes –

(a) a place to which free access is permitted to members of the public with the express or implied consent of the owner or occupier of the place; and

(b) a place to which members of the public are admitted on payment of money while members of the public are present or are permitted to have access to the place; and

(c) a road, street, bridge, footway, footpath, court, alley, passage or thoroughfare which members of the public are allowed to use, notwithstanding that the same may be, or be formed on, private property; and

(d) an aerodrome, whether enclosed or otherwise; and

(e) a passenger vessel or a boat carrying fare – paying passengers; and

(f) a vehicle carrying fare – paying passengers; and

(g) any school building and land or premises used in connexion with any school;

"street sign" includes any sign referred to in Part XI. of the Motor Traffic Regulations, and any sign erected by a public authority in any public place for the assistance or convenience of pedestrians, motorists, cyclists or other persons;

"vehicle" includes any conveyance fitted with wheels or runners for the purpose of carrying persons or things;

"vessel" means a vessel when in the territorial sea or lying or being in any place within Papua New Guinea and includes any cabin of any such vessel.

2 Burden of proof of lawful excuse

Where under the provisions of this Act any act, if done without lawful excuse or lawful cause is an offence, the burden of proof that the act was done with lawful excuse or lawful cause, as the case may be, is on the person charged with the offence.

PART II – DRUNKENNESS

3 Drunkenness

A person who is found drunk in a public place is guilty of an offence.

Penalty: A fine not exceeding K40.00 or imprisonment for a term not exceeding one month.

4 Drunk and disorderly

A person who is found drunk in a public place and who acts in a manner that disturbs a reasonable member of the public or is likely to disturb a reasonable member of the public, is guilty of an offence.

Penalty: A fine not exceeding K100.00 or imprisonment for a term not exceeding three months.

5 Special provisions relating to drunkeness

(1) Notwithstanding this Act or any other law, where a person has been convicted of an offence against Section 3 or 4, the court convicting the person may, instead of imposing a penalty, order that the person convicted be released on his entering into a recognizance, with or without sureties, to be of good behaviour and to comply with such other conditions as the court determines and specifies in the recognizance, for such period as the court orders.

(2) The conditions specified in the recognizance may include a condition that the convicted person subject himself to medical treatment for drunkenness.

PART III – PROTECTION OF PERSONS

[836]6 Assault

(1) In this section, "applies force" includes the application of heat, light, sound, electrical force, gas odour or any other substance or thing if applied to such a degree as to cause any injury or personal discomfort.

(2) For the purposes of this section, a person who –

(a) strikes, touches, moves or otherwise applies force of any kind to the person of another, either directly or indirectly, without his consent, or with his consent if the consent is obtained by fraud; or

(b) by any bodily act or gesture, attempts or threatens to apply force of any kind to the person of another without his consent, under such circumstances that the person making the attempt or threat has an actual or apparent present ability to apply such force,

is deemed to assault that person.

(3) A person who unlawfully assaults another person is guilty of an offence.

Penalty: A fine not exceeding K500.00 or imprisonment for a term not exceeding two years.

(4) Where a court convicts a person of an offence against Subsection (3), it may order him to pay –

(a) to the person, in relation to whom the offence was committed; or

(b) to any other person who suffers bodily injury or damage to property as a result of the commission of the offence,

such amount by way of compensation for bodily injury or damage to the property of the person occasioned by or in the course of the commission of the offence, as it considers just.

---

[836] Section 6 was amended by:
No. 17 of 1983, s1; and
No. 14 of 1985, s1.

[837]7 Provoking a breach of the peace

A person who –

(a) uses threatening, offensive or insulting behaviour; or

(b) uses threatening, abusive or insulting words; or

(c) makes threatening, abusive or insulting gestures,

with intent to provoke a breach of the peace or by which a breach of the peace is likely to take place is guilty of an offence.

Penalty: A fine not exceeding K300.00 or imprisonment for a term not exceeding one year.

[838]8 Causing a fight

A person who causes a fight or behaves in a manner that is likely to cause a fight is guilty of an offence.

Penalty: A fine not exceeding K600.00 or imprisonment for a term not exceeding three years.

[839]9 Inciting to fight

A person who by words, gestures or otherwise incites any other person or persons to fight is guilty of an offence.

Penalty: A fine not exceeding K800.00 or imprisonment for a term not exceeding four years.

[840]10 Fighting

Where two or more persons are fighting in a manner that is likely –

(a) to cause bodily injury to some other person; or

(b) to cause damage to the property of some other person,

they are each and severally guilty of an offence.

Penalty: A fine not exceeding K600.00 or imprisonment for

---

[837] Section 7 was amended by:
No. 17 of 1983, s2; and
No. 14 of 1985, s2.

[838] Section 8 was amended by:
No. 17 of 1983, s3; and
No. 14 of 1985, s3.

[839] Section 9 was amended by:
No. 17 of 1983, s4; and
No. 14 of 1985, s4.

[840] Section 10 was amended by:
No. 17 of 1983, s5; and
No. 14 of 1985, s5

a term not exceeding three years.

11 False reports

A person who spreads false or wilfully misleading reports tending to cause trouble or ill-feeling –

(a) amongst people; or

(b) between the members of a group of people; or

(c) between groups of people; or

(d) between individuals,

is guilty of an offence.

Penalty: A fine not exceeding K100.00 or imprisonment for a term not exceeding three months.

[841]12 Carrying weapons

(1) A person who without reasonable excuse –

(a) carries; or

(b) has in his possession, custody or control,

any offensive weapon is guilty of an offence.[842]

Penalty: A fine not exceeding K2,000.00 or imprisonment for a term not exceeding five years.

(2) Where a person is convicted of an offence against Subsection (1), the court that convicts him may order that the weapon the subject of the charge be destroyed or forfeited to the State.

13 Adding matter to food or drink

A person who adds any matter or thing to food or drink consumed, or intended to be consumed, by another person with intent to cause that other person any physical or mental harm or incapacity is guilty of an offence.

Penalty: A fine not exceeding K100.00 or imprisonment for a term not exceeding three months.

---

[841] Section 12 was amended by:
No. 17 of 1983, s6; and
No. 14 of 1985, s6

[842] The penalty provision of Section 12(1) was repealed and replaced by the *Summary Offences (Amendment) Act* 1993 (No. 16 of 1993), s1.

14 Valueless cheques

(1) A person who obtains, or pays for, any goods, money, valuable security, credit, benefit or advantage by passing a cheque that is not paid on presentation to the bank against which it is drawn is guilty of an offence.

Penalty: A fine not exceeding K400.00 or imprisonment for a term not exceeding one year.

(2) It is a defence to a charge for an offence against Subsection (1) if the person charged proves that he had reasonable grounds for believing that the cheque would be paid in full on presentation.

(3) The fact that at the time the cheque was passed there were some funds to the credit of the account against which the cheque was drawn is not, of itself, a defence to a charge of an offence against Subsection (1).

15 False pretences

A person who solicits, gathers, collects or obtains any money, property, subscription, contribution or advantage for himself or for any other person by means of any false pretence or wilfully misleading conduct, is guilty of an offence.

Penalty: A fine not exceeding K100.00 or imprisonment for a term not exceeding three months.

[843]16 Property reasonably suspected of having been stolen

A person who has in his possession or who is conveying in any manner property reasonably suspected of having been stolen or unlawfully obtained who does not give an account to the satisfaction of the court as to how he came by the property is guilty of an offence.

Penalty: A fine not exceeding K200.00 or imprisonment for a term not exceeding two years.

17 Disguises

A person who –

(a) wears a disguise; or

(b) has on or about his person any article of disguise,

[843] Section 16 was amended by:
No. 17 of 1983, s7; and
No. 14 of 1985, s7.

with intent to commit an offence, is guilty of an offence.[844]

Penalty: A fine not exceeding K500.00 or imprisonment for a term not exceeding two years.

[845]18 Possession of house – breaking implements

(1) A person who has in his possession –

(a) by night – any implement capable of being used for house – breaking, in circumstances that prima facie show an intention to use it for house – breaking; or

(b) by day – any house – breaking implement with intent to commit an indictable offence,

is guilty of an offence.

Penalty: A fine not exceeding K200.00 or imprisonment for a term not exceeding two years.

(2) It is a defence to a charge under Subsection (1)(a) if the person charged proves that he had lawful excuse for having the implement in his possession.

(3) Where a court convicts a person of an offence against Subsection (1), it may order that the house-breaking implement in relation to which the person was convicted be destroyed or forfeited to the State.

[846]19 Loitering with intent to commit indictable offence

A person who –

(a) loiters in or near; or

(b) frequents,

a public place with intent to commit an indictable offence is guilty of an offence.

Penalty: A fine not exceeding K200.00 or imprisonment for a term not exceeding one year.

---

[844] The penalty provision of Section 17 was repealed and replaced by the *Summary Offences (Amendment) Act* 1993 (No. 16 of 1993), s2.

[845] Section 18 was amended by:
No. 17 of 1983, s. 8; and
No. 14 of 1985, s. 8.

[846] Section 19 was amended by:
No. 17 of 1983, s 9; and
No. 14 of 1985, s 9.

[847]20 Unlawfully on premises

A person who, without lawful excuse, is in, on or adjacent to any premises is guilty of an offence.

Penalty: A fine not exceeding K400.00 or imprisonment for a term not exceeding two years.

21 Habitually in the company of thieves

(1) A person who is habitually in the company of persons who have been convicted of false pretences, stealing or other offences relating to property may –

(a) be summoned to appear before; or

(b) be arrested with or without warrant and brought before,

a District Court.

(2) Where a District Court is satisfied after due enquiry that a person to whom Subsection (1) refers, is habitually in the company of persons who have been convicted of false pretences, stealing or other offences relating to property, it may order that person to stay out of the company of the persons who have been convicted of false pretences, stealing or other offences relating to property specified in the order.

(3) A person who fails to comply with an order of a District Court under Subsection (2) is guilty of an offence.

Penalty: For the first offence – a fine not exceeding K100.00 or imprisonment for a term not exceeding three months.

For a second or subsequent offence – a fine not exceeding K200.00 or imprisonment for a term not exceeding six months.

22 Escaping from lawful custody

(1) A person who, being in the lawful custody of a person under any law, escapes or attempts to escape from custody is guilty of an offence.

Penalty: A fine not exceeding K200.00 or imprisonment for a term not exceeding six months.

---

[847] Section 20 was amended by:
No. 17 of 1983, s 10; and
No. 14 of 1985, s 10

(2) A person who escapes from lawful custody is deemed to be continuing to commit an offence under Subsection (1) until he is arrested for that offence, any other offence, or under any other law.

23 Indecent exposure

(1) In this section "private parts", in relation to –

(a) a male person – means his genitals; and

(b) a female person – means her vagina and the area immediately surrounding the vagina.

(2) A person who intentionally exposes his private parts in a public place or within view of any person in a public place is guilty of an offence.

Penalty: A fine not exceeding K50.00 or imprisonment for a term not exceeding one month.

(3) A person who intentionally exposes his private parts with intent to insult or offend any person in any place is guilty of an offence.

Penalty: A fine not exceeding K50.00 or imprisonment for a term not exceeding one month.

(4) A person cannot be convicted of an offence under this section on the uncorroborated testimony of one witness.

(5) It is a defence to a charge of an offence against Subsection (2) if the defendant proves that –

(a) he had no intention to offend public decency; and

(b) it was reasonable for him to have believed that his action would not insult, offend or annoy any other person.

24 Indecent writing

(1) A person who –

(a) in a public place; or

(b) within the view of any person in a public place,

writes any word which grossly offends against accepted standards of public decency is guilty of an offence.

Penalty: A fine not exceeding K40.00.

(2) Where a court convicts a person of an offence against Subsection (1) it may order the person convicted –

(a) to remove or pay for the removal of the writing from any building, wall, fence, tree, pole, structure, roof or footpath, as the case may be, in a public place; and

(b) to restore the building, wall, fence, tree, pole, structure, road or footpath, as the case may be, to its former condition.

25 Indecent drawings, etc

(1) A person who –

(a) in a public place; or

(b) within the view of any person in a public place,

exhibits or causes to be exhibited –

(c) any drawing, etching or painting; or

(d) any photograph or photographic reproduction; or

(e) any sculpture,

that grossly offends against accepted standards of public decency is guilty of an offence.

Penalty: A fine not exceeding K20.00 or imprisonment for a term not exceeding 14 days.

(2) Where a court convicts a person of an offence against Subsection (1) it may order that the drawing, etching, painting, photograph, photographic reproduction or sculpture, as the case may be, be destroyed or forfeited to the State.

(3) In addition to any order made under Subsection (2), where a court convicts a person of an offence under Subsection (1) it may order the person convicted –

(a) to remove or pay for the removal of the drawing, etching, painting, photograph, photographic reproduction or sculpture, as the case may be, from any building, wall, fence, tree, pole, structure, road or footpath, as the case may be, in a public place; and

(b) to restore the building, wall, fence, tree, pole, structure, road or footpath, as the case may be, to its former condition.

(4) It is a defence to a charge of an offence against Subsection (1) if the defendant proves that the article exhibited or caused to be exhibited in a public place had artistic or cultural merit.

(5) The opinion of witnesses as to the artistic or cultural merit of an article may be admitted in evidence in any proceedings under this section to establish or negative a defence under Subsection (4).

[848]25A Possession, etc, of indecent etc, article

(1) A person who –

(a) has in his possession; or

(b) makes; or

(c) produces; or

(d) performs in the making or production of; or

(e) exhibits; or

(f) sells,

an article or articles that –

(g) is or are blasphemous or indecent; or

(h) grossly offends or grossly offend against accepted standards of decency,

is guilty of an offence.

Penalty: A fine not exceeding K2,000.00 or imprisonment for a term not exceeding one year, or both.

(2) It is a defence to a charge of an offence against Subsection (1)(d) that the person charged was not aware that he was performing in the making or production of an article or articles.

(3) For the purposes of this section –

"article" means any description of article containing or embodying matter to be read or looked at or both, any sound record and any film or other record or a picture or pictures;

"film" means –

(a) a cinematograph film, and includes a positive or negative of a cinematograph film; or

(b) a video tape or video disc.

[848] Section 25A was added by the *Summary Offences (Amendment) Act* 1986 (No. 36 of 1986), s3.

PART IV – PROTECTION OF THE NEIGHBOURHOOD

[849]26 Unlawfully disturbing householders

A person who, without reasonable excuse, disturbs –

(a) any occupant of; or

(b) any other person lawfully within,

any building –

(c) by ringing any doorbell, buzzer or other similar device; or

(d) by rapping or knocking on, or throwing stones, sticks or other missiles at,

any part of the building, is guilty of an offence.

Penalty: A fine not exceeding K100.00 or imprisonment for a term not exceeding one year.

[850]27 Allowing disturbances on licenced premises

The holder of a publican's licence, tavern licence, limited hotel licence, club licence, bottle shop licence or restaurant licence, under the Liquor (Licensing) Act, who allows on the licenced premises conduct which causes or is likely to cause alarm, fear or disgust to any reasonable person is guilty of an offence.

Penalty: A fine not exceeding K5,000.00.

28 Use of missiles, firearms, etc

(1) In this section, "firearm" includes –

(a) any gun, rifle or pistol; and

(b) an airgun, starting pistol or imitation firearm whether or not it is capable of projecting any kind of shot, bullet or missile.

(2) A person who, without reasonable cause, discharges, throws or projects any stone, stick or other missile with intent to, or in a manner likely to –

(a) injure, annoy or frighten any person; or

---

[849] Section 26 was amended by:
No. 17 of 1983, s11; and
No. 14 of 1985, s11.

[850] Section 27 was amended by:
No. 17 of 1983, s12; and
No. 14 of 1985, s12.

(b) damage any property,

is guilty of an offence.

Penalty: A fine not exceeding K100.00 or imprisonment for a term not exceeding three months.

[851](3) A person –

(a) who without reasonable cause, discharges a firearm with intent to, or in a manner likely to –

(i) injure, annoy or frighten any person; or

(ii) damage any property; or

(b) who makes, possesses or sells a firearm, without being the holder of a valid licence under the Firearms Act (Chapter 310),

is guilty of an offence.

Penalty: A fine not exceeding K1,000.00 or imprisonment for a term not exceeding two years.

(4) Where a person is convicted of an offence against Subsection (3) the court before which he is convicted may order that the firearm, the subject of the charge, be forfeited to the State.

29 Exploding fireworks, etc, in a public place

A person who, without the written consent of a Provincial Commissioner –

(a) sets fire to or explodes any fireworks or explosive material in a public place; or

(b) throws any fireworks or explosive material into public place so that it explodes in or near the public place,

is guilty of an offence.

Penalty: A fine not exceeding K10.00.

30 Throwing, etc, fireworks or other explosive material

A person who throws, sets fire to, or explodes any fireworks or other explosive material –

(a) so as to injure, frighten or annoy any person; or

(b) in such circumstances that any person is likely to be injured, annoyed or frightened,

is guilty of an offence.

---

[851] Section 28(3) was repealed and replaced by the *Summary Offences (Amendment) Act* 1993 (No. 16 of 1993), s3.

Penalty: A fine not exceeding K50.00.

31 Waterskiing in prohibited area

(1) In this section "area of water" includes any area of inland or coastal water, or any part of such area, within the country.

(2) Where it appears to the Minister to be in the public interest to do so, he may, by notice in the National Gazette, declare any area of water specified in the notice to be a prohibited area for the purposes of this section.

(3) A person who, in a prohibited area –

(a) water skis,[852] or

(b) navigates any boat, motor vessel or powered canoe at a speed greater than five knots,

is guilty of an offence.

Penalty: For the first offence – a fine not exceeding K50.00.

For a second or subsequent offence – a fine not exceeding K100.00.

(4) A member of the Police Force who intends to lay a charge under Subsection (3) against a person may –

(a) advise that person that he intends to lay a charge under Subsection (3) against him; and

(b) ask that person for his name and address.

(5) A person who refuses or fails to provide his name and address when requested to do so under Subsection (4) is guilty of an offence.

Penalty: A fine not exceeding K50.00.

[853]32 Burning rubbish

A person who, without reasonable cause, burns, or causes to be burnt, any substance that interferes with the reasonable comfort of any other person is guilty of an offence.

Penalty: A fine not exceeding K10.00.

---

[852] The Act has ",".

[853] See also Section 38.

[854]33 Yards to be clean and free from offensive smells

A person who –

(a) is the owner or occupier of any premises or area adjacent to a public place; and

(b) fails or neglects to keep the premises or area clean and so causes annoyance to any person in the public place by reason of an offensive smell emanating from the premises or area,

is guilty of an offence.

Penalty: A fine not exceeding K10.00.

Default penalty: A fine not exceeding K1.00.

[855]34 Breaking glass in a public place

(1) A member of the Police Force who –

(a) finds a person wilfully breaking glass in a public place; or

(b) has reasonable cause to believe that a person has just wilfully broken glass in a public place,

may order that person to remove that broken glass from the public place.

(2) A person who refuses or fails to obey an order given under Subsection (1) is guilty of an offence.

Penalty: A fine not exceeding K100.00 or imprisonment for a term not exceeding one year.

[856]35 Dead animals

(1) In this section, "animal" includes any bird, fish or reptile.

(2) A person who leaves, or causes to be left, any dead animal or any part of a dead animal in or near any river, creek, drain or other watercourse that flows through or alongside a public place is guilty of an offence.

Penalty: A fine not exceeding K100.00.

---

[854] See also Section 38.

[855] Section 34 was amended by:
No. 17 of 1983, s13; and
No. 14 of 1985, s13.

[856] See also Section 38.

[857]36 Polluting watercourses, etc

A person who throws or drops any filth or rubbish into, or otherwise pollutes any river, creek, canal, watercourse, well, water – tank or water storage is guilty of an offence.

Penalty: A fine not exceeding K100.00.

[858]37 Obstructing watercourses, etc

(1) A person who, without reasonable excuse, obstructs or diverts from its channel any public sewer, public drain, creek or other watercourse is guilty of an offence.

Penalty: A fine not exceeding K100.00.

(2) It is a defence to a charge against Subsection (1) if the person charged proves –

(a) that he is a member of a customary group or community; and

(b) that it is traditional for members of that customary group or community to divert that creek or other watercourse for the purpose of catching fish.

38 Further orders relating to the removal of rubbish, etc

(1) The court that convicts a person of an offence against Section 32, 33, 35, 36 or 37 may order the person convicted to –

(a) remove, within the time specified in the order; or

(b) pay the cost of the removal of,

the litter, filth, rubbish, refuse or other thing from the land or place on which it was deposited and to –

(c) restore, within the time specified in the order; or

(d) pay the cost of the restoration of,

the sewer, drain, creek or other watercourse to its former channel.

(2) A person who fails to comply with an order made under Subsection (1) is guilty of an offence.

Penalty: A fine not exceeding K100.00.

---

[857] See also Section 38.

[858] See also Section 38.

39 Fencing holes, etc

A person who –

(a) is the owner or occupier of land that is open and exposed to any public place; and

(b) without reasonable excuse, fails to cover, fence or shield any hole or other danger on that land adjacent to a public place; or

(c) without reasonable excuse fails to cover, fence or shield any hole or other danger on that land so as to provide reasonable protection from injury to any person lawfully on that land,

is guilty of an offence.

Penalty: A fine not exceeding K50.00.

Default penalty: A fine not exceeding K5.00.

40 Dangers, etc, in public places to be barricaded, etc

(1) A person who –

(a) digs or causes to be dug, or who leaves or causes to be left, any hole; or

(b) creates or causes to be created, any other danger,

in a public place or in an area adjacent to a public place, must –

(c) immediately construct, or cause to be constructed, a barrier around the hole or danger so as to provide reasonable protection from injury to those members of the public who may reasonably be expected to use that public place or that area; and

(d) between the hours of 6 p.m. and 6 a.m, place and keep, or cause to be placed and kept, at least one visible lamp on the barrier so as to give reasonable warning of the hole or other danger to the members of the public using that public place or that area.

(2) A person who fails to comply with any of the provisions of Subsection (1) is guilty of an offence.

Penalty: A fine not exceeding K50.00.

Default penalty: A fine not exceeding K5.00.

PART V – PROTECTION OF PROPERTY

[859]*Division 1 – Offences Relating to Property*

41 Interpretation of Part V

In this Part, "lawful authority" includes the approval or consent of the owner or person in possession or control of the building, wall, fence, tree, pole, structure, road or footpath to which the offence relates.

42 Posting bills on walls, etc

(1) A person who, without lawful authority, in a public place, attaches any paper, bill, poster or placard to any building, wall, fence, tree, pole, structure, road or footpath is guilty of an offence.

Penalty: A fine not exceeding K50.00.

(2) The court that convicts a person of an offence against Subsection (1) may order the person convicted –

(a) to remove, or to pay for the removal of, within the period specified by the court, the paper, bill, poster or placard, as the case may be; and

(b) to restore the building, wall, fence, tree, pole, structure, road or footpath, as the case may be, to its former condition.

(3) A person who refuses or fails to comply with an order made by a court under Subsection (2) is guilty of an offence.

Penalty: A fine not exceeding K100.00.

43 Writing on or defacing walls, etc

(1) A person who, without lawful authority, in a public place, writes on, soils, defaces or marks any building, wall, fence, tree, pole, structure, road or footpath by any means, is guilty of an offence.

Penalty: A fine not exceeding K50.00.

(2) The court that convicts a person of an offence against Subsection (1) may order the person convicted –

(a) to remove, or to pay for the removal of, within the period specified by the court, the writing, dirt or marks, as the case may be; and

[859] Heading added by No. 35 of 1981.

(b) to restore the building, wall, fence, tree, pole, structure, road or footpath, as the case may be, to its former condition.

(3) A person who refuses or fails to comply with an order under Subsection (2) is guilty of an offence.

Penalty: A fine not exceeding K100.00.

44 Defacing, etc, street signs

(1) A person who, without lawful authority, interferes with, defaces, disfigures, destroys or removes a street sign or any part of a street sign is guilty of an offence.

Penalty: A fine not exceeding K50.00.

(2) The court that convicts a person of an offence against Subsection (1) may order the person convicted to repair or restore, or to pay for the repair or restoration of the street sign, within the period specified by the court.

(3) A person who refuses or fails to comply with an order made under Subsection (2) is guilty of an offence.

Penalty: A fine not exceeding K100.00.

45 Casting boats adrift

(1) In this section, "cast adrift" includes –

(a) the cutting of mooring lines; and

(b) pulling up anchor; and

(c) untying from a pier or buoy.

(2) A person who, without reasonable excuse, interferes with or casts adrift any boat is guilty of an offence.

Penalty: A fine not exceeding K100.00.

(3) Where a person is convicted of an offence against Subsection (2), the court before which he is convicted may, in addition to any penalty that it may impose, order the person convicted to pay such amount, by way of compensation, to the person aggrieved, as the court thinks fit.

46 Interference, etc, with public lighting

(1) A person who, without reasonable cause, removes, obscures, damages or otherwise interferes with any lamp or other means of lighting erected or placed on a public place for the purpose of street lighting or for the safety of members of the public is guilty of an offence.

Penalty: A fine not exceeding K50.00.

(2) Where a person is convicted of an offence against Subsection (1), the court before which he is convicted may, in addition to any penalty it may impose, order the person convicted to pay such amount to replace or to restore to its former condition any lamp or other means of lighting referred to in Subsection (1).

(3) A person who refuses or fails to comply with an order made under Subsection (2) is guilty of an offence.

Penalty: A fine not exceeding K100.00.

[860]47 Damaging property

(1) In this section, "property" includes any personal property, house or other building, garden, crop, tree, fence, road, bridge, animal, reptile, bird or fish.

(2) A person who, without reasonable excuse, destroys, damages or injures any property belonging to another person is guilty of an offence.

Penalty: A fine not exceeding K400.00 or imprisonment for a term not exceeding two years.

(3) Where a person is convicted of an offence against Subsection (2), the court before which he is convicted may, in addition to any penalty that it may impose, order the person convicted to pay such amount, by way of compensation, to the person aggrieved as the court thinks fit.

48 Negligent use of fire

(1) In this section, "property" includes any personal property, house or other building, garden, crop, tree, fence, road, bridge, animal, reptile, bird or fish.

(2) A person who, by the negligent use of fire, destroys, damages or injures any property belonging to any other person is guilty of an offence.

Penalty: A fine not exceeding K100.00 or imprisonment for a term not exceeding three months.

(3) Where a person is convicted of an offence against Subsection (2) the court before which he is convicted may, in addition to any penalty that it may impose, order the person convicted to pay such amount, by way of compensation, to the person aggrieved, as the court thinks fit.

---

[860] Section 47 was amended by:
No. 17 of 1983, s14; and
No. 14 of 1985, s14.

[861]*Division 2 – Stealing*

48A Application of Criminal Code

Sections 363 to 371 of the Criminal Code apply to offences under this Division.

[862]48B Jurisdiction

[Repealed]

48C Stealing

(1) A person who steals or attempts to steal anything, capable of being stolen, of a value not exceeding K500.00, is guilty of an offence under this Act.

Penalty: A fine not exceeding K400.00 or imprisonment for a term not exceeding 12 months.

(2) A person who steals or attempts to steal anything, capable of being stolen, of a value not exceeding K500.00 –

(a) from the person of another; or

(b) the property of his employer or property which came into his possession on account of his employer,

is guilty of an offence under this Act.

Penalty: A fine not exceeding K400.00 or imprisonment for a term not exceeding 12 months.

---

[861] Division 2 added by No. 35 of 1981.

[862] Section 48B repealed by No. 16 of 1982.

PART VI – GAMING AND BETTING

49 Application of Part VI

This Part is subject to and does not derogate from the provisions of –

(a) the Gaming Act; and

(b) the Bookmaking Act; and

(c) the Criminal Code.

50 Declaration of unlawful game

(1) The Head of State, acting on advice may, by notice in the National Gazette, declare any game to be an unlawful game for the purposes of this Part.

(2) A declaration under Subsection (1) has no force or effect until approved by a resolution of the Parliament.

51 Playing unlawful game

A person who plays an unlawful game is guilty of an offence.

Penalty: For the first offence – a fine not exceeding K40.00 or imprisonment for a term not exceeding one month.

For a second or subsequent offence – a fine not exceeding K100.00 or imprisonment for a term not exceeding three months.

52 Gaming in places of public resort

A person who –

(a) has the possession of, or the control of, any premises into which members of the public may enter, whether on payment of money or not; and

(b) allows any unlawful game to be played on those premises,

is guilty of an offence.

Penalty: A fine not exceeding K50.00.

53 Unlawful Betting

A person who, in or near any public place or in or near any premises licensed under the Liquor (Licensing) Act plays or bets or incites or encourages any person to play or bet –

(a) at or with any instrument of gaming at any game or pretended game of chance; or

(b) at or on any trick or sleight of hand; or

(c) at or on any game or trick with any instrument that is so constructed as to be capable of being used for cheating,

for a stake or prize is guilty of an offence.

Penalty: A fine not exceeding K100.00 or imprisonment for a term not exceeding three months.

54 Possession of instruments of gaming

(1) A person who –

(a) loiters in or near any public place or in or near any premises licensed under the Liquor (Licensing) Act; and

(b) has in his possession, without lawful excuse –

(i) an instrument of gaming; or

(ii) an instrument that is so constructed as to be capable of being used as a means of cheating,

is guilty of an offence.

Penalty: A fine not exceeding K100.00 or imprisonment for a term not exceeding three months.

(2) Where a court convicts a person of an offence against Subsection (1), it may order that the instrument in relation to which the person was convicted be forfeited to the State.

PART VII – PROSTITUTION

55 Persons living on the earnings of prostitution

(1) A person who knowingly lives wholly or in part on the earnings of prostitution is guilty of an offence.

Penalty: A fine not exceeding K400.00 or imprisonment for a term not exceeding one year.

(2) The fact that –

(a) a person lives with, or is constantly in the company of a prostitute; or

(b) a person has exercised some degree of control or influence over the movements of a prostitute in such a manner as to show that that person is assisting her to commit prostitution,

is prima facie evidence that that person is knowingly living on the earnings of prostitution.

56 Keeping a brothel

(1) A person who –

(a) keeps, manages or acts or assists in the management of a brothel; or

(b) knowingly supplies, or assists in the supply of money for the maintenance and support of a brothel,

is guilty of an offence,

Penalty: A fine not exceeding K800.00 or imprisonment for a term not exceeding two years.

(2) For the purposes of this section, a person who acts or behaves in such a manner as would lead a reasonable person to believe that he is the person in charge of, or having the care or management of, a brothel, shall be deemed to keep the brothel.

57 Suppression of brothels

A person who –

(a) being the owner, lessee, tenant, occupier or person in charge of any premises –

uses the premises or knowingly permits the premises to be used as a brothel or for any purposes connected with prostitution; or

(b) being the owner or lessee of any premises or the agent of any such owner or lessee – lets or sublets the premises knowing that the premises are to be used as a brothel or for any purpose connected with prostitution,

is guilty of an offence.

Penalty: A fine not exceeding K200.00.

Default penalty: A fine not exceeding K20.00.

PART VIII – OFFENCES RELATING TO POLICE

58 Creating false belief

A person who does any act with the intention of creating a belief or suspicion in any person that –

(a) an offence has been committed; or

(b) a life has or may be lost or is or may be endangered; or

(c) property is, has been or may be endangered,

knowing that the circumstances with respect to which he intends to create the belief of suspicion have not occurred, is guilty of an offence.

Penalty: A fine not exceeding K200.00 or imprisonment for a term not exceeding six months.

59 Delaying or withdrawing an information for reward

A person who –

(a) lays an information or makes a complaint before a Magistrate for any offence, by which he is not personally aggrieved, which is alleged to have been committed against this Act or any other enactment or subordinate enactment; and

(b) directly or indirectly accepts, without the consent of a court, any money or other reward for delaying or withdrawing the information or complaint,

is guilty of an offence.

Penalty: A fine not exceeding K200.00 or imprisonment for a term not exceeding six months.

60 Obstructing, etc, a member of the Police Force

(1) A person who resists, obstructs or hinders a member of the Police Force acting in the execution of his duty, is guilty of an offence.

Penalty: A fine not exceeding K200.00 or imprisonment for a term not exceeding six months.

(2) It is a defence to a charge of an offence against Subsection (1) if the defendant proves that he could not reasonably have known that the person resisted, obstructed or hindered was a member of the Police Force acting in the execution of his duty.

(3) Where a court convicts a person of an offence against

Subsection (1), it may order him to pay to the member of the Police Force, in relation to whom the offence was committed, such amount by way of compensation for bodily injury or damage to the property of the member occasioned by or in the course of the commission of the offence, as it considers just.

(4) A person who refuses or fails to comply with an order made under Subsection (3) is guilty of an offence.

Penalty: A fine not exceeding K100.00.

61 Assaulting a member of the Police Force

(1) A person who assaults a member of the Police Force acting in the execution of his duty is guilty of an offence.

Penalty: A fine not exceeding K200.00 or imprisonment for a term not exceeding six months, or both.

(2) It is a defence to a charge of an offence against Subsection (1) if the defendant proves that he could not reasonably have known that the person assaulted was a member of the Police Force acting in the execution of his duty.

(3) Where a court convicts a person of an offence against Subsection (1), it may order him to pay to the member of the Police Force, in relation to whom the offence was committed, such amount by way of compensation for bodily injury or damage to the property of the member occasioned by or in the course of the commission of the offence, as it considers just.

(4) A person who refuses or fails to comply with an order made under Subsection (3) is guilty of an offence.

Penalty: A fine not exceeding K100.00.

PART IX – OFFENCES RELATING TO CERTAIN TYPES OF VEHICLES

62 Interpretation of Part IX

In this Part, unless the contrary intention appears –

"public street" means any street, road, lane, thoroughfare, footpath, bridge or place open to or used by the public or to which the public have or are permitted to have access whether on payment of a fee or otherwise;

"vehicle" means a vehicle other than a motor vehicle as defined in the Motor Traffic Act.

63 Driving, etc, vehicle at night without light

A person who, in a public street, drives or uses a vehicle between the hours of sunset and sunrise –

(a) without having attached to the vehicle a white light that is, under normal circumstances, visible to a person in front of the vehicle at a distance of not less than 50m; or

(b) without having attached to the back of the vehicle a red reflector light that is under normal circumstances clearly visible to a person behind the vehicle at a distance of not less than 50m,

is guilty of an offence.

Penalty: A fine not exceeding K20.00.

[863]64 Negligent driving, etc

A person who, in a public street, drives or uses a vehicle in a negligent manner is guilty of an offence.

Penalty: A fine not exceeding K400.00 or imprisonment for a term not exceeding two years.

---

[863] Section 64 amended by:
No. 17 of 1983, s15; and
No. 14 of 1985, s15.

[864]65 Dangerous driving

A person who, in a public street, drives or uses a vehicle in a manner dangerous to the public or any member of the public is guilty of an offence.

Penalty: A fine not exceeding K400.00 or imprisonment for a term not exceeding two years.

66 Failure to keep to the left

A person who, without reasonable excuse, drives or uses a vehicle without keeping the vehicle as close as practicable to the left – hand side of the carriageway is guilty of an offence.

Penalty: A fine not exceeding K40.00.

67 Driving, etc, on footpath

A person who, without reasonable excuse, drives or uses any vehicle on a footpath is guilty of an offence.

Penalty: A fine not exceeding K40.00.

68 Failure to comply with directions of member of Police Force

A person who, in any public street, drives or uses any vehicle and fails to comply with any reasonable direction given by a member of the Police Force as to –

[865](a) the manner of approaching or departing from any place; or

(b) the manner of taking up or setting down any passengers or the loading or unloading of goods; or

(c) the regulation of traffic,

is guilty of an offence.

Penalty: A fine not exceeding K40.00.

---

[864] Section 65 was amended by:
No. 17 of 1983, s16; and
No. 14 of 1985, s16.

[865] The Revised Act mistakenly refers to "(b)"

PART X – MISCELLANEOUS

69 Time limit on bringing charges

Notwithstanding Section 22 of the Local Courts Act no charge for an offence against any provision of this Act shall be laid in any court after six months after the offence took place.

70 Regulations

The Head of State, acting on advice, may make regulations, not inconsistent with this Act, prescribing all matters that by this Act are required or permitted to be prescribed, for carrying out and giving effect to this Act, and in particular for prescribing –

(a) the form in which charges under the several sections of this Act may be laid; and

(b) the imposition of penalties of fines not exceeding K100.00 or imprisonment for terms not exceeding three months, or both, for offences against the regulations.

No 37 of 1989

Village Courts Act 1989

PART I – PRELIMINARY

PART II – VILLAGE COURTS SECRETARIAT

PART III – VILLAGE COURTS

Division 1 – Establishment, Suspension and abolition etc

Division 2 – Constitution and sitting of Village Courts

Division 3 – Inspection of Village Courts

Division 4 – Fines

PART IV – VILLAGE COURT OFFICIALS

Division 1 – Provincial Supervising Magistrates and Village Magistrates

Division 5 – Preventive Jurisdiction

Division 6 – Mediatory Jurisdiction

Division 7 – Joint Jurisdiction of Courts

Division 8 – Law to be applied

Division 9 – Enforcement

Division 10 – Procedure

PART X – MISCELLANEOUS

SCHEDULE

INDEPENDENT STATE OF PAPUA NEW GUINEA

No 37 of 1989

Village Courts Act 1989

(Consolidated to Village Courts (Amendment) Act 2000)

Being an Act as authorized by Section 172 of the *Constitution* to provide for a system of Village Courts and Village Peace Officers, their jurisdiction, powers, duties, practice and procedure, and for other purposes,

MADE by the National Parliament, to come into operation in accordance with a notice in the National Gazette by the Head of State, acting with, and in accordance with, the advice of the Minister.

PART I – PRELIMINARY

1 Interpretation

(1) In this Act, unless the contrary intention appears –

[866]"community work order" means an order to perform community work in accordance with Subsections (2) and (3);

"Deputy Provincial Supervising Magistrate" means a Magistrate appointed as such under Section 15(1)(b);

"Deputy Village Court Clerk" means a Deputy Village Court Clerk appointed under Section 22 and, in relation to a Village Court, means a Deputy Village Court Clerk appointed for the Court;

"dispute" includes any case where a person complains of, and is genuinely aggrieved by, the actions or likely actions of another person but does not include any case in which the complaint –

(a) is made in an official capacity; or

(b) is a complaint against an official act;

[866]Definition "community work order" inserted by the *Village Courts (Amendment) Act* 2000, s1.

"land" includes a reef or bank and a house or other structure built on or over water, but does not include things growing on land;

"Local Land Court" has the meaning given to it in Section 2 of the *Land Disputes Settlement Act* (Chapter 45);

"Local Level Government body", in relation to a Village Court, means the Local Level Government body for the area in which the Village Court is established;

"Magistrate" means –

(a) a District Court Magistrate; or

[867](b) . . . [Repealed]

(c) a Reserve District Court Magistrate; or

[868](d) . . . [Repealed]

"Peace and Good Order Committee" means a Peace and Good Order Committee established under Section 5 of the *Inter-Group Fighting Act* (Chapter 344);

"Provincial Executive", in relation to a Village Court, means the Provincial Executive for the province in which the Village Court is established;

"Provincial Gazette", in relation to a Village Court, means the Provincial Gazette for the province in which the Village Court is established;

"Provincial Government", in relation to a Village Court, means the Provincial Government for the province in which the Village Court is established;

"Provincial Land Court" has the meaning given to it in Section 2 of the *Land Disputes Settlement Act* (Chapter 45);

"Provincial Legislature", in relation to a Village Court, means the Provincial Legislature for the province in which the Village Court is established;

[869]"Provincial Minister", in relation to a Village Court, means the Minister of the Provincial Government or person or Committee of the Provincial Government having responsibility for matters relating to Village Courts;

---

[867]This paragraph was impliedly amended when the *Local Courts Act* (Chapter 41) was repealed by the *Local Courts (Repeal) Act* 2000.

[868]This paragraph was impliedly amended when the *Local Courts Act* (Chapter 41) was repealed by the *Local Courts (Repeal) Act* 2000.

[869]The definition of "Provincial Minister" repealed and replaced by the *Provincial Governments and Local-level Governments (Consequential Amendments) Act* 1995 (No. 17 of 1995), s5.

"Provincial Supervising Magistrate" means a District Court Magistrate appointed as such under Section 15(1)(a) and includes a Deputy Provincial Supervising Magistrate exercising or performing any power or function of a Provincial Supervising Magistrate under Section 15(3);

"Provincial Village Courts Officer", in relation to a Village Court, means the Provincial Village Courts Officer for the province in which the Village Court is established;

"Secretary" means the head of the Village Courts Secretariat;

"The Provincial Supervising Magistrate", in relation to a Village Court, means the Provincial Supervising Magistrate for the province in which the Village Court is situated;

"this Act" includes the Regulations;

"Village Court" means a Village Court established under Section 4 and includes a joint sitting of Village Courts under Section 56;

"Village Court Clerk" means a Village Court Clerk appointed under Section 22, and, in relation to a Village Court, means the Village Court Clerk appointed for the Court;

"Village Court Inspector", in relation to a Village Court, means the Village Court Inspector for the District in which the Village Court is established;

"Village Court Officer" includes Provincial Village Courts Officer and Village Court Inspector;

"Village Court Official" means –

(a) a Village Magistrate; or

(b) a Village Court Clerk; or

(c) a Deputy Village Court Clerk; or

(d) a Village Peace Officer;

"Village Magistrate" means a Village Magistrate appointed under Section 17, and, in relation to a Village Court, means a Village Magistrate appointed for the Court;

"Village Peace Officer" means a Village Peace Officer appointed under Section 26, and, in relation to a Village Court, means a Village Peace Officer appointed for the area of the Court.

[870](2) A community work order shall consist of an order for the offender to perform, for community purposes, specified work or work of a specified kind, for a specified period or periods not exceeding –

(a) eight hours in any one day; and

[870]Inserted by the Village Courts (Amendment) Act 2000, s1.

(b) six days in any one week; and

(c) a total period of six months, in such manner, at such times and subject to such conditions as to supervision or otherwise as are specified in the order.

[871](3) Wherever possible, a community work order shall consist of specified work, or work of a specified kind, which in the opinion of the Village Court will be most likely to benefit any person injured or aggrieved by the offence or matter in relation to which the penalty is ordered.

2 Application

(1) Where, pursuant to [872]Section 39 of the Organic Law on Provincial Government, a Provincial Legislature enacts legislation in respect of the establishment and administration of Village Courts, to the extent that that legislation conflicts with this Act, that legislation shall have effect and this Act shall not apply.

(2) Nothing contained in Subsection (1) shall be construed as derogating, or in any way restricting, the power of the Minister to cause an inspection of a Village Court under Section 10.

[871]Inserted by the Village Courts (Amendment) Act 2000, s1.

[872]Note that the Organic Law on Provincial Government has been repealed and replaced by the Organic Law on Provincial and Local-level Governments.

PART II – VILLAGE COURTS SECRETARIAT

3 Village Courts Secretariat

(1) There is established a Village Courts Secretariat, located within the Department responsible for justice matters, comprising such number of officers as are necessary for the carrying out of its function.

(2) The function of the Village Courts Secretariat is the efficient management of the system of Village Courts and Village Peace Officers.

PART III – VILLAGE COURTS

Division 1 – Establishment, Suspension and abolition etc

4 Establishment of Village Courts

The Minister may, by notice in the National Gazette, establish a Village Court in and for an area specified in the notice.

5 Suspension and abolition of Village Courts

The Minister may, by notice in the National Gazette –

(a) suspend a Village Court; or

(b) abolish a Village Court,

established under Section 4.

6 Procedure where Village Court suspended or abolished

(1) Where a Village Court is suspended or abolished under Section 5, the Provincial Supervising Magistrate shall –

(a) take possession and provide for the safe custody of –

(i) the books and records of the Village Court; and

(ii) the badges and other insignia of office issued under Section 106; and

(iii) the certificates of appointment (if any) of the Village Court Officials;

[873](b) in the case of the suspension of a Village Court, transfer to a specified Local Court such proceedings pending in the suspended Village Court at the date of the suspension as he considers necessary, in the interest of justice, so to do; and

[874](c) in the case of the abolition of a Village Court, transfer to a specified Local Court all proceedings pending in the abolished Village Court at the date of the abolition; and

(d) publicize, by notice in the Provincial Gazette and by such other means as he considers appropriate, –

(i) the suspension or abolition of the Village Court; and

(ii) proceedings transferred under Paragraph (b) or (c).

---

[873]This paragraph was impliedly amended or repealed when the *Local Courts Act* (Chapter 41) was repealed by the *Local Courts (Repeal) Act* 2000.

[874]This Subsection was impliedly amended or repealed when the *Local Courts Act* (Chapter 41) was repealed by the *Local Courts (Repeal) Act* 2000.

[875](2) Proceedings transferred under Subsection (1)(b) or (c) shall be heard and determined in the Local Court specified.

(3) Where a Village Court is suspended under Section 5, during the period of suspension, the Village Court Officials shall be suspended without pay.

(4) Where a Village Court is abolished under Section 5, the appointment of all Village Court Officials is deemed to be revoked.

Division 2 – Constitution and sitting of Village Courts

7 Constitution of Village Courts

(1) Subject to Section 8, a Village Court shall be constituted by an odd number (not being less than three) of Village Magistrates.

(2) Subject to Subsection (3), at a sitting of a Village Court, the Chairman of the Village Court shall preside and, in the absence of the Chairman, the Deputy Chairman shall preside.

(3) Where –

(a) the Chairman and the Deputy Chairman are absent; or

(b) there is no Chairman or Deputy Chairman,

the Village Magistrates constituting the Village Court shall appoint one of their number to preside.

(4) A decision of a Village Court shall be by majority vote.

8 One Village Magistrate to constitute Village Court

Notwithstanding Sections 7 and 17(3) where custom provides for a system of chiefs or chieftainship, the Minister may, in respect of a specified Village Court, by notice in the National Gazette, declare that a Village Magistrate sitting alone shall constitute that Village Court.

[875]This Subsection was impliedly amended or repealed when the *Local Courts Act* (Chapter 41) was repealed by the *Local Courts (Repeal) Act* 2000.

9 Place of sittings

A Village Court may sit at any place in the area for which it is established and may adjourn from time to time and from place to place.

Division 3 – Inspection of Village Courts

10 Minister may cause inspection

Where –

(a) an Act of a Provincial Legislature provides for the establishment and administration of Village Courts within a province; and

(b) the Minister wishes to determine whether a Village Court so established is acting within the jurisdiction and powers conferred by this Act,

the Minister may cause an inspection to be made of the Village Court.

11 Secretary may direct inspections

The Secretary may, in respect of a specified Village Court, direct the Provincial Village Courts Officer to ensure that the Village Court and its records are inspected at such intervals as the Secretary may determine and that a report of each such inspection is submitted promptly in accordance with any directions the Secretary may make concerning such reports.

12 Provincial Village Courts Officer may direct inspections

The Provincial Village Courts Officer may, in respect of a specified Village Court, direct a Village Court Inspector –

(a) to inspect the Village Court and its records; and

(b) to inquire into the functioning of the Village Court; and

(c) to point out to the Village Court Officials any defects in practice or procedure; and

(d) to encourage the adoption of practices and procedures recommended under Section 77(2); and

(e) to submit reports of inspections within a specified period.

Division 4 – Fines

13 Disposal of fines

All –

(a) fees chargeable in respect of matters before a Village Court; and

(b) fines, penalties and forfeitures ordered by a Village Court,

are payable to the Provincial Government.

14 Obligation of Provincial Government

The Provincial Government shall, insofar as it is practicable, allocate as a minimum for the maintenance and improvement of Village Courts an amount equivalent to the total amount received under Section 13.

PART IV – VILLAGE COURT OFFICIALS

Division 1 – Provincial Supervising Magistrates and Village Magistrates

15 Provincial Supervising Magistrates

(1) As soon as practicable after a Village Court has been established in a province, the Minister –

- (a) shall appoint a District Court Magistrate to be the Provincial Supervising Magistrate; and
- (b) may appoint such other Magistrates as in his opinion it is desirable so to do, to be Deputy Provincial Supervising Magistrates.

(2) A Provincial Supervising Magistrate and a Deputy Provincial Supervising Magistrate have such powers, functions, duties and responsibilities as are provided by this Act.

(3) A Provincial Supervising Magistrate may direct a Deputy Provincial Supervising Magistrate to exercise or perform any power or function of the Provincial Supervising Magistrate.

16 Recommendations as to appointment of Village Magistrates

As soon as practicable after the establishment of a Village Court, and afterwards as necessary, the Secretary shall, after consultation with –

- (a) any Local Level Government body in whose area the area, or part of the area, of the Village Court is situated or, where there is no Local Level Government body, the Provincial Government; and
- (b) such other bodies or persons, or groups of persons as –
  - (i) he thinks it desirable to consult; or
  - (ii) he is directed by the Minister to consult,

submit to the Minister the names of persons to be appointed Village Magistrates for the Village Court.

17 Appointment of Village Magistrates

(1) Subject to Subsections (2) and (3), within three months after the date of the establishment of a Village Court, and afterwards as necessary, the Minister shall appoint those persons whose names are submitted to him in accordance with Section 16 to be Village Magistrates for the Village Court.

(2) Persons appointed Village Magistrates under Subsection (1) shall, as far as practicable, be representative of the traditional population groupings of the area in which the Village Court is established.

(3) Not less than three Village Magistrates shall be appointed for each Village Court except a Village Court in respect of which the Minister has made a declaration under Section 8.

(4) A person may be appointed a Village Magistrate for more than one Village Court.

18 Chairman and Deputy Chairman

(1) The Minister may appoint a Village Magistrate appointed for a Village Court to be the Chairman, and another such Magistrate to be the Deputy Chairman, of the Village Court.

(2) The Chairman and Deputy Chairman of a Village Court shall exercise general supervision over the work of the Village Court and shall have such other powers, functions, duties and responsibilities as are prescribed.

19 Conditions of service

The terms and conditions of service of a Village Magistrate are as prescribed.

20 Revocation of appointment of Village Magistrates

The Minister may, on the recommendation of the Secretary or a Local Level Government body, revoke the appointment of a Village Magistrate –

(a) for failure to attend to duty; or

(b) for incapacity; or

(c) for misconduct; or

(d) if he resigns; or

(e) if he dies.

21 Suspension of Village Magistrates

The Minister may suspend a Village Magistrate with or without pay for misconduct or failure to attend to duty.

Division 2 – Village Court Clerks and Deputy Village Court Clerks

22 Appointment of Village Court Clerks, etc

(1) The Secretary shall appoint for each Village Court a Village Court Clerk and such Deputy Village Court Clerks as he thinks necessary.

(2) The terms and conditions of Village Court Clerks and Deputy Village Court Clerks are as prescribed.

23 Functions and duties of Village Court Clerks, etc

Village Court Clerks and Deputy Village Court Clerks –

(a) shall keep the prescribed records; and

(b) have such other duties and responsibilities as are prescribed.

24 Revocation of appointment of Village Court Clerk, etc

The Secretary may revoke the appointment of a Village Court Clerk or a Deputy Village Court Clerk –

(a) for failure to attend to duty; or

(b) for incapacity; or

(c) for misconduct; or

(d) if he resign; or

(e) if he dies.

25 Suspension of Village Court Clerk, etc

The Provincial Supervising Magistrate may suspend a Village Court Clerk or a Deputy Village Court Clerk with or without pay for misconduct or failure to attend to duty.

Division 3 – Village Peace Officers

26 Appointment of Village Peace Officers

(1) The Secretary may appoint persons to be Village Peace Officers for a Village Court.

(2) A person may be appointed a Village Peace Officer for more than one Village Court.

(3) The terms and other conditions of service of Village Peace Officers are as prescribed.

27 Area of jurisdiction of Village Peace Officers

The powers of a Village Peace Officer may be exercised only in the area of a Village Court for which he is appointed.

28 General functions and duties of Village Peace Officers

(1) A Village Peace Officer is an officer of the Village Court and his main functions are to assist the Village Court and to enforce the decisions and orders of the Village Court.

(2) In particular, a Village Peace Officer –

(a) shall report to the Village Court or to a Village Magistrate any case in which he knows or suspects that a dispute has arisen or may arise or an offence has been committed or may be committed, that is apparently within the jurisdiction of the Village Court; and

(b) shall, as directed by the Village Court –

(i) serve orders, either oral or in writing, to persons to appear before the Village Court; and

[876](ii) . . . [Repealed]

(iii) where an order for imprisonment is issued but not endorsed, convey to a Magistrate, for endorsement of the order under Section 68, any person whose imprisonment is ordered by the Village Court; and

[877](iv) . . . [Repealed]

[878](v) . . . [Repealed]

[876]Repealed by the Village Courts (Amendment) Act 2000, s2.
[877]Repealed by the Village Courts (Amendment) Act 2000, s2.
[878]Repealed by the Village Courts (Amendment) Act 2000, s2.

[879](vi) where, under Section 65, a warrant of execution is issued, execute that warrant.

29 Functions in relation to keeping the peace

(1) Where –

(a) a fight or violence to the person or property or other breach of the peace occurs; or

(b) a Village Peace Officer has reason to believe that a fight or violence to the person or property or other breach of the peace may occur,

the Village Peace Officer may order any person –

(c) to keep the peace; or

(d) to refrain from doing anything that may cause a breach of the peace.

(2) Prosecution for an offence against this section may be brought in a Village Court.

30 Powers of arrest

(1) Where –

(a) a Village Peace Officer suspects that a person –

(i) is about to commit an offence; or

(ii) is committing an offence; or

(iii) has committed an offence; and

(b) the offence appears to the Village Peace Officer to be within the jurisdiction of the Village Court,

the Village Peace Officer may arrest the person.

(2) A Village Peace Officer shall arrest a person when directed to do so by a Village Magistrate.

(3) Where a Village Peace Officer arrests a person under Subsection (1) or (2), he shall take the person before the Village Court as soon as practicable and in any event within 24 hours of making the arrest.

31 Application of Section 207 of the Constitution to Village Peace Officer assisting Police

A Village Peace Officer appointed under this Act or under an Act of a Provincial Legislature may act under the direction of a member of the Police Force, for the purpose of assisting in the performance of the functions or duties of that member or of the Force.

---

[879]Amended by the Village Courts (Amendment) Act 2000, s2.

32 Revocation of appointment of Village Peace Officer

The Secretary may revoke the appointment of a Village Peace Officer –

(a) for failure to attend to duty; or
(b) for incapacity; or
(c) for misconduct; or
(d) if he resigns; or
(e) if he dies.

33 Suspension of Village Peace Officer

The Provincial Supervising Magistrate may suspend a Village Peace Officer with or without pay for misconduct or failure to attend to duty.

Division 4 – Village Court Officials appointed under Provincial Laws

34 Village Magistrate, etc, appointed under Act of Provincial Legislature

A –

(a) Village Magistrate; or
(b) Village Court Clerk; or
(c) Deputy Village Court Clerk; or
(d) Village Peace Officer,

appointed under an Act of a Provincial Legislature has, and may exercise, all the powers, functions, duties and responsibilities of a Village Magistrate, Village Court Clerk, Deputy Village Court Clerk or Village Peace Officer respectively, appointed under this Act.

PART V – JURISDICTION

Division 1 – Interpretation

35 Interpretation

In this Part, unless the contrary meaning appears –

"Village Court" includes a Village Court established under an Act of a provincial legislature.

Division 2 – General Jurisdiction

36 General jurisdiction

Subject to this Act, a Village Court has jurisdiction in the area for which it is established –

(a) in relation to any dispute where –

(i) the dispute arose within its area; or

(ii) the subject matter of the dispute is within its area; or

(iii) all of the parties to the dispute are normally resident within its area; or

(iv) some of the parties to the dispute are normally resident within its area and the others consent to the jurisdiction; and

(b) in criminal matters as specified in Division 3; and

(c) in civil matters as specified in Division 4.

37 Concurrent jurisdiction of Village Magistrates

The jurisdiction of a Village Court may be exercised by a number of Village Magistrates notwithstanding that the jurisdiction is being exercised at the same time by other Village Magistrates.

[880]38 Local Courts may exercise jurisdiction of Village Court

[Repealed]

---

[880]This section was impliedly repealed when the *Local Courts Act* (Chapter 41) was repealed by the *Local Courts (Repeal) Act* 2000.

39 Limits of general jurisdiction

A Village Court has no jurisdiction in relation to a matter involving an act done –

(a) by authority of an Act of the Parliament; or

(b) by authority of an Act of a Provincial Legislature.

40 Ancillary jurisdiction

In addition to any other orders that it may make under this Act, a Village Court has jurisdiction to make orders –

(a) that are necessary or convenient for the purposes of the exercise of its powers, jurisdiction and authority under this Act; and

(b) that are ancillary to its general orders.

Division 3 – General Criminal Jurisdiction

41 Extent of jurisdiction

A Village Court has criminal jurisdiction –

(a) in respect of offences that are prescribed offences for the purposes of this section; and

(b) in respect of contravention of, or failure to comply with –

(i) a Local Level Government rule; or

(ii) a law made by or under an Act of a Provincial Legislature,

if the rule or law, as the case may be, provides that an offence against it may be dealt with by a Village Court; and

(c) in accordance with Division 5 and Sections 29, 40 and 104.

[881]42 Penalties

In the exercise of the jurisdiction referred to in Section 41, a Village Court may –

(a) in respect of Section 41(a) – order an offender to perform community work; or

(b) in respect of Section 41(b) – order an offender to perform community work for a period of one week for every K50.00 of any monetary penalty which may have been imposed under the rule or the law.

[881]Repealed and replaced by the *Village Courts (Amendment) Act* 2000, s3.

Division 4 – Civil Jurisdiction

43 Disputes in respect of land

A Village Court that has jurisdiction over an area in which there is situated any land that is the subject of a dispute as to –

(a) its ownership by custom; or
(b) the right by custom to its use,

may, on the application of a party to the dispute, make an order –

(c) authorizing the use or occupation of the land by one of the parties to the dispute for such purposes and subject to such conditions as are set out in the order; and
(d) where appropriate, prohibiting the use or occupation of the land referred to in Paragraph (c) except in accordance with an order referred to in that paragraph; and
(e) restraining the other party to the dispute from interfering with the authorized use or occupation,

or for any other purpose, pending a decision by the Local Land Court or the Provincial Land Court.

44 Order to perform work

A Village Court may order a party to a dispute to perform specified work, or work of a specified kind, for the benefit of an injured or aggrieved party, for a period or periods not exceeding –

(a) eight hours in any one day; and
(b) six days in any one week; and
(c) a total period of twelve weeks,

in such manner, at such times and subject to such conditions as to supervision or otherwise as are specified in the order.

45 Orders for compensation, damages and debt

Subject to Section 46 and to Part VI, a Village Court may make an order for –

(a) the payment of compensation or damages; or
(b) the repayment of a debt,

to an amount not exceeding, in cash or in value, the sum of K1,000.00.

46 Bride price etc

In matters relating to –

(a) bride price; or
(b) the custody of children; or
(c) death,

a Village Court may award such amount in compensation or damages as to the Village Court seems just.

47 Custody of children

A Village Court may make an order as to the custody or guardianship of a child if the child is –

(a) born of parents married under customary law; or

(b) illegitimate.

48 Limits of civil jurisdiction

(1) A Village Court has no jurisdiction under this Division in relation to –

(a) subject to Section 43, a matter involving the ownership of land; or

(b) a dispute involving the driving of a motor vehicle.

(2) Nothing contained in Subsection (1)(b) shall be construed as preventing a Village Court from dealing with a motor vehicle offence where such an offence is a prescribed offence under Section 41(a).

Division 5 – Preventive Jurisdiction

49 Interpretation

In this Division, unless the contrary meaning appears –

"dispute" includes a threatened dispute.

50 Exercise of preventive jurisdiction

The preventive jurisdiction may be exercised by –

(a) a Village Magistrate or a number of Village Magistrates notwithstanding that the jurisdiction is being exercised at the same time by another Village Magistrate or other Village Magistrates; or

(b) a Village Court.

51 Preventive orders

(1) Where it appears to a Village Magistrate or a Village Court that a dispute may cause a breach of the peace, the Village Magistrate or the Village Court may –

(a) order the parties to appear before the Village Court with a view to having the dispute dealt with under this Act; and

(b) for the meantime, order the parties or any other person not to –

(i) enter into a further dispute or counsel another person to enter into a dispute; or

(ii) fight, prepare to fight or counsel another person to fight; or

(iii) spread rumours or fears about the existence or imminence of a dispute; or

(iv) make offensive weapons or carry offensive weapons in certain places; or

(v) do any other act or thing, whether or not specified in the order, that might aggravate the dispute or cause a breach of the peace.

(2) Where an order is made under Subsection (1)(b), the Court shall cause the order to be issued in writing and served on each party to the dispute or on any other person.

(3) A person who –

(a) fails, without reasonable excuse (proof of which is on him), to obey an order under Subsection (1)(a); or

(b) fails to obey an order under Subsection (1)(b),

is guilty of an offence.

[882]Penalty: Where the charge is brought before a Village Court – a community work order for a period not exceeding six months;

[883] Where the charge is brought before a Local Court – a fine not exceeding K1000.00 or imprisonment for a term not exceeding six months, or both.

[884](4) . . . [Repealed]

(5) The Minister shall act in accordance with a recommendation under Subsection (4).

[885](6) A charge for an offence under this section may be brought before a Village Court.

---

[882]Amended by the Village Courts (Amendment) Act 2000, s3.

[883]This penalty clause was impliedly amended or repealed when the Local Courts Act (Chapter 41) was repealed by the Local Courts (Repeal) Act 2000.

[884]Repealed by the Village Courts (Amendment) Act 2000, s4.

[885]This Subsection was impliedly amended when the *Local Courts Act* (Chapter 41) was repealed by the *Local Courts (Repeal) Act* 2000.

Division 6 – Mediatory Jurisdiction

52 Primary function of Village Courts

The primary function of a Village Court is to ensure peace and harmony in the area for which it is established by mediating in, and endeavouring to obtain just and amicable settlements of disputes.

53 Exercise of mediatory jurisdiction

(1) The mediatory jurisdiction of a Village Court may be exercised by a single Village Magistrate.

(2) In all matters before it relating to a dispute, a Village Court –

(a) shall, before exercising its jurisdiction under Division 3 or 4, attempt to reach a settlement by mediation; and

(b) may, if it thinks that by doing so a just and amicable settlement may be reached, adjourn any proceedings in which it is exercising jurisdiction under those Divisions.

54 Settlements

Where a dispute is settled in accordance with this Division, the terms of the settlement shall be –

(a) recorded in the prescribed form; and

(b) treated and enforced as an order of the Village Court as between the parties to the settlement and persons claiming through them.

Division 7 – Joint Jurisdiction of Courts

55 Interpretation

In this Division, unless the contrary meaning appears –

"dispute" includes a threatened dispute;

"Village Magistrate" includes a Visiting Village Magistrate;

"Visiting Village Magistrate" means a Village Magistrate appointed to a Village Court other than a Village Court referred to in Section 56(1).

56 Joint sittings

(1) Where –

(a) a dispute or the subject matter of a dispute extends to the area of more than one Village Court; or

(b) parties to a dispute are normally resident in the area of more than one Village Court; or

(c) it appears to the Village Magistrates or the Peace and Good Order Committee that a dispute may cause a breach of the peace,

the Village Courts may –

(d) by agreement between the Chairmen; or

(e) if there are no Chairmen, by agreement between the Village Magistrates; or

(f) at the direction of the Provincial Supervising Magistrate; or

(g) at the request of the Peace and Good Order Committee,

hold a joint sitting for the purpose of dealing with the dispute.

(2) A joint sitting shall consist of –

(a) not less than two Village Magistrates from each Village Court referred to in Subsection (1); and

(b) a Visiting Village Magistrate.

(3) A Visiting Village Magistrate shall be such Village Magistrate as –

(a) the Chairmen, or, if there are no Chairmen, the Village Magistrates, referred to in Subsection (1), by agreement determine; or

(b) the Provincial Supervising Magistrate, where there is no agreement under Paragraph (a), directs to sit.

(4) The Village Magistrates constituting a joint sitting shall appoint one of their number to preside.

(5) The Village Magistrates constituting a joint sitting may sit outside the area of the Village Court to which they are respectively appointed.

(6) A joint sitting under Subsection (5) has jurisdiction to deal with a dispute under this Division.

(7) Subject to this section, this Act applies to and in relation to a joint sitting as though –

(a) it was a sitting of a single Village Court established for the combined areas of the Village Courts concerned; and

(b) the Village Magistrates were Village Magistrates for the combined Village Court.

Division 8 – Law to be applied

57 Application of custom

(1) Subject to Subsections (2) and (3), in all matters before it a Village Court shall apply any relevant custom as determined in accordance with Sections 2, 3 and 7 of the *Customs (Recognition) Act* (Chapter 19).

(2) Custom shall be applied in accordance with Subsection (1) whether or not it is inconsistent with any Act.

(3) The power conferred on a Local Level Government body by the *Local Government Act* (Chapter 57) or an Act of a Provincial Legislature to make rules, extends to making rules declaring what is to be taken as the custom relating to any matter, and such a declaration is binding on Village Courts.

58 General law

(1) In exercising its jurisdiction under this Division, a Village Court is not bound by any Law (other than the *Constitution* and this Act) that is not expressly applied to it, but shall, subject to Subsection (2) and Section 57, decide all matters before it in accordance with substantial justice.

(2) A person charged with an offence before a Village Court is presumed innocent until proved guilty.

59 Evidence, etc

(1) Subject to Subsection (2), in any proceedings before it a Village Court shall not apply technical rules of evidence but shall admit and consider such information as is available.

(2) The powers and procedures of a Village Court shall be exercised in accordance with the principles of natural justice.

[886]*Division 9 – Enforcement*

60 Obstruction, etc

A person, who –

(a) wilfully interrupts, interferes with or disturbs the proceedings of a Village Court; or

(b) wilfully obstructs a Village Court Official or other person acting under this Act,

is guilty of an offence.

Penalty: A community work order for a period not exceeding six months.

61 Failure to obey certain orders

A person, who fails, without reasonable excuse (proof of which is upon him), to obey an order of –

(a) a Village Peace Officer under Section 29; or

(b) a Village Court under –

(c) Section 40; or

(d) Section 43; or

(e) Section 47; or

(f) Section 81,

is guilty of an offence.

Penalty: A community work order for a period not exceeding six months.

62 Failure to pay compensation, etc

(1) A person, who fails, without reasonable excuse (proof of which is upon him) –

(a) to pay compensation; or

(b) to pay damages; or

(c) to pay a debt,

in accordance with an order of a Village Court under Section 45, is guilty of an offence.

Penalty: Subject to Subsection (2), a community work order for a period not exceeding six months.

(2) A community work order under this Section does not operate as a satisfaction or discharge of the amount due on an order, and,

---

[886]Division V.9 repealed and replaced by the *Village Courts (Amendment) Act* 2000, s4.

notwithstanding such community work order, a Village Court may make an order for execution in the prescribed form against the goods and chattels of the person so ordered to perform work.

63 Failure to perform community work order

A person, who fails, without reasonable excuse (proof of which is upon him), to obey an order of a Village Court for the performance of a community work order, is guilty of an offence.

Penalty: A fine not exceeding K50.00 for each week of work not performed.

64 Endorsement of fine

(1) An order made by a Village Court for the payment of a fine under this Act is of no force or effect unless it is endorsed by a Magistrate.

(2) The Village Court that made the order shall immediately cause it to be presented to a Magistrate for endorsement under Subsection (1).

(3) The Magistrate to whom the order for the payment of a fine is presented under Subsection (2) shall, unless he has reason to believe that the Village Court –

(a) acted without jurisdiction; or

(b) acted in excess of its powers, endorse the order.

(4) Where the Magistrate believes the Village Court may have –

(a) acted without jurisdiction; or

(b) acted in excess of its powers, he shall exercise the power of review provided by Division II.

(5) Where an order for payment of a fine is endorsed by a Magistrate under this section, the *District Courts Act* (Chapter 40), with the necessary modifications, applies in all respects as though the order for payment of the fine were an order of the District Court.

65 Order for execution

(1) An order for execution under Section 62 is of no force or effect unless the order is endorsed by a District Court Magistrate.

(2) The Village Court that made the order for execution shall immediately cause it to be presented to a District Court Magistrate for endorsement under Subsection (1).

(3) The District Court Magistrate to whom the order is presented for endorsement under this section shall, unless he has reason to believe that the Village Court –

(a) acted without jurisdiction; or

(b) acted in excess of its powers, endorse the order without delay.

(4) Where the magistrate believes that the Village Court may have –

(a) acted without jurisdiction; or

(b) acted in excess of its powers, he shall exercise the power of review provided by Division II.

(5) Subject to Subsection (7), where an order for execution is endorsed by a District Court Magistrate under this section, the *District Courts Act* (Chapter 40), with the necessary modifications, applies in all respects as though the order were an order of the District Court.

(6) The District Court Magistrate shall ensure that the necessary warrant of execution is issued.

(7) A warrant of execution issued under this section shall be executed by or under the direction of –

(a) a police officer; or

(b) a Village Peace Officer; or

(c) an officer named in the warrant,

and the provisions of the *District Courts Act* (Chapter 40) shall be read and construed accordingly.

66 Where convicted person is under 18 years

Subject to Subsection (2), where –

(a) a community work order is presented to a District Court Magistrate for endorsement under Section 65(2); and

(b) the District Court Magistrate is satisfied that the person is under the age of 18 years,

the District Court Magistrate shall not endorse the order but shall refer the order and the person to a Children's Court to be dealt with by that court.

67 Children's court to deal with offender

Where a person is referred to a Children's Court under Section 66(1), the Children's Court shall –

(a) endorse the community work order; or

(b) make such other order under the *Child Welfare Act* (Chapter 276) as it considers appropriate, and the *Child Welfare Act* (Chapter 276) shall apply to and in relation to that person.

68 Endorsement of order for imprisonment

[Repealed]

[887]69 Where convicted person is under 17 years

[Repealed]

69 Where convicted person is under 18 years

[Repealed]

[888]70 Children's Court to deal with offender

[Repealed]

70 Juvenile Court to deal with offender

[Repealed]

71 Effect of endorsed order for imprisonment

[Repealed]

72 Non-performance of work

[Repealed]

73 Failure to obey certain orders

[Repealed]

74 Order to pay compensation etc

[Repealed]

75 Endorsement of order of execution

[Repealed]

---

[887]The Head Note to Section 69 was amended by the *Juvenile Courts Act* 1991 (Act No. 40 of 1991), s66(2).

[888]The Head Note to Section 70 was amended by the *Juvenile Courts Act* 1991 (Act No. 40 of 1991), s66(2).

76 Effect of endorsed order for execution

[Repealed]

Division 10 – Procedure

77 Procedures generally

(1) Subject to this Division the procedures of a Village Court are as determined by the Court.

(2) The Minister may publish recommended practices and procedures for all or any Village Court.

78 Uniformity of civil and criminal procedures

Subject to Section 77, there is no procedural distinction between the civil and the criminal jurisdiction of a Village Court under this Division and in any proceedings before it a Village Court may make such order under Division 3 or 4 or both, as it thinks fit.

79 Presence of parties

(1) Subject to Subsections (2) and (3), a Village Court shall not proceed in the absence of a party.

(2) Where a party is represented before a Village Court in accordance with Section 80, he is deemed to be present before the Village Court.

(3) Where a Village Court is satisfied that –

(a) a party who is normally resident in the area of the Village Court is deliberately absenting himself from the area of the Village Court; and

(b) Division 7 is inapplicable or its application is impracticable,

the Village Court may proceed in the absence of the party, but, in that case, the Village Court has no power to make an order, other than an order against him under Part V.3.

80 Representation

A party to any proceedings under Division 3, 4 or 9 is entitled to be represented by any person other than a lawyer.

81 Summoning parties and witnesses

(1) In any proceedings under Division 3, 4 or 9, a Village Court may order any person who is, or in its opinion may be, a party to appear before it at a time and place specified in the order.

(2) In any proceedings under Division 3, 4 or 9, a Village Court may order any person –

(a) who, in its opinion, may be able to give any relevant information; or

(b) in whose possession or control there is any document or thing that may, in the opinion of the Village Court, be relevant to the proceedings,

to appear before it at a time and place specified in the order and to answer questions or produce the document or thing to the Court.

(3) An order under Subsection (1) or (2) shall be in the prescribed form.

(4) In addition to any action that may be taken under this Act where a person fails to comply with an order of a Village Court under Subsection (1) or (2), the Village Court may direct a Village Peace Officer appointed for its area –

(a) to arrest the person and bring him before the Village Court; or

(b) to seize and produce to the Village Court any document, or thing, the subject of the order.

82 Exclusion of Local Level Government Councillors, etc

(1) Where any proceedings are brought by, or by authority or direction of, a Local Level Government body, a Village Magistrate who is –

(a) a Councillor; or

(b) an associate member of a Ward Committee; or

(c) an officer or employee of the Local Level Government body,

is not eligible to sit as a member of the Village Court in the proceedings.

(2) A Village Magistrate who has a substantial interest in the subject matter of any proceedings before a Village Court is not eligible to sit as a member of the Village Court in the proceedings.

83 Charges

A charge of an offence may be brought before a Village Court by –

(a) a Village Peace Officer; or

(b) a member of the Police Force; or

(c) in the case of an offence against a Local Level Government rule, an officer authorized by the Local Level Government body for the purpose; or

(d) in the case of an offence against a Law made by or under an Act of a Provincial Legislature, a person authorized for the purpose by or under the Law,

in his official capacity; or

(e) by any other person.

84 Records

(1) As far as practicable, a Village Court shall keep, or cause to be kept, a record of its proceedings in the prescribed form.

(2) Each record of proceedings shall be certified as correct by –

(a) a Village Magistrate; or

(b) a Village Court Clerk; or

(c) a Deputy Village Court Clerk,

and when so certified is *prima facie* evidence of the matters set out in it.

Division 11 – Appeals etc

85 Interpretation of Division 11

In this Division, unless the contrary intention appears, "decision" means a final decision of a Village Court under Division 3, 4 or 6.

86 Appeals

(1) Subject to Subsection (2), a person aggrieved by a decision of a Village Court may, within three months after the day on which the decision is pronounced, appeal, orally or in writing, to a Magistrate.

(2) Subject to Subsection (3), a Magistrate may, in the special circumstances of a particular case, allow such extension of time for appealing, as to the Magistrate seems fit.

(3) No appeal against a decision shall be made after the expiration of twelve months from the day on which a decision is pronounced.

87 Review

A Magistrate may review a decision of a Village Court at any time within a period of 12 months from the day of the decision.

88 Stay of execution

Where –

(a) an appeal is made under Section 86; or

(b) a Magistrate is exercising the power of review, under Section 87,

the Magistrate may, pending the outcome of the appeal or review, as the case may be, order a stay of execution.

89 Hearing of appeals and conduct of reviews

(1) Subject to Section 90, a Magistrate hearing an appeal against, or making a review of, a decision of a Village Court shall appoint two or more Village Magistrates of that Village Court to sit with him.

(2) A Village Magistrate who made the decision that is appealed against or that is under review is eligible for appointment under Subsection (1).

(3) The Village Magistrates shall advise the Magistrate hearing the appeal or making the review –

(a) on custom; and

(b) on other relevant matters within their knowledge,

but shall not otherwise take part in the proceedings and shall not take part in the decision.

(4) The Magistrate hearing the appeal or making the review shall –

(a) consider the records (if any) relevant to the decision; and

(b) receive such evidence (if any) and make such enquiries (if any) as he thinks necessary.

(5) Division 8 applies to and in relation to an appeal or review under this Division as if the Magistrate hearing the appeal or making the review constituted a Village Court.

(6) A party to any proceedings appealed against or under review may –

(a) appear personally; or

(b) be represented by any person other than a lawyer.

90 Single Magistrate may hear appeal or conduct review

(1) Where –

(a) under Section 89 a Magistrate appoints two or more Village Magistrates to sit with him on an appeal or on a review; and

(b) the Village Magistrates, or any one or more Village Magistrates fail to sit,

the Magistrate may, notwithstanding the provisions of that section, hear and determine the appeal or the review, as the case may be.

(2) A decision of a Magistrate under Subsection (1) shall not be challenged in any court of law by reason only of the fact that the provisions of Section 89, other than Subsections (4), (5) and (6), were not complied with.

91 Summoning of witnesses etc

(1) A Magistrate may, for the purpose of hearing an appeal against, or making a review of, a decision of a Village Court, orally or in writing, summon –

(a) parties to the proceedings; or

(b) witnesses.

(2) A person who fails, without reasonable excuse (proof of which is on him), to obey a summons issued under Subsection (1) is guilty of an offence.

Penalty: Subject to Subsection (3), a fine not exceeding K200.00 or imprisonment for a term not exceeding three months.

(3) A Magistrate may, instead of imposing a penalty under Subsection (2), order an offender to perform, for community purposes, specified work or work of a specified kind, for a period or periods not exceeding –

(a) eight hours in any one day; and

(b) six days in any one week; and

(c) a total period of three months,

in such manner, at such times and subject to such conditions as to supervision or otherwise as are specified in the order.

92 Decision on appeal or review

(1) A Magistrate hearing an appeal against, or making a review of, a decision of a Village Court may –

(a) confirm the decision; or

(b) quash the decision; or

(c) order that the matter be dealt with again by the Village Court and, if he thinks fit, give with the order a direction as to how any defect in the earlier proceedings may be overcome.

(2) The decision shall be confirmed unless the Magistrate is satisfied that –

(a) the Village Court acted in contravention of any Constitutional Law, Act or subordinate enactment applying to it; or

(b) the Court was not properly constituted; or

(c) except as provided for by this Act, a party was not present; or

(d) a party was not given a reasonable opportunity to present his case personally or by a representative; or

(e) the Court exceeded its jurisdiction or its powers; or

(f) the Village Magistrates constituting the Court included a Village Magistrate who had a substantial interest in the subject matter of the proceedings such as to disqualify him from adjudicating on the matter,

and there has been a substantial miscarriage of justice.

(3) The decision shall be confirmed where by reason of –

(a) the lapse of time; or

(b) the failure of the aggrieved party to appeal earlier,

it would, in the opinion of the Magistrate, be unjust to reopen the matter.

93 Record of decision

The Magistrate hearing an appeal or making a review shall –

(a) make a record of –

(i) his decision on the appeal or review; and

(ii) his reasons; and

(b) forward a copy of the record to the Provincial Supervising Magistrate.

94 Further review by Provincial Supervising Magistrate

(1) On receipt of a record under Section 93 the Provincial Supervising Magistrate may, unless he was the Magistrate who heard the appeal or made the review, review the decision.

(2) For the purpose of a review under Subsection (1), the Provincial Supervising Magistrate has all the powers and jurisdiction of a Magistrate conducting a review under the preceding provisions of this Division but

is not bound by those provisions (other than Section 89(4) and (5) and Section 92), and those provisions with the necessary modifications, apply accordingly.

95 Custody etc, during appeal or review

While a decision in respect of an order for imprisonment made under this Act by a Village Court is under appeal or review, the convicted person shall be –

(a) held in such custody; or

(b) released on such conditions,

as the Magistrate hearing the appeal or making the review orders.

PART VI – RELATIONSHIP BETWEEN VILLAGE COURTS AND OTHER COURTS

96 Matters dealt with or being dealt with in other Courts

(1) A person shall not be punished by a Village Court for an act for which he has already been punished by another Village Court or other court.

(2) Where a person has been tried for, and acquitted or convicted of, an offence by a Village Court or other court, he shall not be tried again for the same offence, or for an offence that is substantially the same offence, by a Village Court.

(3) When a matter has been dealt with by a Village Court, a plea of *autrefois acquit, autrefois convict* or *res judicata* is available in a court of summary jurisdiction in the same way as if the matter had been dealt with by another court of summary jurisdiction.

(4) Nothing in the preceding provisions of this section prevents proceedings for relief (whether by way of compensation or otherwise) being taken in a Village Court or other court after a decision has been given in a Village Court or other court, where proceedings for such relief were not disposed of in the first proceedings.

(5) Subject to Subsection (7) and to Section 97, where proceedings have been commenced in a Village Court in relation to a matter, proceedings may be taken in another Village Court or another court in relation to the matter, but shall not be concluded until the first mentioned proceedings have been completed.

(6) Subject to Section 97, where proceedings have been commenced in a court other than a Village Court, in relation to a matter, no proceedings shall be taken in a Village Court until the first mentioned proceedings have been completed and –

(a) the time limited for appeal (if any) has expired and no appeal has been instituted; or

(b) the proceedings on any appeal, and on any further appeal, have been dealt with.

(7) Nothing in the preceding provisions of this section prevents proceedings being taken for an indictable offence that has already been

the subject of a decision by, or in respect of which proceedings are pending in, a Village Court, and in that case –

(a) the decision of the Village Court does not give rise to the defence of *autrefois acquit* or *autrefois convict*; and

(b) if an order is made against a person in the Village Court and the person is convicted of an offence in the proceedings for the indictable offence, the court that so convicts him shall take into account, in passing sentence, anything done or suffered under the order.

(8) In a case referred to in Subsection (7)(b), the court that convicts the person may make such order as it thinks reasonable for adjusting rights and liabilities under the order of the Village Court.

97 Reference of matters between Village Courts and other Courts

(1) Where –

(a) proceedings have been commenced in a Village Court; and

(b) it appears to the Village Court that –

(i) the proceedings; or

(ii) any part or aspect of the proceedings,

could more appropriately be dealt with by some other court (including another Village Court) having jurisdiction in the matter,

the Village Court may make an order referring the matter to that other court.

(2) Where –

(a) proceedings have been commenced in a court other than a Village Court; and

(b) it appears to the court that –

(i) the proceedings; or

(ii) any part or aspect of the proceedings,

could more appropriately be dealt with by a Village Court having jurisdiction in the matter,

the court may make an order referring the matter to that Village Court.

PART VII – GROUP RESPONSIBILITY

98 Recognition of groups

For the purposes of proceedings before it, a Village Court may –

(a) recognize a number of persons having a common interest as a group; and

(b) determine in what manner the group may appear or be represented before it.

99 Orders in respect of groups

(1) Where a group is recognised under Section 98 –

(a) the representative of the group shall, for the procedural purposes of this Act, be treated as if he were a party; and

(b) an order may be made for, against, or affecting, the group as if it were a natural person.

(2) Subsection (1) does not make a recognized group liable to conviction for an offence.

100 Effect of orders in respect of groups

(1) Except where –

(a) in accordance with custom, only certain members of a recognized group are personally or fully liable (in which case the Village Court shall so state in its order); or

(b) the Village Court for any other reason, otherwise orders,

an order made by a Village Court in respect of a recognized group has effect as though it were an order made against each member of the group as an individual party to the proceedings.

(2) Sections 44, 45 and 46 apply, in accordance with Subsection (1), to an order affecting a group, and subject to those sections as so applying the Village Court may, by the same or another order, apportion rights and liabilities under the order among members of the group in such manner as it thinks fit.

PART VIII – OFFENCES AT GENERAL LAW

101 Prosecution of offences against Part VIII

A prosecution for an offence against this Part shall not be brought in a Village Court.

102 Application of Criminal Code etc

For the purposes of the *Criminal Code* and of any other law relating to offences by, against, or in connexion with –

(a) persons holding judicial office, a Village Magistrate is a person holding such office; and

(b) persons employed in the Public Service, a Village Court Clerk or a Deputy Village Court Clerk is deemed to be a person so employed; and

(c) Members of the Police Force, a Village Peace Officer is deemed to be such a member,

within the meaning of the *Criminal Code* or other Law.

103 Unauthorized persons wearing insignia etc

(1) A person who, not being a Village Court Official, without lawful excuse (proof of which is on him) –

(a) is in possession of, or wears –

(i) badges of office, or –

(ii) other insignia of office; or

(iii) a colourable imitation of such badges or insignia,

issued under Section 106; or

(b) assumes the description or the designation of a Village Court Official; or

(c) falsely holds himself out to be a Village Court Official,

is guilty of an offence.

Penalty: A fine not exceeding K100.00 or imprisonment for a term not exceeding three months.

104 Supplying etc, unauthorized insignia

A person who unlawfully –

(a) sells or supplies to another person; or

(b) employs or induces another person, not being a Village Court Official, to wear,

badges or other insignia of office issued under Section 106, or a colourable imitation of any such badges or insignia, is guilty of an offence.

Penalty: A fine not exceeding K200.00 or imprisonment for a term not exceeding six months.

105 Promulgation

The Minister may determine in what manner –

(a) the establishment and jurisdiction of Village Courts; and

(b) the appointment of Village Court Officials,

shall be promulgated.

106 Badges and insignia of office

The Minister may cause to be issued to Village Court Officials badges and other insignia of office.

107 Persons in custody

(1) A person in custody under this Act shall –

(a) be supplied with; or

(b) be given reasonable opportunity to supply himself with,

reasonable food and shelter.

(2) For the purposes of Subsection (1), a person who is performing work under an order under Section 42, 44, 73(2) or 91(3) is deemed to be a person in custody.

108 Application of Section 146 of the *Police Force Act*

Subject to Section 68(4), Section 146 of the *Police Force Act* (Chapter 65) (which requires members of the Police Force to execute certain processes and serve certain summonses and warrants) does not apply to or in relation to process of a Village Court.

109 Indemnity

(1) A Village Court Official, or other person acting under or for the purposes of this Act, is not liable for any act done or any omission made, in good faith, for the purposes of this Act whether or not the act or omission was within his lawful power or jurisdiction.

(2) The burden of proof of a lack of good faith is on the person who relies on the lack.

110 Offences with respect to Village Court records

(1) A person who –

(a) without the authority of a Village Court, alters the records of the Village Court; or

(b) wilfully records incorrectly a decision of the Village Court; or

(c) wilfully damages records of a Village Court,

is guilty of an offence.

Penalty: Subject to Subsection (2), a fine not exceeding K200.00 or imprisonment for a term not exceeding 6 months, or both.

[889](2) Prosecution for an offence against this section may only be brought in a Local Court.

111 Village Court Official to be worker, etc

A Village Court Official is a worker within the meaning of "worker" in the *Workers' Compensation Act* (Chapter 179)

112 Additional powers of Head of State

(1) Where there is no provision, or no sufficient provision, in this Act in respect of an, matter or thing that is necessary or desirable to give effect to this Act, the Head of state, acting on advice, may, by instrument, determine in what manner or form the lack of provision or the insufficient provision shall be supplied.

(2) Sections 75, 76 and 91 of the *Interpretation Act* (Chapter 2) apply to a determination under Subsection (1) as if it were a regulation.

113 Regulations

(1) The Head of state, acting on advice, may make Regulations, not inconsistent with this Act, prescribing all matters that by this Act are required or permitted to be prescribed, or that are necessary or convenient to be prescribed for carrying out or giving effect to this Act, and in particular may make Regulations prescribing –

(a) offences for the purposes of Section 41(a); and

(b) the procedure for, and on, the reference of a matter to a Village Court or other court under Section 97; and

---

[889]This Subsection was impliedly repealed when the *Local Courts Act* (Chapter 41) was repealed by the *Local Courts (Repeal) Act* 2000.

(c) penalties of fines not exceeding K200.00 or imprisonment for terms not exceeding three months for offences against the regulations (other than offences referred to in Paragraph (a)).

(2) A prosecution for an offence to which Subsection (1)(c) applies shall not be brought before a Village Court.

(3) Regulations may be made under this section to apply to, and in respect of, the whole of the country and all Village Courts or a part of the country, or some Village Courts.

PART IX – REPEAL, SAVING AND TRANSITIONAL

114 Interpretation

In this part "repealed Acts" means the Acts specified in the Schedule.

115 Repeal and saving

(1) The Acts specified in the Schedule are repealed.

(2) Regulations made under the repealed Acts shall, so far as they are not inconsistent with this Act, remain in force until they have been revoked by Regulations made under this Act and shall be deemed for all purposes to have been made under this Act.

116 Village Courts established under the repealed Act

Village Courts established under the repealed Acts are deemed to have been established under this Act.

117 Appointments under repealed Act

Village Court Officials appointed under the repealed Acts are deemed to have been appointed under this Act and, until appointments are made under this Act, the terms and conditions of employment in force immediately before the commencement of this Act shall have effect.

118 Actions etc, not to abate

Where, immediately before the commencement of this Act, any action or proceeding was pending or existing under the repealed Acts, the action or proceeding, as the case may be, does not, on the commencement of this Act, abate or discontinue but it may be prosecuted, continued or enforced under the repealed Acts as if this Act had not come into operation.

Sec. 115.

SCHEDULE

Repealed Acts

Village Courts Act (Chapter 44)
Village Courts (Amendment) Act 1986 (No. 2 of 1986).

SCHEDULE

CHAPTER No 179

Workers' Compensation Act

PART I – PRELIMINARY

PART II – ADMINISTRATION

PART III – THE WORKERS' COMPENSATION FUND

PART IV – CLAIMS

Division 1 – Workers' Compensation Tribunals

Division 2 – Proceedings of Tribunals

Subdivision A – General

PART VI – AMOUNT OF COMPENSATION

PART VII – PAYMENT AND INVESTMENT OF WORKERS' COMPENSATION

PART VIII – ALTERNATIVE REMEDIES

PART IX – COMPULSORY WORKERS' COMPENSATION INSURANCE

PART X – MISCELLANEOUS

SCHEDULES

SCHEDULE 1

SCHEDULE 2

SCHEDULE 3

INDEPENDENT STATE OF PAPUA NEW GUINEA

CHAPTER No 179

Workers' Compensation Act

(Consolidated to No 11 of 1990)

Being an Act to provide for compensation to workers and their dependants in respect of injuries suffered by workers arising out of or in the course of their employment, and for related purposes.

PART I – PRELIMINARY

1 Interpretation

(1) In this Act, unless the contrary intention appears –

"the Chief Commissioner" means the Chief Commissioner of Workers' Compensation appointed under Section 3(1);

"Commissioner" means a Commissioner of Workers' Compensation appointed under Section 3(3);

"custom" means the customs and usages of the indigenous inhabitants of the country existing in relation to the matter in question at the time when, and the place in relation to which, the matter arose regardless of whether or not the custom or usage had existed from time immemorial;

"dependant" means, in relation to a deceased worker –

(a) those members of the family of the worker who –

(i) were wholly, mainly or partially dependant on his earnings on the date of his death; or

(ii) would, but for the incapacity due to the injury, have been so dependent; and

(b) other than a non-automatic citizen worker – any person who by custom has a right to share in compensation awarded in respect of the death of a worker;

"Deputy Registrar" means a Deputy Registrar of Workers' Compensation appointed under Section 10(1);

"employer" includes –

(a) the State; and

(b) a provincial government; and

(c) an authority or instrumentality constituted under any law in force in the country; and

(d) any body of persons corporate or unincorporate; and

(e) the legal personal representative of a deceased employer;

"the Fund" means the Workers' Compensation Fund established under Section 15;

"husband", in relation to a worker who is a female, includes –

(a) a husband by custom; and

(b) a man who is not married to the worker but who is living with the worker on a permanent basis as her de facto husband;

"injury" means any physical or mental injury and includes –

(a) a disease contracted by the worker in the course of his employment, whether at or away from his place of employment, and to which the employment was a contributory factor; and

(b) the aggravation, acceleration, exacerbation, deterioration or recurrence of any pre-existing injury or disease where the employment was a contributing factor to that aggravation, acceleration, exacerbation, deterioration or recurrence;

"the Insurance Commissioner" means the Insurance Commissioner appointed under the *Insurance Act* 1995;

"members of the family", in relation to a worker –

(a) means the wife or husband, father, mother, grandmother, grandfather, step-father, step-mother, son and daughter whether legitimate or ex-nuptial, grandson, granddaughter, step-son, step-daughter, brother, sister, step-brother, step-sister, half brother, half sister, mother-in-law or father-in-law of the worker; and

(b) includes –

(i) an adopted child, the brother of his father, a son of his father's brother, his brother's son, his brother's daughter, his mother's brother, his mother's sister, a daughter of his mother's sister, a son of his sister, a daughter of his sister and son of his mother's sister; and

(ii) any person in relation to whom the worker stands in place of a parent;

"nominal dependant" means a person who by custom has the right by that custom to determine the distribution of a compensation payment;

"occupational disease" means any of the diseases specified in Column 1 of Schedule 2 and includes any recurrence or consequence of any of those diseases;

"Office" means the Office of Workers' Compensation established by Section 2.

"officer" means –

(a) an officer appointed to the Public Service under Section 25, 27 or 39 of the *Public Services (Management) Act* 1995; or

(b) a person employed to render temporary or casual assistance in the Public Service under the *Public Services (Management) Act* 1995; or

(c) a person who occupies an office for the time being declared by notice under Subsection (6);

"outworker" means a person to whom articles or materials are given out to be treated or manufactured in his own home or on other premises not under the control or management of the person who gave out the articles or materials;

"proceedings", in relation to a tribunal, include all matters, proceedings and enquiries before the tribunal;

"the Registrar" means the Registrar of Workers' Compensation appointed under Section 10(1);

"the repealed Act" means the *Workers' Compensation Act* replaced by this Act;

"seamen" includes a master, officer, apprentice or other person employed or engaged in any capacity on board ship;

"ship" means any ship, vessel, boat or other craft not ordinarily propelled by oars;

"this Act" includes the regulations;

"tribunal" means a tribunal established under Section 22(1);

"wife", in relation to a worker, includes –

(a) a wife by custom; and

(b) a woman who is not married to the worker but who is living with the worker on a permanent basis as his de facto wife;

"worker" means –

(a) a member of a Provincial Assembly; or

(b) a person (including a domestic servant) who has entered into or works under a contract of employment or apprenticeship or otherwise with an employer whether by way of manual labour, clerical work or otherwise and whether the contract is expressed or implied or is oral or is in writing but does not include –

(i) an outworker; or

(ii) a person whose employment is of a casual nature and is not for the purpose of the employer's trade or business.

(2) For the purposes of this Act –

(a) any reference in this Act to a worker who has been injured includes, where the worker is dead, a reference to his legal personal [890]representative or to his dependants or other persons to whom or for whose benefit compensation is payable; and

(b) any reference in this Act to the wife or the widow of a worker shall, where the worker is a female, be read as a reference to the husband or widower, as the case requires, of the worker; and

(c) the exercise and performance of the powers, duties or functions of a statutory body shall be deemed to be the trade or business of that body.

(3) For the purposes of Subsection (2)(c) "statutory body" means any body corporate or unincorporate constituted by an Act in respect of which the Head of State, acting on advice, has the right to appoint one or more of the persons comprising the body or concerned in its management and includes –

(a) a provincial government; and

(b) a Special Purposes Authority or a Local Government Council or any body exercising the powers, duties and functions of a Local Government Council; and

(c) any body similar in nature and function to a Local Government Council established by a provincial government.

(4) In this Act a reference applicable to a worker after the date of injury shall be read as including a reference to a worker whose contract of employment or apprenticeship has expired or been terminated.

---

[890]The Act has "represenative".

(5) For the purposes of this Act, in the case of an injury that is a disease, the injury shall be deemed to have occurred on the day on which the worker became totally or partially physically or mentally incapacitated because of the injury but where a particular day cannot be ascertained then the injury shall be deemed to have occurred on a day certified by a medical practitioner to be the day on which the worker was so incapacitated by reason of the injury.

(6) The Minister may, by notice in the National Gazette, declare an office for the purpose of the definition of "officer" in Subsection (1).

PART II – ADMINISTRATION

2 Office of Workers' Compensation

(1) The Office of Workers' Compensation is hereby established for the administration of this Act.

(2) The Office shall consist of –

(a) the Chief Commissioner; and

(b) the Commissioners (if any); and

(c) the Registrar; and

(d) the Deputy Registrar; and

(e) such other staff referred to in Section 13 as are necessary for the proper administration of this Act.

3 The Chief Commissioner and Commissioners

(1) There shall be a Chief Commissioner of Workers' Compensation who shall be –

(a) an officer; and

(b) appointed by the Minister by notice in the National Gazette.

(2) There shall be such number of Commissioners of Workers' Compensation as the Minister determines.

(3) A Commissioner shall –

(a) if he is an officer – be appointed by the Minister by notice in the National Gazette; and

(b) if he is a person other than an officer – be appointed by the Minister from a panel or panels of names submitted by –

(i) the employer industrial organizations of a national nature registered under the *Industrial Relations Act* in consultation with the Papua New Guinea Insurance Underwriters' Association; and

(ii) the employee industrial organizations of a national nature registered under the *Industrial Relations Act*,

or either of them, as the case requires, by notice in the National Gazette.

(4) Where the number of Commissioners appointed or to be appointed under Subsection (3)(b) permits, 50% of them shall be appointed from the panel or panels of names submitted by the organizations referred to in Subsection (3)(b)(i) and 50% of them shall be appointed from the panel or panels of names submitted by the organizations referred to in Subsection (3)(b)(ii).

(5) If the Minister is not satisfied that there is on a panel or panels of names submitted to him in accordance with Subsection (3) the name of a person suitable for appointment as a Commissioner, the Minister may request the organizations referred to in Subsection (3)(b)(i) or (ii), as the case requires, to submit a further name or names.

(6) In the event of a failure on the part of the organizations referred to in Subsection 3)(b)(i) or (ii), as the case requires, to submit a panel of names in accordance with Subsection (3)(b), or a further name or names under Subsection (5), within, in the opinion of the Minister, a reasonable time after being requested by him to do so, the Minister may appoint a person to be the Commissioner.

(7) This section does not compel the Minister to appoint Commissioners.

4 Persons ineligible for appointment

A person who –

(a) is less than 21 years of age; or

(b) is an undischarged bankrupt or insolvent; or

(c) has been convicted of an offence punishable under a law of Papua New Guinea by death or imprisonment for one year or longer and, as a result of the conviction, is subject to be sentenced to death or is undergoing imprisonment, or is under bond to appear for sentence if called on; or

(d) is of unsound mind as that expression is used in the *Public Health Act*,

shall not be appointed or nominated as a Commissioner.

5 Term of office

(1) Subject to this Act, a Commissioner referred to in Section 3(3)(b) holds office for a term of five years, and is eligible for re-appointment.

(2) Notwithstanding Subsection (1), where a Commissioner is appointed to an office from which a Commissioner has been removed or resigned, the Commissioner so appointed holds office for the balance of the term of office of the previous Commissioner, and is eligible for re-appointment.

6 Removal from office

If a Commissioner referred to in Section 3(3)(b) –

(a) declines to act; or

(b) becomes permanently incapable of performing his duties as a Commissioner; or

(c) becomes a person disqualified under Section 4 from being appointed as a Commissioner; or

(d) without first obtaining the approval of the Minister, engages in paid employment, outside the duties of his office; or

(e) is guilty of misbehaviour,

the Minister may, by notice in the National Gazette, remove the Commissioner from office.

7 Terms and conditions of appointment

The salary and other terms and conditions of appointment of Commissioners referred to in Section 3(3)(b) are as determined by the Minister after consultation with the Departmental Head of the Department of Personnel Management.

8 Leave of absence

The Chief Commissioner may grant leave of absence to a Commissioner referred to in Section 3(3)(b) on such terms and conditions as to remuneration or otherwise as the Minister determines.

9 Resignation

A Commissioner referred to in Section 3(3)(b) may resign his office by writing under his hand delivered to the Chief Commissioner.

10 Registrar and Deputy Registrars

(1) For the purposes of this Act, the Minister may, by notice in the National Gazette, appoint –

(a) a Registrar of Workers' Compensation; and

(b) such Deputy Registrars of Workers' Compensation as the Minister considers necessary,

each of whom shall be an officer of the Public Service.

(2) The powers, functions, duties and responsibilities of a Deputy Registrar are –

(a) as prescribed; or

(b) as directed by the Chief Commissioner with, where the Deputy Registrar is an officer of the Department, the approval of the Secretary of the Department.

11 Acting Registrar

(1) At any time when the position of Registrar is not filled on a permanent basis, or when the Registrar is absent from the country or for any reason is not able to carry out his duties, the Chief Commissioner may appoint a member of the staff of the Office or an officer to act as the Registrar.

(2) The appointment of an Acting Registrar under Subsection (1) continues until a permanent Registrar is appointed or until the Registrar returns to the country or becomes able again to carry out his duties, as the case may be.

(3) An Acting Registrar has and may exercise and perform all the powers, functions, duties and responsibilities of the Registrar.

12 Functions, etc, of Registrar

The Registrar shall –

(a) keep a register in the prescribed form and shall enter or cause to be entered in the register all the prescribed particulars of –

(i) all claims received by the Office for workers' compensation; and

(ii) all determinations, awards and orders of a tribunal that arise out of those claims; and

(b) carry out such other functions and duties as are prescribed or as are directed by the Chief Commissioner.

13 Staff

(1) Subject to Subsection (2), any staff required for the purposes of this Act shall be officers or employees of the Public Service.

(2) Subsection (1) does not prevent any person from being employed, on contract or otherwise, under any other law of Papua New Guinea to perform functions in relation to the Office.

14 Declaration of office

The Chief Commissioner, each Commissioner, the Registrar and each Deputy Registrar shall, before taking up the duties of his office, make a Declaration of Office as set out in Schedule 1.

PART III – THE WORKERS' COMPENSATION FUND

15 The Workers' Compensation Fund

The Workers' Compensation Fund is hereby established, into which shall be paid such moneys as are specified by this Act.

16 Application of *Public Finances (Management) Act* 1995

Except where this Act provides to the contrary, the provisions of the *Public Finances (Management) Act* 1995 relating to Trust Accounts within the meaning of that Act apply to and in relation to the Fund.

17 Contributions to the Fund

(1) Each insurer shall contribute annually to the Fund a sum amounting to a percentage to be fixed by the Chief Commissioner on the total amount of the premium income (whether received by or owing to the insurer) of the insurer in respect of the year ended 31 December immediately preceding in respect of insurance or indemnity indemnifying employers against their liability in relation to workers' compensation under this Act and any other law in respect of persons employed by them, excluding any part of premiums actually paid by way of re-insurance to any other insurer contributing under this Act.

(2) Each public employer who is a self-insurer shall, in respect of any period for which contributions to the Fund are payable by the insurer, contribute to the Fund such amount as the Chief Commissioner determines and as is assessed on the wages paid by the public employer to employees during that period, having regard to the premium payable for insurance or indemnity by employers engaged in the same or any similar trade, occupation, calling or industry.

(3) The percentage shall, for the purposes of Subsection (1), be uniform for all insurers.

(4) The amount of any annual contribution –

(a) shall be paid in quarterly instalments on or before 1 January, 1 April, 1 July and 1 October in each year, or on such other days as the Chief Commissioner determines; and

(b) is recoverable as a debt due to the State in any court of competent jurisdiction.

(5) An insurer who fails to pay an instalment of the annual contribution within 30 days after the date it became payable by him, is guilty of an offence.

Penalty: A fine not exceeding K500.00.

18 Expenditure from the Fund

There shall be paid out of the Fund –

(a) all moneys payable on account of the employment of the Chief Commissioner, Commissioners (if any), the Registrar, the Deputy Registrars and the staff of the Office; and

(b) all moneys payable on account of the functioning and administration of the Office; and

(c) compensation payable under an order of a tribunal where the employer of the worker in relation to whom the order was made –

(i) has not effected insurance or indemnity against his liability to pay compensation under this Act and the compensation is not paid within 30 days after the date of the award; or

(ii) cannot, after diligent inquiry, be found; and

(d) all other money required by the Chief Commissioner for carrying out this Act.

19 Estimates of expenditure

(1) The Chief Commissioner shall, prior to 1 January in each year, prepare estimates of expenditure for that year and submit them to the Minister.

(2) Expenditure shall not be incurred in relation to any estimates of expenditure unless and until those estimates have been approved by the Minister.

(3) Where, in any year, the amount actually contributed to the Fund under Section 17 –

(a) is less than the expenditure actually incurred in that year, the deficit shall be added to the estimated expenditure for the next succeeding year, and the rate of contribution increased proportionately; or

(b) exceeds the expenditure actually incurred in that year, the excess shall be regarded as a credit against contributions for the next succeeding year, and the rate of contribution may be reduced proportionately.

20 Insufficiency of Fund

(1) Where –

(a) the amount standing to the credit of the Fund is, at any time, insufficient to make any payment which is required by this Act to be paid; and

(b) the Minister responsible for financial matters certifies as to the insufficiency,

the payment shall be made from the Consolidated Revenue Fund which to the necessary extent is appropriated accordingly.

(2) Any amount paid out of the Consolidated Revenue Fund under Subsection (1) –

(a) is a charge on the Fund; and

(b) shall, as soon as the Minister responsible for financial matters certifies that sufficient funds are standing to the credit of the Fund, be repaid from the Fund to the Consolidated Revenue Fund.

21 Returns to be furnished by insurers

(1) In January of each year or at such other time as the Chief Commissioner appoints, every insurer shall furnish to the Chief Commissioner –

(a) a return showing the amount of the premium income (whether received or owing to the insurer) in respect of insurance of employers against their liability to pay compensation under this Act and their liability under any other law in respect of persons employed by them during the immediately preceding year, excluding any part of that premium income actually paid by way of re-insurance to any other insurer contributing under this Act; and

(b) a statutory declaration by the insurer or his or its manager, secretary or agent in Papua New Guinea, that he has carefully examined the return and to the best of his knowledge, information and belief, the return is a true return of that amount.

(2) An insurer who fails to furnish a return as required by Subsection (1) is guilty of an offence.

Penalty: A fine not exceeding K50.00 for each day the offence continues.

(3) An insurer who furnishes a return under Subsection (1) which is false or misleading in any material particular is guilty of an offence.

Penalty: A fine not exceeding K500.00.

PART IV – CLAIMS

Division 1 – Workers' Compensation Tribunals

22 Constitution of tribunals

(1) For the purposes of this Act, the Chief Commissioner may, by instrument under his hand, establish Workers' Compensation Tribunals consisting of –

(a) the Chief Commissioner; or

(b) the Chief Commissioner and one or more Commissioners; or

(c) one or more Commissioners.

(2) Where –

(a) a tribunal consists of more than one person; and

(b) a vacancy occurs in the membership of the tribunal,

the tribunal may continue to act notwithstanding the vacancy.

(3) Where a tribunal continues to act after a vacancy occurs in the membership of the tribunal, no act, proceeding, determination, order or award of the tribunal is to be called into question or invalidated merely by reason of the vacancy.

[891]23 Jurisdiction of tribunals

(1) Subject to this Act, a tribunal has exclusive jurisdiction to examine, hear and determine all questions and matters arising under this Act, and the action or decision of a tribunal on any such matter is final and conclusive.

(2) Subsection (1) does not prevent a tribunal from reconsidering any matter which has been dealt with by it, or from rescinding, altering or amending any decision or order previously made by it.

(3) Without limiting the generality of Subsection (1), the jurisdiction of a tribunal extends to determining –

(a) whether an injury has arisen out of, or in the course of, an employment within the meaning of this Act; and

(b) the existence and degree of disability by reason of any injury; and

(c) the permanence of disability by reason of any injury; and

(d) the degree of diminution of earning capacity by reason of any injury; and

(e) the amount of average earnings of a worker; and

---

[891]*See* Section 49(1).

(f) the amounts of any refunds or adjustments of assessments which, in its discretion, it may deem proper to make; and

(g) the existence and extent of dependency; and

(h) whether a person is a worker within the meaning of this Act; and

(i) whether any person or aggregation of persons is or is not an employer of a worker within the meaning of this Act and if so whether such worker is or is not entitled to compensation; and

(j) for the purposes of this Act – the existence of any relationship of any member of the family of a worker; and

(k) all cases of permanent, partial or total incapacity, and making awards of compensation within the limits prescribed in this Act as may appear proper after taking into consideration the circumstances of the case; and

(l) the modification of weekly payments when a partially incapacitated worker resumes or is capable of resuming any employment other than his former employment; and

(m) whether the circumstances of any particular case justify the making of an order for redemption of weekly payments of compensation by payment of a lump sum; and

(n) the liability of any person in respect of the expenses of medical or surgical attendance on an injured worker at the suit of any person –

(i) by whom they have been incurred; or

(ii) entitled to receive payment in respect of them.

(4) An action shall not be brought or maintained against a tribunal or any member of a tribunal in respect of an act or decision done or made in the honest belief that it was within the jurisdiction of the tribunal.

Division 2 – Proceedings of Tribunals

Subdivision A – General

24 Regulation of proceedings

(1) Subject to this Act, the procedure to be followed in any proceedings before a tribunal, the Chief Commissioner, a Commissioner, the Registrar or any other person or court acting as a delegate of a tribunal is as prescribed or, in the absence of prescription, is as determined by the tribunal, Chief Commissioner, Commissioner, Registrar or other person or body, as the case may be.

(2) Any person who is a party to any proceedings before a tribunal may –

(a) appear in person; or
(b) be represented by –
   (i) his lawyer; or
   (ii) some other person duly appointed by the party for the purpose,

and, subject to this Act, every party who appears by his lawyer or other representative is bound by the acts of his lawyer or representative.

25 Questions determined on substantial merits

(1) Subject to this Act, in the hearing and determination of any question, a tribunal, the Chief Commissioner, a Commissioner, the Registrar and any other person or court acting as a delegate of a tribunal –

(a) shall act according to equity and good conscience and the substantial merits of the case; and
(b) is not bound to observe strict legal procedure or to apply technical rules of evidence; and
(c) shall inform itself or himself as to the matter by such means as in the circumstances are considered necessary and just; and
(d) may, by order, require a person –
   (i) to furnish in writing or otherwise, such particulars in relation to the matter as it or he requires; or
   (ii) to attend before it or him and to give evidence on oath or otherwise; or
   (iii) to answer any questions or to produce any documents or thing which in its or his opinion is or may be relevant to the matter.

(2) In considering a question as to whether a person who resides outside the country is a dependant of a worker, a tribunal –

(a) shall require proof by or including documentary evidence that the worker has, wholly or in part, as the case may be, supported the person; and
(b) shall not accept as sufficient proof a statutory declaration or affidavit which is unsupported by documentary evidence to that effect.

(3) The granting of relief or redress under this Act shall not necessarily be restricted to the specific claim made, nor to the subject matter of the claim.

(4) All proceedings before a tribunal are to be conducted in public unless the tribunal otherwise directs.

26 Tribunal may act on report of officer, etc

(1) A tribunal may act on the report of any member of the staff of the Office.

(2) Any inquiry which a tribunal considers necessary to make may be made by –

- (a) the Chief Commissioner; or
- (b) a Commissioner; or
- (c) the Registrar or a Deputy Registrar; or
- (d) a member of the staff of the Office; or
- (e) some other person appointed by the tribunal to make the inquiry, and the tribunal may act on his report as to the result of the inquiry.

(3) A person appointed under Subsection (2) to make an inquiry has, for the purposes of making that inquiry, all the powers of a tribunal.

27 Delegation to Village Courts, etc

(1) A tribunal may delegate all or any of its powers relating to the determination of any question relating to the existence and extent of dependency to –

- (a) a Village Court; or
- (b) where no Village Court has been established for the relevant area, to the Local Court,

but the delegation in each case shall be of a specific and not of a general nature.

(2) A tribunal is not bound to accept a decision of a Village Court or a Local Court made under a delegation under Subsection (1) but such a decision is, in all other respects, as binding and effective as if it were a decision of the tribunal.

(3) Where a Village Court or a Local Court has determined any question under this Section, that Court shall, within 14 days after making the determination, forward, or cause to be forwarded, to the tribunal, a report of its proceedings.

28 Case stated on questions of law

When any question of law arises in any proceeding before it, including any question as to whether or not a person is a worker, a tribunal –

(a) may; and

(b) shall, if requested to do so by any party to the proceedings before it,

state a case for the decision of the National Court.

29 Certified copies, etc, of records to be prima facie evidence

Every copy or extract from an entry of any book or record of a tribunal or of the Office and of any document filed with a tribunal or the Office purporting to be certified by the Registrar to be a true copy or extract shall be received in any court as prima facie evidence of the matter so certified without proof of the Registrars appointment, authority or signature.

30 Issue of certificate of tribunal's finding

The Registrar may, in any case where he considers it necessary to do so, and shall, on the application of any employer or worker interested in any order, award, ruling or decision of a tribunal, issue a certificate embodying the substance of the order, award, ruling or decision.

31 Registrar to inform workers and employers of their rights

The Registrar shall, when requested to do so, furnish workers and employers with information as to their rights and liabilities in respect of injuries sustained by workers in connexion with their employment.

32 Illegal contracts

Where in any proceedings for the recovery under this Act of compensation for an injury it appears to a tribunal that the contract of employment or apprenticeship under which the injured worker was engaged at the time when the injury happened was illegal, the tribunal may, if, having regard to all the circumstances of the case, it thinks it proper to do so, deal with the matter as if the injured person had at that time been a worker under a valid contract of employment or apprenticeship.

Subdivision B – Expeditious Settlement of Disputes

33 Summary list

(1) All proceedings before a tribunal shall, in the first instance, be placed on a list for hearing by the tribunal to be called the "summary list".

(2) Proceedings in the summary list may be heard and determined by a tribunal expeditiously and informally and on the hearing of each proceeding the tribunal may determine the matter at issue without taking evidence on oath except that, if any party to the proceedings requests that any or all evidence be taken on oath, the tribunal shall take that evidence on oath.

34 Removal of proceedings from the summary list

(1) Where, in any proceedings in the summary list before a tribunal, the tribunal considers that difficult or complex questions of fact or law have arisen or are likely to arise, it may order that the proceedings be removed from the summary list and placed on the list for formal determination.

(2) Where proceedings have been removed from the summary list under Subsection (1) and it later appears to the tribunal bearing the proceedings that difficult or complex questions of fact or law have not arisen and that the proceeding could have been expeditiously determined at proceedings in the summary list, the tribunal may order the party responsible for having the matter removed from the summary list –

(a) to pay the costs or any part of the costs involved in the removal and formal determination to the other party; and

(b) where the party so responsible is an employer – it may determine that he has caused an unreasonable delay in the settlement of the claim for compensation and Section 35 applies.

35 Unreasonable delay in settlement of claims

(1) Where, in any proceedings under this Act for the settlement of a claim for compensation, a tribunal is of the opinion that the employer is responsible for or has caused an unreasonable delay in having the claim settled, it may order that the amount of compensation awarded or payable be increased by such amount as it specifies in the order.

(2) An increase in compensation under Subsection (1) shall not exceed –

(a) in the case of a lump sum – 10% of the total amount of the compensation; or

(b) in the case of a weekly payment – 10% of the total amount of the weekly payment accrued at the date of assessment of compensation.

36 Weekly payments

(1) Subject to the succeeding provisions of this Division, unless a tribunal otherwise orders, the first weekly payment to an incapacitated worker provided for by Section 66(1) –

(a) shall be made to the worker as soon as possible but not more than two weeks after the worker has provided evidence of his incapacity; and

(b) shall be made on the day on which the worker would, but for his incapacity, have been paid his wages and afterwards weekly payment shall be made at seven day intervals calculated from that day.

(2) The weekly payment referred to in Subsection (1) shall be made as if the worker were totally incapacitated.

(3) An employer who disputes his liability to pay compensation under this Act may, within the period of two weeks referred to in Subsection (1), or such further time as the Chief Commissioner orders, apply to the Chief Commissioner for an order by a tribunal that Subsection (1) does not apply.

(4) An application under Subsection (3) shall be heard and determined as a proceeding on the summary list and, until the application has been determined, the operation of Subsection (1) is suspended.

(5) On the hearing of an application under Subsection (3) the tribunal may –

(a) dismiss or adjourn the application on such terms as it thinks fit and, if it dismisses the application, make such order as to the modification of the application of Subsection (1) as it thinks fit, and then Subsection (1) applies and has effect accordingly; or

(b) if it considers that a genuine dispute exists concerning the liability of the employer to pay compensation – order that Subsection (1) does not apply.

(6) The fact that an application under Subsection (3) has been dismissed shall not be taken into account by a tribunal in any other proceedings under this Act.

(7) The provisions of this Act which provide for a hearing to be removed from the summary list for formal determination do not apply to any proceedings under this section.

37 Making of weekly payment not an admission of liability

For the purposes of this Act, the making of a weekly payment referred to in Section 36(1) does not of itself constitute an admission of liability to pay compensation.

38 Weekly payments cannot be recovered unless obtained by fraud

Unless it appears to a court that the payment of weekly payments was obtained by fraud or misrepresentation on the part of a worker, the fact that an employer may be found by a tribunal not to be liable for such weekly payments does not entitle any person who made the weekly payments to sue for and recover from the worker the amount of any such weekly payments.

39 Making of weekly payments not to preclude submission of notice of injury

The making of weekly payments under this Division does not preclude the requirement of the submission of a notice of injury under Section 42.

Division 3 – Costs

40 Costs

(1) The costs of and incidental to any proceedings before a tribunal shall –

(a) subject to the regulations – be in the discretion of the tribunal; and

(b) not exceed the limit prescribed; and

(c) be taxed in the manner prescribed.

(2) A taxation of costs under Subsection (1) may be reviewed by the Registrar of the National Court.

Division 4 – Notice of Injuries and Claims

41 Time for taking proceedings

(1) Without limiting the generality of the meaning of the expression "reasonable cause" in this section, it shall be deemed to include –

(a) the making of any payment to a worker which he believes to be a payment of compensation under this Act; and

(b) any conduct on the part of the employer or his insurer or agent, or on the part of an employee purporting to act on behalf of the employer, by which the worker is lead to believe –

(i) that compensation under this Act will or will probably be paid to him; or

(ii) that he is not entitled to any such compensation.

(2) Subject to Section 68, proceedings for the recovery under this Act of compensation are not maintainable unless –

(a) notice of the injury has been given as soon as practicable after the injury occurs and before the worker has voluntarily left the employment in which he was injured; and

(b) the claim for compensation with respect to the injury has been made within 12 months after the occurrence of the injury, or in the case of death within 12 months after the date of death.

(3) For the purposes of Subsection (2)(a), a worker shall not be deemed to have voluntarily left the employment in any case where by reason of the injury he was unable to continue in the employment.

(4) The want of or any defect or irregularity in a notice of injury is not a bar to the maintenance of proceedings for the recovery of compensation –

(a) if the application is made in respect of the death of a worker resulting from an injury which occurred on the premises of the employer, or at any place where the worker at the time of the injury was working under the control of the employer or of any person employed by the employer and the worker died –

(i) on those premises; or

(ii) at that place; or

(iii) on any premises belonging to the employer; or

(iv) without having left the vicinity of the premises or place where the injury occurred; or

(b) if the employer is proved to have had knowledge of the injury from any other source at or about the time of the injury or, if it is found in the proceedings for settling the claim that the employer is not or would not, if a notice or amended notice were then given and the hearing postponed, be prejudiced in his defence by the want or defect or inaccuracy, or that such want, defect or inaccuracy was occasioned by mistake, absence from the country or other reasonable cause.

(5) The notice referred to in Subsection (2) –

(a) may be given in writing or orally to the employer or any one of the employers or to any foreman or other official under whose supervision the worker is employed or to any person designated by the employer for the purpose; and

(b) shall specify the name and address of the person injured; and

(c) shall state in ordinary language the cause of the injury and the date on which the injury occurred.

(6) Where a principal contracts with a contractor for the execution of any work undertaken by the principal, notice of an injury to a worker employed by the contractor given to the contractor or to any foreman or other official under whose supervision the worker is employed or to any person designated for the purpose by the contractor, shall be deemed to be notice to the principal.

(7) The Registrar may receive, and a tribunal may determine, any application for compensation under this Act in any case where –

(a) the required notice has not been given; or

(b) the application has not been made in due time,

provided that the Registrar or tribunal, as the case may be, is satisfied that there was reasonable cause for the failure to give notice or to make the application in due time, as the case may be.

[892]42 Employer to give notice of injury, etc, to Registrar

(1) Where an injury to a worker results –

(a) in the death of the worker within one day after the occurrence of the injury; or

(b) in the total or partial incapacity of the worker for a period exceeding one day,

---

[892]*See*, also, Section 45.

whether or not the injury gives rise to any claim for compensation, the employer must –

(c) not later than seven days after the occurrence of the injury; or

(d) where the employer had no immediate knowledge of the injury, not later than seven days after the occurrence of the injury first came to his notice,

forward to the Registrar a notice in the prescribed form.

(2) Where an injury to a worker results in the death of the worker more than one day after the occurrence of the injury, the employer must, whether or not the death of the worker gives rise to any claim for compensation –

(a) not later than seven days after the death; or

(b) where the employer had no immediate knowledge of the death, not later than seven days after the death first came to his notice,

forward to the Registrar a notice in the prescribed form.

43 Deputy Registrar to ascertain whether claim for compensation may arise and to inform dependants

(1) As soon as practicable after a notice of injury or of death is received by the Registrar he may refer the notice to a Deputy Registrar who shall ascertain whether a claim for compensation may arise out of the injury or death.

(2) Where the Deputy Registrar to whom a notice is referred under Subsection (1) is of the opinion that a claim for compensation may arise, he shall –

(a) in the event of the death of the worker –

(i) ascertain whether there are any dependants of the deceased worker; and

(ii) if there are any such dependants –

(A) inform them of the reported circumstances and cause of the death; and

(B) advise them of their possible rights to compensation under this Act; and

(C) if so required by all or any of them, make a claim for compensation on their behalf; and

(b) in the event of an injury to the worker –

(i) if the claim is in respect of the incapacity of a worker and weekly payments are not being made under Section 36(1); or

(ii) if the claim is in respect of a specific injury under Section 66 or 67,

and if the worker so requests, make a claim for compensation on behalf of the worker.

44 Employer deemed to have knowledge of death of worker on his premises

For the purposes of this Division, where the death of a worker occurs on premises belonging to or under the control of his employer, the employer shall be deemed to have knowledge of the death from the moment at which it occurred.

45 Failure to give notice of injury

An employer who, without reasonable cause (proof of which is on him) fails to give to the Registrar a notice of injury or notice of death as required by Section 42, is guilty of an offence.

Penalty: A fine not exceeding K500.00.

Division 5 – Medical Examinations

46 Employer may require worker to be medically examined

(1) Where a worker –

(a) has suffered an injury that may give rise to a claim for compensation under this Act; or

(b) has given notice of an injury under this Act; or

(c) is receiving weekly payments under this Act,

the worker shall, if so required by the employer, from time to time, submit himself for examination by a medical practitioner provided and paid for by the employer.

(2) Where a worker –

(a) fails or refuses to submit himself for a medical examination when required to do so under Subsection (1); or

(b) in any way obstructs the medical examination,

his right to weekly payments or to other compensation under this Act is suspended until the medical examination has taken place.

(3) The employer shall reimburse the worker the amount of any cost or out of pocket expenses reasonably incurred by the worker for the purpose of submitting himself to any medical examination under Subsection (1).

(4) A worker shall not be required to submit himself for examination by a medical practitioner under Subsection (1) –

(a) otherwise than in accordance with the regulations; or

(b) at more frequent intervals than are prescribed.

47 Cost of medical and surgical treatment

Where, during the period of his incapacity, a worker, at the request of the employer, receives medical or surgical treatment, the cost of, and incidental to, that treatment shall not be regarded as a payment, allowance or benefit within the meaning of this Act.

48 Reports of medical examination

(1) Where a worker is required to submit himself to a medical examination under this Act, the employer must, at the request of –

(a) the worker; or

(b) any representative of the worker,

promptly supply, or cause to be supplied, to the worker or the representative –

(c) a copy of every report furnished to the employer or his representative by the medical practitioner who conducted the examination; and

(d) a written statement of all the facts, conclusions and opinions of the medical practitioner relating to the condition of the worker which have been communicated by the medical practitioner to the employer or to his representative.

(2) An employer who fails or refuses to comply with Subsection (1) is guilty of an offence.

Penalty: A fine not exceeding K200.00.

Division 6 – Appeals

49 Appeal to National Court

(1) Where in any proceedings under this Act a tribunal gives a decision or makes an order or award, either party to the proceedings may appeal from the decision, order or award on a question of law or fact, or both, to the National Court within the time and in accordance with the

conditions prescribed by the Rules of Court for appeals from decisions of the District Court.

(2) An appeal under Subsection (1) may be by way of rehearing.

(3) The National Court shall decide the matter of the appeal and may affirm, quash or vary the decision, order or award appealed from, or substitute or make any decision, order or award which ought to have been made in the first instance, and may make such order as to the costs of the appeal or of the proceedings before the tribunal, or both, as it thinks proper.

Division 7 – Miscellaneous

50 Copies of statements to be given to worker

(1) An employer must, where a worker or his representative so requests, promptly supply, or cause to be supplied, to the worker or his representative a copy of any statement, that has been reduced to writing, made by the worker to the employer, or to any representative of the employer, in connexion with an injury suffered by the worker whilst he was in the employ of the employer.

(2) An employer who fails to comply with Subsection (1) is guilty of an offence.

Penalty: A fine not exceeding K100.00.

51 Inspection of premises, etc

A person who is in charge of –

(a) any premises or place; or

(b) any plant or machinery,

at or in relation to which an injury to a worker has occurred, and who unreasonably refuses to allow the worker, or a person nominated by the worker, to make a reasonable inspection or examination of those premises, that place or that plant or machinery, is guilty of an offence.

Penalty: A fine not exceeding K100.00.

52 Notices, etc, to be displayed

(1) An employer shall display prominently at his place or places of employment such notices in relation to workers' compensation as the Chief Commissioner determines.

(2) An employer shall keep at his place or places of employment and make available at all reasonable times to all persons employed by him all books, pamphlets, and other documents relating to workers'

compensation that may, from time to time, be issued by the Chief Commissioner.

PART V – RIGHT TO COMPENSATION

53 Interpretation of Part V

In this Part, unless the contrary intention appears –

"institution" means trade, technical or other school and university or other place of tertiary education;

"journey" means the passage by any reasonable, direct or convenient route between two places but does not include –

(a) any substantial deviation from that route for purposes unconnected with the employment or other purpose for which the journey was undertaken; or

(b) any substantial interruption of that passage for purposes unconnected with the employment or other purpose for which the journey was undertaken,

unless in the circumstances of that substantial deviation or substantial interruption the nature, extent, degree or content of the risk of injury to the worker was not materially changed or increased by reason only of the deviation or interruption;

"place of abode", in relation to a worker, includes any place at which, under the terms of his employment, or at the request of his employer, he resides temporarily or at which it is necessary or convenient for him to reside temporarily for the purposes of his employment;

"place of employment" includes place of pick-up and where there is no fixed place of employment, the whole area, scope or ambit of employment;

"place of pick-up" means any pre-arranged place at which persons attend and at which employers select and engage persons for employment.

54 Liability of employer to compensate worker for injuries

(1) If in any employment personal injury arising out of or in the course of the employment is caused to a worker, his employer shall, except as provided in this Act, be liable to pay compensation in accordance with this Act.

(2) Without limiting the generality of Subsection (1), an injury shall be deemed to arise out of or in the course of the employment of a worker if it occurs while the worker –

(a) is in the course of a daily or other periodic journey between his place of abode and his place of employment, whether such journey is to or from his place of employment; or

(b) is in the course of a journey between his place of employment or place of abode and an institution which he is required by law to attend, or which he attends at the request of or with the approval of the employer for the purpose of attending a class or undertaking training at such an institution; or

(c) is in attendance at an institution referred to in Paragraph (b) for a purpose referred to in that paragraph; or

(d) is in the course of a journey between his place of abode or place of employment and any other place for the purpose of –

(i) obtaining a medical certificate in connection with any injury for which he has received compensation or for which a claim for compensation has been admitted; or

(ii) receiving attention or treatment in connexion with any such injury, medical, surgical or hospital advice,

or is in attendance at any such place for any such purpose; or

(e) is in attendance at his place of employment for reasons connected with his employment including any period –

(i) before he has commenced his work for the day; and

(ii) after he has concluded his work for the day; and

(iii) during an authorized break in his work,

so long as the worker –

(iv) is not guilty of any misconduct or breach of his employer's instructions; and

(v) did not voluntarily subject himself to any abnormal risk of injury.

(3) While a worker is in the course of a journey from his place of employment under one employer to his place of employment under another employer, this section applies and has effect as if the first-mentioned place of employment were his place of abode.

(4) Notwithstanding any other law, a person who ordinarily engages in employment in connexion with which he customarily attends at a place of pick-up, shall be deemed to be working under a contract of employment –

(a) with the employer who selected and engaged him at the place of pick-up; or

(b) if no employer so selected or engaged him – with the last employer who, within the immediately preceding 21 days, selected and engaged him in that employment.

(5) Notwithstanding anything in this Act, compensation under this Act is not payable –

(a) in respect of any injury that is consequent on or attributable to the serious and wilful misconduct of the worker unless that injury results in the death or permanent total incapacity of the worker; or

(b) in respect of a deliberately self-inflicted injury.

55 Acting in employment

For the purposes of Section 54, a worker shall be deemed to be acting in the course of his employment notwithstanding the fact that –

(a) he was acting in contravention of any statutory or other regulation applicable to the employment; or

(b) he was acting without instructions from his employer,

if he was so acting for the purposes of, and in connexion with, his employment.

56 Compensation for injuries, etc, received outside the country

(1) Where an employer in Papua New Guinea employs a worker and that worker, whilst outside the territorial limits of Papua New Guinea –

(a) receives an injury; or

(b) dies,

under circumstances which, had the injury been received or the death occurred in Papua New Guinea, would entitle him (or, in the case of the death of the worker, his dependants) to compensation in accordance with the provisions of this Act, that worker is (or, in the case of the death of the worker, his dependants are) entitled to receive compensation in accordance with the provisions of this Act.

(2) For the purposes of Subsection (1), the provisions of this Act apply, with the necessary modifications, to and in relation to the injury or death.

(3) This Act shall not be construed so as to entitle a worker (or, in the case of the death of the worker, his dependants) to receive compensation for the same injury (or for the death) under this Act and under the corresponding law of any place other than Papua New Guinea.

(4) If a worker (or, in the case of the death of a worker, his dependants) receives compensation under this Act in respect of an injury (or death) and subsequently receives compensation under a corresponding law in force in a place other than Papua New Guinea in respect of the same injury (or death), the employer is entitled to recover from the worker (or, in the case of the death of the worker, his dependants) the amount of compensation paid by the employer under this Act.

57 Drivers of certain passenger vehicles under contracts of bailment deemed to be employees

Notwithstanding anything in this Act, where a person engaged in driving a vehicle used for carrying passengers or goods for reward has the use of that vehicle under a contract of bailment (not being a bona fide contract for the purchase of the vehicle whether by hire-purchase or otherwise) under which he is required to pay any sum or sums (whether of fixed amount or proportionate to mileage or receipts or otherwise) for the use of that vehicle, then for the purposes of this Act –

(a) such person shall be deemed to be working under a contract of employment with an employer; and

(b) the person from whom the use of the vehicle is obtained under the contract of bailment shall be deemed to be that employer.

58 Services of employee lent by employer

Where the services of a worker are lent or let on hire to another person by the person with whom the worker has entered into a contract of employment or apprenticeship, the latter person shall, for the purposes of this Act, be deemed to continue to be the employer of the worker while he is working for that other person.

59 Sub-contracting

(1) In this section –

"contractor" means a person with whom a principal contracts for the execution by or under the contractor of the whole or any part of any work undertaken by the principal;

"principal" means a person who, in the course of, or for the purpose of his trade or business, contracts with any other person for the execution by or under that person of the whole or any part of any work.

(2) Subject to Subsection (3), the principal is liable to pay to any worker employed in the execution of the work by the contractor, any

compensation under this Act which he would have been liable to pay if that worker had been immediately employed by him.

(3) Where compensation is claimed from, or proceedings are taken against, the principal, then, in the application of this Act, references to the principal shall be substituted for references to the employer except that the amount of compensation shall be calculated with reference to the earnings of the worker under the employer by whom he is immediately employed.

(4) Where the principal is liable to pay compensation under this section he is entitled to be indemnified by any person who would have been liable to pay compensation to the worker independently of this section, and all questions as to the right to, and amount of, any such indemnity shall, in default of agreement, be settled by a tribunal.

(5) This section does not prevent a worker from recovering compensation under this Act from the contractor instead of the principal.

60 Application of Act to seaman

(1) In this section, "Papua New Guinea ship" means a ship which is –

(a) registered in Papua New Guinea; or

(b) owned by a corporation established under the laws of Papua New Guinea or having its principal office or place of business in Papua New Guinea, or in the possession of any such corporation by virtue of a charter; or

(c) owned by a person or corporation whose chief office or place of business in respect of the management of the ship is in Papua New Guinea, or in the possession of any such person or corporation by virtue of a charter.

(2) Subject to the following modifications, this Act applies to a worker who is a seaman employed on a Papua New Guinea ship or a ship whose first port of clearance and whose destination are in Papua New Guinea: –

(a) the notice of injury and the claim for compensation may, except where the person injured is a master, be given to the master of the ship as if he were the employer but, where the injury occurred or the incapacity commences on board the ship, it is not necessary to give notice of the injury; and

(b) in the case of the death of a seaman, the claim for compensation shall be made within 12 months after news of the death has been received by the claimant; and

(c) where an injured seaman is discharged or left behind in a foreign country, depositions respecting the circumstances and nature of the injury, taken by a Judge or magistrate or by a Papua New Guinea diplomatic or consular official in the foreign country, shall, in any proceedings for enforcing the claim, be admissible in evidence if authenticated by the signature of the Judge, magistrate or diplomatic or consular official, without proof of the signature or official character of the person appearing to have signed the deposition; and

(d) in the case of the death of a seaman leaving no dependants, compensation is not payable if the owner of the ship is, under any law in force in Papua New Guinea, liable to pay the expenses of burial; and

(e) the weekly payment shall not be payable in respect of the period during which the owner of the ship is, under any law in force in Papua New Guinea, liable to defray the expenses of maintenance of an injured seaman; and

(f) any sum payable by way of compensation shall be paid in full notwithstanding any limitation of liability in any other law; and

(g) in any proceeding for the recovery of compensation, if it is shown that the ship has 12 months or upwards before the institution of the proceedings left a port of departure, the ship shall, unless it is shown that it has been heard of within 12 months after that departure, be deemed to have been lost with all hands either immediately after the time it was last heard of or at such later time as the tribunal thinks probable; and

(h) any duplicate agreement or list of the crew made out or statement of change of the crew delivered to a public officer at the time of the last departure of the ship from a port or a certificate purporting to be a certificate from a consular or other public officer at any port, stating that certain seamen were shipped in the ship from the port, shall, if produced or purporting to be produced from proper custody, be, in the absence of proof to the contrary, sufficient proof that the seamen named as belonging to the ship were on board at the time of the loss; and

(i) in the case of a ship lost with all hands, proceedings for the recovery of compensation shall be maintainable if the claim is made within 18 months of the date at which the ship is deemed under Paragraph (g) to have been lost with all hands.

61 Insolvency of employer

(1) Where an employer who has entered into a contract with any insurers in respect of any liability under this Act to any worker –

(a) becomes insolvent; or

(b) makes a composition or arrangement with his creditors; or

(c) being a company, has commenced to be wound up,

the rights of the employer against the insurers with respect to that liability shall, notwithstanding any Act relating to insolvency or to the winding-up of companies, be transferred to and vest in the worker.

(2) Where a transfer has been effected under Subsection (1), the insurers have the same rights and remedies and are subject to the same liabilities as if they were the employer, but they shall not be under any greater liability to the worker than they would have been under to the employer.

(3) If the liability of the insurers to the worker is less than the liability of the employer to the worker, the worker may prove for the balance in the insolvency or liquidation.

62 Persons entitled to compensation on death

(1) Where an injury results in the death of a worker, the dependants of that worker are entitled to claim compensation under this Act.

(2) Notwithstanding anything in this Act –

(a) a wife or the wives; and

(b) the children,

of a deceased worker who was or were wholly or mainly dependent for support on the earnings of the worker at the time of death of the worker or at any other relevant time shall be awarded jointly –

(c) not less than 50%; or

(d) such higher percentage as a tribunal considers just,

of the total amount of compensation awarded in respect of the death of the worker.

(3) Subject to this Act and in particular to Subsection (2), any question as to –

(a) who is a dependant of a deceased worker; and

(b) the amount payable to each such dependant,

shall be determined by a tribunal.

(4) Where a tribunal has determined to award compensation to a customary dependant or customary dependants of a deceased worker, the tribunal may award the compensation to a nominee dependant nominated

by it for distribution by him to the persons who by custom have a right to share in any compensation payable in respect of the deceased worker, and the actual distribution by the nominee dependant shall be deemed to be a determination under Subsection (3).

(5) For the purposes of –

(a) Subsection (4), the term "customary dependant" does not include a member of the family of a deceased worker who was mainly, wholly or partially dependent on the earnings of the worker at the date of his death, or would, but for the incapacity due to the injury have been so dependent; and

(b) calculating the total amount of compensation payable under this section, no regard shall be had to any weekly payments awarded under this section.

[893]62A Disbursement of certain monies

(1) Subject to subsection (2), any money held belonging to –

(a) a deceased worker; or

(b) an injured worker; or

(c) in the case of the death of the worker – his defendant,

shall, after three years from the date of the making of the award, be transferred to the Workers Compensation Trust Funds Account to meet payment of any uninsured claims being made.

(2) Where a worker dies after the tribunal makes an award, and the death of the worker is not related to the injury received in the course of his employment, any compensation award to the deceased worker shall be paid to his next-of-kin.

(3) For the purposes of this section, if a worker or his next-of-kin is identified after three years from the date of the making of the award, and the fund had already been transferred to the Workers' Compensation Trust Fund Account, the worker or, as the case may be, the next-of-kin, shall be paid out of the Trust Account.

63 Determination of dependency

Notwithstanding anything to the contrary in this Act –

(a) any child of a worker (including an ex-nuptial child) who is under 16 years of age at the time of the death of the worker or at any other relevant time shall, unless the contrary is proved, be deemed to have been –

[893]Section 62A added by *Workers Compensation (Amendment) Act* 1990 (No. 11 of 1990), s5.

(i) a dependant of the worker (where that fact is relevant); and

(ii) wholly dependent on the worker for support,

at the time of death or other relevant time; and

(b) the amount of –

(i) any child endowment or similar payment made under the laws of any other country; or

(ii) any child allowance paid by the State,

in respect of any child shall be disregarded in ascertaining, for the purposes of this Act, whether or not that child is or was dependent on the earnings of the worker at the relevant time; and

(c) where the wife of a worker has delivered to the employer, or to the Registrar, a statutory declaration made by her declaring that she was wholly, mainly or partially dependent on the earnings of the worker at the time of his death, or at the time of the injury which gave rise to his death or at any other relevant time, the wife shall, unless the contrary is proved, be deemed to have been –

(i) a dependant of the worker (where that fact is relevant); and

(ii) dependent on his earnings,

at the time of death, injury or other relevant time to the extent stated in the statutory declaration.

PART VI – AMOUNT OF COMPENSATION

64 Interpretation of Part VI

In this Part "funeral expenses" includes –

(a) the transportation of the body of the deceased worker from the place of employment to his place of origin or any other place nominated by his dependants or, in the absence of dependants, his relatives, not being of greater expense of transportation than to his place of origin; and

(b) if the worker is a citizen, the costs of customary burial rites (if any).

65 Amount of compensation payable on death of worker

(1) The amount of compensation payable in relation to the death of a worker shall, where the death of the worker results from or is materially contributed to by injury, be calculated as follows: –

(a) where the worker leaves any dependants wholly dependent on his earnings and whether or not there exist persons who by custom have a right to share in compensation awarded in respect of the death of the worker, the amount of compensation payable –

(i) shall, subject to Subparagraphs (ii) and (iii), be an amount equal to eight times the annual earnings of the worker at the time of the injury plus K6.40 per week for each dependant child; and

(ii) shall be not less than K5,750.00 plus K6.40 per week for each dependant child; and

(iii) shall be not more than K17,000.00 plus K6.40 per week for each dependant child; and

(b) where the worker does not leave any dependants wholly dependent on his earnings and whether or not there exist persons who by custom have a right to share in compensation awarded in respect of the death of the worker, the amount of compensation payable shall be such amount as in the opinion of a tribunal is reasonable but shall not exceed the amount specified in Paragraph (a); and

(c) where there are –

(i) total and partial dependants; or

(ii) total and partial dependants and persons who by custom have a right to share in any compensation awarded in respect of the death of the worker,

a tribunal may, subject to Section 62, apportion the compensation between the total dependants and the partial dependants and the persons who by custom have a right to share in the compensation; and

(d) where the worker leaves no dependants totally or partially dependent on his earnings but there are persons who by custom have a right to share in compensation awarded in respect of the death of the worker, the amount of compensation payable shall be such amount as in the opinion of the tribunal is reasonable but shall not exceed the amount specified in Paragraph (a).

(2) If a deceased worker leaves no dependants the employer shall pay –

(a) reasonable funeral expenses of the deceased worker not exceeding K500.00; and

(b) the reasonable expenses of medical attendances on the deceased worker,

to the person or authority properly incurring such expenses.

(3) In addition to any compensation paid or payable to them under Subsection (1), the dependants of a deceased worker who have paid or are liable to pay the funeral expenses of the worker are entitled to the amount of such expenses not exceeding K500.00.

(4) Amounts paid or payable before the death of a worker as weekly payments in respect of his total or partial incapacity for work resulting from the injury shall not be taken into consideration in calculating the amount of compensation payable on his death, but any amount paid before the death of a worker in redemption of the liability for weekly payments or in respect of an injury for which compensation is payable in respect of a specified injury (except so much of that amount as in the opinion of a tribunal is referable to compensation for total or partial incapacity before death) shall be deducted from the amount payable on death.

[894](5) The compensation amount specified in Subsection (1)(a)(ii) shall, in respect of the year specified in Column 1 of the table A below, be not less than the amount specified in column 2 of the table plus the amount specified in Column 3 for each dependant child: –

---

[894]Section 65(5) added by *Workers Compensation (Amendment) Act* 1990 (No. 11 of 1990), s6(d).

TABLE A		
Column 1 YEAR	**Column 2 AMOUNT**	**Column 3 PER WEEK EACH DEPENDANT**
1991	K6,500.00	K7.30
1992	K7,250.00	K8.20
1993	K8,000.00	K9.10
1994	K8,750.00	K10.00

[895](6) The compensation amount specified in Subsection (1)(a)(iii) shall, in respect of the year specified in Column 1 of the table B below, be not more than the amount specified in Column 2 of the table plus the amount specified in Column 3 for each dependant child: –

TABLE B		
Column 1 YEAR	**Column 2 AMOUNT**	**Column 3 PER WEEK EACH DEPENDANT**
1991	K19,000.00	K7.30
1992	K21,000.00	K8.20
1993	K23,000.00	K9.10
1994	K25,000.00	K10.00

[896](7) The funeral expenses specified in Subsection (2) and (3) shall, in respect of the year specified in Column 1 of the table C below, be not more than the amount specified in Column 2.

TABLE C	
Column 1 YEAR	**Column 2 AMOUNT**
1991	K600.00
1992	K650.00
1993	K700.00
1994	K750.00.

[897](8) For the purposes of making a compensation claim under this Act, it is hereby declared that the amount of compensation, benefit or expenses an injured worker is (or, in the case of the death of the worker his defendants are) entitled to claim shall be that amount of

[895]Section 65(6) added by *Workers Compensation (Amendment) Act* 1990 (No. 11 of 1990), s6(d).
[896]Section 65(7) added by *Workers Compensation (Amendment) Act* 1990 (No. 11 of 1990), s6(d).
[897]Section 65(8) added by Workers Compensation (Amendment) Act 1990 (No. 11 of 1990), s6(d).

compensation, benefit or expenses specified in respect of the year during which the worker is injured or killed.

66 Compensation for incapacity

(1) For the purposes of this section "loss of weekly earnings" means the difference between the amount of the average weekly earnings of the worker before the injury and the average weekly amount that the worker is earning or is able to earn from some suitable employment or business after the injury.

(2) For the purposes of this section where the question of the amount that an injured worker is earning or is able to earn arises and a tribunal considers that, because of the injury suffered by the worker (including any physical disfigurement of the worker), the worker is or will be unable to obtain employment or to remain in reasonably regular employment, the tribunal may decide that the worker is incapacitated by the injury –

(a) totally or partially; and

(b) permanently or temporarily,

as the circumstances of the case require and then compensation in accordance with this Act is payable.

(3) The amount of compensation payable in relation to the incapacity for work of a worker shall, where the incapacity results from or is materially contributed to by injury, be calculated as follows: –

(a) in the case of total incapacity for work the amount of compensation payable weekly by the employer shall be –

(i) where the average weekly earnings of the injured worker before the injury was less than K14.00, an amount equal to the average weekly earnings; and

(ii) where the average weekly earnings of the injured worker before the injury was more than K14.00 and the injured worker has no person wholly or mainly dependent on him, an amount equal to –

(A) 80% of the average weekly earnings to a maximum of K45.00; or

(B) K14.00,

whichever is the greater; and

(iii) where the average weekly earnings of the injured worker before the injury was more than K14.00 and the injured worker has a spouse who is wholly or mainly dependent on him for support, an amount equal to –

(A) 80% of the average weekly earnings to a maximum of K55.00; or

(B) K14.00,

whichever is the greater together with, in the case where the injured worker has a child or children who is or are wholly or mainly dependent on him, an additional maximum amount of K6.40 in respect of each dependant child but the total of the additional amount shall not exceed the average weekly earnings of the worker prior to the injury,

and where, under this section, a weekly payment becomes payable in respect of a child who is born and becomes dependent on the earnings of the injured worker during the incapacity, that payment shall be made only from the date of the birth of the child; and

(b) in the case of partial incapacity for work, the amount of the compensation payable weekly by the employer during the incapacity shall be such amount as bears the same ratio to the amount of the weekly payment which would have been payable if the worker was totally incapacitated for work as the worker's loss of weekly earnings bears to the amount of the average weekly earnings of the worker before the injury.

(4) The total liability of an employer in respect of payments to an injured worker under this section shall not exceed –

(a) K14,000.00 unless the injury results in total incapacity; and

(b) in any case, K17,000.00.

[898](5) For a single worker the weekly benefits referred to in Subsection (3)(a)(ii) shall, in respect of the year specified in column 1 of the table D below, be not less than the amount specified in Column 2 of the table and shall be not more than the amount specified in column 3.

TABLE D

Column 1 YEAR	Column 2 MINIMUM AMOUNT	Column 3 MAXIMUM AMOUNT
1991	K14.00	K50.00
1992	K16.00	K55.00

[898]Section 66(5) added by *Workers Compensation (Amendment) Act* 1990 (No. 11 of 1990), s8(c).

Column 1 YEAR	Column 2 MINIMUM AMOUNT	Column 3 MAXIMUM AMOUNT
1993	K16.00	K60.00
1994	K18.00	K65.00

[899](6) For a married worker the weekly benefit referred to in Subsection (3)(a)(iii) shall, in respect of the year specified in column 1 of the table E below, be not less than the amount specified in column 2 and be not more than the amount specified in column 3.

TABLE E

Column 1 YEAR	Column 2 MINIMUM AMOUNT	Column 3 MAXIMUM AMOUNT
1991	K14.00	K60.00
1992	K16.00	K65.00
1993	K16.00	K70.00
1994	K18.00	K75.00

[900](7) The total liability of an employer referred to in Subsection (4) shall, in respect of the year specified in column 1 of the table F below, not to exceed the amount specified in column 2 of the table, unless the injury results in total incapacity, and, in any case the amount shall not exceed the amount specified in column 3.

TABLE F

Column 1 YEAR	Column 2 AMOUNT	Column 3 AMOUNT IN ANY CASE
1991	K16,000.00	K19,000.00
1992	K18,000.00	K21,000.00
1993	K20,000.00	K23,000.00
1994	K22,000.00	K25,000.00.

[899]Section 66(6) added by *Workers Compensation (Amendment) Act* 1990 (No. 11 of 1990), s8(c).

[900]Section 66(7) added by *Workers Compensation (Amendment) Act* 1990 (No. 11 of 1990), s8(c).

[901]66A Children's weekly benefits increase

The additional amount of K6.40 in respect of each dependant child refer to Section 66(3)(iii) shall be increased each year in accordance with this Act.

[902]66B Compensation for incapacity payable not to exceed weekly earnings of worker

Subject to this Act, the amount of compensation payable to a worker in relation to the incapacity for work of the worker shall not exceed the worker's weekly earnings.

67 Fixed rates of compensation for certain injuries

(1) For the purposes of this section –

(a) an annual wage of K625.00 or less shall be deemed to be an annual wage of K625.00; and

(b) an annual wage of K1,875.00 and more shall be deemed to be an annual wage of K1,875.00.

(2) Subject to Subsection (4), the amount of compensation payable for the injuries specified in Column 1 of Schedule 3 shall be assessed in the manner indicated in Column 2 of that Schedule.

(3) Subsection (2) does not apply where, before the amount of compensation is settled, the worker, with the approval of the Registrar, by written notice to the employer, states that he does not desire to have the amount of compensation assessed under that subsection and in that case the amount of compensation shall be calculated as if this section had not been enacted.

(4) Where an injured worker at the time of the injury was receiving an annual salary of K625.00 or more but less than K1,875.00 the amount of compensation payable for the injury shall be calculated in accordance with the formula –

$$C = \frac{(W \times 8) \times P}{100}$$

where –

C is the amount of compensation payable; and

W is the worker's annual wage; and

---

[901]Section 66A added by *Workers Compensation (Amendment) Act* 1990 (No. 11 of 1990), s7.

[902]Section 66B added by *Workers Compensation (Amendment) Act* 1990 (No. 11 of 1990), s7.

P is the percentage specified in Column 2 of Schedule 3 opposite the injury specified in Column 1 of that Schedule.

(5) Subsection (4) does not limit the amount of compensation payable for an injury to which that subsection applies during any period of incapacity resulting from that injury occurring before an assessment of compensation is made in accordance with that subsection.

(6) For the purposes of this section, an eye, a foot or other member shall be deemed to be lost if it is rendered permanently and wholly useless, and a finger shall be deemed to be lost if two joints of the finger are severed from the hand or rendered permanently and wholly useless.

(7) Where a worker suffers injury to any limb, member, faculty, organ, power or sense specified in Schedule 3 so that the worker permanently has less than the full efficient use of it, the worker shall be entitled to the percentage of the compensation payable under this section for the total loss of that limb, member, faculty, organ, power or sense equal to the percentage of the full, efficient use of it lost by the worker.

(8) Subject to Subsection (9) for the purpose of determining the percentage or the full and efficient use lost by the worker of any limb, member, faculty, organ, power or sense specified in Schedule 3, no regard shall be had to the extent to which that loss may be reduced or limited by the use by the worker of any external and removable artificial aid or appliance.

(9) Where a worker has suffered an injury to his eye the percentage of the full and efficient use of that eye lost by the worker shall be determined by reference –

(a) to the vision of that eye as corrected; or

(b) if a refractive error of the eye has been produced or changed by the injury – to the corrected vision or uncorrected vision whichever reference discloses the greater loss.

(10) Where a worker suffers by the same occurrence from more than one of the injuries specified in Schedule 3, he is not entitled in any case to receive in respect of the fixed sums specified in that Schedule more than –

(a) K17,000.00; or

(b) subject to Subsection (4), eight times his annual wage,

whichever is the less.

(11) Notwithstanding Subsection (2), where a worker suffers a subsequent injury in respect of which he is entitled to payment of compensation under this section, the amount of compensation payable is the difference between the amount otherwise payable under this section

and the amount of compensation that has been paid under this section or under the repealed Act in respect of the prior injury.

(12) In Subsection (11) –

"prior injury means any injury or disease in respect of which compensation has been paid under this section or the repealed Act;

"subsequent injury" in relation to a prior injury means an injury or disease that is an aggravation, acceleration, exacerbation, deterioration or recurrence of the prior injury.

[903]67A Fixed rates to be increased every year

The amount specified in Section 67(10)(a) shall, in respect of the year specified in column 1 of the table G be not more than the amount specified in column 2.

TABLE G

Column 1 YEAR	Column 2 AMOUNT
1991	K19,000.00
1992	K21,000.00
1993	K23,000.00
1994	K25,000.00.

68 Occupational diseases

(1) Where a worker contracts an occupational disease which –

(a) results in the total or partial incapacity (whether of a permanent or temporary nature), or the death, of the worker; and

(b) is due to the nature of any employment in which the worker was employed at any time prior to the incapacity or death, whether under one or more employers,

the worker (or, in the case of the death of the worker, his dependants) is entitled to compensation under this Act as if that incapacity or death had arisen out of or in the course of employment in respect of which Section 54 applies, and this Act, with the necessary modifications, applies, subject to the following modifications: –

(c) the incapacity or the death shall be treated as the happening of the injury; and

---

[903]Section 67A added by *Workers Compensation (Amendment) Act* 1990 (No. 11 of 1990), s9(b).

(d) where it is proved that the worker, at the time he entered into the employment, wilfully and with intent to deceive, represented in writing that he had not previously suffered from the disease which resulted in the incapacity or death – compensation is not payable; and

(e) subject to Subsection (4), compensation is recoverable from the employer who last employed the worker in the employment to the nature of which the disease was due, immediately preceding the incapacity or death; and

(f) the amount of compensation shall be calculated with reference to the earnings of the worker under the employer from whom compensation is recoverable under Paragraph (e) or Subsection (4), as the case requires; and

(g) the notice of incapacity or death –

(i) shall be given to the employer who last employed the worker immediately preceding the incapacity or death in the employment to the nature of which the disease was due; and

(ii) may be given notwithstanding that the worker has voluntarily left that employer's employment.

(2) Where a worker suffers incapacity or dies as a result of an occupational disease the worker or his dependants, as the case may be, if required to do so, shall furnish the employer who last employed the worker immediately preceding the incapacity or death in the employment, to the nature of which the occupational disease was due, with such information as he or they possess as to the names and addresses of all other employers who employed him in such employment.

(3) Where information is required to be furnished to an employer under Subsection (2) and that information –

(a) is not furnished; or

(b) is furnished in insufficient detail to enable the employer to take proceedings under Subsection (4),

the employer, on proving that the disease was not contracted whilst the worker was in his employment, is not liable to pay compensation.

(4) Where the employer who last employed the worker immediately proceeding the incapacity or death in the employment, to the nature of which the occupational disease was due, alleges that the disease was contracted whilst the worker was in the employment of some other employer and not whilst in his employment, he may join the other employer as a party to the proceedings in respect of the claim to compensation and, if the allegation is proved, compensation is recoverable from that other employer.

(5) If the occupational disease which results in the incapacity or death of a worker is of such a nature as to be contracted by a gradual process, the other employers (if any) who employed the worker before his incapacity or death in employment, to the nature of which the disease was due, are liable to make to the employer from whom compensation is payable under Subsection (1)(e) or (4) such contribution as, in default of agreement, may be determined by a tribunal.

(6) Subsections (2) and (4) do not prevent a worker or his dependants, as the case may be, from recovering compensation under this section from any other employer who previously employed the worker in employment, to the nature of which the occupational disease was due, in the event of the employer who last employed the worker in such employment proving that the disease in question was not contracted whilst the worker was in his employment.

(7) For the purposes of this section, the date of the incapacity shall, in the absence of agreement, be such date as a tribunal determines as being the date on which the incapacity commenced and a worker shall not be prejudiced in any claim for compensation under this section by reason only that the notice of incapacity given to the employer, specified some other date.

(8) An employer may, before employing a worker in any trade, industry or process specified in Column 2 of Schedule 2, require the worker to undergo a medical examination by a medical practitioner at the cost of the employer.

(9) Subject to Subsection (10) a worker who refuses to undergo a medical examination required under Subsection (8) is not entitled to recover from that employer compensation under this Act for incapacity or death suffered as a result of an occupational disease.

(10) Subsection (9) does not apply unless the refusal referred to in that subsection is evidenced in writing under the hand of the worker.

(11) Where a worker suffers incapacity or death as a result of an occupational disease specified in Column 1 of Schedule 2, and he was, immediately preceding the incapacity or death, employed in a trade, industry or process specified in Column 2 of that Schedule opposite to the disease, it shall be presumed, until the contrary is proved, that the disease was due to the nature of the employment.

(12) This section does not prejudice the right of a worker to recover compensation under this Act in respect of a disease to which this section does not apply if the disease is a personal injury within the meaning of Section 54.

(13) The Head of State, acting on advice, may by order in the National Gazette amend Schedule 2.

69 Additional compensation

(1) In this section –

"ambulance services" means transport by a vehicle to a hospital or other place for medical examination or medical treatment or rehabilitation and, where necessary, on the return journey;

"constant attendance service" means the service, not being nursing services, of a person in any case where the injury is of such a nature that the worker must have the regular or constant personal attendance of another person;

"hospital services" means –

(a) maintenance, attendance and treatment in a hospital; or

(b) the provision by a hospital of medical and nursing services, medical, surgical and other curative materials, appliances and apparatus; or

(c) other usual or necessary hospital services;

"medical services" means –

(a) attendance, examination or treatment of any kind administered by a medical practitioner, by a registered dentist, by a registered optician or on the prescription of a medical practitioner by a registered physiotherapist or by a registered chiropodist; or

(b) the provision and the repair, adjustment or replacement of skiagrams, artificial limbs, eyes or teeth, crutches, splints, spectacles, and other medical and surgical aids and curative appliances or apparatus; or

(c) the repair or replacement of artificial limbs, eyes or teeth, crutches, splints, spectacles or other medical or surgical aids or curative appliances destroyed or damaged at the time of the injury; or

(d) the provision by a registered pharmaceutical chemist of medicines or curative appliances or materials on the prescription of a medical practitioner; or

(e) the provision by a medical practitioner, registered dentist, registered physiotherapist, registered optician or registered chiropodist of any certificate required by the worker, his legal personal representatives or his dependants for the purposes of this Act;

"nursing services" means nursing services rendered by a registered nurse otherwise than as a member of the nursing staff of a hospital;

"reasonable", in relation to any costs or claims, means reasonable having regard not only to the service or provision actually rendered but also to the necessity of that service or provision in the circumstances of the case.

(2) Where a worker is entitled to compensation under the other provisions of this Act or under Subsection (6), the employer is liable to pay as compensation to the worker such reasonable expenses as were incurred by the worker as a result of his injury –

(a) for medical services, hospital services, nursing services, constant attendance services and ambulance services; and

(b) not exceeding K75.00 for repairing or replacing damaged clothing; and

(c) not exceeding K200.00 for repairing or replacing damaged tools of trade.

(3) Where a person or authority –

(a) has rendered to or provided for a worker any medical services, hospital services, nursing services, constant attendance services or ambulance services for the cost of which the employer is required under this section to compensate the worker; and

(b) has not been paid the full amount to which he or it is entitled for those services,

the employer may pay to the person or authority the whole or any part of the amount owing to him or it and such a payment shall, to the extent of the amount paid, be a discharge of the liability of the worker under this section and of the liability of the worker to the person or authority for the service.

(4) The amount for which an employer shall be liable in respect of medical services, hospital services, nursing services, constant attendance services or ambulance services is such as is agreed on by the employer and the worker or, in default of such agreement, as is determined by a tribunal.

(5) The compensation payable under this section is additional to all other compensation payable to the worker and the fact that a worker is entitled to compensation under this section shall not restrict the compensation payable to him under any other provision of this Act.

(6) Where, in any employment, personal injury arising out of or in the course of employment is caused to a worker and the worker is not disabled for at least one day from earning full wages at his work, this section shall apply to the same extent as if the worker was so disabled for at least one day and whether or not the worker is entitled to compensation other than compensation for expenses referred to in this section.

70 Computation of "annual earnings" and "average weekly earnings"

(1) In this Part any reference to the annual earnings of a worker shall be taken to refer to an amount of 52 times his average weekly earnings calculated in accordance with Subsection (2).

(2) In this Part any reference to the average weekly earnings of a worker before an inquiry shall, subject to this subsection, be taken to refer to his average weekly earnings during the period of 12 months immediately preceding the injury if he has been so long employed by the same employer but, if not, then for any lesser period during which he has been so employed and, in the ascertainment of such average weekly earnings, the following provisions shall be observed: –

(a) in computing average weekly earnings, amounts paid for overtime worked by the worker shall be included; and

(b) where, by reason of –

(i) the shortness of time during which the worker has been in the employment of his employer; or

(ii) the terms of the employment,

it is impracticable at the time of the injury to compute the average weekly earnings of the worker under that employer, regard may be had to the average weekly amount which during the 12 months previous to the injury was being earned –

(iii) by a person in the same grade employed at the same work by the same employer; or

(iv) if there is no person so employed – by a person in the same grade employed in the same class of employment and in the same area; and

(c) where –

(i) the worker had entered into concurrent contracts of service with two or more employers under which he worked at one time for one such employer and at another time for another such employer; or

(ii) the worker's employment has been of a casual nature,

his average weekly earnings shall be computed as if his earnings under all such contracts or in the employment of his several employers were earnings in the employment of the employer for whom he was working at the time of the injury; and

(d) employment by the same employer shall be taken to mean employment by the same employer in the grade in which the worker was employed at the time of the injury uninterrupted by absence from work due to illness or other unavoidable cause, and the worker shall be deemed to have been employed in a new grade of employment whenever his rate of payment has been lawfully increased or decreased otherwise than by any cost of living adjustments; and

(e) where the employer has been accustomed to pay to the worker any sum to cover any special expenses entailed on him by the nature of his employment, the sum so paid shall not be reckoned as part of the earnings; and

(f) in computing average weekly earnings, the value of food and accommodation supplied by an employer, the cost of which is not deducted from the wage of the worker, shall be included; and

(g) where the worker delivers to the employer a written statement verified by statutory declaration setting out the amount of his earnings during any period the statement is prima facie evidence that the amount was the earnings of the worker during that period.

71 Allowances, etc, to be taken into account in fixing weekly payment

In fixing the amount of any weekly payment –

(a) regard shall be had to any payment or allowance or benefit the worker may receive from the employer during the period of his incapacity; and

(b) regard shall not be had to any sum paid or payable under any contract of assurance or insurance or of any industrial award or determination providing for additional compensation payments.

72 Cessation of weekly payments in respect of dependant children

A weekly payment in respect of a dependant child referred to in this Part ceases to be payable when the dependant child –

(a) attains the age of 16 years; or
(b) marries; or
(c) dies,

whichever first occurs.

PART VII – PAYMENT AND INVESTMENT OF WORKERS' COMPENSATION

73 Certain purported payments of compensation invalid

(1) A payment, other than a weekly payment under Section 36, shall not be deemed to be a payment of compensation, or valid compromise of any claim under this Act, unless –

(a) the payment is made under an award of a tribunal; or

(b) a tribunal orders that the payment is to be deemed to be a payment of compensation.

(2) Where any person, except in accordance with an award of a tribunal, makes any payment, other than a weekly payment under Section 36, in purported payment of compensation or in purported compromise of any claim under this Act –

(a) the person who makes the payment; and

(b) if that person is an employer or agent of the employer concerned or of that employer's insurer – the employers or insurer, as the case may be,

are each and severally guilty of an offence.

Penalty: For a first offence – a fine not exceeding K100.00.

For a second or subsequent offence – a fine not exceeding K500.00.

(3) It is a defence to a prosecution for an offence against Subsection (2) if the defendant proves that a tribunal ordered that the payment be deemed to be a payment in full settlement of compensation in accordance with or in valid compromise of the whole claim under this Act.

74 Compromise award by consent of parties

Where the parties agree on any claim for compensation under this Act, a tribunal may, after such investigation as it thinks proper, make an award by consent of the parties.

75 Investment of compensation

(1) Unless otherwise ordered, compensation, other than weekly payments, shall be paid into the Office and the receipt of the Registrar shall be sufficient discharge in respect of any amount of compensation so paid in.

(2) If so agreed the payment of compensation in the case of death shall, if the worker leaves no dependants, be made to his legal personal representative or, if he has no such representative, to the person to whom the expenses of medical attendance and burial are due.

(3) The Chief Commissioner may invest, apply or otherwise deal with any sum paid into the Office under Subsection (1) in such manner as in his discretion he thinks fit for the benefit of the person entitled to it under this Act.

(4) The Chief Commissioner in his administration of any moneys paid into the Office under Subsection (1), is not bound by any law relating to the administration or investment of trust funds but he is bound in administering such moneys to act in good faith.

76 Unlawful discontinuance of weekly payments

(1) Except where a provision of this Act specifically provides otherwise, a weekly payment made under this Act shall not be discontinued or diminished without the prior consent of the Registrar.

(2) Where the Registrar has given his consent or refused to give his consent under Subsection (1), the worker or employer, as the case may be, may, within 21 days after giving or refusal of consent, apply to the Chief Commissioner for an order by a tribunal that –

- (a) the weekly payments not be discontinued or diminished; or
- (b) the weekly payments be discontinued or diminished,

as the case may be, and such application is to be heard and determined as a proceeding on the summary list.

(3) On the hearing of an application referred to in Subsection (2), the tribunal may –

- (a) adjourn the application on such terms as it thinks fit; or
- (b) dismiss the application; or
- (c) make such order as to the continuance, discontinuance or diminution of weekly payments as it thinks fit.

(4) Any weekly payment may, on the application of the worker, at intervals of not less than 12 months, be reviewed by a tribunal and where the review takes place more than three months after the injury, the amount of the weekly payment may be increased by an amount not

exceeding 80% of the cost of living increases that would have been granted to the worker but for the injury.

(5) A hearing or review under this section shall be heard and determined as proceeding on the summary list and Section 34(1) does not apply.

(6) If weekly payments are discontinued or diminished otherwise than in accordance with this Act, the employer is guilty of an offence.

Penalty: A fine not exceeding K500.00.

(7) A conviction for an offence against Subsection (6) does not affect any liability for the making of weekly payments under this Act.

77 Weekly payments to worker ceasing to reside in Papua New Guinea

(1) Where a worker who is receiving a weekly payment ceases, without the consent of his employer to reside in Papua New Guinea, he shall cease to be entitled to receive any weekly payment unless a tribunal otherwise orders.

(2) Where, under Subsection (1) –

(a) the employer consents to the worker ceasing to reside in Papua New Guinea; or

(b) a tribunal orders that the worker continue to be eligible to receive the weekly payment,

the weekly payments shall be paid quarterly in arrears for so long as the worker proves his identity and the incapacity in respect of which the weekly payment is payable in such manner and at such intervals as the tribunal directs.

78 Suspension of payment of weekly payments

Where a right to compensation is suspended under this Act, weekly payments are not payable in respect of the period of suspension.

79 Weekly payments not assignable

A weekly payment, or a sum paid by way of redemption of a weekly payment –

(a) is not capable of being assigned, charged or attached; and

(b) shall not pass to any other person by operation of law; and

(c) shall not have any claim set off against it.

80 Weekly sum due to person under a legal disability

Where a weekly payment is payable under this Act to a person under any legal disability, a tribunal may, on application being made to the Chief Commissioner, order that the weekly payment be paid during the disability into the Office, and the provisions of this Act with respect to sums required by this Act to be paid into the Office, apply to the sums so paid into the Office.

81 Lump sum in redemption of weekly payments

(1) The liability for weekly payments or other compensation under this Act may, with the approval of a tribunal on application by or on behalf of either the worker or the employer, be redeemed by the payment of a lump sum to be settled by proceedings under this Act.

(2) Proceedings under Subsection (1) may be in the form of an award by consent of the parties.

(3) Where permanent, total or partial incapacity of the worker results from the injury, any weekly payments made prior to an application under Subsection (1) shall be in addition to any such lump sum and, in settling a lump sum payment, the tribunal shall treat a worker as totally incapacitated for work as a result of the injury if he is fitted only for employment of a kind that is not reasonably available to him.

82 Application for payment of award against uninsured employer out of the fund

(1) Where –

(a) an award of compensation is made or has been made under this Act or the repealed Act in respect of the death, incapacity or disablement of a worker or the costs of medical, hospital, nursing or ambulance services or of cremation or burial, and an employer whose liability in respect of that death, incapacity or disability, or those costs, is not covered by a policy of insurance or indemnity in accordance with this Act; and

(b) any payment required to be made under that award, whether of a lump sum or any weekly payment and whether as compensation or for costs or otherwise, remains unpaid for a period of not less than one month after the due date for its payment,

the person or the agent of the person in whose favour the award was made may, after giving such notices as are prescribed, apply to the Chief Commissioner for an order for payment out of the Fund of all or any of the moneys payable or to become payable under that award.

(2) Where, in or in relation to any application under Subsection (1), it is alleged that the liability of an employer in respect of the death, incapacity or disablement of any worker is not covered by a policy of insurance or indemnity in force under this Act, that liability, unless the contrary is proved, shall, for the purposes of this section, be deemed not to be covered.

(3) Where an application has been made under Subsection (1), the insurance Commissioner shall represent the Fund and is entitled by himself or his representative to show cause to a tribunal why an order should not be made.

(4) Where, on the hearing of an application under Subsection (1), the tribunal is satisfied that the award is not likely to be fully satisfied except under this section –

(a) the tribunal may direct that all or any part of the payments required to be made under the award, whether payable at the date of the order or to become payable afterwards, shall be paid out of the Fund; and

(b) after presentation of a certificate of the tribunal's order to the Secretary for Finance, the payments specified in the order shall be made out of the Fund.

(5) Where any compensation is paid out of the Fund under Subsection (4), the Registrar may institute civil proceedings against the employer for the recovery of the amount of compensation paid, and any moneys received as a result of the proceedings shall be paid into the Fund.

83 Tribunal may make interim awards

(1) Where, in respect of a claim, a tribunal is reasonably satisfied that compensation is payable under this Act but it is unable for any reason to make an award in settlement of the claim promptly, it may, if it is satisfied that the total amount payable will not be less than a specific sum, make an interim award for payment of the whole or any part of that sum.

(2) The making of an interim award under Subsection (1), does not –

(a) preclude a tribunal from later making, in respect of the claim, a further interim award or final award; or

(b) prejudice the rights of either of the parties in respect of any further or final claim.

PART VIII – ALTERNATIVE REMEDIES

84 Liability independently of Act

(1) This Act, except as expressly provided in it, does not affect any liability which exists independently of it.

(2) Where a worker or his dependants, as the case may be, has received or is entitled to receive, compensation under this Act or under the repealed Act, in respect of an injury, he shall not bring an action against the employer for damages in respect of the same injury unless he commences that action within three years from the day on which the injury occurred.

(3) Where a worker has recovered judgement against an employer independently of this Act for damages in respect of an injury, he shall not commence or continue any proceedings for or in relation to compensation under this Act in respect of the same injury.

(4) A worker shall not commence or continue any proceedings against his employer for damages independently of this Act in respect of any injury after he has obtained a final award against his employer, under which his employer is liable to pay compensation under this Act in respect of the same injury.

(5) Any sum received by a worker from an employer by way of damages in respect of an injury shall be deducted from the sum recoverable by the worker from the employer by way of compensation under this Act in respect of the same injury.

(6) Any sum received by a worker from an employer by way of compensation under this Act or under a law of any other country in respect of an injury shall be deducted from the sum recoverable by the worker from the employer by way of damages in respect of the same injury.

85 Action brought for injury under this Act

(1) If, within the time limited by this Act for taking proceedings, an action is brought to recover damages independently of this Act for an injury, and it is determined in that action that the injury is one for which the employer is not liable but that he would have been liable to pay compensation under this Act, the action shall be dismissed, but the court in which the action is tried –

(a) shall, if either party so chooses, proceed to assess the compensation; and

(b) may deduct from the compensation all or part of the costs which, in its judgement, have been caused by the plaintiff bringing the action instead of proceeding under this Act.

(2) If, within the time limited by this Act for taking proceedings, an action is brought to recover damages independently of this Act for an injury and it is determined in the action that –

(a) the person against whom the action was brought would have been liable to pay compensation under this Act in respect of that injury; and

(b) the damages that would have been recovered in that action would have been less than the amount of compensation that the person would have been liable to pay under this Act,

proceedings in the action may be stayed and the court in which the action is tried –

(c) shall, if either party so chooses, proceed to assess the compensation; and

(d) may deduct from the compensation all or part of the costs which, in its judgement, have been caused by the plaintiff bringing the action instead of proceeding under this Act.

(3) In any proceedings under this section, when the court in which the action is tried assesses the compensation it shall give a certificate of the compensation it has awarded and the directions it has given as to the deduction for costs, and the certificate shall have the force and effect of an award of a tribunal under this Act.

(4) A copy of the certificate referred to in Subsection (3) shall be transmitted to the Registrar by the proper officer of the court referred to in that subsection.

86 Remedies against employer and stranger

(1) In this section "the third party" means a person other than the employer having a legal liability to pay damages in respect of an injury for which compensation is payable under this Act.

(2) Where the injury for which compensation is payable under this Act was caused by a third party –

(a) the worker may take proceedings both against the third party to recover damages and against the employer for compensation; and

(b) a worker who receives any money from a third party in respect of an injury and compensation under this Act shall repay to the employer such amount of that compensation as does not exceed the amount recovered from the third party; and

(c) on notice to the third party, the employer shall have a first charge on moneys payable by the third party to the worker, to the extent of any compensation which the employer has paid to the worker; and

(d) if the worker has received compensation under this Act, but no damages or less than the full amount of damages to which he is entitled –

  (i) the third party shall be liable to indemnify the employer against so much of the compensation paid to the worker as does not exceed the damages for which the third party is still liable; and

  (ii) the employer may enforce the indemnity against the third party by action by the employer; and

(e) payment of money by a third party to the employer under Paragraph (d) shall, to the extent of the amount paid, be a satisfaction of the liability of the third party to the worker.

87 Where claim exists elsewhere as well as in Papua New Guinea

(1) If a claim for compensation has already been made by the claimant in respect of the injury under any law not being a law of Papua New Guinea, and compensation has been recovered under that claim, compensation under this Act shall not be allowed to the claimant.

(2) A person referred to in Subsection (1) having a claim under any law not being a law of Papua New Guinea shall not claim under this Act unless he declares in writing that he has not claimed, and will not claim, compensation or damages for the injury under any such law.

88 Contracting out

This Act applies notwithstanding any contract to the contrary.

PART IX – COMPULSORY WORKERS' COMPENSATION INSURANCE

89 Licensed insurers only may carry on workers' compensation business

A person, other than a licensed insurer within the meaning of the *Insurance Act* 1995, who carries on workers' compensation business for the purposes of this Act is guilty of an offence.

Penalty: A fine not exceeding K1,000.00.

90 Compulsory insurance

(1) An employer other than –

(a) the State; or

(b) a statutory authority approved by the Minister responsible for financial matters by notice in the National Gazette,

who employs any worker in any employment unless there is in force in relation to that worker a policy of insurance or indemnity issued by a licensed insurer for the full amount of the liability of the employer under this Act (other than additional liability under Section 35) for any injury to the worker arising out of or in the course of his employment, is guilty of an offence.

Penalty: For a first offence – a fine not exceeding K500.00.

For a second or subsequent offence a fine not exceeding K1,000.00.

(2) Where an employer employs workers, the Chief Commissioner or any person authorized by him may require the employer to produce for inspection by the Chief Commissioner or authorized person any policy of insurance or indemnity effected for the purpose of Subsection (1) or a cover note in respect of such policy of insurance or indemnity.

91 Certain conditions to be of no effect

(1) Any condition in a policy of insurance or indemnity issued for the purposes of this Part which provides that no liability shall arise under the policy or that any liability so arising is to cease in the event of some specified thing being done or omitted to be done after the happening of the injury giving rise to the claim under the policy shall be of no effect on a claim made by a worker under this Act.

(2) Subsection (1) does not render void any provision in a policy of insurance or indemnity issued under this Part requiring an insured

employer to repay to the insurer any such claims which the insurer may have paid under the policy in satisfaction of any such claim.

92 Record of wages, etc, to be kept and supplied

(1) Every employer applying to an insurer to issue or review a policy of insurance or indemnity under this Part must supply to the insurer a full and correct statement of all wages paid to workers in his employment during the period relevant to the determination of the premium payable by him for the policy.

(2) An employer who fails to supply a full and correct statement of wages in respect of his workers as required by Subsection (1) is guilty of an offence.

Penalty: A fine not exceeding K500.00.

(3) Every employer shall keep accurate records of –

(a) all wages paid to workers employed by him; and

(b) the trade, occupation or calling of each worker employed by him; and

(c) such other matters relating to wages as may be prescribed,

and shall retain those records in his possession in good order and condition for three years.

(4) The records required to be kept under Subsection (3) may be combined with other records of wages required by any other Act to be kept by an employer.

(5) The Insurance Commissioner may, on application by an insurer who has issued a policy of insurance or indemnity to an employer, and whether or not the policy is still in force, order the employer –

(a) to supply to the insurer within a time specified in the order –

(i) a full and correct statement of all wages paid during a period so specified, being a period during which the policy was in force and which commenced not more than three years before the making of the application, to the workers in the employment of that employer; and

(ii) such information as to trade, occupation or calling of the workers and other prescribed matters relating to those wages as may be specified; and

(b) to make available at or within such time or times and at such place as is specified in the order for inspection by –

(i) an officer authorized for the purpose by the Insurance Commissioner; or

(ii) a person authorized for the purpose by the specified insurer,

the records required by this subsection to be kept by the employer and, at the time of the order, to be retained by him in respect of a specified period, being a period when the policy was in force.

(6) Any officer or person authorized under Subsection (5) may inspect such records in accordance with the terms of the order and make copies of them and take extracts from them.

(7) An employer who fails to comply with an order issued under Subsection (5) is guilty of an offence.

Penalty: A fine exceeding K1,000.00.

(8) Subsection (7) does not affect the authority of the Insurance Commissioner to make a further order or orders against the employer under Subsection (5).

93 Worker may require name, etc, of insurer

A worker may require his employer to supply him with the name and address of the insurer from whom the employer has obtained a policy of insurance or indemnity under Section 90.

94 Deductions towards compensation not lawful

An employer, insurer or other person on behalf of any employer or insurer shall not directly or indirectly take or receive any money from any worker, whether by way of deduction from wages or otherwise in respect of any liability of an employer to pay compensation under this Act and all moneys so taken or received from any worker, whether with the consent of the worker or not, may be recovered in any court of competent jurisdiction as a debt due to him by the employer, insurer or person who took or received it.

PART X – MISCELLANEOUS

95 Annual report

The Chief Commissioner shall prepare and furnish to the Minister on or before 31 March in each and every year a report for presentation to the Parliament containing –

(a) a statement in detail of the receipts and expenditure of the Fund; and

(b) a statement of the Office's activities relating to the Fund; and

(c) such other matters as the Minister directs,

relating to the preceding year ended 31 December.

96 General penalty

Any person who commits an offence against this Act for which no special penalty is provided in this Act is liable to a fine not exceeding K200.00.

97 Offences to be dealt with summarily

All proceedings in respect of offences against this Act shall be dealt with summarily.

98 Regulations

The Head of State, acting on advice, may make regulations, not inconsistent with this Act, prescribing all matters that by this Act are required or permitted to be prescribed, or that are necessary or convenient to be prescribed for carrying out or giving effect to this Act, and in particular prescribing matters for and in relation to –

(a) the fees and expenses to be paid for medical examinations and medical attendances; and

(b) the forms to be used in connexion with this Act; and

(c) the procedure and practice before a tribunal; and

(d) the matters in which fees shall be paid and the fees to be paid; and

(e) the manner of doing or performing anything by this Act required to be done or performed; and

(f) the imposition of penalties of fines not exceeding K150.00 for offences against the regulations.

SCHEDULES

SCHEDULE 1

Sec. 14.

DECLARATION OF OFFICE

I, . . . , do promise and declare that I will well and truly serve the independent State of Papua New Guinea and its People in the office of . . . and that I will in all things uphold the Constitution and the laws of the independent State of Papua New Guinea and that I will do right to all manner of people in accordance therewith, without fear or favour, affection or ill-will.

SCHEDULE 2

Secs., 1, 68.

OCCUPATIONAL DISEASE.	
Column 1 Description of disease	**Column 2 Nature of trade, industry or process.**
Poisoning by lead	Any occupation involving the use or handling of, or exposure to the fumes, dust or vapour of lead, or a compound of lead or a substance containing lead.
Poisoning by mercury	Any occupation involving the use of or handling of, or exposure to the fumes, dust or vapour of mercury or a compound of mercury or a substance containing mercury.
Anthrax	Any process involving the handling of wool, hair, bristles, hides or skins or other animal products or residues or contact with animals infected with Anthrax or loading and unloading or transport of merchandise.
Silicosis with or without pulmonary tuberculosis	Any process involving exposure to silica dust.
Poisoning by phosphorus	Any occupation involving the use or handling of or exposure to the fumes, dust or vapour of phosphorus or a compound of phosphorus or a substance containing phosphorus.
Poisoning by arsenic	Any occupation involving the use or handling of or exposure to the fumes, dust or vapour of arsenic or a compound of arsenic or a substance containing arsenic.
Poisoning by benzine or a homologue of benzine	Any occupation involving the use or handling of, or exposure to the fumes of, or vapour containing benzine or any of its homologues.

SCHEDULE 2

Poisoning by a nitro-derivative or amido-derivative of benzine or a homologue of benzine	Any occupation involving the use or handling of, or exposure to the fumes of, or vapour containing a nitro-derivative or amido-derivative of benzine or a homologue of benzine.
Poisoning by halogen derivatives of hydrocarbons of the aliphatic series	Any process involving the production, liberation or utilization of halogen derivatives of hydrocarbons of the aliphatic series.
Pathological manifestations due to radium or other radioactive substances or X-Rays	Any process involving exposure to the action of radium, radioactive substances or X-rays.
Primary epitheliomatous cancer of the skin	Any process involving the handling or use of tar, pitch, bitumen, mineral oil, paraffin, or the compounds, products or residues of those substances.

SCHEDULE 3

Sec., 67.

COMPENSATION FOR SPECIFIED INJURIES

Column 1.	**Column 2.**				
Nature of Injury.	**The ratio which the fixed sum payable as compensation under Section 67 bears to: –**				
	1990 K17,000 %	1991 K19,000 %	1992 K21,000 %	1993 K23,000 %	1994 K25,000 %
Permanent and incurable loss of mental capacity resulting in total inability to work	100	100	100	100	100
Total and incurable paralysis of the limbs	100	100	100	100	100
Eye injuries –					
Total loss of sight of both eyes	100	100	100	100	100
Total loss of sight of one eye	50	50	50	50	50
Total loss of sight of one eye, the vision in the other eye being less than 6/60 Snellen type with correction or absent	100	100	100	100	100
Hearing injuries –					
Total loss of hearing	75	75	75	75	75
Speech loss –					
Total loss of the speech	75	75	75	75	75
Sensory loss –					
Total loss of senses of taste and smell	50	50	50	50	50
Total loss of sense of taste	25	25	25	25	25
Total loss of sense of smell	25	25	25	25	25

SCHEDULE 3

Column 1.	Column 2.				
Nature of Injury.	**The ratio which the fixed sum payable as compensation under Section 67 bears to: –**				
Arm injuries –					
Loss of arm at or above elbow	90	90	90	90	90
Loss of arm below elbow	80	80	80	80	80
Hand injuries –					
Loss of both hands	100	100	100	100	100
Loss of hand and foot	100	100	100	100	100
Loss of hand or loss of thumb and four fingers	80	80	80	80	80
Loss of thumb	35	35	35	35	35
Loss of forefinger	25	25	25	25	25
Loss of middle finger	20	20	20	20	20
Loss of ring finger	20	20	20	20	20
Loss of little finger	14	14	14	14	14
Total loss of movement of joint of thumb	15	15	15	15	15
Loss of distal phalanx of thumb	17	17	17	17	17
Loss of portion of terminal segment of thumb involving one-third of its flexor surface without loss of distal phalanx	15	15	15	15	15
Loss of distal phalanx of forefinger	11	11	11	11	11
Loss of distal phalanx of other fingers	9	9	9	9	9
Leg injuries –					
Loss of leg at or above knee	90	90	90	90	90
Loss of leg below knee	80	80	80	80	80
Foot injuries –					
Loss of both feet	100	100	100	100	100
Loss of foot and	100	100	100	100	100

SCHEDULE 3

Column 1.	**Column 2.**				
Nature of Injury.	**The ratio which the fixed sum payable as compensation under Section 67 bears to: –**				
hand					
Loss of foot	75	75	75	75	75
Loss of great toe	25	25	25	25	25
Loss of any other toe	10	10	10	10	10
Loss of two phalanges of any other toe	8	8	8	8	8
Loss of phalanx of great toe	11	11	11	11	11
Loss of phalanx of any other toe	7	7	7	7	7
Miscellaneous –					
Loss of genitals	50	50	50	50	50
Severe facial scarring or disfigurement to a maximum of	80	80	80	80	80
Severe bodily, other than facial, scarring or disfigurement to a maximum of	50	50	50	50	50

CHAPTER No 297

Wrongs (Miscellaneous Provisions) Act

PART I – STATE LIABILITY IN TORT

Division 1 – General

Subdivision D – Regulations

PART II – ACTIONS BETWEEN HUSBAND AND WIFE

PART III – SEDUCTION

PART IV – WRONGFUL ACT OR NEGLECT CAUSING DEATH

PART V – SURVIVAL OF CAUSES OF ACTION

PART VI – COMMON EMPLOYMENT

PART VII – MENTAL OR NERVOUS SHOCK

PART VIII – TORT-FEASORS

PART IX – CONTRIBUTORY NEGLIGENCE

PART X – DAMAGE BY AIRCRAFT

PART XI – DAMAGE TO NAVIGATION WORKS

PART XII – OCCUPIERS' LIABILITY

PART XIII – DAMAGE BY FIRE

INDEPENDENT STATE OF PAPUA NEW GUINEA

CHAPTER No 297

Wrongs (Miscellaneous Provisions) Act

Being an Act relating to various aspects of the law of wrongs.

PART I – STATE LIABILITY IN TORT

Division 1 – General

1 General liability of the State in tort

(1) Subject to this Division, the State is subject to all liabilities in tort to which, if it were a private person of full age and capacity, it would be subject –

(a) in respect of torts committed by its servants and agents; and

(b) in respect of any breach of the duties that a person owes to his servants or agents under the underlying law by reason of being their employer; and

(c) in respect of any breach of the duties attaching under the underlying law to the ownership, occupation, possession or control of property.

(2) Proceedings do not lie against the State by virtue of Subsection (1)(a) in respect of an act or omission of a servant or agent of the State unless the act or omission would, apart from this Division, have given rise to a cause of action in tort against the servant or agent or his estate.

(3) Where the State is bound by a statutory duty that is binding also on persons other than the State and its officers, then, subject to this Division, the State is, in respect of a failure to comply with that duty, subject to all liabilities in tort (if any) to which it would be subject if it were a private person of full age and capacity.

(4) Where functions are conferred or imposed on an officer of the State as such either by a rule of the underlying law or by statute, and the

officer commits a tort while performing or purporting to perform the functions, the liabilities of the State in respect of the tort are such as they would have been if the functions had been conferred or imposed solely by virtue of instructions lawfully given by the Government.

(5) An Act or subordinate enactment that negatives or limits the amount of the liability of a Department of the Government or officer of the State in respect of a tort committed by the Department or officer applies, in the case of proceedings against the State under this section in respect of a tort committed by the Department or officer, in relation to the State as it would have applied in relation to the Department or officer if the proceedings against the State had been proceedings against the Department or officer.

(6) Proceedings do not lie against the State by virtue of this section in respect of anything done or omitted to be done by a person while discharging or purporting to discharge responsibilities of a judicial nature vested in him, or responsibilities that he has in connexion with the execution of judicial process.

2 Application of law as to indemnity, contribution, joint and several tort-feasors and contributory negligence

(1) Where the State is subject to liability by virtue of this Division, the law relating to indemnity and contribution is enforceable by or against the State in respect of the liability to which it is so subject as if the State were a private person of full age and capacity.

(2) Without prejudice to the effect of Subsection (1), Part VIII. binds the State.

(3) Part IX. binds the State.

Division 2 – Liability in Respect of Motor Vehicles

3 Interpretation of Division 2

(1) In this Division, unless the contrary intention appears –

"driver" includes the rider of a motor cycle and a person for the time being in charge of a motor vehicle;

"motor vehicle" means a motor car, motor carriage, motor cycle, motor lorry, motor omnibus, motor tractor or other vehicle propelled wholly or partly by a volatile spirit or by steam, gas, oil or electricity, or by any means other than human or animal power, and includes a trailer or semi-trailer other than a vehicle used on a railway or tramway;

"statutory instrumentality" means a corporation incorporated for a public purpose by a law, but does not include an incorporated company or association;

"third-party policy" means a policy of insurance that is a third-party policy within the meaning of the *Motor Vehicles (Third Party Insurance) Act*;

"uninsured motor vehicle" means a motor vehicle in respect of which a third-party policy is not in force.

(2) This Division does not apply in relation to proceedings arising out of an occurrence that took place outside the country.

4 Conclusive presumption of agency in respect of driving of Government vehicles

(1) In proceedings in which –

(a) a claim is made against the State or a statutory instrumentality for damages in respect of the death of, or personal injury to, a person caused by, or arising out of the use of, an uninsured motor vehicle owned by the State or the instrumentality; or

(b) a claim is made by or against the State or a statutory instrumentality for contribution in relation to liability of the State or the instrumentality for such damages,

the driver of the vehicle shall, for the purposes of the claim, be conclusively presumed to have been at all relevant times, with respect to the driving of the vehicle, the agent of the State or of the instrumentality, as the case may be, acting within the scope of his authority.

(2) Nothing in this Division implies ratification by the State or a statutory instrumentality of the acts of the driver of a vehicle.

Division 3 – Liability in Respect of Aircraft Accidents

Subdivision A – Preliminary

5 Interpretation of Division 3

In this Division, unless the contrary intention appears –

"damages" includes an amount received under a compromise or settlement of a claim for damages, whether legal proceedings had been instituted or not;

"flying pay" includes flying instructional pay, flight pay and flying allowance and any other similar pay or allowance;

"passenger", in relation to an aircraft, does not include –

(a) a member of the crew (including a pilot) of the aircraft; or

(b) a member of the Defence Force, whether a member of the crew of the aircraft or not, who –

(i) is in receipt of flying pay; or

(ii) is included in a prescribed class of members of the Defence Force, being a class as to whom the terms and conditions of their service include provision for risks arising out of the performance of duties in aircraft; or

(c) a person whose carriage in the aircraft is specifically and only for the purpose of his performing in the aircraft –

(i) duties or services for the performance of which he is employed or engaged by the State or an instrumentality of the Government; or

(ii) duties as a member of the Defence Force; or

(d) a person whose carriage in the aircraft is specifically and only for the purpose of his performing duties or services in the aircraft; or

(e) a person who is not lawfully entitled to be on board the aircraft.

6 Application of Division 3

This Division applies both within and outside the country.

Subdivision B – Carriage in Aircraft Operated by the State or an Instrumentality of the Government

7 Application of Subdivision B

This Subdivision applies to the carriage of a passenger in an aircraft operated by the State or an instrumentality of the Government, not being carriage to which Part III. of the *Civil Aviation (Aircraft Operators' Liability) Act* applies.

8 Application of the Civil Aviation (Aircraft Operators' Liability) Act

Subject to this Subdivision, Sections 24, 28(1), 29, 30, 31 (other than Subsection (2)) and 33 to 35 (inclusive) of the *Civil Aviation (Aircraft Operators' Liability) Act* apply to and in relation to carriage to which this Subdivision applies as if those provisions were incorporated in this Subdivision and as if–

(a) references in those provisions to a carrier or the carrier were references to the State or the instrumentality of the Government by which the aircraft was being operated, as the case requires; and

(b) the reference in Section 29 of that Act to Section 27 of that Act were a reference to Section 9 of this Act.

9 Limitation of liability under Subdivision B

(1) The maximum liability under this Subdivision of the State or an instrumentality of the Government in respect of any one person, by reason of his death or injury, is K30,000.00.

(2) The amount of any damages that would, but for this subsection, be recoverable by virtue of this Subdivision by a person from the State or from an instrumentality of the Government, in respect of a death or injury is reduced by any amount received or receivable by him in consequence of the death or injury by reason of–

(a) insurance effected by the State or the instrumentality for the benefit of the deceased or injured person or his estate; or

(b) insurance effected by the deceased or injured person that is referable to an allowance granted by the State or the instrumentality for the purpose of enabling him to effect such insurance.

10 Relief from certain other liabilities

(1) Subject to Section 33 of the *Civil Aviation (Aircraft Operators' Liability) Act* in its application by virtue of this Subdivision, the liability, under this Subdivision, of the State or an instrumentality of the Government in respect of the death of a passenger, or personal injury to a passenger that has not resulted in his death, is in substitution for any other civil liability of the State or the instrumentality in respect of the death or injury other than –

(a) a liability under Division II.1 or Division II.2 of the *Civil Aviation (Aircraft Operators' Liability) Act*; or

(b) a liability arising otherwise than by reason of the operation of the aircraft by the State or the instrumentality.

(2) Notwithstanding Division II.1 and Division II.2 of the *Civil Aviation (Aircraft Operators' Liability) Act* but without prejudice to the operation of Section 11 of this Act, any liability, under this Subdivision, of the State or an instrumentality of the Government is not excluded by reason of the existence of any liability of the State or of the instrumentality under either of those Divisions.

11 Liability of State, etc, independently of Subdivision B

(1) Where, apart from this section, damages in respect of any death or injury are recoverable, under this Subdivision, from the State or an instrumentality of the Government by or for the benefit of a person and such damages are also recoverable from the State or an instrumentality of the Government by or for the benefit of that person otherwise than under this Subdivision –

(a) if damages are recovered otherwise than under this Subdivision – damages are not recoverable under this Subdivision; and

(b) if damages are recovered under this Subdivision – the amount of damages recoverable otherwise than under this Subdivision is reduced by the amount of the damages so recovered.

(2) In Subsection (1), "damages" does not include compensation under the *Workers' Compensation Act.*

(3) This section does not prevent the application of Section 7 of the *Workers' Compensation Act* in relation to damages recovered or recoverable under this Subdivision.

Subdivision C – Carriage in Aircraft not Operated by the State or an Instrumentality of the Government

12 Application of Subdivision C

(1) Subject to this section, this Subdivision applies to the carriage in an aircraft, operated by a person other than the State or an instrumentality of the Government, of a passenger –

(a) who is an employee within the meaning of the *Workers' Compensation Act*, and is travelling in the course of his employment by the State or an instrumentality of the Government; or

(b) the cost of whose carriage has been, or is to be, borne by the State or an instrumentality of the Government; or

(c) who is travelling by air for the purposes of the State or of an instrumentality of the Government under arrangements made or authority given by the State or the instrumentality.

(2) This Subdivision does not apply to carriage to which Part III. of the *Civil Aviation (Aircraft Operators' Liability) Act* applies.

13 Liability of State, etc, for death or injury

Subject to this Subdivision, where this Subdivision applies to the carriage of a person –

(a) the State; or

(b) if the person is employed by an instrumentality of the Government or an instrumentality of the Government has borne, or is to bear, the cost of his carriage or has arranged for or authorized his carriage – the instrumentality,

is liable –

(c) for damage sustained by reason of his death; or

(d) for any personal injury suffered by him,

resulting from an accident that took place –

(e) on board the aircraft; or

(f) in the course of any of the operations of embarking or disembarking.

14 Application of the Civil Aviation (Aircraft Operators' Liability) Act

Subject to this Subdivision, Sections 30, 31 (other than Subsections (2) and (10)), 34 and 35 of the *Civil Aviation (Aircraft Operators' Liability) Act* apply to and in relation to carriage to which this Subdivision applies as if those provisions were incorporated in this

Subdivision and as if references in those provisions to a carrier were references to the State or an instrumentality of the Government.

15 Limitation of liability under Subdivision C

(1) The maximum liability under this Subdivision of the State or an instrumentality of the Government in respect of any one person, by reason of his death or injury, is K30,000.00.

(2) The amount of any damages recoverable, by virtue of this Subdivision, but for this subsection by a person from the State or an instrumentality of the Government in respect of a death or injury is reduced by –

(a) the amount of any damages or compensation –

(i) paid or payable, in respect of the death or injury, to or for the benefit of the person by; or

(ii) recovered or recoverable by or for the benefit of that person from,

the carrier, a servant or agent of the carrier or any other person other than the State or the instrumentality, as the case may be; and

(b) any amount received or receivable by the person, in consequence of the death or injury, by reason of –

(i) insurance effected, for the benefit of the deceased or injured person or his estate, by the carrier or by the State or the instrumentality; or

(ii) insurance effected by the deceased or injured person that is referable to an allowance granted by the State or the instrumentality for the purpose of enabling him to effect such insurance.

16 Liability of State, etc, independently of Subdivision C

(1) Where, apart from this section, damages in respect of any death or injury are recoverable from the State or an instrumentality of the Government by or for the benefit of a person under this Subdivision, and such damages are also recoverable from the State or an instrumentality of the Government by or for the benefit of the person otherwise than under this Subdivision –

(a) if damages are recovered otherwise than under this Subdivision – damages are not recoverable under this Subdivision; and

(b) if damages are recovered under this Subdivision – the amount of damages recoverable otherwise than under this Subdivision is reduced by the amount of the damages so recovered.

(2) In Subsection (1), "damages" does not include compensation under the *Workers' Compensation Act.*

(3) This section does not prevent the application of Section 7 of the *Workers' Compensation Act* in relation to damages recovered or recoverable under this Subdivision.

17 Damages not recoverable under Subdivision C in certain circumstances

(1) Damages under this Subdivision in respect of a death or injury are not recoverable from the State or an instrumentality of the Government by or for the benefit of a person where the person, or a person lawfully acting or entitled to act on behalf of the person –

(a) has failed to take any action that he could reasonably have been expected to take, if this Subdivision had not been enacted, to recover damages in respect of the death or injury from any other person who was, or may have been, liable to pay damages in respect of the death or injury; or

(b) has, without the written consent of the Government or the instrumentality, as the case may be, entered into a compromise, settlement or agreement by which a person other than the State or the instrumentality has been discharged, in whole or in part, from liability to which he was, or might have been, subject in respect of the death or injury; or

(c) has refused to comply with a request under Subsection (2).

(2) The State or an instrumentality of the Government may, in writing, request a person who appears to be entitled to recover damages in respect of a death or injury to which this Subdivision applies against a person other than the State or the instrumentality, or a person lawfully acting or entitled to act on behalf of such a person, to take or continue proceedings (whether in the country or elsewhere) to recover the damages.

(3) Where proceedings are taken or continued in accordance with Subsection (2), the proceedings shall be conducted on behalf of the first-mentioned person at the expense of the State or the instrumentality, as the case may be.

(4) The State or an instrumentality of the Government may, by written notice, revoke a request made under Subsection (2), and, in that

event, it is not liable for any costs or expenses incurred in respect of the continuance of the proceedings after the revocation.

18 Action against State, etc, under Subdivision C when other proceedings pending

An action against the State or an instrumentality of the Government for damages under this Subdivision in respect of a death or injury shall not be heard or determined if an action against a person other than the State or the instrumentality for damages in respect of the death or injury is pending in any court, whether in the country or elsewhere.

Subdivision D – Regulations

19 Regulations

The Head of State, acting on advice, may make regulations, not inconsistent with this Division, prescribing all matters that by this Division are required or permitted to be prescribed, or that are necessary or convenient to be prescribed for carrying out or giving effect to this Division.

PART II – ACTIONS BETWEEN HUSBAND AND WIFE

20 Actions in tort

(1) Subject to this section, each of the parties to a marriage has a like right of action in tort against the other as if they were not married.

(2) Where an action in tort is brought by one of the parties to a marriage against the other during the subsistence of the marriage –

(a) the court before which the action is brought may stay the action if it appears that no substantial benefit would accrue to either party from the continuation of the proceedings; or

(b) if the action is brought in the National Court, the Court –

(i) may stay the action if it appears that the question or questions in issue could more conveniently be disposed of on an application under Section 15 of the *Married Women's Property Act*, and

(ii) may, without the necessity of any further application, exercise any power that could be exercised on an application under that Section, or give such directions as it thinks proper for the disposal under that section of any question arising in the proceedings.

21 Application of Section 20 where marriage annulled, etc

The reference in Section 20(1) to the parties to the marriage includes a reference to persons who were parties to a marriage that has been annulled or dissolved.

22 Application of Part II to certain causes of action

Sections 20 and 21 do not apply to a cause of action that arose or would, but for the subsistence of a marriage, have arisen before 25 June 1970 (being the date of commencement of the pre-Independence *Law Reform (Husband and Wife) Act* 1970).

PART III – SEDUCTION

23 Proof of loss of service in actions of seduction

In an action of seduction brought by a parent or person in *loco parentis* it is not necessary for the plaintiff to allege or give evidence of loss of service to the plaintiff by the woman or girl seduced, or that between them there was the relation of master and servant, but the loss of service and relation shall be conclusively presumed in favour of the plaintiff.

PART IV – WRONGFUL ACT OR NEGLECT CAUSING DEATH

24 Interpretation of Part IV

(1) In this Part, unless the contrary intention appears –

"child" includes son, daughter, grandson, granddaughter, stepson and stepdaughter;

"parent" includes father, mother, grandfather, grandmother, stepfather and stepmother.

(2) For the purposes of this Part, a person shall be deemed to be the parent or child of a deceased person notwithstanding that he was related to him illegitimately or in consequence of adoption, whether under a law of Papua New Guinea or under a law of a place outside Papua New Guinea, and, in deducing a relationship that under the provisions of this Part is included within the meaning of the expression "parent" or "child", an illegitimate person and an adopted person shall be treated as being or as having been the legitimate offspring of his mother and reputed father or of his adopters, as the case may be.

(3) In deducing a relationship for the purposes of this Part, a relationship by affinity shall be treated as a relationship by consanguinity and a relationship of the half-blood as a relationship of the whole blood.

25 Liability for death caused wrongfully, etc

Where the death of a person is caused by a wrongful act, neglect or default and the act, neglect or default is such as would (if death had not ensued) have entitled the party injured to maintain an action and recover damages in respect of it, the person who would have been liable if death had not ensued is liable to an action for damages notwithstanding the death of the person injured and notwithstanding that the death has been caused under such circumstances as amount in law to an offence.

26 Actions under Section 25

(1) An action referred to in Section 25 shall be for the benefit of the wife, husband, parent and child of the deceased person, and a person who is, or is the issue of, a brother, sister, uncle or aunt of the deceased person, and shall be brought by and in the name of the executor or administrator of the person deceased.

(2) In the case of the death of a native within the meaning of the pre-Independence [904]Ordinances Interpretation Act 1949-1973, an action referred to in Subsection (1) may be for the benefit of the persons who by custom were dependent on the deceased immediately before his death, in addition to the persons specified in that subsection.

27 Actions for damages by persons interested

(1) Where in any case to which this Part applies there is no executor or administrator of the person deceased, or where no action referred to in this Part has, within six months after the death of the deceased person, been brought by his executor or administrator, the action may be brought by all or any of the persons for whose benefit the action would have been if it had been brought by the executor or administrator.

(2) An action brought under Subsection (1) shall be for the benefit of the same person or persons and shall be subject to the same procedure as nearly as may be as if it were brought by the executor or administrator.

28 Amount of damages

(1) In an action referred to in Section 25, the court may award such damages as it thinks proportioned to the injury resulting from the death to the respective parties for whom and for whose benefit the action is brought, and the amount so recovered, after deducting the costs not recovered from the defendant, shall be divided amongst those parties in such shares as the court directs.

(2) In an action referred to in Section 25, damages may be awarded in respect of medical expenses incurred as a result of the injury causing the death, together with reasonable expenses of the funeral or cremation of the deceased person (including the cost of erecting a headstone or tombstone over the grave of the deceased person), if those expenses have been incurred by one or more of the parties for whose benefit the action is brought.

29 Solatium to parents of child wrongfully killed

(1) In this section, "parent" means –

(a) where the child has been adopted, the adopted father or mother of the child; and

(b) where the child has not been adopted, the father or mother of a legitimate child and the mother of an illegitimate child.

[904]See now the Interpretation Act, s98.

(2) In an action referred to in Section 25 in relation to the death of a child after 25 July 1968 (being the date of commencement of the pre-Independence *Law Reform (Miscellaneous Provisions) Act* 1967) the court may award such damages, not exceeding K600.00 in the aggregate, as the court thinks just, by way of solatium for the suffering caused to a parent by the death of the child.

(3) When both parents bring an action to recover the sum of money payable under this section, the amount recovered, after deducting the costs not recovered from the defendant, shall be divided between the parents in such shares as the court directs.

(4) Where both parents survive the child and one of them does not join in bringing an action under this section, the other may bring an action for such amount as he claims to be due to him.

(5) In an action brought to enforce a right conferred by this section the court may, in its discretion, refuse to order the payment of any sum by way of solatium if, having regard to the conduct of the plaintiff in relation to the deceased person, or to the relations that existed between the plaintiff and the deceased person, or for any other sufficient reason, it thinks that no such payment should be made.

(6) The rights conferred by this section are in addition to, and not in derogation of, any rights conferred on a parent by any other provision of this Act.

(7) The cause of action conferred on a person by this section does not, on his death, survive for the benefit of his estate.

30 Exclusion of payments by insurers in assessment of damages

In assessing damages in an action under this Part there shall not be taken into account –

(a) any sum (including a return of premiums) paid or payable, on the death of the deceased person, under a contract of assurance or insurance, whenever made; or

(b) any sum paid or payable by way of social service benefit under an Act; or

(c) any sum (including a return of contributions) paid or payable out of a superannuation, provident or like fund, or by way of benefit from a friendly society, benefit society or trade union; or

(d) any benefit or gratuity, in cash or in kind, received, as a result of the death, by a person for whose benefit the action is brought.

31 Limitation of actions under Part IV

Only one action under this Part lies for and in respect of the same subject-matter of complaint, and every such action must be commenced within three years after the death of the deceased person.

32 Particulars of demand

In an action under this Part, the plaintiff on the record must deliver, together with the statement of claim, to the defendant or his lawyer full particulars of the person for whom and on whose behalf the action is brought, and of the nature of the claim in respect of which damages are sought to be recovered.

33 Payment into court

(1) In an action under this Part, the defendant may pay money into court as compensation in one sum to all persons entitled under this Part for the wrongful act, neglect or default, without specifying the shares into which the sum is to be divided by the court.

(2) No portion of the sum paid in shall be paid out of court except under the order of a Judge, but otherwise the rules of the court for the time being in force relating to payment into and out of court and tender, and matters associated with such payment and tender, with any necessary modifications, apply.

PART V – SURVIVAL OF CAUSES OF ACTION

34 Effect of death on certain causes of action

(1) Subject to this section, on the death of a person after 1 January 1963 (being the date of commencement of the pre-Independence *Law Reform (Miscellaneous Provisions) Act* 1962) all causes of action subsisting against or vested in him survive against or for the benefit of, as the case may be, his estate.

(2) Subsection (1) does not apply to causes of action for defamation or seduction or for inducing one spouse to leave or remain apart from the other, or to claims for damages on the ground of adultery.

(3) Where a cause of action survives under this section for the benefit of the estate of a deceased person, the damages recoverable for the benefit of the estate –

(a) do not include exemplary damages; and

(b) in the case of a breach of promise of marriage, are limited to such damages (if any) to the estate of the person as flow from the breach of the promise to marry; and

(c) where the death of the person has been caused by the act or omission that gives rise to the cause of action, shall be calculated without reference to any loss or gain to his estate consequent on his death, except that a sum in respect of funeral expenses may be included.

(4) No proceedings are maintainable in respect of a cause of action in tort that, by virtue of Subsection (1), has survived against the estate of a deceased person unless –

(a) proceedings against him in respect of the cause of action were pending at the date of his death; or

(b) proceedings are taken in respect of the cause of action not later than 12 months after his personal representative took out representation.

(5) Where damage has been suffered by reason of an act or omission in respect of which a cause of action would have subsisted against a person if the person had not died before, or at the same time as, the damage was suffered, there shall be deemed, for the purposes of this section, to have been subsisting against him before his death such cause of action in respect of the act or omission as would have subsisted if he had died after the damage was suffered.

(6) The rights conferred by this section for the benefit of the estates of deceased persons are in addition to and not in derogation of any rights conferred on the dependants of a deceased person by any other law, and this section applies in relation to causes of action under that law as it applies in relation to other causes of action not expressly excepted from the operation of Subsection (1).

PART VI – COMMON EMPLOYMENT

35 Abolition of doctrine of common employment

(1) It is not a defence to an employer who is sued in respect of personal injuries caused by the negligence of a person employed by him, that the person was at the time when the injuries were caused in common employment with the person injured.

(2) A provision in a contract of service or apprenticeship, or in an agreement collateral to any such contract, is void so far as it would have the effect of excluding or limiting the liability of the employer in respect of personal injuries caused to the person employed or apprenticed by the negligence of persons in common employment with him.

PART VII – MENTAL OR NERVOUS SHOCK

36 Mental or nervous shock

In an action for injury to the person, the plaintiff is not debarred from recovering damages merely because the injury complained of arose wholly or in part from mental or nervous shock.

PART VIII – TORT-FEASORS

37 Proceedings against, and contribution between, joint and several tort-feasors

(1) In this section –

"child" has the same meaning as in Part IV.;

"dependant" means a person for whose benefit an action could be brought under Part IV.;

"judgement first given" means, where a judgement is reversed on appeal, the judgement first given that is not so reversed or, where the judgement first given is varied on appeal, that judgement as so varied;

"parent" has the same meaning as in Part IV.;

"plaintiff" means the person suffering the damage referred to in Subsection (2), whether or not he has commenced an action for recovery of judgement in respect of the damage;

"third party" means a tort-feasor from whom any other tort-feasor is entitled to recover contribution under Subsection (2)(c).

(2) Where damage is suffered by a person as a result of a tort (whether it is also an offence or not) –

(a) judgement recovered against a tort-feasor liable in respect of the damage is not a bar to an action against any other person who would, if sued, have been liable as joint tort-feasor in respect of the same damage; and

(b) if more than one action is brought in respect of the damage by or on behalf of the person by whom it was suffered, or for the benefit of the estate or of the wife, husband, parent or child of that person, against tort-feasors liable in respect of the damage (whether as joint tort-feasors or otherwise) –

(i) the sums recoverable under the judgements given in the actions by way of damages shall not in the aggregate exceed the amount of the damages awarded by the judgement first given; and

(ii) in any of the actions, other than the one in which judgement is first given, the plaintiff is not entitled to costs unless the court is of opinion that there was reasonable ground for bringing the action separately; and

(c) a tort-feasor liable in respect of the damage may recover contribution from any other tort-feasor who is, or would if sued have been, liable in respect of the same damage (whether as a joint tort-feasor or otherwise), but no person is entitled to recover contribution under this section from a person entitled to be indemnified by him in respect of the liability in respect of which the contribution is sought; and

(d) a tort-feasor liable in respect of the damage may recover contribution from a third party or commence proceedings for the recovery of contribution notwithstanding that –

(i) judgement in an action founded on the tort has not been given determining the tort-feasor's liability in respect of that damage; or

(ii) the plaintiff has released the third party from his liability to the plaintiff for the damage or any part of it; or

(iii) the liability of the tort-feasor to the plaintiff has been extinguished in whole or in part by payment before proceedings for contribution under this section are commenced.

(3) In any proceedings for contribution under this section, the amount of the contribution recoverable from a person is such as is found by the court to be just and equitable, having regard to the extent of his responsibility for the damage, and the court may exempt a person from liability to make contribution, or direct that the contribution recovered from a person amounts to a complete indemnity.

(4) No execution for the recovery of contribution under this section shall issue without the leave of the court or a Judge, and on application for leave the court or Judge may direct that payment to the original plaintiff is sufficient satisfaction of the order for contribution.

(5) Notwithstanding any law requiring notice to be given before action or prescribing the time within which an action may be brought, proceedings for contribution under this section may, although no such notice has been given or the time has expired, be commenced at any time within 12 months after –

(a) the receipt by the party seeking the contribution of written notice of the claim of the original plaintiff against him in respect of the damage; or

(b) settlement of the claim,

whichever first occurs, but at the expiry of that period of 12 months the right to recover contribution is extinguished.

(6) In a case referred to in Section 54 of the *Motor Vehicles (Third Party Insurance) Act* and Section 20 of the *Motor Vehicles (Third Party Insurance) (Basic Protection Compensation) Act* the Trust shall be deemed, for the purposes of this Part –

(a) to be a tort-feasor in relation to the death or bodily injury in question, if the insured person was a tort-feasor in relation to the death or injury; and

(b) to be responsible for the damage to the same extent as the insured person would have been held to be responsible if sued.

(7) Nothing in this section –

(a) applies with respect to a tort committed before 1 January 1963 (being the date of commencement of the pre-Independence *Law Reform (Miscellaneous Provisions) Act* 1962); or

(b) affects any criminal proceedings against a person in respect of a wrongful act; or

(c) makes enforceable an agreement for indemnity that would not have been enforceable if this section had not been made.

PART IX – CONTRIBUTORY NEGLIGENCE

38 Application of Part IX

This Part does not apply to any case where the acts or omissions giving rise to the claim occurred before 1 January 1963 (being the date of commencement of the pre-Independence *Law Reform (Miscellaneous Provisions) Act* 1962).

39 Interpretation of Part IX

In this Part, unless the contrary intention appears –

"court", in relation to a claim, means the court or arbitrator by or before whom the claim falls to be determined;

"damage" includes loss of life and personal injury;

"dependant" means a person for whose benefit an action could be brought under Part IV.;

"employer" includes –

(a) the State, an authority constituted by or under a law, a body of persons, corporate or unincorporate, and the legal personal representative of a deceased employer; and

(b) where the services of a worker are temporarily lent or let on hire to another person by the person with whom the worker has entered into a contract of service or apprenticeship, the person so lending the services or letting them on hire;

"fault" means negligence, breach of statutory duty or other act or omission that gives rise to a liability in tort or would, apart from this Part, give rise to the defence of contributory negligence;

"worker" means a worker within the meaning of the *Workers' Compensation Act*.

40 Apportionment of liability in case of contributory negligence

(1) Subject to Subsection (2), where a person suffers damage as the result partly of his own fault and partly of the fault of any other person, a claim in respect of the damage shall not be defeated by reason of the fault of the person suffering the damage, but the damages recoverable in respect of it shall be reduced to such extent as the court thinks just and

equitable, having regard to the claimant's share in the responsibility for the damage.

(2) Notwithstanding Subsection (1) –

(a) that subsection does not operate to defeat a defence arising under a contract; and

(b) where a contract or enactment providing for the limitation of liability is applicable to the claim, the amount of damages awarded to the claimant by virtue of that subsection shall not exceed the maximum so applicable; and

(c) where an action is brought in a court of limited jurisdiction, the court may award damages up to the limit of its jurisdiction even though the damages have first been reduced under that subsection.

(3) Where damages are recoverable by any person by virtue of Subsection (1) subject to a reduction under that subsection or under Subsection (5) or (6), the court shall find and record the total damages that, apart from any limitation referred to in Subsection (1)(b) or (c), would have been awarded if the claimant had not been at fault.

(4) Part VIII. applies where two or more persons are liable or would, if they had all been sued, be liable by virtue of Subsection (1) in respect of the damages suffered by a person.

(5) Where a person dies as the result partly of his own fault and partly of the fault of any other person, and accordingly if an action were brought for the benefit of the estate under Part V. the damages recoverable would be reduced under Subsection (1), any damages recoverable in an action brought for the benefit of the dependants of a deceased person under Part IV. shall be reduced to a proportionate extent.

(6) Where a person dies as a result partly of the fault of one of his dependants and partly of the fault of any other person, any damages recoverable in an action brought for the benefit of the dependants of the deceased person under Part IV. shall be reduced, so far as the share in them of the negligent dependant is concerned to such extent as the court thinks just and equitable, having regard to the share of the negligent dependant in the responsibility for the death of the deceased person.

(7) Where –

(a) a person (in this subsection called "the injured person") suffers damage as a result partly of his own fault and partly of the fault of any other person; and

(b) by reason of the damage to the injured person a third person suffers damage (whether by way of the loss of the society or services of the injured person or otherwise), then, in any claim by the third person for the damage so suffered by him the fault of the injured person shall be taken into account under Subsection (1) for the purpose of reducing the damages recoverable by the third party as if it were the fault of the third party.

(8) Where in a case to which Subsection (1) applies one of the persons at fault avoids liability to any other such person or the personal representative of any other person by pleading any enactment limiting the time within which proceedings may be taken, he is not entitled to recover any damages or contributions from the other person or the representative by virtue of that subsection.

41 Provisions as to workers and employers

(1) Where, within the time limited for the taking of proceedings under the *Workers' Compensation Act*, an action is brought to recover damages independently of that Act in respect of an injury or disease giving rise to a claim for compensation under that Act, and it is determined in the action that –

(a) damages are recoverable, independently of that Act, subject to reduction under Section 40(1); and

(b) the employer would have been liable to pay compensation under that Act,

Section 22 of the *Workers' Compensation Act* applies as if the action had been dismissed, and if the claimant chooses to have compensation assessed and awarded in accordance with that section no damages are recoverable in the action.

(2) Where a worker or his personal representative or dependant has recovered compensation under the *Workers' Compensation Act* or any corresponding previous enactment in respect of an injury caused in circumstances that would give a right to recover reduced damages in respect of it by virtue of Section 40 from some person other than the employer (in this subsection referred to as "the third party"), any right to be indemnified by the third party that is conferred by Section 23 of that Act on –

(a) the person by whom the compensation was paid; or

(b) any person called on to pay an indemnity under Section 6 of that Act,

is limited to a right to be indemnified in respect of such part only of the sum paid or payable by the person as bears to the total sum so paid or payable the same proportion as the reduced damages bear to the total damages that would have been recoverable if the worker had not been at fault.

[905]PART X – DAMAGE BY AIRCRAFT

42 Interpretation of Part X

In this Part, unless the contrary intention appears –

"article" includes a mail or postal article and an animal;

"loss or damage" includes, in relation to persons, loss of life and personal injury.

43 Limitation of liability in respect of trespass or nuisance by flying over property

An action does not lie in respect of trespass or nuisance by reason only of the flight of an aircraft over any property at a height above the ground that, having regard to the wind, the weather and all the circumstances, is reasonable, or of the ordinary incidents of such a flight, so long as the *Civil Aviation Act* is complied with.

44 Liability for damage by aircraft or articles falling from aircraft

(1) Subject to Subsection (2), where material loss or damage is caused to any person or property on land or water by or by a person in, or by an article or person falling from, an aircraft while in flight or taking off or landing, then, subject to this Part, damages in respect of the loss or damage are recoverable from the owner of the aircraft, without proof of negligence or intention or other cause of action, as if the loss or damage had been caused by the wilful act, neglect or default of the owner.

(2) Where material loss or damage referred to in Subsection (1) is caused in circumstances in which –

(a) damages in respect of the loss or damage are recoverable from the owner by virtue only of Subsection (1); and

(b) a legal liability to pay damages in respect of the loss or damage is created in some person other than the owner,

the owner is entitled to be indemnified by the other person against any claim in respect of the loss or damage.

(3) Where the aircraft concerned has been bona fide demised, chartered, let or hired, out for a period exceeding 14 days, by the owner to any other person, and no pilot, commander, navigator or operative member of the crew of the aircraft is in the employment of the owner, Subsections (1) and (2) have effect as if for references to the owner there

[905]See, also, the *Civil Aviation (Aircraft Operators' Liability) Act*. The Civil Aviation Bill 2000 proposes to repeal this Part.

were substituted references to the person to whom the aircraft has been so demised, chartered, let or hired out.

PART XI – DAMAGE TO NAVIGATION WORKS

45 Interpretation of Part XI

In this Part, unless the contrary intention appears –

"harbour works" includes all wharves, piers, jetties, embankments, lights and other constructions for the improvement, protection, management or utilization of a port or harbour, that are –

(a) owned or controlled by the State or the Harbours Board; or

(b) private harbour works;

"private harbour work" means a construction declared under Section 47 to be a private harbour work for the purposes of this Part;

"vessel" includes a ship, boat, lighter, floating plant or other craft, whether propelled by mechanical means or otherwise, but does not include an aircraft.

46 Liability under other laws

This Part does not limit the liability of any person under any other law.

47 Private harbour works

The Minister may, by notice in the National Gazette, declare a construction for the improvement, protection, management or utilization of a port or harbour, being a construction that is owned or controlled by a person other than the State or the Harbours Board, to be a private harbour work for the purposes of this Act.

48 Liability for damage to harbour works

(1) Subject to this section, the owner of a vessel or a float of timber is liable for any damage done to a port or harbour or to harbour works by the vessel or float, or by a person employed on or about the vessel or float.

(2) Where damage to a port or harbour or to harbour works is caused by a vessel or float of timber through the wilful act or negligence of the master or the person having charge of the vessel or float, or of a person employed on or about the vessel or float, the master or person is jointly and severally liable with the owner for the damage.

(3) This section does not impose liability on the owner of a vessel or float of timber –

(a) that is derelict; or

(b) where the damage is caused by act of God.

49 Owner may recover from master, etc

If the owner of a vessel or float of timber makes satisfaction under Section 48 for damage wilfully or negligently done by the master or person having charge of the vessel or float, or by a person employed on or about the vessel or float, the master or person shall repay to the owner the amount paid in satisfaction, together with the costs of the proceedings to enforce the repayment.

50 Seizure of vessel, etc, doing damage

In addition to any other remedy given by any other law –

(a) the State, in relation to harbour works owned by it; or

(b) the Harbours Board, in relation to harbour works owned by it; or

(c) the owner or person in control of any private harbour works, in relation to those works,

may at any time detain a vessel or float of timber that has done any damage to a port or harbour, or to any harbour works, whether or not the vessel or float has left the place where the damage was done, until satisfaction has been made or sufficient security has been given for the amount of damage done by the vessel or float.

PART XII – OCCUPIERS' LIABILITY

51 Preliminary

(1) The rules prescribed by this Part –

(a) have effect to regulate the duty that an occupier of premises owes to his visitors in respect of dangers due to the state of the premises or to things done or omitted to be done on the premises; and

(b) subject to Subsection (3), regulate the nature of the duty imposed by law in consequence of the occupation or control of premises by a person and of an invitation or permission that he gives (or is, under this Part, to be deemed to give) to another to enter or use the premises.

(2) The rules prescribed by this Part in relation to an occupier of premises and his visitors, also apply, in the same manner and to the same extent as the principles applicable in accordance with the underlying law to an occupier of premises and his invitees or licensees would apply, to regulate –

(a) the obligations of a person occupying or having control over any fixed or moveable structure, including a vessel, vehicle or aircraft; and

(b) the obligations of a person occupying or having control over any premises or structure in respect of damage to property, including the property of persons who are not themselves his visitors.

(3) This Part does not alter the rules of the underlying law as to the persons on whom a duty is so imposed, or to whom it is owed.

52 Extent of occupier's ordinary duty

(1) An occupier of premises owes the same duty (in this section referred to as "the common duty of care") to all his visitors, except so far as he is free to, and does, extend, restrict, modify or exclude his duty to a visitor by agreement or otherwise.

(2) The common duty of care is a duty to take such care as in all the circumstances of the case is reasonable to see that the visitor will be reasonably safe in using the premises for the purposes for which he is invited or permitted by the occupier to be there.

(3) The relevant circumstances for the purposes of this section include the degree of care, and of want of care, that would ordinarily be looked for in such a visitor, so that, amongst other things, in proper cases –

(a) an occupier must be prepared for children to be less careful than adults; and

(b) an occupier may expect that a person, in the exercise of his calling, will appreciate and guard against any special risks ordinarily incident to it, so far as the occupier leaves him free to do so.

(4) In determining whether the occupier of premises has discharged the common duty of care to a visitor, regard shall be had to all the circumstances, so that, amongst other things –

(a) where damage is caused to a visitor by a danger of which he had been warned by the occupier, the warning shall not be treated without more as absolving the occupier from liability unless, in all the circumstances, it was enough to enable the visitor to be reasonably safe; and

(b) where damage is caused to a visitor by a danger due to the faulty execution of any work of construction, maintenance or repair by an independent contractor employed by the occupier, the occupier shall not be treated without more as answerable for the danger if, in all the circumstances, he had acted reasonably in entrusting the work to an independent contractor and had taken such steps (if any) as he reasonably ought in order to satisfy himself that the contractor was competent and that the work had been properly done.

(5) The common duty of care does not impose on an occupier an obligation to a visitor in respect of risks willingly accepted as his by the visitor, and the question whether a risk was so accepted shall be decided on the same principles as in other cases in which one person owes a duty of care to another.

(6) For the purposes of this section, persons who enter premises for any purpose in the exercise of a right conferred by law shall be deemed to have been permitted by the occupier to be there for that purpose, whether they in fact have his permission or not.

53 Effect of contract on occupier's liability to third party

(1) In this section –

"stranger to the contract" in relation to a contract, means a person not for the time being entitled to the benefit of the contract as a party to it or as the successor by assignment or otherwise of a party to it, and includes a party to the contract who has ceased to be so entitled;

"tenancy" includes a statutory tenancy that does not in law amount to a tenancy, and "landlord" has a corresponding meaning.

(2) Where an occupier of premises is bound by contract to permit persons who are strangers to the contract to enter or use the premises, the duty of care that he owes to them as his visitors may be restricted or excluded by the contract, but (subject to any provision of the contract to the contrary) includes the duty to perform his obligations under the contract, whether or not undertaken for the protection of those strangers, so far as those obligations go beyond the obligations otherwise involved in that duty.

(3) Unless it expressly so provides, a contract does not, by virtue of this section, have the effect of making an occupier who has taken all reasonable care answerable to strangers to the contract for dangers due to the faulty execution of any work of construction, maintenance or repair or other such operation by persons other than himself, his servants and persons acting under his direction and control.

(4) Where by the terms or conditions governing a tenancy the landlord or the tenant is bound, otherwise than by contract, to permit persons to enter or use premises of which he is the occupier, this section applies as if the tenancy were a contract between the landlord and the tenant.

(5) So far as it prevents the common duty of care within the meaning of Section 52 from being restricted or excluded, this section applies to contracts entered into and tenancies created at any time, but so far as it enlarges the duty owed by an occupier beyond the common duty of care it has effect only in relation to obligations that are undertaken after 1 January 1963 (being the date of commencement of the pre-Independence *Law Reform (Miscellaneous Provisions) Act* 1962) or that are renewed by agreement (whether express or implied) after that date.

54 Landlord's liability by virtue of obligation to repair

(1) Where premises are occupied by a person under a tenancy that imposes on the landlord an obligation to the person for the maintenance or repair of the premises, the landlord owes to all persons who or whose goods are from time to time lawfully on the premises the same duty, in respect of dangers arising from a default by him in carrying out that obligation, as if he were an occupier of the premises and the persons or their goods were there by his invitation or permission (but without a contract).

(2) Where premises are occupied under a sub-tenancy, Subsection (1) applies to a landlord of the premises (whether the immediate or a

superior landlord) on whom an obligation to the occupier for maintenance or repair of the premises is put by the sub-tenancy, and for that purpose an obligation to the occupier that the sub-tenancy imposes on a mesne landlord of the premises, whether of its own force or under this section, shall be deemed to be imposed by it also on a landlord on whom the tenancy of the mesne landlord puts the same obligation towards the mesne landlord.

(3) For the purposes of this section, where –

(a) premises comprised in a tenancy (whether occupied under the tenancy or under a sub-tenancy) are put to a use not permitted by the tenancy; and

(b) the landlord of whom they are held under the tenancy is not debarred by his acquiescence or otherwise from objecting or from enforcing his objection,

no persons or goods whose presence on the premises is due solely to that use of the premises shall be deemed to be lawfully on the premises as regards the landlord or any superior landlord of the premises, whether or not they are lawfully there as regards an inferior landlord.

(4) For the purposes of this section, a landlord shall not be deemed to have made default in carrying out an obligation to the occupier of the premises unless his default is such as to be actionable at the suit of the occupier or, in the case of a superior landlord whose actual obligation is to an inferior landlord, his default in carrying out the obligation is actionable at the suit of the inferior landlord.

(5) This section does not impose on a landlord of premises a greater duty than the occupier to persons who or whose goods are lawfully on the premises by reason only of the exercise of a right of way.

(6) Nothing in this section relieves a landlord of any duty that he is under apart from this section.

(7) For the purposes of this section, obligations imposed by an Act or subordinate enactment in virtue of a tenancy shall be deemed to be imposed by the tenancy.

(8) This section applies to tenancies whenever created.

PART XIII – DAMAGE BY FIRE

55 Accidental fires

(1) Subject to Subsection (2), an action for damage caused by fire does not lie against a person in whose buildings or on whose land the fire accidentally begins.

(2) Subsection (1) does not operate to defeat or make void a contract or agreement made between a landlord and his tenant.

LaVergne, TN USA
02 February 2010
171801LV00005BC/1/P

9 789980 939